CONTENT AREA READING

CONTENT AREA READING

SECOND EDITION

RICHARD T. VACCA
JO ANNE L. VACCA
Kent State University

Little, Brown and Company
BOSTON   TORONTO

Library of Congress Cataloging-in-Publication Data

Vacca, Richard T.
  Content area reading.

  Bibliography: p.
  Includes index.
  1. Content area reading. I. Vacca, Jo Anne L.
II. Title.
LB1050.455.V33 1986   428.4'3   85-19807
ISBN 0-316-89490-7

Library of Congress Catalog Card No. 85-19807

9 8 7 6 5

ALP

Published simultaneously in Canada by Little, Brown & Company (Canada) Limited

Printed in the United States of America

CREDITS

The colleagues, teachers, and friends listed below contributed generously to the development of this book.

Chapter 2

Judith W. Irwin and Carol A. Davis for items on pages 41–44 from the Understandability and Motivation sections of the Readibility Checklist. From "Assessing Readability: The Checklist Approach." *Journal of Reading*, November 1980, 124–130. By permission of Judith W. Irwin and Carol A. Davis and The International Reading Association.

Chapter 3

Judith A. Langer for steps in the Prereading Plan (PreP) on pages 74–75. From "From Theory to Practice: A Prereading Plan." *Journal of Reading*, November 1981, p. 154. By permission of Judith A. Langer and The International Reading Association.

Candice Brickley, home economics teacher, Durham, Connecticut, prereading assessment activity for food faddism, p. 75.

Chet Hollister, earth science teacher, Algonquin, Illinois, prereading assessment activity for weather conditions, p. 76.

(continued on page 471)

Courtney,

. . . constant as the Northern Star,
Of whose true-fixed and resting quality
There is no fellow in the firmament.

—*Julius Caesar*
Act III, Sc. I

Preface

Reading development continues throughout life. Little did we realize when we began the second edition of *Content Area Reading* that so does our development as authors! We've discovered the double edge of the lifelong learning sword these past several years. As we continued to work with teachers and to participate with other colleagues in various professional activities, we too were changing and growing. So when it became time to revise *Content Area Reading* we felt compelled to give it an overhaul in light of what we've learned, experienced, and come to believe since 1981.

We've learned from teachers how they've gone about putting into practice the information contained in the first edition. Numerous persons have shared what features of the book they liked, what worked for them, and what might need changing. As teachers used the strategies, they mostly reported their successes and the satisfaction of knowing that reading can become a *workable* and *sensible* part of content area learning. Well aware of an old saying, "If it works, don't fix it," we kept the plaudits in mind. Yet . . .

Changes permeate the second edition. They are neither subtle nor enumerable. They are interlaced throughout the book. Instead of two separate chapters, the present chapter on vocabulary now provides a comprehensive treatment of word meaning and concept development. This certainly makes more sense from an instructor's point of view as does the new position of the chapter on evaluating students' reading needs, which is now contained in the first part of the book. This chapter considers a full array of informal evaluation procedures and advocates a *naturalistic* approach because it is most useful in making decisions about content area instruction. Moreover, we have expanded the discussion of structure and organization in text and the evaluation of text difficulty.

To further underscore the importance of the *context* in which reading to learn occurs, we chose to emphasize the three way relationship that exists among teacher–student–text. Moreover, throughout the book, we reiterate the balanced presentation of theory and practice characteristic of the first edition. The instructional strategies presented here are practical and powerful tools that are theoretically-based. They give students a sense of accomplishment and self-confidence as readers. Teachers can put students into a strategic position to take charge of their own learning. We've added two major areas to this edition to further help students learn how to learn.

Research on *metacognition* has direct implications for developing self-knowledge and self-monitoring behavior for reading and studying. By showing students how to study text purposefully and deliberately, they will learn to adapt study strategies to their own needs. *Writing to learn* is a powerful strategy for helping students understand what they are reading and studying. Students who write to learn are involved in a process of manipulating, clarifying, discovering, and synthesizing ideas.

Teachers as well as students benefit from being in a strategic position to take charge of their own learning, hence, updated information on staff development is now a chapter rather than an appendix. Teachers, too, need more than knowledge and enthusiasm to learn and grow. Just as content area reading provides support and reinforcement essential to learning in the classroom context, staff development provides support and reinforcement essential for change in the school context.

Content Area Reading is divided into three parts. Part One, "Establishing a Context for Instruction," deals with the nature of instruction in content areas and factors inherent in reading to learn. The necessity of understanding the teacher as decision maker regarding texts and textbooks, as well as students' knowledge, attitudes, and performance sets the tone. "Reading, Writing, and Studying," Part Two, contains a multitude of theory-based, practical strategies for instruction in content area reading. From developing frames of reference during prereading, to questioning at different levels of comprehension, to constructing and using reading guides or vocabulary activities, their purpose is similar: help students construct meaning and expand their thinking. In the chapters "Writing to Learn" and "Study Strategies," we explore the process of writing and studying along with relevant, meaning-based strategies. In Part Three "Organizing and Guiding the Content Area Reading Program," the focus shifts somewhat to the teacher in the roles of planner, manager, facilitator, and, in a role we can really relate to, lifelong learner.

Each chapter begins with a quotation, a chapter overview, in which the relationships among important ideas are visually depicted, and an organizing principle. At a glance, these organizing principles should capture the major themes in the second edition:

1. Reading to learn is greatly influenced by classroom interactions that occur among the teacher, students, and the text.
2. The difficulty of text material is the result of factors residing in both the reader and the text.
3. Evaluating for instruction is a continuous process which uses informal procedures in the natural context of the classroom.
4. A teacher reduces the uncertainty students bring to content material by helping them to use background knowledge, raise questions and make predictions about what they will be reading.

5. How, when, and where a question is used to guide reading determines its effectiveness.

6. Teacher-made adjunct instructional materials that accompany reading assignments help students experience the satisfaction of learning content from texts.

7. Writing to learn is a catalyst for reading and studying course material.

8. As students become more aware of reading processes—for example, how to identify important ideas in text—they become better able to use and monitor strategies for studying.

9. Vocabulary taught and reinforced within the framework of concept development enhances reading comprehension.

10. Teaching involves putting a plan to work in actual classroom situations.

11. Participating in planned staff development in content area reading leads to continued professional growth and improved instruction.

Many people deserve our thanks and merit recognition for demonstrating the care that reveals a true professional. Kudos are extended to our secretaries, Karen Brothers and Carolyn Brothers, for their fine and meticulous work. Applause also goes to our editor at Little, Brown and Company, Mylan Jaixen, and to our reviewers: Kathleen Jongsma of Texas Woman's University, Judith Meagher of The University of Connecticut, Anthony Manzo of University of Missouri, Kansas City, and Doris Jakubek of Central Washington University. Your response to our writing was invaluable. We can't repay you for the insights you provided but thought you'd enjoy a laugh at our expense as you read this quote from Annie Dillard:

> You know when you think about writing a book you think it is overwhelming. But, actually, you break it down into tiny little tasks any moron could do.

Richard T. Vacca
Jo Anne L. Vacca

CONTENTS

Chapter 3.　Evaluating for Instruction　62

Part Two: Strategies for Reading, Writing, and Studying

Chapter 4.　Prereading Strategies　98

Chapter 5.   Questions and Questioning   138

Chapter 6.   Reading and Study Guides   174

Part Three: Translating Knowledge into Practice

Part One

Establishing a Context for Instruction

CHAPTER ONE

Reading to Learn

*There are two ways of spreading light: to be the candle
or the mirror that reflects it.*
—EDITH WHARTON

Organizing Principle

Content area reading is driven by the discovery of meaning through the study of texts. Why and how students pursue knowledge is always a personal matter. Yet the search for meaning and knowledge can be informed through effective teaching. Reading to learn is influenced by many *meaning sources* in the classroom. This book is about the classroom interactions that occur among three of these sources: the teacher, the students, and the text. Each is at once the candle for spreading light and the mirror that reflects it.

The message that is all too clear to today's classroom teacher is that tomorrow's illiterate is the student who has not learned how to learn. Although content is king in many classrooms, it's never absolute. Reading is a *process* whose value lies in its use. Although textbook pages are assigned in content classrooms, showing students how to read to learn infrequently enters into the plans of teachers. The text is a valuable source of meaning and knowledge, yet its true potential has not been realized. When students become too dependent on

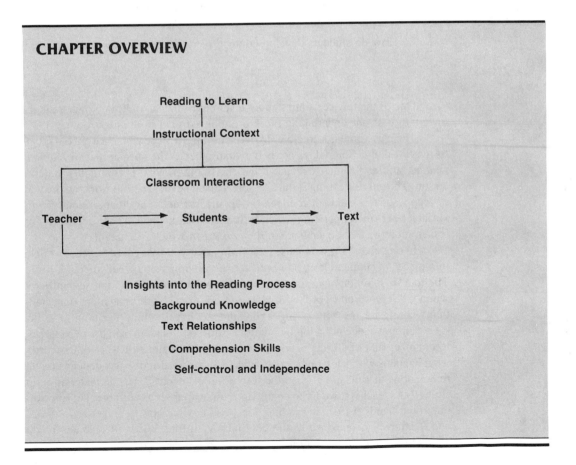

CHAPTER OVERVIEW

Reading to Learn

Instructional Context

Classroom Interactions

Teacher   ⇄   Students   ⇄   Text

Insights into the Reading Process

Background Knowledge

Text Relationships

Comprehension Skills

Self-control and Independence

teachers as their only meaning source, they rarely learn how to learn. How students interact with text, other students, and the teacher is reflected in the organizing principle of this chapter: *Reading to learn is greatly influenced by the classroom interactions that occur among the teacher, the students, and the text.*

Before reading, study the Chapter Overview. It's your map to the major ideas in the chapter. The overview shows the relationships that exist among the concepts you will study.

When you finish reading the chapter, you should be able to fully respond to the following questions:

1. How is reading to learn influenced by the context in which lessons are taught? Explain the social and communicative context of reading to learn.
2. What do readers do when they interact with text?
3. How does background knowledge influence comprehension?
4. Why should readers look for structure in what they read?
5. Why should reading comprehension be taught as a process rather than as a set of separate skills?
6. How do students develop control over and satisfaction with text?

One of the few certainties about teaching is its uncertainty. Nowhere is the uncertainty of our undertaking more pronounced than in the classroom.

The classroom is a crucible. In one sense, it's a place where we put ourselves to the test daily. Some days are better than others. The special mix of *teacher, student,* and *text* comes together in the classroom in what is commonly called a lesson. The only sure thing about a lesson is that it never seems to work out the way it's supposed to. And with good reason. In any instructional situation, intervening variables are often operating which influence what happens. The success of any lesson more or less depends upon the *context* in which it's taught.

In one class, a lesson jells. Everything that you *thought about doing* clicks into place. In another class, however, the lesson limps along. So you cut it short. The four or so remaining minutes before the bell rings are a kind of self-inflicted wound. "Serves you right," your alter ego cries out. Nothing is more unnerving than waiting for the bell to ring when students have nothing meaningful to do.

Circumstance has a lot to do with the different outcomes in the two classes. Recognize, first of all, that any instructional event is situational. In other words, what happens with a lesson in a particular class on a particular day depends on the interactions that occur between the teacher, the students, and the material being studied. As teachers, we try to control as many variables as possible, but some are out of our hands. Effective teaching for us is knowing how to orchestrate "plans" and "actions" in response to the continually shifting needs of students in the context of a learning situation.

Consider a science teacher's reflection on the way things went in one of her classes. "Something was missing," she explained. "Excuse the pun, but the chemistry wasn't there today. I know what my students can do, but maybe the material was too hard. Maybe I could have done something differently. Any suggestions?" The teacher, like most good teachers, cares about what she does. She's inquisitive. She doesn't talk about it in these terms, but she thinks about the *instructional context* in her class. She wants to know how to make her situation better. She knows that when the "chemistry" is there, teaching is its own reward.

The instructional context is a source of study and fascination for teachers who search for meaning in what they do. Teaching is tough for most of us; it doesn't get easier with time, just better. It gets better because we're learners. In the process of plying our craft, we get smarter about the things we do. Anyone who investigates the contextual factors which influence classroom learning soon appreciates how incredibly complex teaching is.

On one level, for example, the *physical context* of learning influences what happens in the classroom. Space may constrain or restrict participation depending on how a teacher interprets the situation. You see, the decision is still the teacher's to make. A math teacher explained why she didn't decide on small group work in one class but permitted it in another: "I didn't go with group problem solving in my second period class . . . too many rowdies, and not enough room to spread them apart." Other factors in the physical environment may be out of the teacher's control. "Why," an English teacher once lamented, "did I wait until May when the heating system is working at its best to teach my favorite novel?" Some teachers use their surroundings to promote learning. Bulletin boards reflect themes or topics being studied; a display area prominently arrays students' written work for others to read. Of course, other teachers remain oblivious to the physical space that they and students cohabitate. A room, after all, is just a room. It's the interaction that counts. Interactions are first and foremost social. And because they are social, interactions involve language, both verbal and nonverbal.

The *social* and *communicative context* of learning has tremendous effect on what happens during any instructional event. The social context depends on what teachers and students do together. Classroom learning is as much collaborative as it is individual. It often involves on-the-spot decision making: Who gets to do what? with whom? when? where? Because most learning situations in the classroom are face-to-face encounters, they necessarily entail language. As Labov (1972) noted, all communication is social. Most instructional contexts, therefore, build upon a series of conversational acts between teacher and students, and students and students. These acts are governed by rules (Green and Harker, 1982). Students quickly learn the rules and interact with the teacher or other students accordingly. The teacher orchestrates the conversational flow in the class by how or what he or she says and does.

A third variable, *the text*, adds to the social and communicative complexity of the classroom. How teachers orchestrate interactions with texts is part of the context of learning. Reading, therefore, is a social process as much as it is a cognitive and communicative process (Bloome, 1985). *Text authors* are the invisible and often neglected participants in classroom interactions.

What teachers do to show students how to think *in response to* texts is the subject of this book. Let's take a closer look at the "realities" of textbook use in the classroom.

Using Texts in the Classroom

Textbooks remain silent for too many students, even though teachers attempt to use texts with the best of intentions. Hinchman (1984) examined the perspectives held by secondary teachers toward reading. Through extensive classroom observation and interviews, she explored how three teachers in particular think about reading when they plan for instruction. Hinchman found that the teachers seldom spoke of reading. Instead, they viewed it as one of many classroom activities. For these teachers, reading was a means of covering material required in the curriculum. It was a way of helping students acquire information. Our hunch is that showing students how to use reading to think about content doesn't really enter into most teachers' plans.

We have never known a teacher who didn't believe in earnest that the essence of teaching is to show students how to think through the vehicle of his or her content. *Intention,* however, no matter how earnest, is one thing; effect is another. What really matters is what we do in the name of instruction to mediate between intention and effect. To simply tell students to think is not enough. To exhort them to think about what they read or to use reading to learn won't do either, even though

> Reading has the power to carry the (student) further and deeper . . . than any other educational medium . . .he can analyze more thoroughly . . .; he can compare passages for corroboration or to check seeming inconsistencies; he can stop for reflection . . .; he can choose a time for reading that will fit in with his mood and personal needs. . . . *(Preston, 1968, pp. 241–242)*

Such discussion about what reading can do for students falls flat on its face, unfortunately, when a teacher notices that they "just don't read assigned material anymore." Yet it's not that the majority of students can't read. Most choose not to, primarily because they have never been shown how to explore and interpret text effectively.

There must be carefully planned teacher "actions" between good intentions and teachers' ultimate effects in the content classroom. Rieck (1977) reported the findings of interviews with content teachers and their students. These findings show how some teachers unwittingly telegraph messages against reading. English, science, social studies, mathematics, physical education, art, and home economics teachers were asked a series of questions about their actions in relation to reading. On two of the questions asked, here is how they responded:

1. Do you require reading in your course? 97% yes, 3% no.
2. Do most of your students read their assignments? 58% yes, 42% no.

Approximately three hundred students of the teachers who responded "no" to the second question were then asked these questions:

1. Do you like to read? 52% yes, 38% no, 10% no response.
2. Do you read your assignments in this class? 15% yes, 81% no, 4% no response.
3. Do your tests cover mainly lecture and discussion or reading assignments? 98% lecture and discussion, 2% reading.
4. Are you required to discuss your reading assignments? 23% yes, 70% no, 7% no response.
5. Does your teacher give you purpose for reading or are you only given the number of pages to read? 95% pages, 5% purpose.
6. Does your teacher bring in outside material for you to read and recommend books of interest for you to read? 5% yes, 95% no.
7. Does your teacher like to read? 20% yes, 33% no, 47% don't know.

As a result of the contrast between teacher and student responses in the interviews, Rieck (1977) concluded,

> Out loud, these teachers are saying: "I require reading in this course. All students are to read the assignments. Students are to read X number of pages from the textbook." However, their nonverbal attitude said to students: "You really don't have to read the assignments because you aren't tested on them and probably won't have to discuss them. You should read X number of pages but there is no real reason to do so. Reading really isn't important. Outside reading is of little value in this class. My students will have no way to tell whether or not I like to read." *(p. 647)*

Smith and Feathers (1983) essentially reached a similar conclusion in their study of content area reading practices. Reading simply was not an important component of teaching or learning in the classrooms they investigated. Teachers who are wedded to a discipline walk a tightrope between content and process. It's certainly a balancing act every time the attempt is made to influence what is learned (content) and how it should be learned (process). Someone once said that teaching a set of ideas without regard to how students are to acquire those ideas is like blowing air into a punctured balloon. The harder you blow. . . .

Just the reverse is true when an effort is made to develop skills without meaningful content. Teaching skills for the sake of skills is as purposeless as teaching ancient history in a vacuum. It's all Greek to students.

When it comes to reading, then, a content teacher's job is not to teach skills per se but to show students how to use reading effectively to comprehend and learn from text materials. Therein lies the real value of content area reading instruction.

Clarifying the Content Teacher's Role

As you read this book, keep in mind that the notion that reading be taught in content areas is by no means new. The charge to teach reading through content can be traced to at least the 1920s (Moore, Readence, and Rickelman, 1983). But the reading field then was still in its infancy. Content area reading was too ephemeral to have substantial impact on educational practice.

Today, however, the enthusiasm for content area reading can be felt everywhere. Particularly since 1970, the topic consistently dominates the program of the annual convention of the International Reading Association and is a welcome addition to the proceedings of national and state conferences in each of the subject fields. Not a day goes by that a school- or college-based consultant isn't asked to conduct staff development sessions on reading for classroom teachers.

There are good reasons why content area reading has grown in the dramatic fashion that is evident today. Certainly it's reasonable to presume that content teachers are in a very strategic position to show students how to use reading to handle the demands of text. But we also believe that content area reading has "grown up" because its practices have caught up with its underlying rationale. To put the matter plainly, there's a lot more known today about how to teach reading in content areas without fragmenting the instructional process. And this makes sense to content teachers.

Having said this, it's somewhat ironic that the charge to teach content area reading is in many ways still an empty imperative to teachers. Despite the dramatic increase in enthusiasm, content area reading instruction has yet to win wide acceptance by subject matter specialists. That idealistic cliché "every teacher a teacher of reading" causes confusion and often conveys little meaning. The confusion over teaching reading in content areas is apt to be caused by the traditions associated with subject matter instruction, the misconceptions that content teachers have about reading instruction, and their role expectations in general.

Once traditions and conceptions of reading instruction are put into perspective, confusion begins to fade and the expectations that classroom teachers hold for teaching reading through content take on new meaning. Let's examine why.

Content as King

Content is the *what* of instruction. And *what* is learned in the presence of a teacher has been the time-honored tradition of schools since the Middle Ages. As Malcolm Knowles (1973) said, in those days novices entered monasteries to prepare for religious life, and as a result, "The teaching monks based their instruction on assumptions about what would be required to control the development of these children into obedient, faithful and efficient servants of the church" (p. 42). Out of this origin developed traditions which have heavily influenced the secular schools of Europe and America.

Schooling in America, for example, can be traced to the Puritans, whose schools "were definitely instruments of the church at the outset. . . . The schools the children attended were laced with religious experience. Inherent in this vision of the school was the supremacy of content" *(Samples et al., 1977, p. 168).* Content was king, the teacher the authoritative source. Vestiges of this tradition are still felt whenever a ninth grader, or for that matter a graduate student, looks to the teacher for the "right answer."

In many schools today content is still king—the stuff of learning—in many classrooms where teachers have been prepared to teach a discipline. And that's okay—to be content with content. Sometimes reading specialists in their zeal to get reading techniques across to content teachers forget the centuries-old tradition of a discipline and wind up stepping on toes in the process.

The term *discipline* has an interesting etymological background. Its roots can be traced to the Latin noun *discipulus,* which, in turn, is derived from the verb *discere,* "to know." In other words a discipline can be defined as "knowledge organized for instruction." Bruner (1961) and others proposed that the implicit organization or structure of any discipline is the only proper source of learning content. The student who discovers and understands a discipline's structure will be able to contend with its many detailed aspects. Understanding structure means seeing the big picture, developing the superordinate concepts and powerful ideas that are part of each discipline. Nevertheless, the feeling of having to "get through the curriculum" is still omnipresent for many teachers.

It's not difficult to recognize why teachers don't readily commit themselves to teaching reading. To do so is viewed as one more burden on the llama's back. When a llama is overburdened, it gets ornery. It resists. For many content teachers, reading is perceived as one more distraction from their concept of teaching a discipline.

"I've got too much to cover already." "I've got four weeks to get through this unit."

Lay these very real concerns alongside another artifact of tradition—that teachers tend to teach the way they have been taught—and what emerges is a blockbuster of a mental set to break through. Teachers look to former teachers for their models.

Perhaps someone particularly special to you has entered (or will enter) your teaching persona and has influenced (or will influence) your concept of what teaching is about. To impose reading upon that concept of teaching is always difficult until "reading instruction" is clarified.

Misconceptions about Reading

Resistance to content area reading also may occur because of the concepts or, more appropriately, misconcepts that are developed over what reading instruction entails. If, for example, our only experiences with reading instruction are what we can recollect from childhood, what conclusions might we draw? Quite possibly these: (1) reading instruction is reading aloud; (2) reading instruction is learning how to sound out words; (3) reading instruction is doing endless worksheet drills; (4) reading instruction is boring.

Depressing? Outlandish? Johns and Galen (1977) wrote an intriguing article entitled "Reading Instruction in the Middle 50's: What Tomorrow's Teachers Remember Today," in which advanced education majors were asked to record their early impressions of reading. Here's some of what was recalled.

> It's amazing how every year "reading" seemed to get farther away from something we were supposed to be enjoying. If it weren't for the good feeling I had when I first started reading, I never would have survived the rest of the progression through formal reading instruction.

> . . . each person took his turn reading aloud. You would nervously fumble with your book. . . . When your turn came around you prayed that you wouldn't make any mistakes, for fear of being called "one of the dummies."

> While we waited for our turns, most of us became bored and fidgety. . . . So I learned to be real sneaky and feel guilty every time I got bored and started reading ahead again.

> I had to stay after school because I was not reading the words on the flash cards correctly.

> The teacher used to catch people off guard and then ask them to read.

> When a child stumbled over a word—our teacher would correct him in a bored and impatient voice. *(pp. 252–254.)*

Times may have changed; the technology for teaching reading has vastly improved since the 1950s. But on a personal note we can tell you this: if you were to ask our daughter Courtney if she liked reading when she was in elementary school, she would have unflinchingly responded, "I hate it!" Now Courtney is an accomplished reader; she devours books. Why, then, would she have responded so negatively to the question "Do you like reading?" As an elementary student Courtney didn't distinguish between reading and reading instruction. To her, the question implied "Do you like your reading period in school?" She didn't. Reading books, however, was something that she did outside school!

What are your early impressions of reading instruction? Many teachers will have little to do with teaching reading in their disciplines if it means even coming close to doing the things that were done to them in the name of instruction in elementary school.

Happily, it doesn't. Instead, the essence of content area reading is comprehending texts. Most teachers do not need (or want) a comprehensive treatment addressing the many detailed facets related to reading instruction. They do need (and want) to develop skills and understandings that are of immediate and intimate concern to them: they want to know how to facilitate reading comprehension and concept development through text materials. This is the heart of the matter.

Nevertheless, confusion often arises in the minds of content teachers over their role in a schoolwide reading program. The expectations that teachers have about their role and the role of reading specialists contribute to content teachers' dissatisfaction when they are called upon to teach reading through content. Once these expectations are put into perspective, resistance to content area reading is likely to shrink.

The Content Teacher as Process Helper

Although content traditionally has been king to many teachers, process has achieved the stature of prime minister in today's classroom. Showing students how to learn comes with the territory. When textbooks are the vehicle for learning, the teacher has a significant role to perform. In effect, the classroom teacher is a "process helper," bridging the gap that often exists between students and the text.

No doubt a corner has been turned in the perceptions most of us have of reading as a "subject" fit only for the elementary grades. This perception should accompany an even greater awareness that reading cannot be taught entirely as a separate subject at any level of instruction. It defies common sense to think that reading is something taught for one hour every day. Many teachers recognize the dangers inherent in teaching reading as if it were a content area in itself, when in fact reading is a process and should be thought of and taught as such.

Margaret Early, a major voice in secondary reading, has maintained that once the difference between a skills-centered approach to reading, *direct instruction,* and a content-centered approach, *functional instruction,* is explained, the expectations of content teachers will change, and confusions will begin to fade. Early (1964) suggested that a spiral concept of learning can be adapted to provide insights into the meaning of reading instruction through the grades. In Figure 1.1 two cone-shaped spirals superimposed upon one another signify direct and functional instruction in reading. At the base of the direct instructional cone—in the elementary grades—the spiral is tight and wide to represent heavy emphasis on skills development. As direct instruction continues into the secondary grades, the spiral gradually tapers off to suggest less emphasis.

Direct instruction usually centers around a set of reading skills, arranged according to "scope and sequence" and taught systematically by a reading teacher or specialist. Reading materials are selected for their value in teaching the skills and providing practice and reinforcement once they are taught.

But that's only half the picture. Consider the overlapping spiral which begins narrow in the elementary grades and broadens as it moves through the secondary grades. This spiral represents the functional nature of reading. It emphasizes the application of skills that readers must make to learn content from a variety of sources and materials. A functional approach suggests that classroom teachers are in a better position than reading specialists to guide the application of reading skills. Skills aren't taught or applied in isolated drill apart from the mainstream of content area instruction. Nor are "artificial" workbook materials used as a guise for skills development in the content areas. Such materials tend to become exercises in themselves and little else.

An inspection of these overlapping spirals shows that some form of direct teaching of reading skills should continue through the grades but should be superseded by a functional approach to instruction in every subject where reading is an important vehicle for learning. Early (1964) said teachers should draw three implications about their role:

1. They have something important to contribute to the reading development of students, but they need not become reading specialists to contribute it.

2. They should not be held responsible for direct reading instruction, since a qualified reading teacher will be in a better position to deliver a program that meets the specialized needs and abilities of learners at every band in the spiral.

3. A reading program works best when reading specialists and content teachers respect and understand each other's roles.

More and more students will learn how to read textbooks effectively as content teachers put traditions and old expectations into perspective and build healthy concepts of reading instruction. Progress will also depend on how well teachers use insights into the reading process to plan their actions in the classroom.

Insights into the Reading Process

This book is designed to deal with nuts-and-bolts issues related to instruction in content area reading. But the book is also based on the premise that teachers who search for meaning in what they do can go infinitely beyond the nuts and bolts proposed here. Moffett and Wagner (1976) were quite right when they said, "To act without understanding is never practical" (p. 2). Effective teachers are theoretically minded but might not think of themselves that way. Yet they have reasons or rationales for what they believe "works" in the classroom.

We won't deal with theory in a vacuum; nor will we deal with practice in a cookbook manner. Instead, our intent is to integrate theory with practice and avoid the dichotomy that has been created between the two. This dichotomy has had unfortunate consequences in the field of education. There seems to be a backlash by classroom teachers against anything that smacks of the theoretical. But we suspect that teachers object to "theorizers" who "talk at" them. When explanations are presented out of the context of real classroom situations, they are rejected out of hand. "What can I do on Monday morning?" is the often-heard appeal of those disenchanted teachers who are "fed up" with ivory tower theorists—and, we imagine, with good reason. Teachers are tired of empty theorizing. "Show me what to do on Monday morning" is a legitimate concern. But teachers also want to know why; they just phrase it differently: "Why should I do this rather than that?" Knowing why is crucial to understanding how. Probably the single most important question that teachers ask about reading to learn is how to help students understand

Figure 1.1 The Total Reading Curriculum: Direct and Functional Instruction

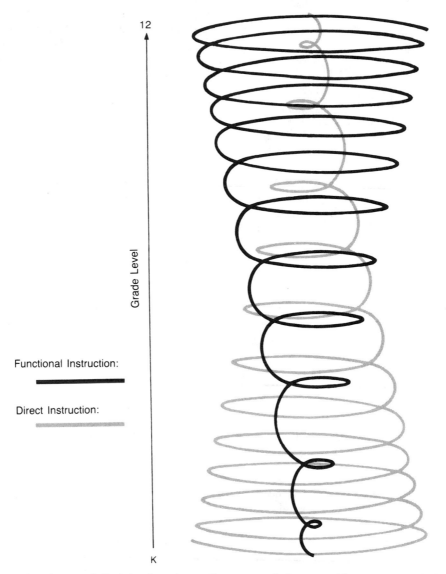

what they read. Insights into the reading process help to provide some answers to the question.

Reading—What's It All About?

The question begs explanation, but none may be in the offing. We are fond of a story that Bill Bernhardt recounts in the book *Just Writing*. A captive African on a slave ship studied the relationship between his master (the ship's captain) and the books that the master read:

> I had often seen my master employed in reading and I had a great curiosity to talk to the books as I thought they did . . . for that purpose I have often taken up a book and have talked to it and then put my ears to it, when alone, in hope it would answer me; and I have been very much concerned when I found it remained silent. (From *Interesting Narrative of Olaudah Equiano, 1789 as quoted in Bernhardt, 1977*)

Reading is a process that in many ways remains as much a mystery today as it did for the African slave almost two hundred years ago. Based on what is known about reading today, the African slave was on the right track. Recent explanations of the reading process suggest that the meaning of a text does not reside in the material itself, but in the transactions and interactions that take place between the reader and the text. Reading is not a passive, "roll-your-eyes-over-the-text" activity, but an active process which mainly takes place behind the eyes. The reader searches for and constructs meaning from the text. The text is more or less a blueprint for understanding; readers build meaning by connecting new knowledge to knowledge they already possess.

We have been in the midst of an information explosion that has contributed unprecedented theorizing and research on the process of reading. The assault on reading has been multidisciplinary. Scholarship in psycholinguistics, information processing, and cognitive psychology has focused on how people comprehend text.

Early positions established by Goodman (1976) and Smith (1978), two of the leading advocates of a psycholinguistic view of reading, have maintained that reading is a language process and not merely the sum of various decoding and comprehension subskills. A reader interacts with print in an effort to understand the author's message. Reading is an active process of deriving meaning.

Suppose you were asked to read the following passage:

The Kindom of Kay Oss

Once in the land of Serenity there ruled a king called Kay Oss. The king wanted to be liked by all his people.

So onx day thx bxnxvolxnt dxspot dxcidxd that no onx in thx country would bx rxsponsiblx for anything. Zll of thx workxrs rxstxd from thxir dzily lxbors. "Blxss Kzy Oss," thxy xxclzimxd. Now, thx lzw mzkxrs wxrx vxry wvsx. But zs wvsx zs thxy wxrx, thxy dxcvdxd thzt thx bxst form of govxrnmxnt wzs nonx zt zll.

Zs tvmx wxnt qn, thx kvngdqm og Kzy qss bxgzn tq splvt zt thx sxzms znd vt lqqkxd lvkx thvs: Bcx dqufghj klzm nqxp qqt rqst vqxwxxz bqxc dqf ghzj kqlxmnxp.

As you read "The Kingdom of Kay Oss," did the progressive substitution of consonants for vowels stymie your efforts to understand the passage? Probably not. Perhaps it slowed down your rate of reading a bit, but chances are you were still able to interact with the passage and construct meaning from it.

According to advocates of a psycholinguistic view, a reader is a user of language whose task is to make sense out of what he or she reads. To do this, readers make use of their background knowledge as well as their expectations and interactions with written language. Upon reading about King Kay Oss, you searched for and processed different types of language cues which helped you build meaning from the passage.

For example, you probably made some use of cues among the letter/sound associations in the passage. Part of your ability to read the phrase "thxy dxcvdxd thzt thx bxst" depended on the recognition of some of the consonants or consonant combinations and the sounds that they represent. However, these letter/sound associations in and of themselves provide no clues to meaning. In order to get at meaning, you had to process other types of information in the passage. Your knowledge of grammar, whether that knowledge is intuitive or overt, undoubtedly helped you anticipate some of the words in the passage which "had to come next." For instance, as you began to read the last paragraph and said to yourself, "As time _____ _____," you probably predicted almost automatically that "went" and "on" would follow. This is partially due to your knowledge of how language works. It is also due to the general knowledge that you brought to bear as you read.

Readers use their knowledge to anticipate the meanings of known words or build meaning for unknown words—or even unknown strings of words. When you read the last paragraph in the passage and perceived, "As time went on, the Kingdom of Kay Oss began to split at the seams and it looked like this:" you probably made the inference that "this" referred to the chaotic string of words that followed. These words convey no letter/sound or grammatical cues. Some of you probably decided that the fablelike nature of the passage dictated a moral at the end. Such a decision is based on what you know already or believe to be so.

Background Knowledge

The knowledge structures that students bring to learning have important implications for content area reading. We can grasp the importance of prior knowledge in reading by reviewing the findings of the research conducted under the direction of Richard C. Anderson at the Center for the Study of Reading at the University of Illinois. The scientific enterprise undertaken at the Center for the Study of Reading has in large measure developed support for a *schema theory* of reading and language comprehension. Readers activate existing knowledge structures (schemata) to interpret text. Comprehension involves the matching of what the reader already knows to a new message.

To illustrate this point, we will use a workshop activity. In workshops for content teachers we occasionally read the short story "Ordeal by Cheque" by Wuther Grue (first published in *Vanity Fair* magazine in 1932). The story is extraordinary in that it is told entirely through the bank checks of the Exeter family over a twenty-eight-year span. The workshop participants interact in small groups, with each group assigned the task of constructing the meaning of the story. At first glance the participants don't know what to make of the story. "You must be kidding!" is a typical response. After initial puzzlement, however, they begin to "read."

Here is the essential information contained in the first few checks in the story.

Entry Date	Paid to	Amount	Signed by
8/30/03	A baby shop	$ 148.00	Lawrence Exeter
9/2/03	A hospital	100.00	Lawrence Exeter
10/3/03	A physician	475.00	Lawrence Exeter, Sr.
12/10/03	A toy company	83.20	Lawrence Exeter, Sr.
10/6/09	A private school for boys	1250.00	Lawrence Exeter, Sr.
8/6/15	An exclusive military academy	2150.00	Lawrence Exeter, Sr.
9/3/21	A Cadillac dealer	3885.00	Lawrence Exeter, Sr.
9/7/21	An auto repair shop	228.75	Lawrence Exeter, Sr.

Analyze these bits of information and the relationships established among the events depicted by the checks. Are you able to construct what has taken place thus far in the story? Team up with one or two persons and discuss your versions. What do they have in common? What inferences did you make about the characters? Were there differences in your retellings? If so, why?

Here are some typical responses to these questions:

"A baby boy was born. He's named after his father."

"The Exeters must be 'fat cats.' The old man's loaded."

"He spends $83 for toys in 1903! He probably bought out the toy store."

"Lawrence Jr. must be a spoiled brat!"

"Yeah, how can any kid born with the proverbial silver spoon in his mouth not turn out spoiled?"

"Let's not jump to conclusions. Why is he spoiled?"

"Look, the family sent him to a military academy after he screwed up at the private school."

"No, no. It was fashionable in those days to first send your child to a private school until he was old enough for military school. The super-rich send their children to exclusive schools—it's as simple as that."

"Maybe so, but the kid is still a spoiled brat. His father buys him a Cadillac, probably for graduation from the academy, and four days later, it's in the body shop for repair."

"The father overindulges his son. I wonder what will happen to 'Junior' when he has to make it on his own?"

Although readers attempt to retell an author's message, they also attempt to construct meaning as well. In other words, we not only read the lines to determine what an author says, but we also read between the lines to infer meaning and beyond the lines to elaborate upon the message. If the entire display of checks from "Ordeal by Cheque" were in front of you, you would undoubtedly soon find yourself involved in the process of reading: raising questions, predicting, searching for relationships among the pieces of information contained in each check, inferring, judging, and elaborating.

Text Relationships

Another important aspect of reading merits consideration. Participation in the "Ordeal by Cheque" activity not only reinforces the powerful role that one's background knowledge plays in interpreting text but also illustrates the importance of the text itself. The conceptual and structural demands in a text selection influence comprehension. Readers must search for and find relationships among pieces of information (often called propositions) and concepts.

Pearson and Johnson (1978) bemusedly wished that the readers of their book *Teaching Reading Comprehension* had encountered "the word *relation* so often that you are near the point of hoping you never see it again. We have used it often, because that is what we think comprehension is about—seeing relations among concepts and propositions" (p. 228). Most authors do not write carelessly or aimlessly. They impose structure—an organization among ideas—on their writings. Perceiving structure in text material improves learning and retention. When students are shown how to see relationships among concepts and propositions, they are in the proverbial driver's seat. That is, they are in a better position to respond to meaning and to distinguish important from less important ideas. In the next chapter, the concept of text structure is developed more fully.

The insights into comprehension presented here will be developed in succeeding chapters within the framework of instructional practices related to content area reading. What these insights tell the classroom teacher is this: readers must "work" with print in an effort to explore and build meaning. Reading is first and foremost an interplay, a give and take, between the reader and the text. However, the burden for learning is always on the reader. As a result, content area reading instruction should center around a search for meaning in text materials. The teacher guides comprehension and helps students develop ideas through varied forms of instructional activity—all of which are to be presented in the remainder of this book.

Comprehension Skills

The conventional wisdom in the reading field today is that reading cannot take place unless meaning is involved in the transaction between reader and writer, that comprehension is the bottom line. Yet until recently comprehension has been the least investigated area of reading research over the years—and the least understood by practitioners.

A discussion of reading comprehension is somewhat analogous to Humpty Dumpty's conversation with Alice on the use of a word in *Alice's Adventures in Wonderland:* "When I use a word," says Humpty Dumpty, "it means just what I choose it to mean—nothing more or less." Likewise, in a discussion of *comprehension,* the term has often meant whatever a speaker or writer has chosen it to mean. All too often reading authorities and cognitive psychologists confuse classroom teachers by personalizing comprehension terms with their own unique labels. However, in its broadest sense, particularly for instructional purposes, we will define reading comprehension in ordinary language as the act of exploring and making meaning.

In order to make the teaching of comprehension manageable, the major thrust over the past several decades has been to identify and to isolate the skills commonly thought to be involved in reading comprehension. Davis (1941, 1944, 1968, 1972) spent his professional lifetime determining whether comprehension among mature readers was a unitary process or a set of distinct mental skills. In his 1968 study, Davis used complex statistical analyses to examine the uniqueness of eight skills thought to be discrete:

1. recalling word meanings;
2. drawing inferences from context about the meaning of a word;
3. finding answers to questions answered explicitly or in paraphrase in the passage;
4. weaving together ideas in the content;
5. drawing inferences from the content;
6. recognizing a writer's purpose, attitude, tone, and mood;
7. identifying a writer's techniques;
8. following the structure of a passage.

Davis (1972) concluded that reading comprehension is not a unitary mental process: "It is, apparently, a composite of at least five underlying mental skills" (p. 655). These are skills 1, 3, 5, 6, and 8 in the list above. An important contribution of Davis's work is the recognition that discrete skills aren't independent of one another, that comprehension skills are highly interactive. More often than not, however, comprehension has been viewed as a collection of uncorrelated skills. The teaching emphasis usually has been on systematic instruction and practice in each of the individual skill areas.

Proponents of skills instruction in content areas have gone a step further. They affirm that there are comprehension skills that are peculiar to various subject matters. Burmeister (1974), for example, listed "the most commonly needed skills for reading in specific content areas" (p. 80). An analysis of her lists for comprehension reveals among other things a significant amount of overlap among the separate skills *within and across* the content areas of science, mathematics, social studies, and English. How unfortunate it would be if teachers were to conclude that reading comprehension is mainly a pattern of distinct skills that varies from one content field to another and that their job is to teach each of these skills separately.

This skills approach merits caution. There's the implicit danger of imparting to students the sense that reading comprehension is not a thoughtful, cognitive process but rather a series of individual skill performances. What's worse, however, is that this approach to comprehension in content areas runs the risk of fostering the belief that the distinct skills are uncorrelated with one another—that a particular skill, once taught and practiced, can be used independently of the others. This idea just doesn't make sense. Davis (1972), drawing upon psychometric research conducted over several decades, concluded that the concept of comprehension as a body of separate, independent skills should be soundly rejected.

What, then, is an alternative way of viewing "skills instruction" in comprehension? According to Vacca and Johns (1976), reading may be expressed symbolically as

$$R > S_1 + S_2 + S_3 + \cdots + S_n$$

In this equation, R (reading) is greater than $S_1 + S_2 + S_3 + \cdots + S_n$ (the sum of "teachable" skills). It implies that reading is a meaning-deriving process and places skills within that context. The comprehension process may indeed be a composite of skills, but the skills are so interactive that they cannot be separated from one another during reading.

Goodman and Burke (1972) suggested that individual skills, no matter how identified or labeled, do not necessarily result in effective reading. They explained that:

> You cannot know a process by listing its ingredients or labeling its parts; you must observe the effect of the parts as they interact with each other. Acting together, the parts compose an entity which is uniquely different from the identity of any of the separate parts. Flour, sugar, baking soda, salt, eggs and water can all be listed as ingredients of a cake. Yet the texture, weight, flavor and moistness of a cake cannot be related directly to any one of the ingredients, but only to the quality and result of the interaction. *(p. 95)*

Although it's likely that a composite of comprehension skills does exist, it's just as likely that the interaction among these skills is what really matters.

As a result, the *skillful* use of reading to learn is one of the most important goals of reading instruction. Students need to be shown how to *stick with print* and *work with* an author's ideas. One of our tasks is to plan instruction so that they will experience the satisfaction of learning from text. However, keep in mind that the long-term payoff is that students learn to control and regulate their own reading activities.

Self-Control and Independence

If students are going to read on their own, then teachers must gradually shift the burden of learning from their shoulders to students'. Some students will find any excuse to avoid reading. Others will read an assignment purposelessly, "getting through" to satisfy the teacher's requirements rather than their own. Nevertheless, most students do want to read but have been turned off by their experiences. If they make no attempt to read they cannot fail or be humiliated. Motivation to read is always a dimension of personality. But it is important to recognize that motivation is also the product of the classroom context that we create. A teacher can make a "will" reader out of a "won't" reader by applying an important principle of content area reading: Students must experience some control over reading before they will use it on their own for learning and pleasure.

Students progress along the path of independent learning with teacher support and guidance. Through our strategic use of questions, demonstration and modeling techniques, and teacher-made instructional materials, students develop an awareness of and skill in handling the demands inherent in various kinds of reading tasks. For example, teacher-made materials which accompany reading assignments help students experience the satisfaction of learning content from texts. A teacher builds in the guidance and structure students need to handle difficult reading materials. "Guide materials" give students a sense of what it means to interact with the text. The form and function of guides vary with the reading situation, and with the teacher's instructional purposes.

The prereading activities and materials in Chapter 4 will help students "get into" the text by establishing purpose and sustaining interest and motivation in an assigned reading. We will study how materials can be developed to arouse curiosity and help students make predictions about content before reading. These materials activate schemata. Students clarify and organize what they know and believe prior to reading. Those readers who have trouble matching schemata to text information or who lack sufficient knowledge to bring to bear on an assignment will profit especially from materials which activate reading.

Guide materials will also help students focus their attention on relevant segments of a text selection. Materials which guide reading show students how to search for and interpret information. The reading guides in Chapter 6, the use of questioning strategies as explained in Chapter 5, and the writing and study strategies in Chapters 7 and 8 emphasize how to find and use information during and after reading.

Most students lack the sophistication needed to read text effectively because they are still in the process of maturing as readers. The conceptual and stylistic demands of text are often greater than the levels of reading maturity that students bring to the task. Yet by the time they reach the middle grades, students have a need and a capacity to be self-directing and independent. The whole idea of guide materials is to provide enough instructional support for students to gain confidence and to develop strategies to read effectively on their own.

But to read independently students need to know what to do when they run into trouble with a reading task. They must become aware of *what* the demands are of the task and *how* to handle them. In the process of doing so, students must learn to recognize *when* or *why* they are not comprehending. Self-knowledge is a key factor in learning how to learn from text. With self-knowledge comes the ability to *monitor* or *regulate* reading. In other words, when students get into a jam, they know how to rectify or "fix" it by using appropriate reading and study strategies.

As you can see, independent learning requires knowledge and awareness of cognitive processes. The psychological term for such knowledge is *metacognition*. The more skilled the student, the more easily he or she will be able to use metacognitive abilities to handle the task demands inherent in reading. Maturing readers, the ones likely to be in your classroom, will benefit from instruction that *shows them how*. In other words, metacognitive strategies for reading develop from extended experiences with text, process explanations, and modeling.

The message that is all too clear to today's classroom teacher is that tomorrow's illiterate is the student who has not learned how to learn. So what can a teacher do? Let's read to find out.

Looking Back, Looking Forward

This chapter provided a frame of reference for reading to learn in content areas. The context for classroom learning involves the unique interactions which prevail among the teacher, the students, and the text. Teachers orchestrate plans and strategies in response to the shifting needs of students in any learning situation. The decisions that teachers make about instruction are based on their knowledge of students in relation to the material being studied. The teacher's job is not to exhort students to read, but rather to show them how.

Despite the dramatic increase in enthusiasm over content area reading in the 1970s, this aspect of reading instruction has not been received with open arms by content teachers. Teaching traditions as well as teachers' conceptions of reading instruction and their role expectations have contributed to the confusion over what it means to teach reading in content areas. Once the role of the teacher is clarified, confusion will fade.

The value of integrating theory with practice in this book was also discussed. Knowing why will lead to knowing how, because understanding why is the basis for making instructional decisions. In a sense, knowing why provides the "bag" for an infinite number of instructional procedures that go beyond the practical suggestions which will be made in this book. Therefore, some brief but important insights were discussed related to the reading process. Teaching students how to comprehend text is the heart of content area reading instruction.

There is much that teachers need to know about the nature of text. The next chapter examines the way ideas are organized in text material. It also investigates the factors that contribute to text difficulty. How to assess the difficulty of a text is never an easy chore. To what extent should professional judgment be used to determine difficulty? What is the role of readability measures?

Suggested Readings

Adler, M. (1972). *How to Read a Book*. New York: Simon and Schuster.

Anderson, R. C. (1977). The notion of schemata and the educational enterprise. In R. C. Anderson, R. J. Spiro, and W. E. Montague (eds.), *Schooling and the Acquisition of Knowledge*. Hilldale, N.J.: Erlbaum.

Berger, A., & Robinson, H. A. (eds.). (1982). *Secondary School Reading*. Urbana, Ill.: National Council of Teachers of English.

Bloome, D. (1983). Reading as a social process. In B. Hutson (ed.), *Advances in Reading/Language Research*, Vol. 2. Greenwich, Conn.: JAI Press.

Duffy, G., Roehler, L., & Mason, J. (eds.). (1984). *Comprehension Instruction: Perspectives and Suggestions*. New York: Longman.

Henry, G. (1974). *Teaching Reading as Concept Development*. Newark, Del.: International Reading Association.

Herber, H. (1978). *Teaching Reading in Content Areas* (2nd ed.). Englewood Cliffs, N.J.: Prentice-Hall.

McNeil, J. (1984). *Reading Comprehension: New Directions for Classroom Practice*. Glenview, Ill.: Scott, Foresman and Company.

Pearson, D., & Johnson, D. (1978). *Teaching Reading Comprehension*. New York: Holt, Rinehart and Winston.

Peterson, P., Wilkinson, L., & Hallinan, M. (eds.). (1984). *The Social Contexts of Instruction*. New York: Academic Press.

Rosenblatt, L. (1978). *The Reader, the Text, the Poem*. Carbondale: Southern Illinois University Press.

Smith, F. (1982). *Understanding Reading* (3rd ed.). New York: Holt, Rinehart and Winston.

Smith, S., Carey, R., & Harste, J. (1982). The contexts of reading. In A. Berger and H. A. Robinson (eds.), *Secondary School Reading*. Urbana, Ill.: National Council of Teachers of English.

Vacca, R. & Vacca, J. (1983). Recent research on enhancing reading comprehension in content areas. In B. Hutson (ed.), *Advances in Reading/Language Research*, Vol. 2. Greenwich, Conn.: JAI Press.

CHAPTER TWO

Texts and Textbooks

*This is the sort of impertinence up with which
I will not put.*
—WINSTON CHURCHILL

Organizing Principle

When a sentence which had ended with a preposition was "corrected" on one of the galley proofs of his memoirs, Winston Churchill restored the original order of the words with the marginal comment quoted above. Writers are funny that way. Their ideas are important; their style matters. For Churchill, ending a sentence with a preposition was irrelevant—how his ideas flowed from sentence to sentence in a coherent manner is what really mattered. The way writers tie ideas together in a passage is one of the most important factors affecting text difficulty.

Texts and textbooks are an important part of the classroom context. Classroom life is more than the interactions and transactions between teacher and student and student and student. The three-way relationship among teacher, student, and text must be taken into consideration in any discussion of reading and learning in the content classroom. The level of difficulty of writing (readability) is never easy to assess. Yet the evaluation of content materials through readability formulas has received a great deal of attention from educators and publishers.

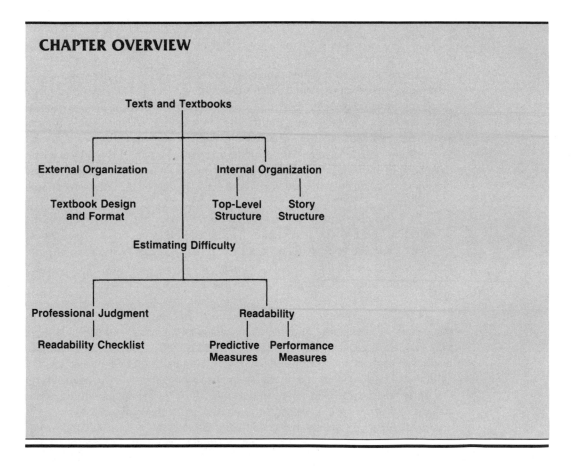

CHAPTER OVERVIEW

Texts and Textbooks

External Organization — Internal Organization

Textbook Design and Format — Top-Level Structure — Story Structure

Estimating Difficulty

Professional Judgment — Readability

Readability Checklist — Predictive Measures — Performance Measures

However, the organizing principle of this chapter warns against a narrow view: *The difficulty of text material is the result of factors residing in both the reader and the text.*

As you study the Chapter Overview and prepare to read, keep in mind that the questions below are pivotal to understanding the chapter's content. When you finish the chapter, you should be able to answer the following:

1. How is the external organization of texts different from their internal organization?

2. What is top-level structure in expository writing? Why must students develop the habit of looking for structure in most everything they read?

3. What do most well-developed stories have in common? Why is understanding a story's structure important?

4. How and when might teachers use professional judgment in analyzing the difficulty of textbooks?

5. How and when are predictive measures of readability useful? How do predictive measures differ from performance measures of readability?

That students have trouble reading content assignments is no longer front-page news to the classroom teacher. Reading workshop leaders and college professors invariably call attention to the *readability* of text material. Teachers know the textbooks they use are difficult. They also know that there's often a significant mismatch between the reading abilities that students bring to text material and the estimated readability of the text itself. Perhaps this is why teachers have become less dependent upon books in their classrooms. The cartoon below hits home. In some content classrooms books may indeed be the latest educational innovation.

In some classrooms the text *is* the curriculum. The teacher follows its organization and content presentation faithfully. In classroom situations where this is the case, the textbook is the teacher's primary source of information, *and* the teacher becomes the students' primary source of information. It doesn't take long for students to figure out that the textbook need not be read to do well.

On the other hand, there are classrooms in which the teacher operates completely independently of the textbook. Parents, students, and administrators may view the teacher's performance as quite effective. Instead of the textbook, instruction centers around prepared notes and activities. Although the teacher may assign readings on a regular basis from the course textbook, students soon recognize that the text is inconsequential. It has little to do with classroom life or successful performance as measured by end-of-unit achievement tests.

Other teachers openly, not unwittingly, circumvent textbooks. Circumvention is a coping strategy commonly used to deal with students who can't or won't study books on their own. Early (1973) claimed that some classroom teachers

"I'm taking an innovative approach to teaching this semester. I'm using BOOKS!"
[SOURCE: Reprinted from *Phi Delta Kappan* 59 (1978): 416. © 1978 Randy J. Glasbergen.]

recognize that a reading dilemma exists, but rather than tackle it head on, their tactic is to avoid the problem:

> The science teacher says: "They can't read the textbook anyway. So I do the experiment, or I set it up for them to do." The social studies teacher says: "They can't read the textbooks. Maybe they shouldn't anyway—the truth is so distorted. So I lecture. Or I set up a simulation." The math teacher says: "I have to read most of the problems to them. . . . If they can't read the ditto, I explain it to them." *(pp. 367–368)*

The "way out" for some teachers is to abandon difficult materials or to avoid reading altogether as a vehicle for learning. This is unfortunate.

While we're not suggesting that books are the only source for learning, or that they should be, they will continue to be indispensable tools for increasing knowledge and understanding, sharing the experiences and feelings of others, and gaining new insights and perspectives. Avoiding books in the classroom isn't the solution to the reading dilemma that frustrates most content specialists. It only compounds the problem.

The practical questions become: How does the textbook meet the goals of the course? Is the conceptual difficulty of the text beyond students' grasp? How well organized are the ideas in the text? Does the author have a clear sense of the intended audience? Certainly other questions of a critical nature are worth asking. However, answers to these kinds of questions provide a sturdy basis for making decisions about text-related instruction. Moreover, *seeking* the answers will put teachers "in touch" with their text materials.

Our hunch is that books are such an accepted aspect of schooling that teachers generally do not give textbooks a second thought. The textbook comes with the territory. To what degree are textbooks taken for granted? Are they part of the physical makeup of the classroom just as desks, chalkboards, and bulletin boards are? One can only speculate.

We raise these issues because the text is an integral part of the communicative context of the classroom. The interactions and transactions among the teacher, the student, and the text author form the very basis for comprehending and learning. Whereas one precept of teaching must surely be, "Teacher know thy students," another, just as surely, is, "Teacher know thy text."

It is little wonder that Terrel H. Bell, former Secretary of Education, voiced his concern about textbook quality in a speech before the American Association of School Administrators (Toch, 1984). He warned school administrators that "textbooks and other tools of learning and teaching must be upgraded and updated to assure more rigorous content (p. 11)." In his speech, Bell referred to the "dumbing down" of textbooks.

"Dumbing down" robs textbooks of a rich content base by making widespread use of readability formulas to rewrite text. Readability formulas are one way, as we'll discuss later in the chapter, to estimate and predict the difficulty of reading material. Textbook publishers "dumb down" a textbook presumably to make it easier for readers to handle. That is, they urge authors or "in-house" editors to write (rewrite) text copy according to readability formula prescriptions. Most formulas manipulate certain text variables associated with text difficulty—usually word difficulty and sentence length. Hence, texts are rewritten with the substitution of smaller words for longer words and shorter, simpler sentences for longer, more complex syntactical structures. Such use of readability formulas borders on educational malpractice. Readability formulas were never intended to be used to rewrite text.

Instead of seeking texts which have been "dumbed down," we agree with Campbell (1979): "There is no need to discard texts because they are difficult. There is a need for teachers to become aware of possible difficulties" (p. 687). Becoming aware of possible text difficulties puts you in a better position to compensate instructionally so that the difficulties do not become insurmountable obstacles to comprehension and learning.

In the remainder of this chapter, we explore a major source of difficulty—the way ideas in texts are organized. We examine how expository texts and narrative stories can be analyzed so that instructional decisions can be facilitated. We also emphasize the need to exercise professional judgment in making decisions about texts. Exercising professional judgment involves the thoughtful consideration of factors which may influence text difficulty. And, finally, more traditional measures of estimating text difficulty are discussed, measures which predict difficulty based on readability formulas and measures which rely on actual student performance with the material.

Text Organization

Although the terms *text* and *textbook* are used synonymously in this book, a broader definition of *text* suggests that it may refer to printed material of any length. Whether it represents a single sentence, a paragraph, a passage of several paragraphs, a chapter, or a book, a text is often discernible by its *structure* or *organization.*

Common sense tells us that most reading materials should have structure, or organization among the ideas. Authors aren't in the business of presenting ideas aimlessly—at least they shouldn't be. Mature readers follow the way an author structures ideas and ties together information. They look for text organization in everything they read. A good reader recognizes that there are relationships among ideas and also that some ideas are more important than others.

Educational psychologists from Thorndyke (1917) to Kintsch (1977) and Meyer and Rice (1984) have shown that organization is a crucial variable in learning and memory. Moreover, such noted reading educators as Rachel Salisbury (1934), Nila Banton Smith (1964), and Olive Niles (1964) underscored the recognition of patterns of organization in text as a key strategy for comprehension and retention. Smith (1964), for example, warned that "If a student . . . failed to identify these patterns and continues to use the same approach in reading . . . his resulting understanding and concepts discussed in class will undoubtedly be extremely limited" (p. 37). Niles (1964) claimed that there are three abilities that clearly differentiate between the good and the poor reader, among them the "power to find and understand various kinds of thought relationships that exist . . . in single sentences, in paragraphs and in selections of varying length" (p. 5).

Shepherd (1978) and Robinson (1983) provided a number of elaborate classifications by which teachers could identify patterns in the writings of their disciplines. They also provided excellent detailed analyses of how patterns work in individual paragraphs and short segments of text. While the many elaborate classifications and close distinctions have value, particularly in the experimental study of text structure per se, they can be counterproductive to content area reading instruction. As Niles (1965) maintained, ". . . elaborate classifications are not only unnecessary but actually a hazard to meaningful teaching" (p. 60). Elaborate classification often leads to overlap and to the labeling of patterns which essentially depict similar kinds of thought relationships. This labeling can only tend to confuse teachers with minimal background in reading instruction who are genuinely interested in helping students read better. According to Niles, teachers must show students how to look for structure in everything they read and know what to do when they find it. What, then, do teachers need to know about the structure of text?

The primary purpose of a textbook is to provide users with information. To make information readily accessible, authors make use of external and internal structural features. External organization is characterized by the textbook's overall instructional design—its format features within chapters as well as at the front and end of the textbook; internal organization, by the interrelationships among ideas in text as well as by the subordination of some ideas to others. Internal organization is referred to as the *top-level structure* or the *pattern of organization* of text.

External Organization

Textbooks contain certain format features—organizational aids—which are built into the text to facilitate reading. This book, for example, contains a *preface*, a *table of contents, appendices,* a *bibliography*, and an *index*. These aids are called the *front* and *end matter* of a book along with the *title page, dedication, list of tables and illustrations,* and *glossary*. Of course, textbooks vary in the amount of front and end matter that they contain. Nevertheless, these aids (the preface, table of contents, and index in particular) can be valuable tools for prospective users of a textbook. Yet the novice reader hardly acknowledges their presence in texts, let alone uses them to advantage.

In addition to the front and end matter, each chapter of a textbook usually has *introduction/summary statements, headings, graphs, charts, illustrations,* and *guide questions*.

Organizational aids such as these are potentially valuable—if they are not skipped or glossed over by readers. Headings, for example, are inserted in text to divide a chapter into logical units. Headings strategically placed in text should guide the reader through a chapter by highlighting major ideas.

In Chapter 8, we suggest strategies which focus attention on external organizational aids. How students learn to preview a text by riveting attention on external organizational cues often sets the stage for active reading. How students learn to study graphic aids such as charts, pictures, and tables can make the difference between superficial and thoughtful reading.

Within each chapter, authors may use top-level structure to logically connect ideas into a coherent whole. Top-level structure might vary from text passage to text passage depending on the author's purpose. These structures or patterns of organization within text are closely associated with expository writing.

Top-Level Structure in Expository Writing

Content area textbooks are written to inform. This is why exposition is the primary mode of discourse found in texts. This is not to say that some authors won't at times attempt to persuade or entertain their readers. They may. However, their primary business is to *tell, show, describe,* or *explain*. It stands to reason that the more logically connected one idea is to another, dependent on the author's informative purpose, the more coherent is the description or the explanation.

Patterns of organization represent the different types of logical connections among the important and less important ideas in expository material. Meyer (1975) suggested that the pattern which ties together these ideas is often located at the "top level" of the author's content presentation. Meyer explained that an author may

Figure 2.1 Hierarchical Relationships among Ideas in Expository Text

CONTENT PRESENTATION

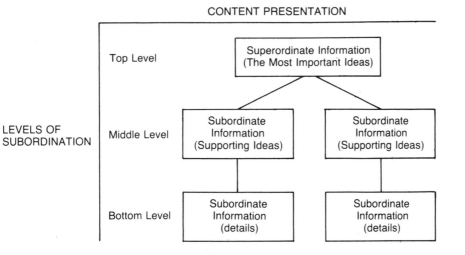

organize content in such a way that there is a *hierarchical relationship* among ideas in the text passage. Therefore, the most important or *superordinate* ideas should be located at the top levels of the content presentation and have many supporting ideas and details below them. According to Meyer, "These top-level ideas dominate their subordinate ideas. The lower-level ideas describe or give more information about the ideas above them . . ." (pp. 13–14). Figure 2.1 provides a general depiction of the structure of hierarchical relationships among ideas in a text passage.

The "flow of meaning" from author to reader is enhanced when the reader recognizes the structure of thought relationships in a text and can readily differentiate the important ideas from less important ideas in the material. Research has shown that good readers know how to look for major thought relationships (Taylor, 1980; Meyer, Brandt, and Bluth, 1980). They approach a reading assignment looking for a predominant top-level structure which will tie together the ideas contained throughout the text passage.

Types of Top-Level Structure

A case can be made for several organizational patterns or top-level structures that seem to predominate in expository writing: *enumeration, time order, comparison-contrast, cause-effect,* and *problem solution.* Here are descriptions and examples for these top-level structures.

   1. *Enumeration.*   Listing information about a topic, event, object, person, etc. (facts, characteristics, traits, features), usually qualifying the listing by criteria such as size or importance. Meyer (1975) labeled this organizational scheme as the *attribution* pattern because it connects ideas through description by listing the important characteristics or attributes

of the topic under consideration. Niles (1965) and Bartlett (1978) found the enumeration pattern to be the most common textbook organizaton. An example follows:

There were several points in the fight for freedom of religion. One point was that religion and government should be kept apart. Secondly, Americans did not want any form of a national church as was the case in England. Finally, Americans made sure that no person would be denied his or her religious beliefs.

2. *Time order.*   Putting facts, events, or concepts into a sequence, using references to time (like dates) to order them. An author will trace the development of the topic or give the steps in the process. Time reference may be explicit or implicit, but a temporal sequence is evident in the pattern. The following paragraph illustrates the pattern:

John F. Kennedy was the Democratic candidate for President when in October 1960 he first suggested there should be a Peace Corps. After he was elected, Kennedy asked his brother-in-law, Sargent Shriver, to help set up a Peace Corps. In March 1961 Kennedy gave an order to create the organization. It wasn't until September that Congress approved the Peace Corps and appropriated the money to run it for one year.

3. *Comparison-contrast.*   Pointing out likenesses (comparison) and differences (contrast) among facts, people, events, concepts, etc., Meyer (1975) labeled this pattern as the *adversative* structure. Study the example below:

Castles were built for defense, not comfort. In spite of some books and movies that have made them attractive, castles were cold, dark, gloomy places to live. Rooms were small and not the least bit charming. Except for the great central hall or the kitchen, there were no fires to keep the rooms heated. Not only was there a lack of furniture, but what there was was uncomfortable.

4. *Cause-effect.*   Showing how facts, events, or concepts (effects) happen or come into being because of other facts, events, or concepts (causes). This top-level structure is labeled *covariance* by Meyer (1975). Examine the paragraph below for cause and effects:

The fire was started by sparks from a campfire left by a careless camper. Thousands of acres of important watershed burned before the fire was brought under control. As a result of the fire, trees and the grasslands on the slopes of the valley were gone. Smoking black stumps were all that remained of tall pine trees.

5. *Problem-solution.*   Showing the development of a problem and the solution(s) to the problem. Problem-solution is called the *response*

5. structure by Meyer (1975). In many ways, problem-solution organization schemes are a special case of the cause-effect pattern. The problem (in this case, a "cause") *leads to* an attempt(s) at solution [the attempt(s) or the solution(s) represent "effects"]. Because many different types of content area textbooks rely on the problem-solution pattern to represent text relationships we have treated it as a separate pattern of organization. Consider the following example:

The skyrocketing price of oil in the 1970s created a serious problem for many Americans. The oil companies responded to the high cost of purchasing oil by searching for new oil supplies. This resulted in new deposits being found in some third world nations such as Nigeria. Oil companies also began drilling for oil on the ocean floor, and scientists discovered ways to extract oil from a rock known as oil shale.

Most textbook authors give readers clues or signals that will help them figure out the structure they are using. Readers usually become aware of the structure if they are looking for the signals. A signal may be a word or a phrase that helps the reader follow the writer's thoughts. Linguists call these words *connectives* or *ties* because they connect one idea to another (Halliday and Hasan, 1976).

Study Figure 2.2 for connectives that authors use to call attention to the organizational patterns just defined.

Figure 2.2 Reading Signals

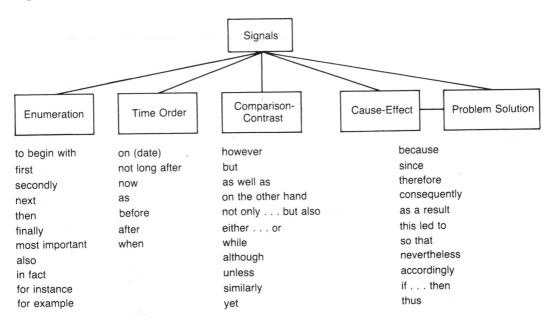

Enumeration	Time Order	Comparison-Contrast	Cause-Effect
to begin with	on (date)	however	because
first	not long after	but	since
secondly	now	as well as	therefore
next	as	on the other hand	consequently
then	before	not only . . . but also	as a result
finally	after	either . . . or	this led to
most important	when	while	so that
also		although	nevertheless
in fact		unless	accordingly
for instance		similarly	if . . . then
for example		yet	thus

Awareness of the internal organization of *long stretches* of text is especially helpful in planning reading assignments. In selecting a text passage of several paragraphs or several pages from the textbook, teachers first need to determine whether a predominant pattern of organization is contained in the material. This is no easy task.

Analyzing Structure in a Text Passage

Expository writing is complex. Authors do not write texts in neat, perfectly identifiable patterns. Within individual paragraphs of a text assignment, several kinds of thought relationships often may exist. Suppose an author begins a passage by stating a problem. In telling about the development of the problem, the author describes (through *enumeration*) a set of events that contributed to the problem. Or, perhaps, the author *compares* or *contrasts* the problem under consideration to another situation. In subsequent paragraphs, the solution(s) or attempts at solution(s) to the problem are stated. In presenting the solution(s), the author uses heavy description and explanation. These descriptions and explanations are logically organized through a *temporal sequence*.

The difficulty that teachers face is one of analyzing the overall pattern of organization of a text selection, even though several types of thought relationships are probably embedded within the material. Analyzing a text for a predominant pattern depends in part on how clearly an author represents the structure in the top level of the content presentation.

Several guidelines follow for analyzing text organization. First, look for the most important idea in the text selection. Are there any explicit signal words that indicate a pattern which will tie together the ideas throughout the passage? Second, study the content presentation for additional important ideas. Are these ideas logically connected to the most important idea? Is a pattern evident? Third, outline or diagram the relationships among the superordinate and subordinate ideas in the text selection. Use the diagram to specify the major relationships contained in the top-level structure and to sort out the important from less important ideas.

Excerpts from five pages of text in a chapter on "Northern North America" are presented below. The chapter is from a junior high level textbook by Drummond (1978) called *The Western Hemisphere*. The excerpts provide a "flavor" of the top-level structure contained in the text selection. Read the excerpts. Then study the diagram in Figure 2.3. It outlines the top-level structure and the subordination of ideas in the material.

> The people of the United States and Canada are alike in many ways. They are similar in their language and religion. Most of the people in the United States and Canada speak English. In the Canadian province of Quebec, however, most of the people are French-speaking. In the American Southwest, many U.S. citizens speak Spanish. . . . Minor differences in pronunciation and speech habits exist from one place to another in the two countries. . . .

Many different religions are found in the United States and Canada. There are more Protestants than Catholics in both countries. . . . Many Jewish people also live in the United States and Canada. Religious freedom is provided every person in both countries.

Economic life is similar throughout Northern North America. Most city dwellers work in manufacturing plants or in service or sales occupations. Most people living in rural areas use power-driven tools and machines. . . .

Both the United States and Canada use a *monetary*, or money system based on dollars and cents. In recent years a dollar. . . .

. . . both the United States and Canada enjoy political stability. The governments of both countries are federal systems—with national governments and state or provincial governments. . . .

Both countries have a Supreme Court. . . .

Both the United States and Canada have developed a high standard of living by making efficient use of available natural resources. There are two main reasons for this efficiency. . . . *(pp. 268–274).*

Figure 2.3 Diagram of Top-Level Structure (Comparison-Contrast) and Subordination of Ideas

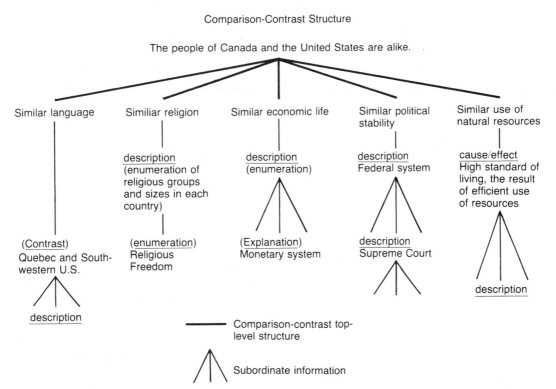

Comparison-Contrast Structure

The people of Canada and the United States are alike.

Analyzing a reading selection for top-level structure helps teachers decide how expository text is put together. In Chapter 6 we show that knowledge of text structure pays off in large instructional dividends. Through the use of *modeling activities*—procedures designed to make readers aware of the importance of perceiving text organization and to show them how to recognize specific patterns in text assignments—students will approach content area texts with the expectation of finding structure in everything they read. Also, we explain the use of *pattern guides*. Pattern guides give students a feel for what it means to recognize and use a predominant pattern of organization in a reading assignment to better understand and remember the material.

Whereas top-level structure specifies the logical connections among ideas in expository text, *story grammar* defines the basic elements of a well-developed story. Recently, various story grammars have been proposed by researchers to analyze a story's structure—the way it is put together.

Story Structure

Most simple stories in Western culture actually aren't as "simple" as they might appear on the surface. During the past decade, cognitive psychologists have demonstrated how complex the underlying structure of a story can be. These psychologists have attempted to identify the basic elements that make up a well-developed story (Mandler and Johnson, 1977; Thorndyke, 1977; Stein and Glenn, 1979). Their efforts have led to the development of several variations of *story grammar*. Just as sentence grammar provides a way of describing how sentences are constructed, story grammar helps to specify the basic parts of a story and how those parts tie together to form a well-constructed story.

What do most well-developed stories have in common? While individual story grammars may differ in their level of specificity, most researchers would agree that a story's structure centers around a *setting, plot,* and *theme*.

Setting and Plot

The setting introduces the main character(s) [protagonist(s)] and situates the character(s) in a time and place. The plot of a story is made up of one or more *episodes*. The intricacies of a story are often manifested in its episodic structure. A simple story has a single episode. More complex stories may have two, several, or many episodes as well as different settings. However, even a single-episode story is defined by an intricate causal chain of elements. These basic elements or events include:

— *An initiating event:* either an idea or an action that sets further events into motion.

— *An internal response:* the protagonist's inner reaction to the initiating

— event, in which the protagonist sets a *goal* or attempts to solve a *problem.*

— *An attempt:* the protagonist's efforts to achieve the goal or alleviate the problem. Several attempts, some failed, may be evident in an episode.

— *A consequence:* an action or state of affairs that evolves from the protagonist's success or failure to achieve the goal or alleviate the problem.

— *A reaction:* an idea, an emotion, or a further event which expresses the protagonist's feelings about success or failure of goal attainment/ problem resolution or which relates the events in the story to some broader set of concerns.

Box 2.1 contains an analysis of a popular short story often taught in a sophomore level English course, "The Sniper" by Liam O'Flaherty.

Box 2.1

ANALYZING STORY STRUCTURE*
Story: "The Sniper"
Author: Liam O'Flaherty

PLOT	THEME

Episode
　Setting: The story takes place on a June night 50 years ago in Dublin, Ireland on a rooftop near O'Connell Bridge.
　Character(s): Two snipers opposing one an-other

The moral dilemma inherent in war

Chain of Events
　Initiating event: A Republican sniper is spotted and shot by an enemy sniper. The sniper is hit in the arm, so consequently he is unable to fire his rifle.
　Internal response: The Republican sniper swears to himself in anger and resolves to shoot the enemy (Free Stater) sniper. He must eliminate the sniper in order to escape before morning's light.
　Attempt: The Republican sniper crawls to a new position where he replaces his cap on his rifle muzzle, raises it, and consequently draws fire from the enemy sniper. He pretends to be dead.
　Consequence: The enemy sniper falls for the trick, stands up, and the Republican sniper is able to kill him with his revolver. (The enemy's body falls to the street below.) He has survived.
　Reaction: After taking a drink, the sniper's nerves are steadied and he decides to look at the enemy sniper to see if he had known him before the army split. He also admires him for being such a good shot. Turning over the dead body, the sniper looks into his brother's face.

*Analyzed by Kathy McDonnell, English teacher, Cuyahoga Falls, Ohio.

The episodic events in the story form a causal chain. Each event leads to the next one as the main character moves toward goal attainment or problem resolution. Pearson (1982) noted that children as young as eight are successful at "flow charting" the causal chain of events in a story. He recommended the flow chart procedure (similar to the *cognitive maps* and *semantic webs* that are introduced in Chapter 8) as a way of building a general framework for understanding stories.

Theme

The theme of a story involves moral, psychological, or philosophical judgment on the part of the reader. When readers evaluate the theme they are "making meaning" or "constructing knowledge" as suggested in Chapter 1. Involving students in the thematic content of stories is a personal process. Students' awareness of how profound the theme is will vary, depending on the background knowledge and experiences they bring to the story. However, a reader must learn to deal with theme in relation to the story's plot: What does the story *mean* to you in addition to what it tells? What is the author *trying to say* to you through the protagonist's actions? What do you see in the story regardless of what the author may have meant?

To have students evaluate the profundity of an author's theme, Sargent, Huus, and Andresen (1971) proposed the use of the Profundity Scale. The scale consists of five levels of evaluation of the theme. The least profound level is to react to the story on a *physical plane*. Here the reader is primarily aware of only the physical actions of the character as embodied in the different episodic events of the story. The most profound level of awareness of a story is at the *philosophical plane*. The reader is aware of the universal truth suggested by the author. Box 2.2 outlines the five planes of thought on the Profundity Scale and shows how the scale may be applied to Margaret Mitchell's *Gone With the Wind*. Instructional applications of the Profundity Scale are described by Sargent, Huus, and Andresen in *How to Read a Book* (1971), an excellent monograph in the International Reading Association's Reading Aids Series.

Developing a Story Map

Teachers who analyze a story's structure for setting, plot, and theme are in a better position to make decisions about instruction. According to Gillet and Temple (1982), teachers can make good use of story structure depending on whether (1) there is access to reading materials that are written around perceivable story structures; (2) students have developed a sense of story structure (i.e., students have developed a schema for how stories are put together); and (3) students use their schema for stories to predict what is coming next in a new story. However, before teaching a story, Beck and her associates (1979) recommended developing a *story map*.

Box 2.2

THE PROFUNDITY SCALE FOR THE EVALUATION OF LITERATURE AS APPLIED TO GONE
WITH THE WIND *BY MARGARET MITCHELL**

Physical Plane
  Reader is aware primarily only of the physical actions of the characters. Example: The battle
  scenes and the burning of Atlanta.

Mental Plane
  Reader is aware of the physical and intellectual actions of the characters. Example: The
  machinations of Scarlet O'Hara.

Moral Plane
  Reader is aware of the physical and intellectual actions of characters in light of an ethical code.
  Example: Scarlet's endeavor to win the affections of Ashley Wilkes.

Psychological Plane
  Reader is aware of the psychological forces influencing the characters' physical and intellectual
  actions in light of an ethical code. Example: Scarlet's rebellion against the social mores of the
  Old South.

Philosophical Plane
  Reader is aware of the universal truths expounded by the author through the physical, in-
  tellectual, and ethical behavior of the characters under the influence of psychological forces.
  Example: The pageant of the decline of the way of life of the Old South.

*Reproduced with permission of the International Reading Association and Eileen Sargent, Helen Huus,
and Oliver Andresen, *How to Read a Book*. Newark, Del.: IRA, 1971.

A story map is a planning tool. It helps teachers analyze the story so that the
questions asked during discussion will create a coherent framework for understanding and remembering the text. Therefore, a story map defines what most
stories have in common—its key structural elements. The analysis of the story
elements in "The Sniper" in Box 2.1 represents a story map. An adaptation of the
map format in Box 2.1 can be found in Chapter 5, page 153. This adaptation has
the teacher consider the following key elements in a story:

— *setting* (time, place, main character),
— *problem/goal* (the problem and goal of the story are intertwined since
   most stories represent attempts of the character to achieve a goal based
   on a problem that has arisen),
— *major events* (the set of attempts to achieve the goal),
— *resolution* (the attainment of the goal and alleviation of the problem)

Beck (1979) and her colleagues argued that teachers should first establish a
line of questions which allows readers to grasp the explicit and implicit elements of
the story. Once students understand the general framework of the story, broader
questions can be raised related to the main character's motives and intentions, the
author's theme, the level of profundity of the story, and conflict situations.

Suggestions follow for the kinds of questions which may be posed from the story map.

	Beginning-of-Story Questions
Setting:	Where did the story take place? When did the story take place? Who is the main character? What is _____ like?
Problem:	What is _____'s problem? What did _____ need? Why is _____ in trouble?
	Middle-of-Story Questions
Goal:	What does _____ decide to do? What does _____ have to attempt to do?
Attempts:	What did _____ do about _____? What happened to _____? What will _____ do now?
	End-of-Story Questions
Resolution:	How did _____ solve the problem? How did _____ achieve the goal? What would you do to solve _____'s problem?
Reaction:	How did _____ feel about the problem? Why did _____ do _____? How did you _____ feel at the end?
Theme:	What is the moral of the story? What did you learn from the story? What is the major point of the story? What does this story say about *(unusual truth)*?

The importance of knowing the internal and external organization of texts and textbooks is evident in the next section. One of the ways to analyze text difficulty is to use professional judgment. Knowledge of the reading process as outlined in Chapter 1 and knowledge of text organization come together in making decisions about the difficulty of text material.

Using Professional Judgment to Make Decisions about Texts

Evaluating text is a critical task for the content area teacher—one which calls for sound professional judgment and decision making. One of the best reasons we know for making decisions about the quality of texts is that the evaluation process puts teachers "in touch" with their textbooks. To judge well, you must approach textbook evaluation in much the same manner as you make decisions about other aspects of content area instruction. Any evaluation suffers to the extent that it relies on a single source of information rather than on multiple sources or perspectives. Therefore, in order to make effective decisions based on professional judgment, the teacher needs to take into account different types of information.

One perspective or source of information to consider is publisher-provided descriptions of the design, format, and organizational structure of the textbook along with grade-level readability designations. Another perspective is the teacher's acquired knowledge of and interactions with the students in the class. A third perspective or source of information is the teacher's own sense of what makes the textbook a useful tool.

Making decisions about texts calls for teachers to articulate *how* the textbook will be used in their curriculum. As Guthrie (1981) noted, you must take into consideration the intended goal or function of the textbook. Will it be used as the primary knowledge source (sole basis of information)? as a knowledge supplement (extension of information)? as a reference (one of a number)? or as a laboratory guide (activities with guidelines)? If, for example, a text is intended to function as the sole knowledge base, you'll want to evaluate it for some of these characteristics:

— vocabulary that is either known to the readers or clearly explained,

— coherent sentences which help connect new information with prior information,

— aids which assist with questioning and review, to hold the reader's attention,

— length appropriate to course time limits,

— content expressed in terms of major concepts and principles with aesthetically pleasing examples and illustrations.

If, on the other hand, you intend a text to be used as a primary reference, an evaluation should take into consideration the following:

— a comprehensive information base in the course content,

— good access structure through clear and consistent topics and subtopics,

— cross-referencing for available definitions,

— factual detail to supplement principles and abstractions (Guthrie, 1981).

Despite the many factors to consider in text evaluation, *teachers ultimately want texts that students will understand, be able to use, and want to use.* To help guide your assessment and keep it manageable, a checklist that focuses on three crucial areas—*understandability, usability, and interestability*—is particularly useful.

One such checklist is presented in Box 2.3. It is an adaptation of the Irwin and Davis (1980) Readability Checklist.

Box 2.3

GENERAL TEXTBOOK READABILITY CHECKLIST

Understandability		Yes	To some extent	No (or does not apply)
Are the assumptions about students' vocabulary knowledge appropriate?	1			

Are the assumptions about students' prior knowledge of this content area appropriate?   2

Are the assumptions about students' general experiential backgrounds appropriate?   3

Does the teacher's manual provide the teacher with ways to develop and review the students' conceptual and experiential backgrounds?   4

Are new concepts explicitly linked to the student's prior knowledge or to their experiential backgrounds?   5

Does the text introduce abstract concepts by accompanying them with many concrete examples?   6

Does the text introduce new concepts one at a time with a sufficient number of examples for each one?   7

Are definitions understandable and at a lower level of abstraction than the concept being defined?   8

Does the text avoid irrelevant details?   9

Does the text explicitly state important complex relationships (e.g., causality, conditionality, etc.) rather than always expecting the reader to infer them from the context?   10

Does the teacher's manual provide lists of accessible resources containing alternative readings for the very poor or very advanced readers?   11

Is the readability level appropriate (according to a readibility formula)?   12

Usability

External organizational aids

Does table of contents provide a clear overview of the contents of the textbook?   1

Do chapter headings clearly define the content of the chapter?   2

Do chapter subheadings clearly break out the important concept in the chapter?   3

Do topic headings provide assistance in breaking the chapter into relevant parts?   4

Does the glossary contain all the technical terms of the textbook?   5

Are graphs and charts clear and supportive of the textual material?	6				
Are illustrations well done and appropriate to the level of the students?	7				
Is print size of the text appropriate to the level of student readers?	8				
Are lines of text an appropriate length for the level of the students who will use the textbook?	9				
Is teacher's manual available and adequate for guidance to the teacher?	10				
Are important terms in italics or boldfaced type for easy identification by readers?	11				
Are end-of-chapter questions on literal, interpretive, and applied levels of comprehension?	12				

Internal organizational aids

Are concepts spaced appropriately throughout the text, rather than being too many in too short a space or too few words?	1				
Is an adequate context provided to allow students to determine meanings of technical terms?	2				
Are the sentence lengths appropriate for the level of students who will be using the text?	3				
Is the author's style (word length, sentence length, sentence complexity, paragraph length, numbers of examples) appropriate to the level of students who will be using the text?	4				
Does the author use a predominant structure or pattern of organization (compare-contrast, cause-effect, time order, problem-solution) within the writing to assist students in interpreting the text?	5				

Interestability

Does the teacher's manual provide introductory activities that will capture students' interest?	1				
Are chapter titles and subheadings concrete, meaningful, or interesting?	2				
Is the writing style of the text appealing to the students?	3				
Are the activities motivating? Will they make the student want to pursue the topic further?	4				

Does the book clearly show how the knowledge being learned might be used by the learner in the future?   5

Are the cover, format, print size, and pictures appealing to the students?   6

Does the text provide positive and motivating models for both sexes as well as for other racial, ethnic, and socioeconomic groups?   7

Does the text help students generate interest as they relate experiences and develop visual and sensory images?   8

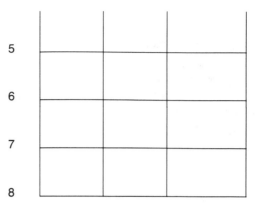

Summary Rating

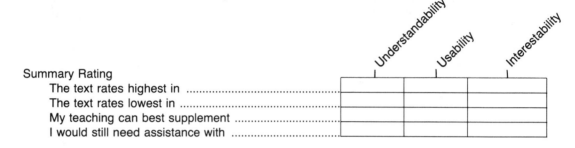

The text rates highest in ....

The text rates lowest in ....

My teaching can best supplement ....

I would still need assistance with ....

Statement of Strengths:

Statement of Weaknesses:

Understandability

The domain of *understandability* is the first, yet often neglected, information needed. It provides information about how likely a given group of students is to understand, to adequately comprehend the text. It helps the teacher to assess relationships between students' own schema and conceptual knowledge and the text information. In Chapter 1 the importance of the reader's schema was underscored. When teachers judge textbooks for possible difficulties, it is imperative to decide whether the author has taken into consideration the knowledge students will bring to the text. The match between what the reader knows and the text will have a strong influence on the understandability of the material.

Armbruster and Anderson (1981) indicated that one way to judge the author's assumptions about students' background knowledge and experiences is to decide if enough relevant ideas are presented in a text to satisfy the author's purpose. Often authors use a heading to suggest their purposes for text passages. Convert the headings to questions. If the passage content answers the questions then the authors have achieved their purposes.

Armbruster and Anderson (1981) contrasted sets of paragraphs to show the differences between enough information provided and insufficient information. For example, study the heading of the text passage below and convert it to a question. The purpose of the passage, as you can infer, is to explain a process. Now read the selection to determine if enough information is provided to satisfy this purpose.

How Blood is Transported Through the Body
The numerous arteries that branch off the aorta carry blood to various organs and systems. The veins return the blood to the heart. Among these pathways are those to the digestive organs, the limbs, the head, the kidneys, and the walls of the heart.

Armbruster and Anderson contended that the passage above is *inconsiderate*. The author's implied purpose is to explain a process — how blood is transported through the body. Yet the author hasn't provided enough information to make the process meaningful. A maturing reader for whom the passage was intended may not possess enough background to fill in the gaps in the author's explanation.

Contrast the above passage with the one below.*

How Blood is Transported Through the Body
Blood is transported by the circulatory system which is composed of networks of tubes (arteries, veins, and capillaries), a pump (the heart), and a fluid (blood) which moves. The heart pumps the blood by a series of contractions and expansions from its chambers into the arteries. Arteries take the blood to all organs of the body (brain, muscles, kidneys, etc.) except the lungs. Blood enters an organ from the artery through capillaries or tiny tubes. Blood also exits the organ through the capillaries which are connected to the veins. Veins then conduct the blood back to the heart.

The second passage is more considerate. It provides enough relevant information in light of the author's purpose to make the process explained in the text passage potentially more understandable to the reader.

In responding to some of the items under *understandability*, teachers should put themselves in the shoes of their students. Take the illustration above. If you were a student, which of the two passages above would have better helped you answer the question, "How is blood transported through the body?" Also, consider the author's assumptions about vocabulary knowledge in the same manner — from the student's perspective: If you were a student in your class, would the words in the text be beyond your present level of vocabulary knowledge? Other aspects of *understandability* should be judged from the teacher's perspective, especially items concerned with the introduction of new concepts, concept abstraction, and the teacher's manual.

*Both passages are from B. Armbruster and T. Anderson, *Content Area Textbooks,* Center for the Study of Reading, Reading Education Report No. 23. Urbana-Champaign, Ill.: University of Illinois, 1981, p. 41.

Usability

The second major domain is *usability*. Is the text coherent, unified, and structured enough to be usable? Divided into two subsections, on external and internal organizational aids, this section provides information about the presentation and organization of content. It helps assess pertinent factors that contribute to the teacher's day-to-day use of the text in teaching and the students' use in learning. These items help pinpoint for a teacher exactly what needs supplementing or what might take additional preparation time or class time to compensate.

Many of the items under *usability* pertain directly to the discussion of text organization in the previous section. Essentially, a teacher's response to these items is another way of deciding if a text is considerate or inconsiderate. A considerate text not only fits the reader's background knowledge, but also helps "the reader to gather appropriate information with minimal cognitive effort"; an inconsiderate text "requires the reader to put forth extra effort" in order to compensate for poorly developed material (Armbruster and Anderson, 1981, p. 3). The items in the usability section of the General Textbook Readability Checklist provide the following indicators of a considerate text: To what extent are the relationships among ideas clear? Is there a logical transition from one idea to another? Does the author use signal words (connectives) to make relationships explicit?

Interestability

The third domain, *interestability,* is intended to ascertain whether features of the text have appeal for a given group of students. Often, it's not possible to identify the real interests of students. They may, for example, respond to written questions in ways they believe will please teachers. Also, student interests may well change over the semester. Yet using student interests is a definite factor in motivating; it's an important way to improve attitudes toward reading and subject matter instruction. While a teacher cannot "make" students interested, there are ways to facilitate this.

One way is to examine certain features of the text. Do the cover design and other artwork convey up-to-date, refreshing images? Print size and face should vary on the pages, with the boldface lettering used for headings contrasting with the lighterface lettering often used for the main narrative. Italics and numbering of words and phrases in lists are two other devices that, in effect, liven up the printed page and make it more appealing to students. Illustrations and pictures should have instant appeal; students can relate to drawings and photographs depicting persons similar to themselves. The more relevant the textbook, the more interesting it will be to students.

Once you've completed the checklist, summarize your placement of checks on the brief rating chart at the end. Does the text rate high in understandability, usability, or interestability? Is a low rating in the area you can supplement well through your instruction or is it in an area in which you could use more help? Also, summarize the strengths and weaknesses of the textbook. If you check two areas in which you'd still need assistance, this text is less likely than another to meet your needs. Finally, decide how you take advantage of the textbook's strengths and compensate for its weaknesses.

Professional judgment is not a substitute for a quantitative analysis of text material but a complement to it. The science of readability prediction and analysis, with its extensive literature spanning half a century, can make some contributions to a teacher's understanding of text difficulty. But aim for a perspective. There are things that readability measures can do and can't do. Let's take a closer look.

Readability

There are over thirty readability formulas that can be used by classroom teachers to estimate textbook difficulty. Most of the popular formulas today are quick and easy to calculate. They typically involve a measure of sentence length and word difficulty to determine a grade-level score for text materials. This score supposedly indicates the reading achievement level that students need to comprehend the material. Because of their ease, readability formulas are used to make judgments about instructional materials. These judgments are global, to be sure, and are not intended to be precise indicators of text difficulty.

Beware and Be Aware of Limitations

A readability formula can best be described as a "rubber ruler" because the scores that it yields are estimates of text difficulty, not absolute levels. These estimates are often determined along a single dimension of an author's writing style: sentence complexity (as measured by length) and vocabulary difficulty (also measured by length). These two variables are used to predict text difficulty. But even though they have been shown to be persistent correlates of readability, they only indirectly assess sentence complexity and vocabulary difficulty. Are long sentences always more difficult to comprehend than short ones? Are long words necessarily harder to understand than short ones?

A series of short sentences in running text may even complicate the reader's ability to comprehend. Pearson (1974–1975) clarified the problem that arises when a readability formula is used to write or rewrite materials. He showed how the inferential burden of the reader actually increases when a long sentence is artificially broken into two short sentences:

> *version 1:* Because the new king clamped down on the public meetings, many residents emigrated to a new land.
> *version 2:* The new king clamped down on public meetings. Many residents emigrated to new lands.

Since the causal relationship in version 2 is not explicit, the reader must infer the connection between the separate ideas presented in each sentence. In version 1, however, the connective "because" makes the causal relationship explicit. The inferential burden is greater in 2 than in 1.

And while we're examining inferential burden, keep in mind that a readability formula doesn't account for the experience and knowledge that readers bring to content material. Hittleman (1973) characterized readability as a moment in time. He maintained that readability estimates should include the reader's emotional, cognitive, and linguistic backgrounds. A person's "human makeup" interacts at the moment with the topic, the proposed purposes for reading, and the semantic and syntactic structures in the material. Formulas are not designed to tap the variables operating in the reader. Our purpose, interest, motivation, and emotional state as well as the environment that we're in during reading contribute to our ability to comprehend text.

Nelson (1978) underscored the importance of viewing a readability formula as a rubber ruler by using the following example:*

> Take the following social studies sentences as an example: "The leader often becomes the symbol of the unity of the country. No one will run against him." These sentences are relatively short and they contain few multisyllabic words. According to readability criteria, the sentences would appear to be appropriate for junior high school text material. However, the difficulty an eighth grade reader might experience in comprehending these sentences has little to do with readability criteria. Consider the information that the student must integrate:
>
> 1. The special meaning of *leader* in the social studies content.
>
> 2. The word *often* used to mean "in many cases" rather than "repeatedly."
>
> 3. The sense of *becomes* as meaning "grows to be" rather than "is suitable to."
>
> 4. The abstract concept of *symbolism*.
>
> 5. The abstract concept of *unity*.
>
> 6. The word *country* as a political unit rather than as a rural area.
>
> 7. The idea of *run against* as in an election.
>
> 8. The implication of a cause and effect relationship between the ideas presented in the two sentences.   *(p. 622)*

The danger, according to Nelson, is not in the use of readability formulas: "The danger is in promoting the faulty assumptions that matching the readability score of materials to the reading achievement scores of students will automatically yield comprehension" (p. 622). She made these suggestions to content teachers:

> 1. Learn to use a simple readability formula as an aid in evaluating text material for student use.

*This and the following quote are reprinted from Joan Nelson, "Reabability: Some Cautions for the Content Area Teacher," *Journal of Reading,* April 1978, by permission of Joan Nelson and the International Reading Association.

2. Wherever possible, provide materials containing the essential facts, concepts, and values of the subject at varying levels of readability within the reading range of your students.

3. Don't assume that matching readability level of material to reading achievement level of students results in automatic comprehension. Remember there are many factors that affect reading difficulty besides those measured by readability formulas.

4. Don't assume that rewriting text materials according to readability criteria results in automatic reading ease. Leave rewriting of text material to the linguists, researchers, and editors who have time to analyze and validate their manipulations.

5. Recognize that using a readability formula is no substitute for instruction. Assigning is not teaching. Subject area textbooks are not designed for independent reading. The best way to enhance reading comprehension in your subject area is to provide the kind of instruction which prepares students for the reading assignment, guides them in their reading, and reinforces the new ideas through rereading and discussion. *(p. 624–625)*

Within the spirit of these suggestions, let's examine three readability formulas and two alternatives, the *cloze* and *maze* procedures. We selected the formulas because of their current popularity, their ease of calculation, and their high degree of reliability with more complex formulas such as the Dale-Chall (1948).

Fry's Readability Graph

The readability graph developed by Edward Fry (1968, 1977) is a quick and simple readability formula. The graph was designed to identify the grade-level score for materials from first grade through college. Two variables are used to predict the difficulty of the reading material: sentence length and word length. Sentence length is detemined by the total number of sentences in a sample passage. Word length is determined by the total number of syllables in the passage. Fry recommended that three 100-word samples from the reading material be used to calculate its readability. The grade-level scores for each of the passages can then be averaged to determine an overall readability level. According to Fry, the readability graph predicts the difficulty level of the material within one grade level. The graph and expanded directions for the Fry formula are presented in Box 2.4.

Raygor Readability Estimate

Raygor (1977) developed a formula using a graph quite similar to Fry's. However, in the Raygor readability estimate word difficulty is measured by counting long words (six letters or more) rather than by counting syllables. Counting syllables

Box 2.4

FRY READABILITY GRAPH*

Graph for Estimating Readability—Extended

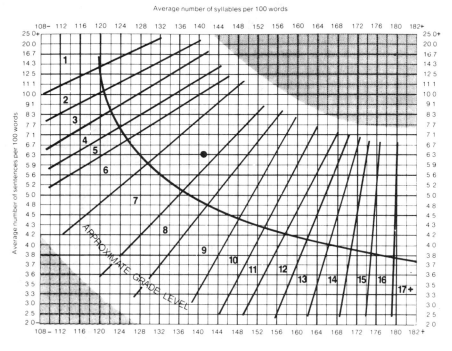

Expanded Directions for Working Readability Graph

1. Randomly select three (3) sample passages and count out exactly 100 words each, beginning with the beginning of a sentence. Do count proper nouns, initializations, and numerals.

2. Count the number of sentences in the hundred words, estimating length of the fraction of the last sentence to the nearest one-tenth.

3. Count the total number of syllables in the 100-word passage. If you don't have a hand counter available, an easy way is to simply put a mark above every syllable over one in each word, then when you get to the end of the passage, count the number of marks and add 100. Small calculators can also be used as counters by pushing numeral 1, then push the + sign for each word or syllable when counting.

4. Enter graph with *average* sentence length and *average* number of syllables; plot dot where the two lines intersect. Area where dot is plotted will give you the approximate grade level.

5. If a great deal of variability is found in syllable count or sentence count, putting more samples into the average is desirable.

6. A word is defined as a group of symbols with a space on either side; thus, *Joe, IRA, 1945,* and *&* are each one word.

7. A syllable is defined as a phonetic syllable. Generally, there are as many syllables as vowel sounds. For example, *stopped* is one syllable and *wanted* is two syllables. When counting syllables for numerals and initializations, count one syllable for each symbol. For example, *1945* is four syllables, *IRA* is three syllables, and *&* is one syllable.

*SOURCE: Edward Fry, "Fry's readability graph: clarifications, validity, and extension to level 17." *Journal of Reading,* **21** (1977): 242–252. Reproduction permitted—no copyright.

can prove difficult and time consuming. It often results in introducing the most human error to an estimate of readability. Baldwin and Kaufman (1979) tested the speed and accuracy of the Raygor formula against that of the Fry. Indeed, they found the Raygor readability graph to be faster to calculate and just about as accurate as the Fry formula. The graph and directions for the Raygor formula can be found in Box 2.5.

Box 2.5

*RAYGOR READABILITY ESTIMATE**

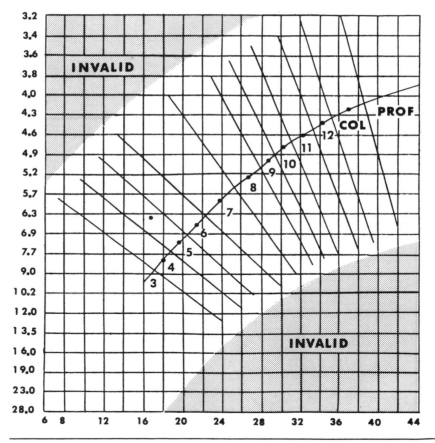

Directions: Count out three 100-word passages at the beginning, middle, and end of a selection or book. Count proper nouns, but not numerals.

1. Count sentences in each passage, estimating to nearest tenth.
2. Count words with six or more letters.
3. Average the sentence length and word length over three samples and plot the average on the graph.

Example	Sentences	Words
A	6.0	15
B	6.8	19
C	6.4	17
Total	19.2	51
Average	6.4	17

Note mark on graph: Grade level is about 5.

*SOURCE: Scott Baldwin and Rhonda Kaufman, "A concurrent validity study of the Raygor readability estimate." Journal of Reading 23 (1979): 148–153. This graph is not copyrighted.

SMOG Grading

The Simple Measure of Gobbledygook (SMOG) is another quick and easy readability formula to compute (McLaughlin, 1969). Unlike the Fry and Raygor formulas, SMOG grading doesn't involve plotting points on a graph to yield a grade-level score. It indirectly relies on sentence length and word difficulty to predict the difficulty of reading material.

To compute a SMOG grade-level score follow these four steps.

1. Count ten consecutive sentences near the beginning of the text to be assessed, ten in the middle, and ten near the end. Count as a sentence any string of words ending with a period, question mark, or exclamation point.

2. In the thirty selected sentences count every word of three or more syllables. Any string of letters or numerals beginning and ending with a space or punctuation mark should be counted if you can distinguish at least three syllables when you read it aloud in context. If a polysyllabic word is repeated, count each repetition.

3. Estimate the square root of the number of polysyllabic words counted. This is done by taking the square root of the nearest perfect square. For example, if the count is 85, the nearest perfect square is 81, which yields a square root of 9. If the count lies roughly between two perfect squares, choose the lower number. For instance, if the count is 110, take the square root of 100 rather than 121.

4. Add 3 to the approximate square root. This gives the SMOG grade, which is the reading grade that a person must have reached if he is to understand fully the text assessed.

A worksheet such as the one illustrated in Box 2.6 can be employed to facilitate the calculation of the SMOG formula.

Box 2.6

WORKSHEET FOR FIGURING SMOG GRADING*

1. Number of polysyllabic words for sample 1 (first set of ten sentences):   _____
2. Number of polysyllabic words for sample 2 (second set of ten sentences):   _____
3. Number of polysyllabic words for sample 3 (third set of ten sentences):   _____
4. Total number of polysyllabic words (add 1, 2, and 3):   _____
5. Nearest perfect square to number 4 above: _____
6. Square root of the perfect square given in number 5:   _____
7. Add 3 to the result of number 6:   _____

Final number is the SMOG grade—the reading grade that an individual must have reached to fully understand the text assessed.

*SOURCE: Jerry Johns. Mimeographed. Northern Illinois University, 1976.

The SMOG is so incredibly easy to calculate that you may think that it's a put-on. Yet McLaughlin, the originator of SMOG, employed an intricate set of statistical procedures to determine its feasibility as a measure of readability. The key to interpreting a SMOG grade-level score is the author's claim that the score indicates the reading achievement level students must have to comprehend the material completely (90% comprehension or better). By way of contrast, the Fry graph claims to determine a grade score that is "suitable" for comprehension (65–75% comprehension).

In summary, readability formulas are predictive techniques. Hypotheses about text difficulty are based on an analysis of the material using selected variables which have been statistically determined to correlate with comprehension difficulty. The reader is not a variable in predicting difficulty from a formula. This is one of the reasons why you should approach these readability formulas with a healthy skepticism.

There are readability measures which aren't based on a prediction of text difficulty but on actual reader performance with the material. The *cloze* procedure and the *maze* technique will help you judge students' ability to cope with content material.

Cloze Procedure

The cloze procedure does not make use of a formula to estimate the difficulty of reading material. "Cloze" refers to the psychological principle of closure. Closure is a Gestalt term which applies to the human tendency to complete a familiar but not-quite-finished pattern. An example of the closure principle is for an individual to perceive a broken circle as a whole, or, in the case of listening and reading, to supply a missing word in a familiar language sequence.

The cloze procedure was originated by Taylor in 1953, but its roots can be traced to the work of Ebbinghaus, who developed a "completion method" test in 1897. A cloze test determines how well students can read a particular text or reading selection as a result of their interaction with the material. Simply defined, then, the cloze procedure is a method by which you systematically delete words from a text passage and then evaluate students' ability to accurately supply the words that were deleted. An encounter with a cloze passage should reveal the interplay between the prior knowledge that students bring to the reading task and their language competence. Knowing the extent of this interplay will be helpful in selecting materials and planning instructional procedures. Box 2.7 presents a sample portion of a cloze procedure.

Box 2.7

SAMPLE PORTION OF CLOZE TEST

Everybody sleeps—everybody, that is, except for an Italian and an Australian. These two men, according (1) twentieth-century medical literature, (2) slept at all. On (3) other hand, not long (4) *The New York Times* (5) on a professor who (6) to have fourteen hours (7) sleep a night. If (8) woke after even thirteen (9), he spent the day (10) foggy and tense. Apart (11) their sleeping patterns, though, (12) three men, according to (13) experts on such matters, (14) to be perfectly normal. (15) why, by inference, assume (16) their sleep habits were (17)? Indeed, when it comes (18) sleep, what is normal (19), by contrast, abnormal? Who's (20) say that what's perfectly natural for me might not be absurd for you?

Answers:

1. to	6. had	11. from	16. that
2. never	7. of	12. these	17. abnormal
3. the	8. he	13. the	18. to
4. ago	9. hours	14. appeared	19. and
5. reported	10. feeling	15. Yet	20. to

Here is how to construct, administer, score, and interpret a cloze test.

1. Construction
   a. Select a reading passage of approximately 275 words from material that students have not yet read, but that you plan to assign.
   b. Leave the first sentence intact. Starting with the second sentence, select at random one of the first five words. Delete every fifth word thereafter, until you have a total of 50 words for deletion. Retain the remaining sentence of the last deleted word. Type one more sentence intact. For children below grade four, deletion of every tenth word is often recommended.
   c. Leave an underlined blank fifteen spaces long for each deleted word as you type the passage on a ditto master.

2. Administration
   a. Inform students that they are not to use their textbooks or work together in completing the cloze passage.
   b. Explain the task that students are to perform. Show how the cloze procedure works by providing several examples on the board.
   c. Allow students as much time as they need to complete the cloze passage.

3. Scoring
   a. Count as correct every *exact* word students supply. *Do not* count synonyms even though they may appear to be satisfactory. Counting synonyms will not change the scores appreciably, but it will cause unnecessary hassles and haggling with students. Accepting synonyms also affects the reliability of the performance criteria since they were established on exact word replacements.
   b. Multiply the total number of exact word replacements by two in order to determine the student's cloze percentage score.
   c. Record the cloze percentage scores on a single sheet of paper for each class. For each class you now have from one to three instructional groups that can form the basis for differentiated assignments. See Box 2.8.

Box 2.8

---

*CLOZE PERFORMANCE CHART**

Subject _____

Period _____

Teacher _____

Below 40%	Between 40% and 60%	Above 60%

*Source: Robert Baker. Mimeographed. Syracuse, N.Y.: Syracuse University, 1972.

---

4. Interpretation
   a. A score of 40–60% indicates that the passage can be read with some competence by students. The material will challenge students if they are given some form of reading guidance.
   b. A score of 60% indicates that the passage can be read with a great deal of competence by students. They may be able to read the material on their own without reading guidance.
   c. A score below 40% indicates that the passage will probably be too difficult for students. They will need either a great deal of reading guidance to benefit from the material or more suitable material.

The cloze procedure is an alternative to readability formulas, because it gives an indication of how students will actually perform with course materials. But two potential problems may have a negative effect on the results of student performance on a cloze test. First, the nature of the test itself will probably be foreign to students. They will be staring at a sea of blank spaces in running text, and having to provide words for them can seem a formidable task. Don't expect a valid score the first time you administer the test. It's important to discuss the purpose of the cloze test and give students ample practice and exposure to it.

A second source of difficulty may be students' reactions to the criteria for successful performance. An excellent score on a cloze test means that a student can respond incorrectly to twenty out of fifty test items — a mind-boggling standard of success that may cause unnecessary anxiety among students.

Maze Technique

Because of the above two precautions, the maze technique seems to us to be a promising modification of the cloze procedure. The maze readability technique is similar to the cloze, with one major alteration: instead of leaving a blank space in place of a deleted word, the student can choose from three alternatives. For example: Air comes into the body through the mouth or (1) feet, (2) loses, (3) nostrils. Number 3, of course, is the correct choice. "Feet" is in the same grammatical word class (noun) as nostrils, but it doesn't make sense. The second choice, "loses," neither is grammatically correct nor makes sense. An example of a maze test passage is presented in Box 2.9.

Box 2.9

ALICE IN WONDERLAND MAZE PASSAGE

Directions: The following exercise will help determine if you will have any trouble reading *Alice in Wonderland*. Every fifth word in the passage has three choices. Underline the word choice that makes the most sense. The passage begins with our Alice chasing a rabbit right into his rabbit hole.

In another moment down went Alice after it, never once considering how in the world she was to get out.

		turn		rather	
The rabbit hole went straight somewhere like a tunnel for six				way and then dipped	
		on		some	
blue				if	
suddenly	down, so suddenly that boy	him	had not a moment to	think about stopping herself	
wonderfully		Alice		and	
falling		nowhere		a	
quickly she found herself falling down			what seemed to be	these very deep well.	
before		her		but	

```
            well                                    it                    or
Either the house was very deep, or search fell very slowly, for she   had plenty of time dark
        given               she                think                    as
          run             wonder               with
she went down to candle about her and to sew     what was going to happen next. First she tried
        look              homely                       dive
know              in                  under              dark
of    look down and make out    what she was coming to       but it was too damp  to see any-
to                  them                  sweetly              rock
        drafty              up            fast
thing: then we    looked at the sides an the well, and noticed which they were filled with
        she                of                that
cupboards             where                briefly
cars        and book-shelves: here and until   she saw maps and pictures hung upon pegs. She
wisely              there              germs
took              twelve              dirty              "orange
jumped down a jar from rusted of the shelves as them passed: it was labeled "empty   Marma-
earth              one                she                "help
        sour                  iron              inside
lade" but to her great disappointment it was empty: you   did not like to learn    the jar for fear
        fly                  she                drop
of                  sleepy            me                shoes
this killing somebody underneath, so colored    to put it into those of the cupboards as him
until                managed          one                she
fell past it.
```

"Well!" thought Alice to herself "After such a fall as this I shall think nothing of tumbling down stairs!"

Here is how to construct, administer, score, and interpret a maze test.

1. Construction
   a. Choose a passage from the content material that students have not yet read.
   b. Leave the first sentence intact. Starting with the second sentence, select at random one of the first five words. Delete every fifth or tenth word thereafter, until you have at least twenty deletions.
   c. Substitute three alternative words for each deletion: (1) the correct word, (2) an incorrect word that is *syntactically acceptable* (from the same word class, such as noun, verb, adjective, as the correct word) but *semantically unacceptable* (not meaning the same as the correct word), (3) an incorrect word that is syntactically and semantically unacceptable.
   d. The order of the three word choices should be changed at random for each deletion.
2. Administration (same as in the cloze procedure)

3. Scoring
   a. Count the number of correct word responses.
   b. Determine the student's comprehension score by dividing the total number of deleted words into the number of correct responses made:

$$\text{Comprehension score} \quad = \frac{\text{total number of choices}}{\text{number of correct responses}}$$

4. Interpretation
   a. A score above 85% indicates that the passage can be read with a great deal of competence by students. They may be able to read the material on their own without reading guidance.
   b. A score between 60 and 85% indicates that the passage can be read with some competence by students. The material will challenge students, but they should be given some form of reading guidance.
   c. A score below 60% indicates that the passage will probably be too difficult for students. They will need either a great deal of guidance to benefit from the material or more suitable material.

Guthrie (1973) originated the maze technique, but validated it with primary grade children only. Further validation studies with secondary students may yield a new set of criteria to help make interpretations about student performance. From a common-sense point of view, however, the maze technique has much potential.

Also from a common-sense point of view, cloze and maze procedures may be adapted as teaching devices. They will stimulate a close reading of an important text passage that the teacher earmarks for discussion. When used as teaching tools, cloze and maze passages need not have systematic word deletions. As we show in Chapter 9, the teacher may wish to alter only key concept terms or only a certain combination of word classes to suit your instructional purposes. Synonyms or reasonable word replacements need not be "incorrect" either because you will not be using a passage to test comprehension but to guide its development.

Looking Back, Looking Forward

In the context of the classroom, texts and textbooks are part of a three-way interaction. Teacher-student-text interact in ways that form the very basis of comprehension and learning of content subject matter. Knowing about the texts and textbooks that students will use is a necessary aspect of content area reading instruction. Evaluating the difficulty of text material requires both professional judgment and quantitative analysis. Text evaluation must take into account various factors within the reader and the text. Exercising professional judgment is as useful as calculating readability formulas in evaluating the difficulty of content material. Teachers, therefore, must be concerned with the quality of the content, format, organization, and appeal of the material. Seeking answers to the practical questions they raise puts teachers in touch with their text materials. This in turn puts teachers in a position to compensate instructionally for difficulties rather than discarding texts.

Two major themes were explored in this chapter: first, how ideas in texts are organized; and second, how professional judgment and traditional measures may be used to estimate the difficulty of texts. The external organization of a textbook includes such factors as the overall instructional design, front and end matter, and within-chapter organizational aids. The internal organization of text deals with predominant interrelationships among ideas as reflected in top-level structures or patterns of organization peculiar to expository writing. Teachers concerned with the structure of a story can use story grammar techniques to analyze how well a story is organized.

The second part of this chapter, making decisions about general textbook readability, called for teachers to articulate how the textbook will be used with students. We cited several factors which need consideration when making these decisions: *understandability* (how likely are my students to comprehend this text?); *usability* (is this text coherent, unified and structured enough to be usable with my class?); and *interestability* (will features of this text have appeal for my students?).

Finally, the Fry readability graph, the Raygor readability estimate, and SMOG grading were examined. Predictive techniques such as these are based on sentence complexity and vocabulary difficulty of the material. Other measures are based on actual reader performance with the material and are alternatives to readability formulas. The cloze procedure and maze technique were reviewed for their utility in helping teachers judge students' ability to handle text material in a specific content subject.

Evaluation takes center stage in the next chapter as we explore multiple ways to assess students in the content classroom. Here too, it quickly becomes apparent that to rely solely on quantitative assessment is unnecessarily limiting. In the next chapter, the emphasis is on informal procedures for assessing background knowledge, reading attitudes, and performance with text in content area reading situations.

Suggested Readings

Bormuth, J. (1966). Readability: A new approach. *Reading Research Quarterly*, **1,** 79–132.

Calfee, R., & Curley, R. (1984). Structures of prose in content areas. In J. Flood (ed.), *Understanding Reading Comprehension*. Newark, Del.: International Reading Association.

Klare, G. (1974). Assessing readability. *Reading Research Quarterly*, **10,** 62–102.

Klare, G. (1982). Readability. In H. Mitzel, *Encyclopedia of Educational Research* (5th ed.). New York: Free Press.

McConaughty, S. (1980). Using story structure in the classroom. *Language Arts*, **57,** 157–165.

Meyer, B. J. F. (1984). The structure of text. In P. D. Pearson (ed.), *Handbook of Reading Research*. New York: Longman.

Stein, N., & Glenn, C. (1979). An analysis of story comprehension in elementary school children. In R. Freedle (ed.), *New Directions in Prose Processing*. Norwood, N.J.: ABLEX.

CHAPTER THREE

Evaluating for Instruction

We are as entranced by numbers as crows are by shiny objects.

—ANNE RONEY

Organizing Principle

Content area teachers constantly make decisions about instruction. To do this effectively, they need to know two things: what kinds of information to collect about students within the natural context of the classroom, and how to obtain that information. Examining differences between a formal, standardized approach and an informal, naturalistic approach to evaluation helps to delineate various methods of assessment. Tests, observations, checklists, interviews, inventories, scales, and text materials themselves are some of the means by which teachers can collect useful information. Evaluating for instructional purposes provides the opportunity to consider information about students' background knowledge, their attitudes toward reading and subject matter, and their ability to use reading to learn from texts. The organizing principle of this chapter underscores the importance of informal evaluation procedures in making decisions about content area reading instruction: *Evaluating for instruction is a continuous process which uses largely informal procedures in the natural context of the classroom.*

CHAPTER OVERVIEW

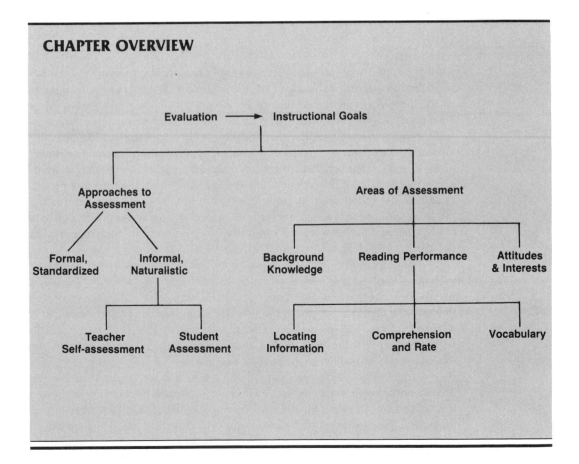

As you approach this chapter, notice that an informal, naturalistic approach to evaluation will be emphasized. The following questions will be answered as a result of reading:

1. How does evaluation aid in setting instructional goals?
2. What is an informal, naturalistic approach to evaluation? How does it differ from a formal, standardized approach?
3. Why should assessment be on-going and occur within the natural context of the classroom?
4. In addition to student assessment, why should teachers engage in self-assessment?
5. How can the teachers assess background knowledge?
6. Why and how should teachers assess students' attitudes and interests toward reading?
7. How does the teacher assess reading performance within the context of classroom instruction?

Reading diagnosis—the very concept is formidable, sometimes even bewildering, to content area teachers. The medical connotation of *diagnosis* suggests a search for deficiencies and factors associated with failure in students. Most classroom teachers—sensibly—see their role as one of emphasizing the strengths students bring to learning situations. The prospect of diagnosing reading behavior is formidable because it suggests expertise and specialization beyond the domain of the classroom teacher. A diagnostic mystique doubtlessly contributes to whatever bewilderment or misgivings teachers have about evaluating reading performance. What is the diagostic mystique? Sawyer (1974) described it as "the prevailing attitude that a skill-oriented assessment of . . . reading behavior by a reading expert is the last word in diagnostic workups. That if we can zero in on skill deficiencies the child will progress" (p. 561).

The diagnostic mystique is more "mythifying" than mystifying; yet it prevails in school. It also promotes faulty assumptions. As a result, *diagnosis* invariably evokes in the minds of teachers what is wrong with students. According to Hittleman (1977), it "seems to exclude assessing a reading performance that is not marked by failure" (p. 86). Teachers may also assume that they have little to do with assessing reading performance, when in fact their contributions to the evaluation process will enhance reading and learning.

Perhaps it's only a question of semantics, but we prefer to make the distinction between diagnosis and evaluation in content areas. Diagnosis is a restrictive term. It smacks too heavily of examining deficiencies and fragmenting the reading process for instructional purposes. Content area teachers are quick to reject this notion. One very important way to put the results of evaluation to work for you is to use assessment data to plan instruction. What does a content area teacher need to know about students to develop goals and objectives for text-related teaching?

As you go about the task of planning for and making decisions about instruction, at least two areas of evaluation become clear. You will, first of all, want to assess students' background knowledge in relation to specific instructional units and text assignments. And, second, you will want to assess how well they use reading strategies to learn from texts. Given these two areas of assessment, teachers for the most part find that an informal, naturalistic approach to evaluation is more useful than a formal, standardized one. Let's examine why this is so.

A Naturalistic Approach to Evaluation

Teachers sometimes intuitively know that what they do in class is working. More often, however, information to make decisions is best obtained through careful observation of students as they engage in tasks in the content classroom. Their strengths and weaknesses as they interact with one another and with content reading material can be evaluated as students participate in small groups, contribute to class discussions, respond to questions, and complete written assignments. This approach to evaluation is informal and naturalistic.

A naturalistic approach to evaluation has two main elements. First, it is based on the responses of those directly involved. Second, it uses methods within the natural context of the classroom. The presence of these two criteria ensures that evaluation will begin with classroom-centered concerns.

Naturalistic methods may include personal observation, interviews, and record and student product review. The information gained from a naturalistic evaluation can be organized into a rich description or portrait of your content area classroom. Concerns that emerge, whether about individual students or the delivery of instructional strategy, are likely to make sense because they came directly from the classroom context.

Consider how a naturalistic approach differs from a more formal, standardized one. In Table 3.1 the two approaches are compared by adapting Stake's (1975) descriptions to reading evaluation. Certainly there are many gray areas—areas in an evaluation where the standardized and naturalistic approaches overlap. In this table, however, differences between the two approaches are emphasized. The design, methods, and feedback of formal evaluation are product oriented. They are more tangible and can be obtained at specific points in time. This is not the case when informal evaluation is stressed; design, methods, and feedback are ongoing and less concrete.

The Limited Utility of Standardized Tests

An assessment based on standardized test information is different from an assessment which evolves from naturalistic methods. A standardized reading test is more formal, may be administered at the beginning of the school year, and uses test

Table 3.1 Comparison of Two Approaches to Evaluation

	Standardized	*Naturalistic*
Orientation	Formal	Informal
Design	At the beginning of the school year	Continuously evolving throughout an instructional unit
Methods	Objective; standardized reading tests	Subjective; observations, interviews, informal, teacher-made tests
Feedback	Report, printout with summary of strong and weak subareas of reading performance	Notes, profiles, recommendations which continuously evolve throughout instructional unit

methods that are considered to be objective. Moreover, schools may purchase a computer printout or report of students' strengths and weaknesses in reading subskills along with the test results.

Today, pressures for accountability have led many schools to rely on standardized tests as a means of assessment. According to Moore (1983), standardized tests help to satisfy the public's demand that assessment be objective, exact, and convenient. As a result, school officials often want "hard" data which are statistically validated and reliable. Enter the standardized test! Standardized reading tests are formal, usually machine-scorable instruments in which scores for the tested group are compared with standards established by an original normative population. The purpose of a standardized reading test is to show where students stand in relation to other students based on a single performance.

Reading researchers have studied the relationships between standardized tests of reading and student performance on reading tasks in specific content areas (Artley, 1948; Peters, 1975). They have generally concluded that specific factors not accounted for on a test of general achievement influence the reading of subject matter materials. In fact, Peters (1975) said a standardized reading test may not provide the information that content teachers desire.

Performance on standardized reading tests can yield only rough estimates at best as to how students will apply reading to textbooks in a particular subject. A student who is a good reader of social studies may be a poor or mediocre reader of math or science. It's safe to say that teachers who consult standardized reading tests should do so judiciously and with reasonable expectations.

What Standardized Tests Tell and Don't Tell

Standardized test results are probably most useful at the building or district, not the classroom level. A school, for instance, may wish to compare itself for reading performance against a national norm. Or local norms may be compared with national norms, which is sometimes necessary in applying for federal or state funds. In general, information from standardized tests may help to screen for students who might have major difficulties in reading, to compare general reading achievement levels of different classes or grades of students, to assess group reading achievement, and to assess reading growth of groups of students (Allington and Strange, 1980).

However, content area teachers need useful information about students' text-related behavior and background knowledge. A teacher would be guilty of misusing standardized test results if he or she were to extrapolate about students' background knowledge or ability to comprehend course materials on the basis of standardized reading test performance.

Alternatives to standardized reading assessment are found in an informal, naturalistic approach to evaluation. One of the most useful assessment tools for naturalistic inquiry is observation.

Evaluating Students Through Observation

"How am I doing?" Every student wants to know, yet fears finding out the answer to this question. Content area teachers, too, want to know about their students in order to provide ongoing feedback. Observation is the primary method they can use to do what needs to be done—"evaluate something that matters" (Little, 1982, p. 43). Consequently, we observe relevant interactive and independent behavior (of students) as they learn in the content classroom.

Observation is one unobtrusive measure that ranges from occasional notice of unusual student behavior, to frequent anecdotal jottings, to regular and detailed written field notes. Besides the obvious opportunity to observe students' oral and silent reading behaviors, there are other advantages to observation. Observing students' appearance, posture, mannerisms, enthusiasm, or apathy may reveal information about self-image. However, unless teachers make a systematic effort to tune in to student performance, they may lose valuable insights. The teacher has to be a good listener and a good watcher of students. Accurate observations should be a natural outgrowth of teaching; it increases teaching efficiency and effectiveness. Instructional decisions based on accurate observation help the teacher zero in on what and how to teach in relation to reading tasks.

However, before this can happen, classroom teachers must view themselves as participant-observers. They need to systematically collect as much information as possible in relation to instructional goals.

For example, a science teacher is beginning a unit on plants and plant life. She probably approaches the unit with certain preconceptions about the difficulty of the reading material, the work and study habits of the students, and the students' ability to use reading as a vehicle for learning. But she suspends these preconceptions; she purposely tries not to let presuppositions interfere with class presentations until actual classroom events and experiences during the unit suggest that her preconceptions are relevant.

The science teacher responds to the happenings that unfold before her. She guides daily observations by asking herself questions which reflect her objectives: How did students react to the class presentation? Which students had trouble with the reading assignment? How did students respond to instructional procedures and materials? Were students bored with the lesson? Did they grasp the concept related to man's dependence on green plants? What adjustments should I make in class presentations for the remainder of the unit?

This teacher is a participant-observer. She searches for the meanings of events that happen in class. To safeguard against the limitations of memory, the observer-teacher records in a notebook what happens in class. These field notes aid in classifying information, inferring behavior, and making predictions about instructional procedures, and as they accumulate, they become anecdotal records which provide documentary evidence of students' behavior over long stretches of time. Robinson (1975) recommended that

> Students should be observed as they work independently, as they respond to questions, . . . and as they interact with their peers. The teacher should concentrate on one or at most a few students at one time and record dated impressions. In this way the instructor is able to compare observations for given students over time while coping with specific reading-study tasks. *(pp. 17–18)*

You can record and date observations in a notebook or on 3″ by 5″ cards. A chronicle of informative notes gradually will emerge. According to Robinson (1975), "the instructor then has a product—dated written comments—to view in conjunction with other evaluative evidence" (p. 18).

Or, you can use a time sample format such as the one outlined in Figure 3.1. This provides an efficient way to collect data about what individuals or groups of students are doing in the classroom. For example you might select a five-minute time interval and describe behavior you observe at three successive intervals. An

Figure 3.1 Time Sample

Date _10/16/85_   Time: Start _11:05_ Stop _11:10_
School _Notre Dame_   Grade _10_
Class _English_
Other pertinent information
Time intervals Used: _2 min_
Time _11:05_ Behavior: Lisa joins group working on Act II in Julius Caesar.
Time _11:07_ Behavior: She seems bored and is staring out the window.
Time _11:09_ Behavior: Rick and Jim begin arguing about a scene and Lisa takes part in the group discussion.

activity such as an anticipation guide (which will be discussed in Chapter 4) which demands both individual student input and small group discussion is a good opportunity to use time sampling.

Listening and discussing are two other assessment tools that go hand in hand with observing students. Many students want to establish a personal rapport with their teacher. They may talk of myriad subjects, seemingly unrelated to the unit. It is often during this informal chatter, however, that teachers find out about the students' background, problems, and interests. This type of conversation, in which teachers assume the role of active listeners, can provide suggestions about topics for future lessons and materials. It should be encouraged, but kept within ethical bounds (Vacca and Sparks, 1981). In other words, teachers need to ignore extraneous information.

Discussion, both casual and directed, is also an integral part of evaluation. Teachers need to make themselves available, both before and after class, for discussion about general topics, lessons, and assignments. For assessing reading comprehension, nothing replaces one-to-one discussion of the material, whether before, during, or after the actual reading. Teachers and students soon become adept at asking pertinent questions that go beyond the literal or factual level into the interpretive, even applied levels of comprehension. Finally, you may even encourage students to verbalize their positive and negative feelings about the class itself as well as topics, reading, and content area activities.

Checklists

Other informal evaluation methods such as checklists and content area reading inventories, discussed later in this chapter, are different from natural, open-ended observation. They often consist of categories and subcategories which have already been determined; they impose an *a priori* classification scheme on the observation process. A checklist is designed to reveal categories of information the teacher has preselected. When constructing a checklist you should know beforehand which reading and study tasks or attitudes you plan to observe. Individual items on the checklist then serve to guide your observations in a selective manner.

The selectivity that a checklist offers is both its strength and weakness as an observational tool. Checklists are obviously efficient because they guide the teacher's observations and allow him or her to zero in on certain kinds of behavior. But a checklist can also restrict observation by limiting the breadth of information recorded—excluding potentially valuable raw data.

Box 3.1 presents sample checklist items that may be adapted to specific instructional objectives in various content areas.

Observation and checklists reveal enough information in most cases to help classroom teachers make good decisions about instruction. They provide ongoing indicators of student behavior. Instructors should also consider assessing their own behavior in the classroom environment.

Box 3.1

SAMPLE CHECKLIST ITEMS FOR OBSERVING READING AND STUDY BEHAVIOR

Reading and Study Behavior	Fred	Pat	Frank	JoAnne	Jerry	Courtney	Mike	Mary
Comprehension								
1. Follows the author's message	A	B	B	A	D	C	F	C
2. Evaluates the relevancy of facts								
3. Questions the accuracy of statements								
4. Critical of an author's bias								
5. Comprehends what the author means								
6. Follows text organization								
7. Can solve problems through reading								
8. Develops purposes for reading								
9. Makes predictions and takes risks								
10. Applies information to come up with new ideas								
Vocabulary								
1. Has a good grasp of technical terms in the subject under study								
2. Works out the meaning of an unknown word through context or structural analysis								
3. Knows how to use a dictionary effectively								
4. Sees relationships among key terms								
5. Becomes interested in the derivation of technical terms								
Study Habits								
1. Concentrates while reading								
2. Understands better by reading orally than silently								
3. Has a well-defined purpose in mind when studying								
4. Knows how to take notes during lecture and discussion								
5. Can organize material through outlining								
6. Skims to find the answer to a specific question								
7. Reads everything slowly and carefully								
8. Makes use of book parts								
9. Understands charts, maps, tables in the text								
10. Summarizes information								

Grading Key: A = always (excellent)
B = usually (good)
C = sometimes (average)
D = seldom (poor)
F = never (unacceptable)

Teacher Self-Evaluation

If teachers are using a naturalistic approach to assess students it seems logical to extend the process and collect some useful information about yourself in the context of the classroom environment. It is a marvelous opportunity to ask that important question, "How am I doing?"

Teachers who want to deal with real concerns within their own classrooms can use a couple of straightforward self-reporting techniques. They can do these individually or, after a while, get together and share with one another.

The first self-reporting technique is a systematic reflection about teaching behavior. As illustrated in Box 3.2, the content area teacher asks a series of questions about his or her behavior in relation to a specific class or even a particular topic or unit of study.

This may be done almost any time, but we suggest asking the questions before or within a week of beginning a new unit or semester. Jotting down the answers on a card or in a small notebook makes it even more useful because the answers will be easy to locate as time goes on. This keeps the process of self-evaluation going and takes a minimal amount of time.

Box 3.2

QUESTIONS FOR TEACHER SELF-EVALUATION

1. *Focus on Present*
   What unit (or class, or part of the day) do I want to look at?

2. *Identify Behaviors*
   What do I usually do now?

3. *Analyze Behaviors*
   What results am I getting?

4. *Expose Alternatives*
   What additional possibilities exist?

5. *Set Goals*
   Where do I hope to go?

6. *Plan Change*
   How will I get there?

7. *Practice for Effectiveness*
   What can I do to assure getting there?

8. *Evaluate*
   Did I get there?

The second self-reporting technique is not as systematic but is more personal: keeping a daily journal. The content area teacher writes down her or his thoughts about what happened in class that day. Regular notebook paper will suffice; what's important is that there is an entry for each school day. Teachers find that setting a certain time aside each day, whether morning, afternoon, or evening, ensures that this becomes a habit.

In the beginning, a few advance questions may be needed just to get the writing flow started. Were you satisfied with the way you presented the strategies today? What did you do for the class that was most helpful to them? What did students do that helped you with your teaching? Is there anything you wish you could do over?

Initial entries will tend to be mundane, dealing with classroom management and describing what happened in the class. As time goes on and teachers become used to writing in this way, what they write about often changes (Holly, 1984). They write more personally, reacting with feelings to certain events and students and colleagues. They are able to identify real issues and concerns about their own teaching. What could be more useful to a teacher?

Another purpose of self-evaluation is for content area teachers to find out what adjustments need to be made in the strategies and adjunct materials they use. If instructional strategies and materials are going to be used on a regular basis, take a few minutes to assess their strengths and weaknesses. Two quick assessments are outlined in Box 3.3.

Box 3.3

EVALUATION OF INSTRUCTIONAL STRATEGIES AND ADJUNCT MATERIALS

I. Assessing an Adjunct Material

1. Type of adjunct material: _____

2. Date, time implemented: _____

3. Number of times used: _____

4. Class or period: _____

5. Strengths: _____

6. Weaknesses: _____

7. Modifications: _____

II. Assessing an Instructional Strategy

1. Think of a specific incident in class within the last two weeks that caused you to feel that the _____ strategy was effective with your students. Exactly what happened?

2. Think of a specific incident in class within the last two weeks that caused you to feel that the same strategy was ineffective. Exactly what happened?

Date: / Class: / Period:

Assessing Background Knowledge

Students' prior knowledge, what they already know about a topic, contributes a great deal to text comprehension. Therefore, assessing the background knowledge, experiences, beliefs, and values that students bring to a unit of study or a text selection becomes invaluable to content area teachers. As we discussed in Chapter 1, one of the reasons for the recent increase in attention given to background knowledge is the popularization of a schema-theoretic view of reading. Understanding the role of schema in reading comprehension provides insights into why students may fail to comprehend text material. Pearson and Spiro (1982) argued that "schema inadequacies" are responsible for a great many roadblocks to reading comprehension.

Three kinds of schema-related problems can interfere with understanding. The first deals with *schema availability. Students may lack the relevant background knowledge and information needed to comprehend a text assignment.* A teacher might ask, "Does my student have the schema necessary to make sense of a particular text selection?"

A second schema inadequacy is *schema selection. Students who have sufficient background knowledge may fail to bring it to bear as they read.* For example, students may be unaware that what they know already about the selection is of any importance in the reading process. How a teacher evaluates and activates available schema is essential to effective reading instruction in content areas.

A third type of schema inadequacy involves *schema maintenance. Students may not be aware or skilled enough at recognizing when shifts in schema occur during reading.* They may not know how or when to adapt and change schema as a particular reading situation demands. In other words, how does a teacher help students to maintain reader-text interactions during reading? The question implies that readers may have a schema available for a text selection and that it has been activated for reading. But somewhere during reading, the reading process breaks down. Students may get lost in a welter of details or bogged down in the conceptual complexity of the selection. Or they may be unable to interact with the text because of the way it is written—the author's language is too complex, convoluted, or stylized. As a result, readers only process bits and pieces of the text and fail to grasp in any coherent way the author's broad message or intent.

Determining whether students possess, select, or maintain schema helps the teacher to make decisions about content area reading instruction. For example, one critical decision involves how much prereading preparation students will need for a text assignment. Another might be to decide how much background building and skill direction will be necessary. Seeking information to help make decisions such as these requires that teachers adapt and use the informal, naturalistic procedures that we have already outlined.

One assessment strategy might be to informally test students' knowledge of the material to be learned. The teacher should construct a background knowledge inventory according to the content objectives, i.e., the major ideas and concepts, to be covered in a unit of study. The inventory or "pretest" can be a short-answer assessment or a set of open-ended essay questions. Many teachers combine short-answer questions with open-ended ones.

The pretest should not be graded, but it should be discussed with the class. In fact, use the pretest to introduce students to the major concepts that will be developed in the unit. Explain why you chose to ask certain questions. Share your content objectives with the class. Students will get a sense of what they already know as a result of the discussion. But the discussion should also underscore *what students need to know* in relation to the new material to be studied.

Alternatives to background knowledge pretesting include assessment procedures which are instructionally based. Consider the following strategies and activities.

Prereading Plan (PreP)

The Prereading Plan (PreP) may be used diagnostically to estimate levels of background knowledge that students bring to text assignments. Judith Langer (1981) recommended PreP as an assessment/instructional activity which fosters group discussion and an awareness of the topics to be covered. She suggested that PreP works best with groups of about ten students.

Before beginning the PreP activity, the teacher should examine the text material for key words (which represent a major concept to be developed), phrases, or pictures, and then introduce the topic that is to be read, following the three-phase plan that Langer (1981, p. 154) outlined:

1. *Initial associations with the concept.* In this first phase the teacher says, "Tell anything that comes to mind when . . ." (e.g., ". . . you hear the word "Congress"). As each student tells what ideas initially came to mind, the teacher jots each response on the board. During this phase the students have their first opportunity to find associations between the key concept and their prior knowledge. When this activity was carried out in a junior high school class, one student, Bill, said "important people." Another student, Danette, said "Washington, D.C."

2. *Reflections on initial associations.* During the second phase of the PreP the students are asked, "What made you think of . . . [the response given by a student]." This phase helps the students develop awareness of their network of associations. They also have opportunity to listen to each other's explanations, to interact, and to become aware of their changing ideas. Through this procedure they may weigh, reject, accept, revise, and integrate some of the ideas that came to mind. When Bill was asked what made him think of important people, he said, "I saw them in the newspaper." When Danette was asked what made her think of Washington, D.C., she said, "Congress takes place there."

3. *Reformulation of knowledge.* In this phase the teacher says, "Based on our discussion and before we read the text, have you any new ideas about . . . [e.g., Congress]?" This phase allows students to verbalize associations that have been elaborated or changed though the discussion. Be-

cause they have had a chance to probe their memories to elaborate their prior knowledge, the responses elicited during the third phase are often more refined than those from phase one. This time Bill said, "lawmakers of America" and Danette said "U.S. government part that makes the laws."

Through observation and listening during the PreP, content area teachers will find their students' background knowledge can be classified into three broad levels. On one level are students who have *much* prior knowledge about the concept. These students are often able to define and draw analogies, make conceptual links, and think categorically. On another level are students who may have *some* prior knowledge. These students can give examples and cite characteristics of the content but may be unable to see relationships or make connections between what they know and the new material. On the third level are students who have *little* background knowledge. They often respond to the PreP activity with words that sound like the concept word and may attempt to make simple associations, often misassociating with the topic.

Once this PreP assessment is complete the teacher has information to adjust or focus instruction more effectively. It provides useful information because of its "process orientation" (Sanacore, 1983). In process-oriented activities, there are usually opportunities for discussion and sufficient time is allocated. The teacher has practical information about the extent to which students' language and concepts match up with the text and may promote comprehension.

Assessing Through Prereading Instruction

In addition to PreP, teachers can use many of the prereading strategies and activities described in Chapter 4 to observe and assess students' knowledge about a subject. These strategies may be used as background knowledge inventories because they will stimulate reaction to and discussion about the content to be studied. During the discussion, teachers can gain many insights and pose hypotheses about the existing knowledge, experience, and values your students have about the topic.

Rather than pose questions to be answered, certain prereading activities invite reaction and discussion through value-laden statements. A high school home economics teacher, for example, began a unit on food faddism by having students react to a series of statements. The purpose behind the activity was to assess the attitudes and concepts that students would bring to the unit. The teacher informed class members that they would be reading and studying about food faddism and some basic misconceptions about foods. The students were then directed to read the statements below and put a check mark next to those that they agreed with.

    ——   1.   Eating garlic can reduce high blood pressure.

    ——   2.   Chemical fertilizers poison the land and any crops that grow on it.

—   3. Yogurt contains no special qualities not found in other foods.

—   4. Some people's deaths have been attributed to following certain fad diets.

—   5. Natural sugars are better for you than refined sugars.

—   6. There are few diseases in the United States today that are caused by dietary deficiencies.

—   7. Vitamin E is valuable for fertility, muscular strength, and control of heart disease.

—   8. Modern food processing methods can preserve or restore foods to their original nutritional value.

—   9. Vitamin supplements are usually unnecessary.

— 10. Vitamin supplements can be dangerous.

— 11. Consumers spend more than half a billion dollars a year on unnecessary vitamin supplements, minerals, and health foods.

In a similar activity an eighth-grade science teacher evaluated understandings that students would bring to a text chapter on the weather. Before assigning text selections from the chapter, the teacher asked students to examine the picture on the chapter's title page. After studying the photograph of a real weather condition, the students had to decide which of the following statements were true:

—   1. The picture is a photograph of a real condition.

—   2. The shoreline is on one of the Great Lakes.

—   3. The shoreline is on an ocean.

—   4. The land is actually part of a small island.

—   5. There is a road of some sort visible in the picture.

—   6. The white area covering the shoreline is a cloud.

—   7. The white area covering the shoreline is a fog.

—   8. A breeze is blowing from right to left in the picture (from the water toward the land).

—   9. The water is cooler than the land.

— 10. There is a deep valley near the center of the land area.

At a point where students began to exhibit some uncertainty with several of the statements, the teacher had them consider what kinds of information they would need to know in order to figure out what the picture was about. The class discussion not only made the teacher aware of students' background knowledge but the students themselves recognized what they needed to know more about as they began chapter study.

In the next chapter you will be introduced to many prereading strategies similar to those just described. Each of these has a built-in assessment/

instructional purpose which will help you to evaluate, build, and activate background knowledge for reading.

Assessing Reading Attitudes

When students learn to analyze a reading assignment by questioning what they know and don't know about the subject matter, they are taking a giant step toward self-awareness. Knowledge of *self* in relation to *texts* and reading *tasks,* as noted in Chapter 1, puts students in a strategic position to learn. Although "knowledge about one's own knowledge" plays an important role in this respect, a teacher needs to help students to be "in touch" with another aspect of *self*—attitudes toward reading. Do students value reading as a source of pleasure? a tool for acquiring knowledge? Do they believe that reading can help them solve problems? Do they read text assignments with confidence? Or do they feel helpless when faced with a textbook assignment?

Attitude is a primary determinant of whether students will approach or avoid textbooks. On one hand, attitude can be defined globally as the internal position one takes for or against something or someone (Quandt, 1977). However, reading attitude is a much more complicated issue than simply knowing how one feels about reading.

A review of the 1979–1980 reading assessment conducted in the United States by the National Assessment of Educational Progress (NAEP) reveals rather startling findings related to the attitude component of the assessment. The NAEP reading assessment tested more than 100,000 nine-, thirteen-, and seventeen-year-old students from all geographic areas and socioeconomic levels and found the following:

— about 10% of the students in each age group did not read at all;

— less than half of the thirteen and seventeen year olds reported that they like to read "very much";

— students liked reading less as they got older;

— almost half of the seventeen year olds chose reading as their least favorite leisure time activity;

— when the students read, it was for short periods of time;

— students valued reading as a source of information, not as a source of pleasure or a means of understanding themselves or cultural values. *(Lehr, 1982)*

The appalling nature of these findings begs an explanation. Lehr (1982) suggested that the results may be the effect of the "back to basics" movement in which an entire generation of students may have been bombarded with too many worksheets and too much meaningless practice and drill—all in the name of reading instruction.

Whatever the case may be, the NAEP findings suggest that attitude toward reading is a more complex construct than may have been previously realized. In fact, Lewis and Teale (1980) proposed a multidimensional view of reading attitude which included such factors as (1) the value placed on reading as a means of gaining insight into self, others, and/or life in general; (2) the value placed on the role of reading for attaining educational or vocational success; and (3) the pleasure derived from reading. Reading attitude, based on these factors, consists of three components: a *cognitive component* (one's beliefs or opinions about reading), an *affective component* (one's evaluations of or feeling about reading), and a *behavioral component* (one's intentions to read and actual reading behavior).

Students' interests and self-concepts are interwoven into the fabric of reading attitude. What students *like* to read—their interests—impacts on when they read, why they read, and how often they read. Moreover, how students *view* their prior experiences with reading and reading instruction also affects reading attitude. The perceptions that they hold about themselves as readers can make or break a positive attitude toward reading. McNeil (1984) put it this way: "Learners have perceptions and feelings about themselves as readers that affect their performance. 'Learned helplessness'—the perceived inability to overcome failure—is particularly self-defeating" (p. 83). Depending on whether students view a reading task as "within reach" or "out of their control," they will probably approach it in a positive or negative fashion.

In this book, we show how students can achieve success with textbooks. Developing a positive reading attitude is one of the keys to that success. Teachers can influence positive attitudes toward reading through effective planning, instructional strategies that bridge the gap between students and textbooks, enthusiastic teaching, and a classroom context that supports reading and writing activity. Students may not learn to love reading in some generic sense, but they will learn to (1) value reading as a source of information and knowledge, (2) believe that it can help them do well in school and everyday life, and (3) use reading to solve problems and develop insights.

Identifying Attitudes

Reading attitudes are never easy to identify. However, as teachers accumulate information about students' strengths and limitations in relation to content area texts, it would be difficult to *ignore* their attitudes, interests, or self-concepts.

Observational techniques and attitude scales are the two major ways to assess reading attitude. Indeed, observation is the method most widely used by teachers to assess reading attitudes (Heathington and Alexander, 1984). Focused teacher observations in which anecdotal notes or checklists are used can be valuable in identifying and recording attitude, interests, and students' self-perception. So too can individual conferences with students. Any of these methods will elicit data about typical attitude-related behavior, including the following:

— willingness to receive instruction,

— class participation,

— quality of work performed,

— library habits,

— independent reading,

— amount and kind of free reading,

— personal goals related to learning.   *(Readence, Bean, and Baldwin, 1981)*

Unfortunately, time constraints often impede continuous informal observation, especially for content area teachers who see five or six different classes each day.

An alternative or partner to observational techniques is a paper-and-pencil attitude survey. An attitude survey, according to Heathington (1975), should meet certain requirements such as reliability and validity and take minimal time for administering and scoring. Certainly one use of an attitude survey is to document changes in student attitude through pre- and post-test scores. The survey should be given early in the school year. Data from the assessment should give teachers a better sense of how students in a particular class approach reading in different situations. This is particularly the case when specific survey items "cluster" around different areas of reading activity in and out of school. By paying attention to students' *cluster scores,* teachers can begin to make plans related to their classroom reading environment. Post-testing later in the year may show that positive changes in attitude occurred for some students in conjunction with the creation of a reading environment and the application of content area reading strategies.

Awareness of the complexity of reading attitudes can be enlightening for some students. Begin a class discussion of a survey's results by explaining how feelings toward reading may vary from situation to situation. Use the case of two students that is presented by Lewis and Teale (1980). One doesn't enjoy reading and never reads in her spare time, but she sees that reading is valuable to her in achieving success in school. The other student reads for pleasure outside of school but doesn't consider reading to be valuable in school or for career success.

The discussion can lead to an awareness that negative attitude is situation specific. With whom did the class members identify in the above example? What can be done, if anything, to change a negative attitude to a positive one? How can the teacher help? The teacher may even want to profile the class results without indicating individual scores. What can be done in this class to make reading a more positive experience?

A Reading Attitude Assessment Scale

Tullock-Rhody and Alexander (1980) reported the development of an attitude scale which yields cluster scores and can be used readily in content classrooms. The *Rhody Secondary Attitude Assessment* in Box 3.4 was carefully validated and has adequate reliability (.84) for classroom purposes. Items from the scale cluster into the following groups: *school-related reading* (items 11, 18), *library reading* (items 9, 20), *recreational reading* (items 5, 7, 22, 24, 25), and *general reading* (items 1, 2, 3, 6, 7, 8, 12, 13, 14, 15, 16, 19, 21, 23). Directions for scoring this scale are also found in Box 3.4.

Box 3.4

RHODY SECONDARY READING ATTITUDE ASSESSMENT*

Directions: This is a test to tell how you feel about reading. The score will not affect your grade in any way. You read the statements silently as I read them aloud. Then put an X on the line under the letter or letters that represent how you feel about the statement.

SD - Strongly Disagree
  D - Disagree
  U - Undecided
  A - Agree
SA - Strongly Agree

	SD	D	U	A	SA
1. You feel you have better things to do than read.	____	____	____	____	____
2. You seldom buy a book.	____	____	____	____	____
3. You are willing to tell people that you do not like to read.	____	____	____	____	____
4. You have a lot of books in your room at home.	____	____	____	____	____
5. You like to read a book whenever you have free time.	____	____	____	____	____
6. You get really excited about books you have read.	____	____	____	____	____
7. You love to read.	____	____	____	____	____
8. You like to read books by well-known authors.	____	____	____	____	____
9. You never check out a book from the library.	____	____	____	____	____
10. You like to stay at home and read.	____	____	____	____	____
11. You seldom read except when you have to do a book report.	____	____	____	____	____
12. You think reading is a waste of time.	____	____	____	____	____
13. You think reading is boring.	____	____	____	____	____
14. You think people are strange when they read a lot.	____	____	____	____	____
15. You like to read to escape from problems.	____	____	____	____	____
16. You make fun of people who read a lot.	____	____	____	____	____
17. You like to share books with your friends.	____	____	____	____	____
18. You would rather someone just tell you information so that you won't have to read to get it.	____	____	____	____	____
19. You hate reading.	____	____	____	____	____
20. You generally check out a book when you go to the library.	____	____	____	____	____
21. It takes you a long time to read a book.	____	____	____	____	____

22. You like to broaden your interests through reading.   ____ ____ ____ ____ ____
23. You read a lot.   ____ ____ ____ ____ ____
24. You like to improve your vocuabulary so you can use   ____ ____ ____ ____ ____
    more words.
25. You like to get books for gifts.   ____ ____ ____ ____ ____

Scoring: To score the *Rhody Secondary Reading Attitude Assessment,* a very positive response receives a score of 5, and a very negative response receives a score of 1. On items 4, 5, 6, 7, 8, 10, 15, 17, 20, 22, 23, 24, and 25, a response of "strongly agree" indicates a very positive attitude and should receive a score of 5. On the remaining items, a "strongly disagree" response indicates a very positive attitude and should receive the 5 score. Therefore, on the positive item, "strongly agree" receives a 5, "agree" receives a 4, "undecided" receives a 3, "disagree" receives a 2, and "strongly disagree" receives a 1. The pattern is reversed on the negative items. The possible range of scores is 5×25 (125) to 1×25 (25).

*Reprinted from R. Tullock-Rhody and J. Alexander, "A Scale for Assessing Attitudes Toward Reading in Secondary Schools," *Journal of Reading,* April 1980, by permission of the authors and the International Reading Association.

Exploring Interests and Self-Perceptions

When emphasis is placed on identifying reading attitudes, teachers soon find themselves dealing with students' reading interests and their perceptions about reading. As we explained in Chapter 2, the *interestability* of text material should be evaluated. A textbook with a low interestability level always complicates matters from an instructional point of view. If, on the other hand, a textbook does appear to be high in interestability, this is still no guarantee that students will be interested in reading it.

This does not mean that textbooks should be banished to student lockers for the entire school year. Nor does it necessarily mean that a teacher must seek out "high interest/low vocabulary" material to serve as a "vitamin supplement" for the textbook. Some high interest/low vocabulary texts have been "watered down" to a point where key concepts are merely mentioned rather than developed to a substantive degree.

An alternative is to help students realize that interest is not inherent in the material, but instead is a state of mind (Ortiz, 1983). When they express little interest in the material or say that it is "boring," it may represent a masking of what students would really like to say, that "this textbook is difficult, and I'm having trouble making sense out of what I'm reading." If this is the case, adjustments can be made within the context of instruction to help students approach the material more positively.

Ortiz (1983) recommended that students need to reflect on how they become involved or interested in reading material. The teacher might begin the discussion with an exaggerated circumstance: "You're locked in a telephone booth with a disconnected phone for two hours and only the telephone book to read. How would you make it interesting?" After several minutes of suggestions on making the telephone book interesting, switch the topic to textbooks. "Which part of the chapter do you usually find most interesting? Have you ever been bored by one part of a textbook and later became interested in another part? What are some things you can do to make the textbook more interesting?"

The discussion should provide valuable insights for the teacher. It can lead to additional activities which will build and reinforce students' awareness of their own interest-generating capability:

— Have students analyze their present reading habits. How do they decide what to read? Where does interest come from? Who controls interest?

— Have students select a passage that interests them from several available. Ask them to analyze why they selected a particular passage over the others. Have them read and reflect on what they found themselves doing as they read the passage that was of interest.

— Have students scan a table of contents and select items of interest. Analyze why they found them interesting.

— Have students lightly dot a passage with a pencil as they read whenever they begin to lose interest. Why?

— Have students read a passage they are not interested in and have them find one item they understand. Then have them find another and so on. Evaluate how understanding relates to interest.   *(Ortiz, 1983)*

Although students must learn to generate interest in materials that are required for course study, the power of choice should also play a major role in content area reading. Students must have the leeway to read course-related texts of their own choosing. In Chapter 10, we discuss how to organize units of study so that students have the opportunity to explore interest areas within the framework of the major concepts under study.

Students' Perceptions of Reading

If content area reading strategies are aimed at involving students in taking control of their own learning, then it becomes critical to know about students' perceptions of reading and what they are doing in the classroom. How do students' perceptions of reading and reading activities affect their ability to study effectively?

One technique developed to interview students about the comprehension process is the Reading Comprehension Interview (Wixson *et al.*, 1984). Designed for grades 3–8, it takes about thirty minutes per student to administer in its entirety. The RCI explores students' perceptions of (1) the purpose of reading in different instructional contexts and content areas, (2) reading task requirements, and (3) strategies the student uses in different contexts.

The RCI's main uses are to help identify patterns of responses (for the whole group and individuals) which could then serve as guides to instruction and to analyze an individual's flexibility with different reading activities.

Several questions on the RCI are particularly appropriate for content area reading situations. Although the RCI was developed for grades 3–8, high school teachers can make good diagnostic use of some of the questions.

Rather than interview each student individually, we suggest the following adaptation. Have students keep a learning log. The uses of learning logs are described in greater detail in Chapters 7 and 8. In these logs, students maintain a regular record (daily, weekly, or at the end of a unit) of personal learning as it happens. That is, the main purpose for keeping a log is to have students write to themselves about what they are learning. For example, they can choose to focus on problems they are having with a particular reading assignment or activity. A variation on this general purpose would be to ask students to respond to some of the more pertinent questions on the RCI—perhaps one or two at any one time over several weeks.

In relation to a particular content area textbook, examine the kinds of questions students can write about from the RCI*:

1. What is the most important reason for reading this kind of material? Why does your teacher want you to read this book?
2. a. Who's the best reader you know in (content area)?
   b. What does he/she do that makes him/her such a good reader?
3. a. How good are *you* at reading this kind of material?
   b. How do you know?
4. What do you have to do to get a good grade in (content area) in your class?
5. a. If the teacher told you to remember the information in this story/chapter, what would be the best way to do this?
   b. Have you ever tried (name a strategy, i.e., outlining)?
6. a. If your teacher told you to find the answers to the questions in this book what would be the best way to do this? Why?
   b. Have you ever tried (name a strategy, i.e., previewing)?
7. a. What is the hardest part about answering questions like the ones in this book?
   b. Does that make you do anything differently?

Having students respond to these questions in writing does not deny the importance of interviewing individuals. However, it does save an enormous amount of time while providing a teacher with a record of students' perceptions of important reading tasks related to comprehension.

Another way to get at some of the same perceptions students hold about reading activities is through a questionnaire. Hahn (1984) developed a ten-item

---

*Reprinted from Karen Wixson *et al.*, "An Interview for Assessing Students' Perceptions of Classroom Reading Tasks," *The Reading Teacher*, January, 1984, with permission from the authors and the International Reading Association.

questionnaire based on modifications of a research instrument used by Paris and Meyers (1981). Five items on the questionnaire represent positive reading strategies (procedures students should use to comprehend effectively) and five items depict negative strategies (those which are ineffective and should be avoided). See Box 3.5.

Students who rate positive strategies as not very helpful can easily be identified upon scoring the questionnaire. These students may benefit from some explicit instruction in the strategies. Also, a good point of discussion would be why the negative strategies are not helpful for effective studying.

Box 3.5

QUESTIONNAIRE ON READING STRATEGIES

Does it help to understand a text selection (or a story) if you . . .
1. Think about something else while you are reading?
   _____ Always   _____ almost always   _____ almost never   _____ never
2. Write it down in your own words?
   _____ Always   _____ almost always   _____ almost never   _____ never
3. Underline important parts of the selection?
   _____ Always   _____ almost always   _____ almost never   _____ never
4. Ask yourself questions about the ideas in the selection?
   _____ Always   _____ almost always   _____ almost never   _____ never
5. Write down every single word in the selection?
   _____ Always   _____ almost always   _____ almost never   _____ never
6. Check through the selection to see if you remember all of it?
   _____ Always   _____ almost always   _____ almost never   _____ never
7. Skip the parts you don't understand in the selection?
   _____ Always   _____ almost always   _____ almost never   _____ never
8. Read the selection as fast as you can?
   _____ Always   _____ almost always   _____ almost never   _____ never
9. Say every word over and over?
   _____ Always   _____ almost always   _____ almost never   _____ never
10. Ask questions about parts of the selection that you don't understand?
   _____ Always   _____ almost always   _____ almost never   _____ never

Positive Strategies: Questions 2, 3, 4, 6, 10
Negative Strategies: Questions 1, 5, 7, 8, 9

Teachers can develop other questionnaires for specific purposes. For example, examine the Vocabulary Attitude Survey in Box 3.6. It is designed to assess students' perceptions about learning new words. Chapter 9 explains many of the vocabulary strategies that are implicit in the items on the survey.

Box 3.6

VOCABULARY ATTITUDE SURVEY

Directions: Put a check mark under the answer that best tells how you feel.

	Always	*Sometimes*	*Never*
1. When I hear or read a word that I don't know or understand, I look up the meaning in a dictionary.			
2. I try to use new words when I talk.			
3. I try to use new words when I write.			
4. I work crossword puzzles or word puzzles at home for fun.			
5. I try to analyze strange words by separating them into prefixes, suffixes, and roots to discover the meaning.			
6. I play word games at home like "Scrabble."			
7. I can discover the meaning of strange words from studying the sentence of which they are a part and guessing at the possible definition.			
8. I am good at "unscrambling" words.			
9. Reading my textbook is hard for me because the words are hard.			
10. Learning the meanings of new words and using them makes me feel happy and satisfied.			

Assessing Reading Performance

Teacher-made tests are another important indicator of student reading performance in content areas. A teacher-made *content area reading inventory* (CARI) is an alternative to the standardized reading test. The CARI is informal. As opposed to the standard of success on a norm-referenced test, which is a comparison between the performance of the tested group and the original normative population, success on the CARI test is measured by performance on the task itself. The CARI measures performance on reading materials actually used in a course. The results of the CARI can give a teacher some good insights into *how* students read course material.

Administering a CARI invoves several general steps. First, explain to students the purpose of the test. Mention that it will be used for evaluation only—to help you plan instruction—that grades will not be assigned. Second, briefly introduce the selected portion of the test to be read and give students an "idea direction" to guide silent reading. Third, if you want to find out how the class uses the textbook, consider an open book evaluation; but if you want to determine students' ability to retain information, have them answer test questions without referring back to the selection. And, finally, discuss the results of the evaluation individually in conferences or collectively with the entire class.

Table 3.2 organizes the objectives and procedures for the development of CARIs based on two different informal testing situations. The objectives and procedures in Table 3.2 are common to all content areas.

A CARI, whether it is developed for use at the beginning of a course or for a unit of study, can be administered piecemeal over several class sessions so that large chunks of instructional time will not be sacrificed. The bane of many content instructors is spending an inordinate amount of time away from actual teaching.

Table 3.2 Informal Text Situations for Content Area Reading Inventories: Objectives and Procedures

Test Situations

Beginning-of-Course Inventory		Assessment of Instructional Unit Inventory	
Objectives	*Procedures*	*Objectives*	*Procedures*
To determine if students will:		To determine if students will:	
1. Locate information efficiently and effectively	1. Locate Information: Construct 15–20 questions which assess students' ability to use a. Book parts b. Textbook aids c. Graphic aids d. Library resources	1. Bring background knowledge to unit materials	1. Background Knowledge: a. Ask several open-ended questions that tape students' understanding of important ideas in unit b. Construct a knowledge-based assessment test that reflects content objectives in the unit c. Construct a prereading guide to assess concepts/attitudes/values related to the important ideas in the unit d. Guide students through the Prereading Plan procedure
2. Read textbook assignments at different levels of comprehension	2. Levels of Comprehension: Select a representative text selection of 500–1000 words. Construct 10–15 questions that test students' ability to read at a. literal level b. inferential level c. applied level	2. Read text material at different levels of comprehension	2. Levels of comprehension: Same steps as in Procedure 2 for Beginning-of-Course Inventory

3. Use independent vocabulary skills to predict the meaning of difficult terms	3. Vocabulary Inquiry: Construct questions to test students' ability to analyze technical terms through a. context b. structure c. dictionary/glossary	3. Recognize the meaning of technical terms in a unit of study	3. Familiarity with technical vocabulary: Construct an inventory of students' knowledge of technical terms
4. Read textbook material at an appropriate rate of comprehension	4. Rate of Comprehension: Determine the number of words in passage that is selected for the levels of comprehension test. Note the time it takes individual students to complete reading. Determine words-per-minute (wpm) performance. Compare rate with percentage of correct comprehension answers	4. Read textbook material at an appropriate rate of comprehension	4. Rate of Comprehension: Same steps as in Procedure 4 for Beginning-of-Course Inventory

Informal instructional tests administered at the beginning of a course elicit the information a teacher needs to adjust instruction and meet student needs. A beginning-of-course inventory should focus on students' ability to (1) locate information, (2) comprehend text, (3) use vocabulary skills, and (4) read at an appropriate rate of comprehension. A unit-of-study assessment should emphasize students' (1) background knowledge as previously discussed, (2) familiarity with technical vocabulary terms, and (3) ability to comprehend text.

Some authorities suggest that teachers should also evaluate additional competency areas such as study skills—skimming, scanning, outlining, taking notes, and so forth. We believe, however, that the best use of reading inventories in content areas is on a much smaller scale. A CARI at the beginning of a course should seek information related to basic reading tasks. For this reason, we recommend that outlining, note taking, and other useful study techniques be assessed through observation and analysis of student work samples. Chapter 8 presents a lesson plan organization for teaching study strategies in which assessment through observation is an internal component.

Assessing the Ability to Locate Information

Locating information is essential to studying textbooks and to working with library materials effectively. Every teacher should know early in the course or school year whether or not students can successfully use book parts, library materials, maps, graphs, or charts. Questions which tap students' ability to locate information, such as those asked (about a social studies text) in Box 3.7 can easily be adapted to any content area. The questions can be asked orally or distributed on dittoed sheets. Examine the test items in Box 3.7. A short evaluative session at the beginning of a course screens students who cannot locate information with some degree of competence. These students will profit from instruction.

Box 3.7

TEST ITEMS FOR CARI ON LOCATIONAL SKILLS*

I. Using Parts of a Book
   1. On what page does the chapter on Southern Europe begin?
   2. On what page would you find a population map of Africa?
   3. Of what value is Table III in the Appendix in helping you understand the material in the textbook?
   4. Where would you look to find a list of the longest rivers in the eastern hemisphere?
   5. On what pages would you look to find information about the Simplon Tunnel?

II. Using Library Materials
   6. What library aid will tell you the library number of a book?
   7. What is an almanac?
   8. Name one set of encyclopedias. How are the topics in it arranged?
   9. Where would you look to find the political boundaries of countries in Europe in 1812?
  10. Where would you look to find a picture of a flag of a country and the history of a flag?

III. Using Maps, Graphs, and Charts
  11. What information is given on the map on page _____?
  12. What does the color red on the map on page _____ represent?
  13. Why are longitude and latitude lines drawn on maps?
  14. What information is given by the graph on page _____?
  15. Using the graph on page _____ tell how many tons of cement were produced in the USSR in 1959.
  16. Using the population graph on page _____, tell which ten-year period Japan's population increased the most.
  17. Using the chart on page _____, list the form of government and the religion of Turkey.

*SOURCE: Adapted fron David Shepherd, *Comprehensive High School Reading Methods.* Columbus, Ohio: Charles E. Merrill, 1973.

Assessing Levels and Rates of Comprehension

Early in the school semester teachers should gauge their students' ability to comprehend text material at different levels of comprehension as a science teacher did with the inventory in Box 3.8. The science teacher assessed whether students were able to respond at literal (getting the facts), inferential (making some interpretations), and applied (going beyond the material) levels of comprehension. These levels are discussed in detail in Chapter 5. At this time you can also determine a measure of reading rate in relation to comprehension.

Box 3.8

AN EXAMPLE OF A COMPREHENSION INVENTORY IN SCIENCE

General Directions: Read pages 228–233. Then look up at the board and note the time that it took you to complete the selection. Record this time in the space provided on the response sheet. Close your book and answer the first question. You may then open your textbook to answer the remaining questions.

STUDENT RESPONSE FORM

Reading Time: _____ min _____sec

I. A. *Directions:* Close your book and answer the following question.
      1. In your own words, what was this selection about? Use as much space as you need on this page. Continue on the opposite side if you should need more room to complete your answer.

II. A. *Directions:* Open your book and answer the following questions.
      1. An insect has six legs and a three-part body.
        a. true
        b. false
        c. can't tell
      2. Insects go through changes called metamorphosis.
        a. true
        b. false
        c. can't tell
      3. Most insects are harmful.
        a. true
        b. false
        c. can't tell
      4. Bees help flowers by moving pollen from flower to flower.
        a. true
        b. false
        c. can't tell

   B. *Directions:* Answers to these questions are not directly stated by the author. You must "read between the lines" to answer them.
      1. How is a baby cecropia moth different from a full-grown moth?

      2. Why does a caterpillar molt?

      3. What are the four stages of a complete metamorphosis?

C. 1. Why do you suppose the caterpillar spins a long thread of silk around itself?
_____
_____

2. During which season would the full-grown cecropia moth leave the cocoon? Why?
_____
_____

3. Why do you think they leave in that season rather than another?
_____
_____
_____

You can construct a comprehension inventory using these steps:

1. Select an appropriate reading selection from within the second fifty pages of the book. The selection need not include the entire unit or story but should be complete within itself as to overall concept. In most cases two or three pages will provide a sufficient sample.

2. Count the total number of words in the excerpt.

3. Read the excerpt and formulate ten to twelve comprehension questions. The first part of the test should ask an open-ended question like "What was the passage you read about?" Then develop three or more questions at each level of comprehension.

4. Prepare a student response sheet.

5. Answer the questions and include specific page references for discussion purposes after the testing is completed.

While students read the material and take the test, the teacher observes, noting work habits and student behavior, especially of those students who appear frustrated by the test. The science teacher of Box 3.8 allowed students to check their own work as the class discussed each question. Other teachers prefer to evaluate individual students' responses to questions first and then discuss them with students either individually or during the next class session.

To get an estimate of students' rates of comprehension, follow these steps:

1. Have students note the time it takes to read the selection. This can be accomplished in an efficient manner by recording the time in five-second intervals by using a "stopwatch" that is drawn on the board (see Figure 3.2).

2. As students complete the reading, they look up at the board to check the stopwatch. The number within the oval represents the minutes that have elapsed. The number that the teacher is pointing to along the perimeter of the oval represents the number of seconds.

3. Later on, students or the teacher can figure rate of reading in words per minute.

Example:

Words in selection: 1500

Figure 3.2 "Stopwatch" for Marking Time to Determine Rate of Reading

Reading time: 4 minutes, 30 seconds
Convert seconds into a decimal fraction. Then divide time into words.

$$\frac{1500}{4.5} = 333 \text{ words per minute}$$

4. Determine the percentage of correct or reasonable answers on the comprehension test. Always evaluate and discuss rate of reading in terms of students' comprehension performance.

Vocabulary Inquiry

In Chapter 9 we discuss the skills that students need to inquire into the meanings of troublesome content area vocabulary terms. The extent to which they effectively use content and word structure often allows students to continue reading without getting "stuck" on difficult words. A beginning-of-course inventory of vocabulary skills can be helpful to teachers in planning vocabulary activities that will reinforce these skills.

Evaluating Context

Select five to ten difficult words from the textbook passage used for the comprehension inventory or from an assignment that students are about to read. These words should have enlightening context—sufficient semantic and syntactic information clues to reveal meaning. Before students read the selection, write the words on the blackboard and ask students to define each one on a sheet of paper. Then instruct them to read the textbook selection. After the reading, ask them to refer back to their original definitions and go back to the text to change any of the original definitions in light of information gained through reading. This procedure is an effective informal way of evaluating students' ability to use context. It quickly tells you which students are proficient, which have some competence but will need reinforcement, and which have trouble and will need assistance to use context effectively.

Evaluating Word Structure

Words carry meaning-bearing units that provide readers with clues. You can select for evaluation content terms which are polysyllabic and are made up of affixes and recognizable English roots. Before testing, be sure students know what prefixes, suffixes, and roots are.

Provide each student with a list of representative words from the subject matter and direct the class to underline the recognizable stems and double underline the prefixes and/or suffixes. Then ask them to explain how the prefix and/or suffix affects the meaning of each content area term. Box 3.9 illustrates sample test items using vocabulary terms in various content areas.

Box 3.9

SAMPLE ITEMS FOR WORD STRUCTURE INVENTORIES

Directions: Below is a list of terms from the course. Each word is made up of a recognizable root and a prefix and/or suffix. For each word:
1. Underline the root
2. Double underline prefix and/or suffix
3. Explain in the column next to the word how the prefix and/or suffix influences the definition of the word

Example: undemocratic = not democratic

	Content Area Terms	Meaning Explanation
Social Studies	coexistence	To exist or live together
	postglacial	
	reconstructionist	
	interdependent	
	exploitation	
Science	decompose	
	relationship	
	thermoplastics	
	humidity	
	transformer	
Mathematics	replacement	
	midpoint	
	equidistant	
	conceptualize	
	segmentation	
Business	absenteeism	
	malpractice	
	unethical	
	transaction	
	consignment	
Industrial Arts	hazardous	
	alignment	
	electromagnetic	
	demonstrator	
	countersink	
Home Economics	perishable	
	biodegradable	
	antisocial	
	inferiority	
	salable	

English   demonic
                                         =====
                                         reiteration
                                         eccentricity
                                         infamous
                                         peradventure

Evaluating Dictionary Usage

Dictionary usage is another valuable skill that aids vocabulary development. During informal testing situations, keep an observant eye on how students actually work with dictionaries in class. Does a student, for instance, select the most appropriate definition from multiple entries in the dictionary entry? Does the student translate formal definitions into his or her own words?

Evaluating Familiarity with Technical Vocabulary Terms

A procedure which gives the teacher a measure of students' familiarity with the content area terms is called the discriminative self-inventory (Dale, O'Rourke, and Bamman, 1971). Using the symbols $+$, $\sqrt{}$, $-$, 0, students indicate how well they know a set of terms: $+$ means "I know it well, I use it"; $\sqrt{}$ means "I know it somewhat"; $-$ means "I've seen it or heard of it before"; and 0 means "I've never seen it or heard it before."

The self-inventory items below were developed by a high school mathematics teacher for terms associated with quadratic functions and systems of equations:

Self-Inventory:
How Well Do You Know These Terms?

___ 1. exponent	___ 7. intersection	___ 13. origin
___ 2. coefficient	___ 8. abscissa	___ 14. vertex
___ 3. reals	___ 9. domain	___ 15. slope
___ 4. integers	___ 10. intercept	___ 16. parabola
___ 5. irrationals	___ 11. linear	___ 17. solution
___ 6. union	___ 12. mapping	

In summary, information you glean from a CARI at the beginning of an instructional unit will help you organize specific lessons and activities. You can decide the background preparation needed, the length of reading assignments, and the reading activities when you apply your best judgment to the information you have learned from the assessment.

A beginning-of-unit CARI can be designed to evaluate (1) background knowledge that students bring to the unit, (2) students' familiarity with technical terms, (3) students' ability to comprehend the material to be read, and (4) rate of comprehension.

Looking Back, Looking Forward

Evaluating for instruction is a continuous process in which teachers collect and analyze information about students' background knowledge and reading performance. In order to obtain useful results, content area teachers need methods which they can use within their classrooms. An informal, naturalistic approach is therefore more likely to be useful than a formal, standardized one. With this approach, decision making can be informed by careful observation of students' strengths and weaknesses as they interact with one another and with content-specific materials.

In this chapter, observation techniques, checklists, and self-evaluation for teachers were explained. Contrasts were drawn to standardized assessment through tests, which provide statistically valid but less useful information to the content area teacher.

Major purposes for evaluation for instruction are to assess students in several areas. Suggestions for assessing the background knowledge of students included pretesting or the use of instructionally based strategies such as PreP. Attitude assessment, to determine impact of a program upon student attitudes, relies on the interpetation of attitude scales and teacher observation.

Content area reading inventories—teacher-made, informal tests—were discussed and several examples given. They not only measure performance on reading materials actually used in a course, but the results can give teachers insights into how students learn from text material.

In Part II of this book numerous instructional strategies are suggested. The next chapter explains how teachers can ready students for reading tasks. Prereading preparation, often neglected or underestimated in the content classroom, is as important to the reader as warm-up preparation is to the athlete. Let's find out why.

Suggested Readings

Estes, T. H., & Vaughan, J. L., Jr. (1985). *Reading and Learning in the Content Classroom* (2nd ed.). Boston: Allyn and Bacon.

Guba, E., & Lincoln, Y. (1981). *Effective Evaluation*. Washington, D.C.: Jossey-Bass.

Readence, J., Bean, T., & Baldwin, R. S. (1981). *Content Area Reading: An Integrated Approach*. Dubuque, IA: Kendall/Hunt.

Shepherd, D. (1978). *Comprehensive High School Reading Methods* (2nd ed.). Columbus, Ohio: Merrill.

Summers, E. G. (1977). Instruments for assessing reading attitudes: A review of research and bibliography. *Journal of Reading Behavior, 9,* 137–155.

Part Two

Strategies for Reading, Writing, and Studying

CHAPTER FOUR

Prereading Strategies

They can because they think they can.
—VIRGIL

Organizing Principle

Confident readers think positively about print. They have their goals in front of them. They know where they are going in a text selection and how to get there. In short, they can (read successfully) because they think they can. If there is one imperative in this chapter it is to prepare students to think positively about what they will read in textbook assignments. Preparing students to read can be easily neglected in a classroom teacher's hurry-scurry efforts to cover the content. Yet the payoffs of prereading preparation are immense. Students learn to bring to the text what they know already about the subject matter. By arousing curiosity and expectations about the meaning of text material, the content teacher helps students read with anticipation and purpose. Therefore, the organizing principle of this chapter can be stated this way: *A teacher reduces the uncertainty students bring to content material by helping them to use background knowledge, raise questions, and make predictions about what they will be reading.*

We will be exploring how to get students ready to learn from texts. Study the

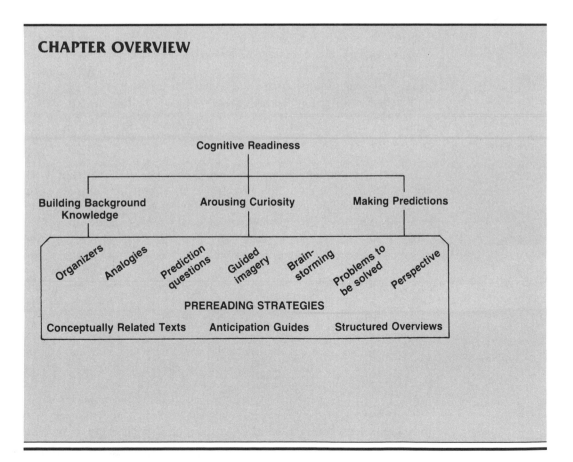

CHAPTER OVERVIEW

Cognitive Readiness

Building Background Knowledge   Arousing Curiosity   Making Predictions

Organizers   Analogies   Prediction questions   Guided imagery   Brain-storming   Problems to be solved   Perspective

PREREADING STRATEGIES

Conceptually Related Texts   Anticipation Guides   Structured Overviews

Chapter Overview before you begin reading. It shows the interrelationships of the major ideas to be developed. In this chapter, the questions below are crucial to your understanding of the material. You should be able to answer each question by the time you finish reading.

1. What is cognitive readiness and how does it apply to reading?

2. How does building background knowledge, arousing curiosity, and making predictions prepare students to approach text reading in a critical frame of mind?

3. How and why do prereading strategies facilitate reading comprehension?

Explanations of reading tend to be complex. Yet as intricate a process as reading may be, it's surely just as magical and mysterious to most of us. After all, who ever really knows a covert process—one that takes place in the head?

Huey (1908) recounted a fascinating tale about the African adventurer Livingstone:

> Livingstone excited the wonder and awe of an African tribe as he daily
> perused a book that had survived the vicissitudes of travel. So
> incomprehensible, to these savages, was his performance with the book,
> that they finally stole it and *ate* it, as the best way they knew of
> "reading" it, of getting the white man's satisfaction from it.   *(p. 2)*

The preliterate natives acted in the only way they knew how. Eating Livingstone's book was a response, somewhat magical, to their uncertainty over the process that we call reading.

Magic and uncertainty go hand in hand. According to Malinowski (1954), people resort to magic in situations where they feel they have limited control over the success of their activities. This is so in primitive cultures such as the African tribe described by Huey or in highly technological societies such as ours.

We believe an element of magic will always be a part of reading, even though it appears second nature to many of us. For most teachers reading just happens, particularly when there is a strong purpose or need to read in the first place. However, a great deal of uncertainty pervades reading for many students. The reading process remains a mystery, a lot of hocus-pocus, for students who believe they have limited control over their chances for success with a reading assignment.

You can do a great deal to reduce the uncertainty that students bring to textbook assignments. In fact, you must. You can take the voodoo out of reading textbook material by helping students link the given—what they know already or the skills they have—with the new—what they are about to learn through reading.

The basis for effective reading instruction in the content areas may very well come before students read. Hansell (1976) underscored the necessity for prereading instruction when he asserted,

. . . teachers may help students to read texts, articles, or books by helping them understand the content before they deal with it in print. . . . The problem of content teachers then becomes, in the words of an eighth grade teacher in Boston, one of "convincing the students that they know more than they think they do about my subject." *(p. 309)*

In a sense, the *feedforward effect* is what prereading instruction is all about.

Feedforward is different from feedback. Feedback is one of those well-established, valuable concepts in learning. It refers generally to the information learners use to guide their actions. Feedback helps individuals to modify, refine, or redirect behavior so that they will learn. Feedforward, on the other hand, is a relatively new concept. It categorizes a wide range of important acts during learning generally and reading specifically. Stauffer (1975) first offered the term "feedforward" to describe the reader's *anticipation* of what will be learned through print: "Each pupil must learn how to raise questions. . . . The feedforward effect of questions raised keeps a reader on course" (p. 34).

Two of the most appropriate questions that students can ask about a reading selection are "What do I need to know?" and "How well do I already know it?" "What do I need to know?" prompts readers to reflect on their background knowledge, to make predictions and set purposes. It gets them thinking positively about the reading material. "How well do I already know it?" helps readers to search their experience and knowledge to give support to tentative predictions and to help make plans for reading.

As simple as these two questions may appear on the surface, maturing readers rarely *know enough* about the reading process to ask them. "What do I need to know?" and "How well do I already know it?" require, as we discussed in Chapter 1, *metacognitive awareness* on the part of learners. However, these two questions, when consciously raised and reflected upon, put students on the road to regulating and monitoring their own reading behavior. It is never too early (or too late) to begin showing students how to raise questions about text.

The psychological principle behind prereading preparation involves *cognitive readiness*. Generally speaking, readiness refers to the ability of a learner at a given age to cope adequately with the demands of a cognitive task (Ausubel et al. 1978). Part of the readiness principle suggests that students must know certain things before they can learn specific new ideas, or that they must develop certain skills before they can develop others.

Cognitive readiness is intrinsic to reading at every instructional level. Instructional lessons which include activity and discussion before reading prepare readers to approach the material in a critical frame of mind so that as they read they will seek answers to questions they have raised about the reading assignment. The major limitation of assigning reading without preparing students to read is evident in the observation that Harste (1978) made:

The old, but still common practice of giving a reading assignment in preparation for a discussion is, unfortunately, backwards. Because what the reader brings to the process greatly influences what he/she gets out of the process, teachers can ensure more successful processing of print through the reverse procedure—discussion first, reading second.   *(p. 22)*

Our observation of an English teacher illustrates Harste's point. We watched as she skillfully prepared students to read William Cullen Bryant's poem "Thanatopsis." Before assigning the poem, the teacher raised students' expectations for meaning by having them respond to value statements about death. She polled students as to whether they agreed or disagreed with propositions such as these:

— Death is inevitable, so there is no need to fear it.

— Nature can comfort a person facing death.

— It is important to accept death as a natural occurrence.

— Death is like a pleasant dream.

— A person fears death because it is unknown.

— When a person dies, others continue their lives as usual.

By a show of hands, the students quickly recognized the extent to which they agreed or disagreed on certain statements. The students wondered why some of the statements achieved greater consensus than others. The teacher asked students to explain why they agreed or disagreed. At first, it struck the class as odd that three students who agreed with the statement, "Death is like a pleasant dream," had totally different reasons for their agreement. But additional discussion drove home the point that each student brings different background knowledge, beliefs, and perceptions to learning situations.

The discussion also provided the opportunity for the teacher to give some pertinent background information as to why Bryant wrote "Thanatopsis." She asked if anyone knew what the title meant. Then the class analyzed the structure of the word. The teacher made the connection between the activities the students had completed and the poem. Then she said, "As you read the poem some of the ideas on death that we have discussed will be expressed by the poet. Which ones? Read to find out." Now the stage was set for reading the poem.

The English teacher's strategy for prereading helped students anticipate meaning in the poem they were about to read. She recognized that just as athletes need to "warm up" before a contest, so do readers need to get ready for text.

Since the 1960s, readiness to read texts has been studied from many perspectives, not the least of which has been a *schema-theoretic view* of the reading process. The essence of cognitive readiness in content area reading is to prepare students to make connections between what they know and what they will learn, to anticipate what will be read, and to help them raise questions about the material under study.

Activating and Building Background Knowledge

Comprehension embodies the very complexity (and magic) of reading. The best anyone can do to understand reading comprehension is to examine it indirectly, by inference, as we did with the "Ordeal by Cheque" demonstration in Chapter 1. In recent years two areas of study—*information processing* and *psycholinguistics*—

have generated inferences about comprehension that can be applied to what we as classroom teachers do in the name of instruction.

Psycholinguistics combines an understanding of how language works with how people learn. Information processing proposes that the brain functions actively to seek, select, organize, store, and, when necessary, retrieve and utilize information about the world (Smith, 1975). A line of inquiry emerging from both fields has examined how background knowledge (schema)—experience, knowledge, beliefs, attitudes, and skills—affects comprehension. What people know, feel, and believe determines the extent to which they will make sense out of events in any situation.

As we suggested earlier, experiences and knowledge are cumulative and integrated into what cognitive psychologists call *schema* or *cognitive structure*. Ausubel (1978), for instance, believed that a person's wealth of knowledge is organized hierarchically—that information is stored in the brain in highly generalized concepts, less inclusive concepts, and specific facts. He asserted that "an individual's organization, stability and clarity of knowledge in a particular subject matter field at a given time" is a major factor in learning and retaining new information. Learning is easier for a person whose knowledge is clear, stable, and organized. But don't think of schema or prior knowledge of a topic as passive. It's dynamic, enlarging, and changing constantly as new information and experiences are assimilated into it.

In the introductory remarks to *Comprehension and Learning* Smith (1975) asserted, "The only effective and meaningful way in which anyone can learn is by attempting to relate new experiences to what he knows (or believes) already" (p. 1). There must be a point of contact between the reader's knowledge of the world and the ideas communicated by the textbook author. Reader and text must interact for comprehension and learning to take place. This is why what students know influences the kinds of questions they will ask about content under study.

Anderson and his associates (1977) illustrated the dynamic role that schema plays in reading comprehension. As part of an experiment, they asked college-level students to read the following passage:

> Rocky slowly got up from the mat, planning his escape. He hesitated a moment and thought. Things were not going well. What bothered him most was being held, especially since the charges against him had been weak. He considered his present situation. The lock that held him was strong but he thought he could break it. He knew, however, that his timing would have to be perfect. Rocky was aware that it was because of his early roughness that he had been penalized so severely—much too severely from his point of view. The situation was becoming frustrating; the pressure had been grinding on him for too long. He was being ridden unmercifully. Rocky was getting angry now. He felt he was ready to make his move. He knew that his success or failure would depend on what he did in the next few seconds. *(p. 372)*

How do you interpret the passage? Would you choose one of these statements to reflect your interpretation?

This passage is about a convict planning his escape from prison.

This passage is about a wrestler trying to break the hold of an opponent.

Or, if neither statement works for you, use this space to write your interpretation of the passage:

This passage is about _____

_____

The "typical person," according to Anderson, would interpret the passage as about a convict planning his escape. Nevertheless, the majority of the students in the experiment who had a physical education background and a special interest in wrestling recalled and interpreted the passage as a description of wrestling. The experimenters concluded that "personal history, knowledge, and belief influence the interpretations that they will give prose passages . . . high-level schemata provide the interpretive framework for comprehending discourse . . . language comprehension always involves using one's knowledge of the world" (pp. 376–378).

When understandings such as these are integrated with what you know (and believe) about teaching effectively, you will develop fresh perspectives on content area reading instruction.

As noted in the previous chapter, "schema inadequacies" may exist among students. Schema-based obstacles to text comprehension may result from a student's lack of available schema for a topic, the inability to select or activate a schema, or the inability to maintain a schema during reading. Our predominant concern throughout the remainder of this chapter is with potential obstacles to reading comprehension. In the sections which follow we examine more closely how to build and activate background knowledge.

Developing Frames of Reference for New Material

As students get ready to read, they need to build a frame of reference for new ideas that will be encountered in the upcoming material. A frame of reference is an anchor point; it reflects the schema or cognitive structure students need to relate new information to existing knowledge. Students need to recognize how new material "fits" into the conceptual frameworks that they already have.

Thelen (1984) likened an individual's cognitive structure to a personal filing cabinet. She noted that, "As students encounter new ideas, they need appropriate filing systems for storing the information" (p. 12). In other words, learning takes place when students' existing cognitive structures are organized for efficient information processing. Helping students to organize what they know is a critical step in preparing them to read. Moreover, showing them *where* and *how* new ideas "fit" into existing knowledge structures is essential for active learning to take place.

Teachers can help students anchor new ideas by giving them a frame of reference for studying the new material. Students can develop frames of reference through a variety of learning activities which build and activate background knowledge. In this section, we emphasize strategies involving *conceptually related readings, advance organizers, previews, analogies,* and *structured overviews.*

Conceptually Related Readings

Reading should be an integral part of learning in the content classroom. Yet it is one thing to assign reading selections, and it is another for students to read them. It is not uncommon for classroom teachers to eschew reading in favor of lecture and other modes of verbal presentation as the dominant means of getting across content. However, students need to recognize that *reading strengthens the reading process,* that reading about a topic under study can dramatically improve comprehension of related readings on the same topic.

Crafton (1983) found that this was indeed the case when high school students read two different articles on the same subject. Not only did comprehension of the second article improve, but students read more actively. Thus, the act of reading in itself can be an important strategy for generating background knowledge and building a frame of reference. As Crafton (1983) noted, "Natural reading experiences allow readers to construct background knowledge which can be used to comprehend other discourse" (p. 590). Two strategies which stimulate conceptually related readings of similar topics involve the use of multiple textbooks and popular books, pamphlets, and magazine selections.

Multiple Textbooks

As we discuss in Chapter 10, the use of more than one textbook in the content classroom is an effective organizational strategy. The purpose behind multiple textbooks typically is to bridge the gap between students of varying reading abilities and materials of varying text difficulty. Multiple textbooks are used because they have different readabilities, and as a result, teachers feel that they are able to make better reading assignments across groups of students.

Crafton (1983) suggested that there is no reason why the multiple textbook strategy could not also have a multiple reading component: ". . . development of a key but unfamiliar concept can be achieved by reading more than one selection on the same topic . . ." (p. 591). The idea of multiple readings is instructionally sound in that "Students are encouraged to expand and refine their growing understanding of a particular concept by encountering it textually in various styles and organizations and from different perspectives" (p. 591). Popular books, pamphlets, and magazine articles serve a similar function.

Popular Books, Pamphlets, and Magazine Selections

In social studies and history, the reading of primary source material and documents (in place of or in addition to textbook selections) has frequently been touted as a strategy which builds multiple perspectives and background knowledge for concept development. Likewise, a variety of reading materials ranging from popular books (fiction and nonfiction) to magazine articles can be used effectively to help students become aware that reading is one major source of knowledge that they have at their command. Pamphlets and magazine articles are particularly helpful in building specific background information needed to understand textbook topics.

In areas such as science, social studies, and history, popular books help to bridge knowledge gaps that textbooks may not cover and to pique interest in a unit of study. Heinly and Hilton (1982) noted the effect of historical literature on middle school students in their school district:

> Reading realistic stories about people in historical settings has helped our students understand societal cause-effect relationships . . . strengthen our students' chronology of time . . . develop a sense of somehow fitting into a broader scheme of life and time.

Brown and Abel (1982) proposed revitalizing American history through literature. They recommended the use of biography, historical fiction, and fiction with applicability to historical content. Biographies, for example, present insights into a particular period of time and often spotlight conflicts which the subject of the biography had to deal with and overcome. Historical fiction, likewise, deals with conflicts which characters must resolve in a particular period. Actual historical figures are likely to give authenticity to a piece of historical fiction. Brown and Abel, for example, suggested Michener's *Chesapeake* and *Centennial* for a high school American history class.

Cianciolo (1981) summed up the role of historical literature when she stated that historical stories provide a fine vehicle for gathering a wide range of knowledge. As a result, readers acquire a *framework for remembering and understanding* historical content. The same holds for science content as well as content from other subject areas. As Dole and Johnson (1981) indicated, popular science books—either fact or fiction—can provide background knowledge for science concepts covered in class, and can help students relate these concepts to their everyday lives.

Natural reading experiences help illustrate the power of the reading process in helping students to generate their own background information. In addition, teacher-made materials can be devised for similar purposes. One of the most studied instructional devices for preparing readers for text material is the *advance organizer* and its many variations.

Organizers, Analogies, and Previews

David Ausubel's major contributions to the field of instructional psychology preceded developments in schema theory and research. However, Ausubel's theory of meaningful verbal learning provided a sound basis for understanding the important role that background knowledge plays in comprehension and learning. As a result of his work, researchers have studied extensively the use of *advance organizers* as an aid to learning and retaining concepts.

Advance organizers attempt to maximize the cognitive readiness of learners prior to a new task. Ausubel maintained that advance organizers, if constructed and used properly, enhance learning and aid retention because they tend to clarify and organize an individual's schema prior to a learning task.

An advance organizer, then, is defined by Ausubel (1968) as "preparatory paragraphs which . . . enhance the discriminability of the new learning material from previously learned related ideas. . . . *To be maximally effective they* [advance organizers] *must be formulated in terms of language, concepts, propositions already familiar to the learner, and use appropriate illustrations and analogies"* (p. 214, italics added).

In everyday terms, organizers have been devised in varied and sundry formats—as introductory paragraphs, graphic displays, and as part of verbal presentations. What the formats have in common is their attempt to influence the predictability of text by providing a frame of reference for readers to link what they know to what they will learn. Although it is highly recommended in many reading textbooks and journal articles, the advance organizer has produced mixed results in classroom-centered research. Sometimes organizers "work" effectively; sometimes they don't. In our opinion they can be highly effective in activating background knowledge and aiding students to link what they know to what they will learn—but organizers don't run by themselves. The effectiveness of an organizer in a content area reading situation depends on how well it is constructed and how actively students are engaged in discussing it before reading the text assignment.

Therefore, we recommend the following guidelines for constructing and using organizers during prereading preparation:

1. Construct an organizer for difficult text material only. As a rule of thumb, an organizer should be about one-tenth as long as the actual text selection to be used.

2. Devise the organizer so that it reflects the top-level or superordinate ideas in the text to be assigned. In Chapter 2 we showed how to analyze expository text for main ideas. Make sure that these ideas are prominent and easily identifiable in the organizer. If narrative texts such as short stories are to be read, key elements of plot and theme should be introduced in the organizer.

3. Use real-life incidents, anecdotes, examples, or illustrations in the organizer to which readers can relate. These devices serve as a basis for

comparing or contrasting what readers know already with unfamiliar material.

4. In a similar vein, use analogies to help readers bridge the "known" with the "new." Hayes and Tierney (1982) reported that analogies have a strong influence on the activation of background knowledge necessary for understanding text.

5. Raise questions in the organizer which will arouse curiosity and pique interest. Questions help students to reflect on the material to be read and to relate it to background knowledge and experience. Questions inserted at key points in the organizer will engage students in thinking about the text to be read.

Let's take a closer look at two types of organizers that have been studied—the analogy and the preview.

Analogies as Organizers

An analogy establishes a comparison contrast between concepts familiar to the reader and unfamiliar ideas which will be encountered in text. For example in the Hayes and Tierney (1982) study, readers compared what they already knew about the game of baseball with information from a text passage on the English sport cricket. Activating readers' knowledge of baseball served as a frame of reference for understanding the cricket passage.

Analogies can be created for almost any content area. In reading a literary work, for example, an English or language arts teacher may devise an analogous situation in which students compare their approach to a problem with a problem that the protagonist of the story must resolve. Or the teacher may create an analogy around the theme of the selection. If students were to read "The Gift of the Magi" they might examine their own beliefs and understandings about giving and receiving in relation to the story's theme.

Study the analogy in Box 4.1, which was prepared for a junior high school science lesson on the Earth's physical makeup.

Box 4.1

AN EXAMPLE OF AN ANALOGY

The Orange and the Earth*

The Earth's physical makeup is very similar to the makeup of an orange. Sometimes an orange has one seed at its center. The Earth's single central, "giant seed," about 760 miles in radius, is called the inner solid iron core. This inner core serves to give our planet life just as the orange's seed gives life.

Earth's interior is as liquid as the interior of an orange. However, the liquid in an orange is what we call orange juice, while the liquid in the Earth is liquid iron and is known as the outer liquid core. This liquid core is about 1400 miles in depth. The liquid iron is confined by what is called a rocky mantle; the juice of the orange is confined by a white spongy cellulose material.

The difference is that the white cellulose is only a small fraction of the orange's radius, while the mantle of the Earth accounts for about a third of the Earth's radius, about 1300 miles.

As you may have guessed by now, both the orange and the Earth have a crust or skin which serves to protect the interior. The Earth's skin actually has two components: the asthenosphere, a layer of fudgelike consistency that extends about 300 miles, and the lithosphere, which is the Earth we walk on and see. The Earth's lithosphere is as thin as the skin of an orange by comparison. As you read more about the Earth's physical makeup, what other comparisons can you make between the orange and the Earth?

*Devised by Dora Bailey, Kent State University.

As the students discussed the analogy in Box 4.1, the teacher used an orange and a facsimile of the Earth as props. The discussion led to the clarification of key concept words introduced in the analogy passage. It also created the organizational framework that students needed to fit new information into existing knowledge.

Previews as Organizers

Previews function as organizers in that they also provide students with a frame of reference in which to understand new material. Previews should be used, like other advance organizers, for difficult reading selections. Graves, Cooke, and LaBerge (1983) examined previews as a prereading strategy for difficult short stories. They found that when a preview was read by the teacher to students, it had a significant influence on low-achieving junior high school students' comprehension and recall of the stories.

The preview passage should provide much more substantive information than the brief introductory statements which usually accompany selections found in reading and literature textbooks. However, the real value of previews are that they build a frame of reference for the story by telling students a good deal about it.

To construct a preview, follow these guidelines:

1. Begin with a series of short statements and one or more questions which spark interest, provide a link between a familiar topic and the topic of the story, and encourage students to actively reflect upon the theme.

2. Provide a synopsis of the story which includes key elements in the story structure (without signaling the resolution or outcome of the plot).

3. Define several key terms within the context of the preview passage.

According to Graves, Prenn, and Cooke (1985), using a preview for pre-reading instruction is a relatively straightforward procedure. They recommended the following steps:

1. Tell students you're going to introduce the upcoming selection.

2. Read the first few sentences of the preview.

3. Give students two or three minutes to discuss the question or questions.

4. Read the remainder of the preview.

5. Have students begin reading immediately after you complete the preview. *(p. 597)*

Study the example in Box 4.2 of a preview developed for a Ray Bradbury novel, *Farenheit 451*. If you teach (or are planning to teach) in a content area other than English, think of ways you can adapt the preview for non-narrative material.

Box 4.2

AN EXAMPLE OF A PREVIEW FOR FARENHEIT 451, *BY RAY BRADBURY*

Some of you like to read. Do you find that your free time is spent reading a good story? Reading books about your hobby? Reading magazines that interest you? Some of you probably don't like to read. Is reading a book or a magazine the last thing you would choose to do?

Even if you do not personally like to read, you probably value the uses of reading. If you were to buy a stereo, for example, it comes with a set of written instructions which must be read. When you go to a restaurant you are handed a menu to read. What other daily activities require reading? Our society values the ability to read and demands that its citizens use this skill for various purposes and situations.

Imagine an advanced human civilization where reading was not valued. In fact readers and books would be persecuted and burned. Imagine a state in which to read was considered a crime of insanity. Why would this be the case? People caught with books in their possession would be sent to an asylum because only an insane person would want to read. The books found would be burned.

The novel we are about to read presents just such a view of the place reading has. In this future society, the greatest antisocial act is to read and the greatest offense is to own books. Books are destroyed by the fire brigade, who instead of putting out fires, start fires.

The main character of the story is Guy Montag, a fireman who at first does his duty without raising either objections or questions. He accepts that books and houses in which they are found should be burned and stamped out as something evil. His position as a fireman is one of power, and it is not until he encounters the comments of a seventeen-year-old girl, Clarisse, that he starts to think. Clarisse plants a seed of doubt about life in this society and Montag's role in it when she asks him, "Is it true that long ago fireman put out fires instead of going to start them?"

As Montag searches himself and examines the values of his society, he is filled with frustration and cries out, "Nobody listens anymore. I can't talk to the walls because they are yelling at me. I can't talk to my wife: she listens to the walls. I just want someone to hear what I have to say. And maybe if I talk long enough, it'll make sense." Montag's desire to communicate is something you probably have felt. But in Montag's society communication is not valued. It is not done.

Many other ideals that you think are valuable are also considered negatively in this upside down world. A sense of loyalty, caring about another person, and respect for human life are several examples.

Under these circumstances, how can you tell the "good guys" from the "bad guys" in Montag's world? Clarisse is trying to get Montag to grow as a human being. Yet she is enticing him away from his society's values. On the other hand, Montag's boss, Beatty, tries to have Montag see the necessity and value behind their society's point of view.

The story opens with, "It was a pleasure to burn." The firemen's symbols were the number 451 (the temperature in farenheit at which paper burns) and the salamander (the Greek mythological reptile said to live in fire).

The story is peppered with such symbols in addition to being a running stream of similes and metaphors. For example, ". . . he searched for a simile, found one in his work (people were like)—torches, blazing away until they whiffed out." It helps to know that many of the story's ideas and thoughts are presented in metaphors. For example, "He felt she was walking in a circle about him, turning him end for end, shaking him quietly, and emptying his pockets, without once moving himself." This sentence means that Clarisse was finding out about him without any real information being exchanged. There is also quite a good deal of high imagery used. For example, "The trees overhead made a sound of letting down their dry rain" sets the tone for the disturbing events that follow.

You should be aware that kerosene is the fuel used for burning books, probably because it is not as dangerous to transport to the sites of the burning as gasoline.

The word *identification* in this story is used to mean almost an empathy. Clarisse knows Montag's inner feelings and thoughts—even better than he does himself.

The "parlor walls" are wall-sized TV screens. We usually have one TV screen. In the world of Montag, it is common to have a screen on each of the four walls; thus a person can be immersed in the TV show.

Previews, analogies, and other types of organizers make excellent writing assignments. Consider assigning students to write a preview in order to "advertise a reading assignment" for future groups of students. You might suggest that students put themselves in the shoes of the teacher or the author. The writing task might be introduced in this manner: "If you were the author of (title of text selection how would you introduce readers to the major ideas in the reading selection?" To accompany the written organizer, students may use pictures, posters, book jackets, slogans, or bumper stickers to capture the unifying idea of the text selection and to arouse interest. As students compose organizers they should be aware of their audience—other students. Impress upon students that these organizers will be read and used by students in future classes.

The teacher may need to model how organizers are constructed as part of prewriting discussion. This perhaps may entail reflecting upon a teacher-constructed organizer that students had previously experienced. Which major ideas received the most prominence? Why did the teacher select these over others? Why were questions or examples or analogies included in the model organizer?

The Structured Overview

At the start of each chapter we have asked you to organize your thoughts around the main ideas in the text. These ideas are presented within the framework of a structured overview—or graphic organizer, as it is sometimes called—a chart which uses content vocabulary to help students anticipate concepts and their relationships to one another in the reading material. These concepts are displayed by arranging key technical terms relevant to the important concepts to be learned. As Figure 4.1 illustrates, the graphic outline that results shows the hierarchical nature of the concepts to be studied. A concept may be designated as *superordin-*

ate, coordinate, or *subordinate* depending on its relationship to other concepts. (For an extended discussion of the hierarchical nature of concepts, see Chapter 9.)

Figure 4.1 Hierarchical Relationships among Concepts

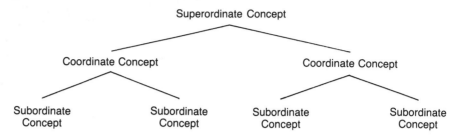

Thelen (1979) illustrated a hierarchical arrangement of mathematical concepts having similar attributes and characteristics. See Figure 4.2.

Figure 4.2

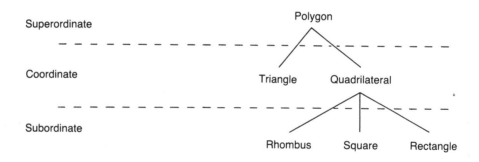

The concept *quadrilateral* is subordinate to *polygon*; coordinate to *triangle*; and superordinate to *rhombus, square,* and *rectangle*. *Polygon* is the most inclusive concept and subsumes all of the others.

A structured overview is a prereading activity which has its roots in Ausubel's theory of meaningful reception learning. A structured overview always shows vocabulary in relation to more inclusive vocabulary concepts. The diagram showing the hierarchical arrangement among vocabulary terms acts as an advance organizer—that is, readers develop a set to learn in advance of the text material. The structured overview is another format for an advance organizer. Let's take a closer look at its construction and application in the classroom.

Constructing the Structured Overview

Barron (1969) suggested the following steps for developing the structured overview and introducing the vocabulary diagram to students:

1. Analyze the vocabulary of the learning task and list all the words that you feel are important for the student to understand.

2. Arrange the list of words until you have a scheme which shows the interrelationships among the concepts particular to the learning task.

3. Add to the scheme vocabulary terms which you believe the students understand in order to show relationships between the learning task and the discipline as a whole.

4. Evaluate the overview. Have you clearly shown major relationships? Can the overview be simplified and still effectively communicate the idea you consider to be crucial?

5. Introduce the students to the learning task by showing them the scheme and telling them why you arranged the terms as you did. Encourage them to contribute as much information as possible to the discussion of the overview.

6. As you complete the learning task, relate new information to the overview where it seems appropriate.

Suppose you were to develop a structured overview for a text chapter in a psychology elective in a high school social studies program. Let's walk through the steps involved.

1. *Analyze the vocabulary and list the important words.* The chapter yields these words:

hebephrenia	neurosis	personality disorders
psychosis	schizophrenia	catatonia
abnormality	mental retardation	phobias

2. *Arrange the list of words.* Choose the word that represents the most inclusive concept, the one superordinate to all the others. Then choose the words classified immediately under the superordinate concept and coordinate them with one another. Then choose the terms subordinate to the coordinate concepts. Your diagram may look like Figure 4.3.

Figure 4.3

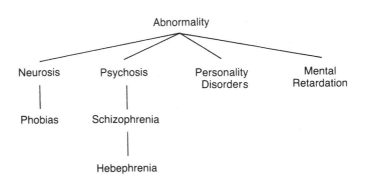

3. *Add to the scheme vocabulary terms which you believe the students understand.* You add the following terms: *antisocial, anxiety, in-*

tellectual deficit, Walter Mitty, depression, paranoia. Where would you place these words on the diagram?

4. *Evaluate the overview.* The interrelationships among the key terms may look like Figure 4.4 once you evaluate the vocabulary arrangement.

Figure 4.4

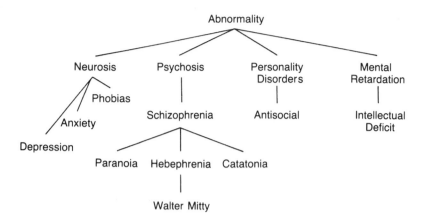

5. *Introduce the students to the learning task.* As you present the vocabulary relationships shown on the structured overview, create as much discussion as possible. Draw upon students' understandings and experiences with the concepts the vocabulary terms label. You might have students relate previous study or learnings to the terms. For example, *Walter Mitty* is subsumed within *hebephrenia.* If students were familiar with James Thurber's short story "The Secret Life of Walter Mitty," they would have little trouble bringing meaning to *hebephrenia* — a schizophrenic condition characterized by excessive daydreaming and delusions. The discussion might also lead to a recognition of the implicit comparison-contrast pattern among the four types of abnormality explained in the text. What better opportunity to provide direction for the skills to be applied during reading than to have students visualize the pattern. The discussions you will stimulate from the structured overview will be worth the time it takes to construct it.

6. *As you complete the learning task, relate new information to the overview.* This is particularly useful as a study and review technique. The overview becomes a study guide that can be referred to throughout the discussion of the material. Students should be encouraged to add information to flesh out the overview as they develop concepts fully.

Classroom Examples

Use a structured overview to show the relationships in an entire text, in a unit covering several chapters, in one chapter, or in a subsection of a chapter. The classroom scenario that follows provides further insight into its utility as a prereading vocabulary activity.

An eighth-grade social studies teacher constructed the structured overview in Figure 4.5 for twelve pages of his text. The purpose of the structured overview was to introduce students to the propaganda terms used in the textbook. Before having the class read the assigned pages, he placed the overview on the board and asked his class to copy it into their notebooks for future reference. Then he explained that propaganda is a word used to describe one way people try to change the opinions of others. He gave an example or two and then asked students to contribute other examples. As part of the development of the concept of propaganda, with the help and participation of students, he derived explanations for all the methods shown in the overview. As these explanations developed, students also saw how each method related to the two categories Name Calling and Name Using. The explanations which developed are as follows:

1. Bad names: calling a person an unpleasant name to make people feel angry or fearful. No facts are given about the person.

2. Glad names: calling a person a pleasant name to make people feel good. No facts are given about the person.

3. Half Truths: presenting only good or only bad information about something or someone. Only one side of the story is told.

4. Bandwagon: telling people that "everyone is doing it" to get them to follow the crowd.

5. Testimonial: getting a well-known person to say he or she likes or dislikes something or someone.

Figure 4.5 Structured Overview

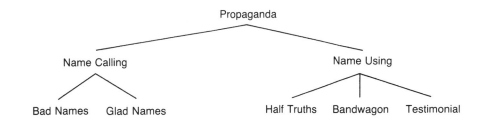

The students recorded these definitions in their notebooks. At this point they began to grasp the difference between methods and started to give examples of propaganda they saw being used in advertising. Then the teacher gave them nine sentences and asked them to identify the propaganda method used in each:

1. "Everyone in town is going to vote for Dan Ray."

2. "The present leaders are criminals and should be put it jail."

3. "She is a noble woman, capable in every way."

4. "As a football player, I know how important it is to wear Brand X hair cream."

5. "The young fighter is faster than the champ and will win the fight."

6. "My opponent is a coward, afraid of solving problems."

7. "Before my TV show, I always use Brand X toothpaste."

8. "Come to the fair and see everyone you know."

9. "The new political party is well organized. It will win the election."

Sentences 2 and 6 prompted considerable discussion as to whether the method was Bad Names, Half Truths, or both. After completing this exercise the students read the assigned pages of the text. The reading went rapidly, because the students quickly recognized the different methods of propaganda used in the textbook. The class discussion that followed was lively: the students were confident of their decisions and were eager to share them with their peers. According to the teacher, the lesson had a lasting effect on the students: in subsequent lessons not dealing specifically with propaganda they recognized the use of propaganda and shared it with the rest of the class.

So much for the testimonial of one teacher. As you study the following illustrations consider the adaptations that might be made if you were to develop a structured overview for material in your content area.

The overview in Figure 4.6 was developed for a high school class in data processing. It introduced students to the different terms of data processing, delineating causes and effects.

Figure 4.6 Structured Overview

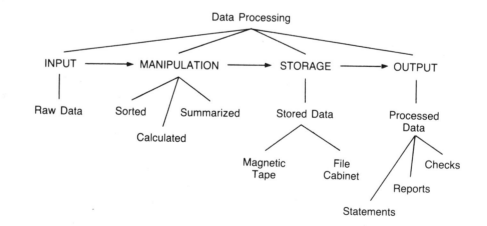

With Figure 4.7 an art teacher showed the relationships among key concepts associated with firing ceramics.

Figure 4.7 Structured Overview

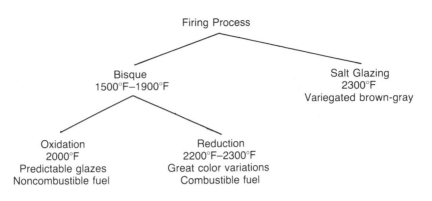

A teacher of ninth-grade English students studying character analysis and development in short fiction made the pictorial structured overview in Figure 4.8. During discussion of the overview, students referred to a short story they had read to provide examples.

Adapting the Structured Overview as a Concept Attainment Strategy

Use the structured overview to show relationships among key concepts. In addition, Thelen (1982) recommended incorporating aspects of a concept attainment model (Frayer, Frederick, and Klausmeier, 1969) into the class presentation of a structured overview. In doing so, the teacher singles out one or two key concepts to teach in detail. Once the target concepts are identified, elicit from the students as many *examples* and *nonexamples* of the concept(s) as possible as well as the *relevant* and *irrelevant attributes* of the concept(s). As we show in Chapter 9, an *example* is any instance of the concept being considered; a *nonexample* is anything not an instance of that concept. Likewise, *relevant* traits, features, and characteristics are those associated with the concept. *Irrelevant attributes* are not associated with the concept.

Thelen (1982) suggested that the teacher construct a structured overview as previously outlined in this chapter, and then proceed with the following steps:*

1. Decide upon the target concept in the structured overview. In the structured overview that Thelen used as an example (Figure 4.9) the teacher singled out *mammals* for discussion.

2. Define the concept so that you will be sure of the relevant attributes. For example, *Mammal—any vertebrate . . . that feeds its young with milk from the female mammary glands, that has the body more or less covered with hair, and that, with the exception of the montremes, brings forth living young rather than eggs (Random House Dictionary of the English Language).*

*Adapted from Judie Thelen, "Preparing Students for Content Reading Assignments," *Journal of Reading*, March 1982, pp. 546–547.

Figure 4.8 Structured Overview: Ways the Author Develops a Character

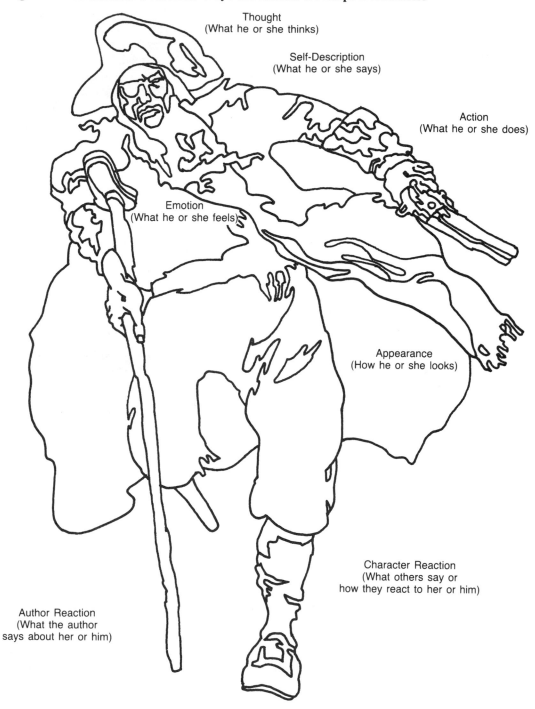

Thought
(What he or she thinks)

Self-Description
(What he or she says)

Action
(What he or she does)

Emotion
(What he or she feels)

Appearance
(How he or she looks)

Character Reaction
(What others say or
how they react to her or him)

Author Reaction
(What the author
says about her or him)

3. Tell the students what the name of the concept is that you're going to teach and ask them to contribute any examples that they may have. This can be accomplished by having students break into small groups of no more than five and making a list. After a specified period of time, usually no more than five to ten minutes, ask for the longest list. While the other groups listen, a representative of the group dictates the list as you write it on the board or overhead. Begin organizing the examples into categories. Other groups are then invited to add to, or challenge, the examples of their peers. Nonexamples are usually examples under coordinate concepts; that is, if students give the name of birds as mammals, write those examples under the slot that will be later labeled as birds, a coordinate concept of mammal.

4. Finish constructing the structured overview by explaining why you are placing the terms where you are.

5. Guide the students in discovering what characteristics are common to all examples. These will be the relevant attributes. This is the part of the lesson where you can clear up any misconceptions.

6. Next, guide the students in finding the differences among the concept examples. For instance, mammals differ in their habitat, height, weight, hair, etc.

7. When you feel that the students understand the concept, supply them with examples and nonexamples not previously discussed. These could be the concepts that will be encountered in the reading assignment. If the students can discriminate and generalize to the new, you can feel confident that they understand the concept.

Figure 4.9 A Structured Overview of Animals with Target Concept Mammals (Thelen, 1982)

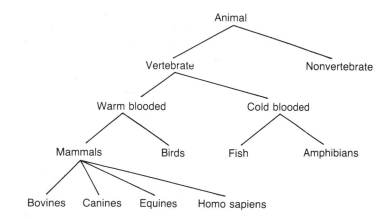

Examples:
    Bovines (cows, bulls)
    Canines (collies, German shepherds)

Equines (stallions, pintos)

Homo sapiens (monkeys, apes, humans)

The strategies that we have suggested for developing frames of reference are unquestionably linked to raising students' expectations about upcoming reading material. In this respect they have a stake in motivating students to want to read. Arousing curiosity about topics to be read and studied in a content classroom is an important motivational tool.

Arousing Curiosity

The "curioser and curioser" Alice became, the further she plunged into her adventures in Wonderland. The greater students' curiosity about a reading selection, the greater their motivation to read.

Arousing curiosity and activating background knowledge are closely related instructional activities. Curiosity arousal gives students the chance to consider what they know already about the material to be read. Through your guidance they are encouraged to make connections—to relate their knowledge to the text assignment. And further, they will recognize that there are problems—conceptual conflicts—to be resolved that they can best resolve through reading. In short, arousing curiosity helps students raise questions that they can answer only by giving thought to what they read.

Brainstorming

In Chapter 3, we noted that brainstorming techniques may be used diagnostically to assess students' levels of background knowledge. From a diagnostic *and* instructional point of view, brainstorming is a valuable tool for prereading. It will help students generate ideas which can then be used to "think about" the upcoming reading material. Brainstorming involves two basic steps which can be adapted easily to content objectives: (1) identify a broad concept that reflects the main topic to be studied in the assigned reading and (2) have students work in small groups to generate a list of words related to the broad concept in x number of seconds.

These two steps help you instantly discover what knowledge your students possess about the topic they are going to study. Furthermore, Herber (1978) suggested:

> The device of having students produce lists of related words is a useful
> way to guide review. It helps them become instantly aware of how
> much they know, individually and collectively, about the topic. They
> discover quickly that there are no right or wrong answers. . . . Until the
> students reach the point in the lesson where they must read the passage
> and judge whether their predictions are accurate, the entire lesson is
> based on their own knowledge, experience, and opinion. This captivates

their interest much more than the more traditional, perfunctory review. *(p. 179)*

When the brainstorming activity is over, and lists of words have been generated, consider these two follow-up activities: (1) Have students in small groups arrange their lists of words into subcategories. They must be prepared to identify the subcategories and the logic behind each arrangement. (2) Once the brainstormed word lists have been compared and discussed, have students make predictions about the content to be studied. You might ask, "Given the list of words and subcategories that you have developed, what do you think the reading assignment will be about? How does the title of the selection relate to your subcategories? Why do you think so?"

A teacher in New Haven, Connecticut, initiated a brainstorming activity with a class of "low-achieving learners." The students, working in small groups, were asked to list in two minutes as many words as possible that were related to the Civil War. Then the groups shared their lists of Civil War words. The teacher then created a master list on the board from the individual entries of the groups. He also wrote three categories on the board—North, South, Both—and asked the groups to classify each word from the master list under one of the categories. Here's how one group responded:

North	South	Both
blue	gray	soldiers
Lincoln	farms	armies
Grant	Rebel	guns
factories	Booth	cannons
Yankee	slavery	Gettysburg Address
Ford Theater		roots
We won		death
		horses
		assassination

Note that in this example the teacher provided the categories. He recognized that students needed the additional structure to be successful with this particular task. The activity led to a good deal of discussion and debate. Students were put in the position of "authority," sharing what they knew and believed already with other class members. As a result of the activity, they were asked to raise questions about the Civil War that they wanted to have answered through reading and class discussion.

Creating Conceptual Conflicts

We once observed a class of eighth graders form small groups before reading a selection from the book *African Elephants* by B. F. Beebe. The selection, entitled "Today's Stone Age Elephant Hunters," was part of a social studies unit on African life and history. The teacher assigned the groups a hypothetical problem to solve

before reading the selection. The problem: if you were a Pigmy, alone and with a spear as your only weapon, how would you hunt and kill an elephant?

The students began to chatter enthusiastically. The problem seemed to be at an intermediate level of familiarity—that is, the hypothetical situation suggested by the question was not outside the students' realm of experience. Nor was it so unfamiliar to the students that the conceptual conflict created by the question would be nonexistent. Rather, they appeared to be intrigued and somewhat perplexed and baffled by the problem yet aroused enough to pursue possible solutions.

The teacher facilitated discussion by keeping the groups on the task— prodding, playing devil's advocate, asking open-ended questions. After several minutes of discussion, the teacher asked each group to share its solution with the whole class. The gist of many of the solutions, as you might expect, was predictable:

"Dig a big hole and lure the elephant into it."
"Climb a tree and wait for the elephant to pass under it."
"Lead the elephant off a cliff."

As each group provided its solution, members of other groups were invited to respond, to find loopholes or additional problems unaccounted for. The teacher, meanwhile, remained nondirective but kept the discussion going, trying to get students to relate their world to the problem. As a result, several of the students shared their knowledge of hunting. Others recognized the element of surprise as the Pigmy's best offense. As one likely future military tactician noted, "When he [the elephant] least expects it, he better expect it."

Next the teacher asked, "Would you like to find out how a lone Pigmy with a spear as his only weapon actually *does* hunt and kill an elephant?" The students leaped on the question. They were off and reading in no time flat.

How *do* Pigmies kill elephants? Read Box 4.3 and find out for yourself.

Box 4.3

TODAY'S STONE AGE ELEPHANT HUNTERS*
B. F. Beebe

Some pigmies of the western Congo use a system of concealing their scent when hunting elephants. Few of these little jungle dwellers hunt elephants but those that do have chosen about the most dangerous way to secure food in today's world.

Hunting is done by a single man using a spear with a large metal spearhead and thick shaft. After taking the trail behind an elephant herd the hunter pauses frequently to coat his skin with fresh elephant droppings for several days until he has lost all human scent.

Closing on the herd the pigmy selects his prey, usually a young adult. He watches this animal until he is aware of its distinctive habits—how often it dozes, eats, turns, wanders out of the herd, and other individual behavior.

Then he moves toward his huge prey, usually at midday when the herd is dozing while standing. The little hunter moves silently between the elephant's legs, braces himself and drives the spear up into the stomach area for several feet. The elephant snaps to alertness, screaming and trying to reach his diminutive attacker. Many pigmy hunters have lost their lives at this moment, but if the little hunter is fast enough he pulls out the spear to facilitate bleeding and ducks for safety.

Death does not come for several days and the hunter must follow his wounded prey until it stops. When the elephant falls the pigmy cuts off the tail as proof of his kill and sets off for his village, which may be several days away by now.

*Source: B. F. Beebe, *African Elephants*. New York: McKay, 1968, pp. 91–92.

One of the keys to motivation through curiosity arousal is conceptual conflict (Berlyne, 1976). Should students be presented with prereading situations that take the form of puzzlement, doubt, surprise, perplexity, contradiction, or ambiguity, they will be motivated to seek resolution in order to maintain equilibrium.

Shablak and Castallo (1977) asserted, "The need within the person becomes one of information-seeking in an attempt to resolve the conflict; to fill the gap between known and unknown" (p. 53). The search for knowledge becomes a driving force. When a question begins to gnaw, searching behavior is aroused; learning occurs as the conceptual conflict resolves itself.

The instructional possibilities for creating conceptual conflict are legion. Several broad strategies can be adapted to arouse curiosity and sustain interest prior to reading content materials.

Establishing Problematic Situations

Creating a problem to be solved provides an imaginative entry into a text selection, as was the case with the illustration from *African Elephants*. The teacher's role in creating problematic situations is one of (1) providing the time to discuss the problem, raising questions, and seeking possible solutions prior to reading, and then (2) assigning the reading material that will help lead to resolution and conceptual development.

Collette (1973) offered an excellent example of a "teachable moment" which helped students get "curioser" about reading science materials:

An unusual fall thunderstorm killed one of two men who sought shelter under a tree. The ninth grade students immediately were curious about the reason for the death of only one man while his companion only a couple of feet away was unharmed. The science teacher explained that man did not know much about the action of lightning and suggested that the pupils make a list of questions that would likely be answered by looking in books and other references.

In addition to the "teachable moment," consider "keying" a problematic situation directly to specific text selections. For example, a social studies teacher and her students were exploring the development of early American settlements in a unit on Colonial life. Here is how she presented the problematic situation to students:

> Suppose the time is 1680, and the place Massachusetts. Imagine that you are early European settlers. You will want to try to think as you believe they may have thought, act as they might have acted. You and your group have petitioned the Great and General Court to be allowed to form a new town. After checking to make sure you are of good character and the land is fertile and can be defended, the court says yes. They grant you a five-mile square of land. As proprietors of this land, you must plan a town. What buildings would you put in first? Second? Third? Later? Why? How would you divide the land among the many people who want to live there? Why? As proprietors would you treat yourselves differently from the way you treated the others? Why? How would you run the government?

The series of questions promoted an interest-filled discussion, putting students into a situation in which they had to rely on background knowledge for responses.

Asking the students in the social studies class to approach reading by imagining that they were early European settlers placed them in a particular role. With the role comes a perspective. Creating such a perspective has its underpinnings in a schema-theoretical view of the reading process.

Influencing a Reader's Perspective

One of the earlier studies from the Center for the Study of Reading at the University of Illinois pointed to the powerful role of perspective in comprehending text (Pichert and Anderson, 1977). They showed just how important the reader's perspective can be. Two groups of readers were asked to read a passage about a house from one of two perspectives, that of either a burglar or a house buyer. When readers who held the perspective of a house burglar read a story about going through a house, they recalled different information than those readers who approached the story from the perspective of a house buyer.

Creating a perspective (a role) for the student is one way to get "into" reading. Students in these roles find themselves solving problems that force them to use their knowledge and experience.

A high school teacher created a perspective for students before assigning a reading selection from an auto mechanics manual.

The Perspective:
You are the only mechanic on duty when a four-wheel-drive truck with a V-8 engine pulls in for repair. The truck has high mileage, and it appears that the problem may be a worn clutch disk. What tools do you think you will need? What procedures would you follow? Put your answers to these questions under the two columns below.
   Tools needed   Procedures

In preparation for reading the short shory, "Alas Babylon," an English teacher set up a perspective in which students' curiosity was aroused and expectations for the story raised:

> The year is 1990. We are on the verge of a nuclear disaster. Through inside sources you learn that the attack will occur within five days. What preparations will you consider making before the nuclear attack occurs?

The class considered the orienting question. After some discussion, the teacher then suggested the following:

> Assuming that your town and house will not be destroyed by the bomb and that you have enough time to prepare for the attack, which twelve items from the list provided will you choose?

The students then formed small groups in which each group was directed to come to consensus on the twelve items they would choose. Those items were as follows:

____ a. buy a gun and ammunition to protect against looters

____ b. cash in all savings bonds and take all the money out of your checking and savings accounts

____ c. build a fireplace in your house

____ d. buy firewood and charcoal

____ e. buy extra tanks of gasoline and fill your car up

____ f. purchase antibiotics and other medicines

____ g. dig a latrine

____ h. buy lumber, nails, and various other supplies

____ i. plant fruit trees

____ j. notify all your friends and relatives of coming nuclear attack

____ k. invest in books on canning, making candles, and soap

____ l. buy a few head of livestock from a farmer

____ m. buy fishing equipment and a boat

____ n. buy seeds of several different kinds of vegetables for a garden

____ o. make friends with a farmer who has a horse and wagon

____ p. shop at antique stores for kerosene lamps and large cooking pots

____ q. buy a safe to hide your money in

____ r. buy foodstuffs

From the small group discussions came the recognition that the values and attitudes readers bring to text shape their perspective as much as their background knowledge on a topic. For this reason, we suggest that building motivation for text to be read take into account the examination of values and attitudes.

Examining Beliefs and Attitudes

Prereading discussion can be sparked through an examination of the beliefs and attitudes that students bring to reading assignments.

Study the exercise in Box 4.4 which was developed for a social studies class. The teacher helped to connect students' beliefs and feelings about war to the study of American involvement in the Mexican War. He began by informing students that for the next couple of days they would be reading about President Polk's war message in which he gave his reasons for asking Congress to declare war against Mexico. Before beginning that assignment, the students examined their beliefs and feelings about war. They were directed to put a check mark along a continuum next to each of the statements below to indicate the extent to which they "agreed" or "disagreed."

Box 4.4

AMERICAN INVOLVEMENT IN THE MEXICAN WAR

Directions: Place a check along the continuum next to each of the statements to indicate the extent to which you "agree" or "disagree."

Strongly   Strongly
agree   disagree

←————————————→

_____   1. A nation must protect the property of its people, even if war is necessary.

_____   2. If a country expects to be attacked by a foreign power, it is justified in attacking that power first in its own defense.

_____   3. Only when a nation is invaded does it have the right to go to war.

_____   4. The government of the U.S. must defend American-owned businesses in foreign countries.

_____   5. Even though some Americans may oppose war with another country, once war is declared each person should give the government his or her full support.

_____   6. When two countries are at war, there should be no distinction between the civilian population and the military.

_____   7. There are situations facing a nation where war is the only alternative.

_____   8. A nation has the right to resort to war to obtain the natural resources it lacks and needs for its own well-being.

_____   9. When called upon to approve a declaration of war, a Congressman should decide the matter according to his conscience rather than according to the wishes of his or her constituents.

_____   10. During time of war, a person should put his country ahead of his or her personal beliefs.

To conclude this section, we offer one more example of arousing curiosity. The strategy is another alternative to consider for your teaching repertoire during prereading preparation.

Guided Imagery

Guided imagery allows students to explore concepts visually. Described here as a feedforward activity, guided imagery can also be incorporated into a variety of instructional situations for a variety of purposes.

Samples et al. (1977, p. 189) recommended guided imagery, among other things, as a means for

1. building an experience base for inquiry, discussion, and group work;
2. building self-image;
3. exploring and stretching concepts;
4. solving and clarifying problems;
5. exploring history and the future;
6. exploring other lands and worlds;
7. creative writing.

Guided imagery works like this. The teacher, according to Samples et al., structures a daydream: "You use *words* to get into the process—but once there, images take over" (p. 188). After you read the following illustration, close your eyes and do it:

> Close your eyes . . . tell all your muscles to relax. You are entering a space capsule ten minutes before takeoff. Soon you feel it lift off . . . you look over at your companions and check their reactions. Now you are ready to take a reading of the instrument panel. As you relay the information to ground control, it is eleven minutes into the flight . . . you settle back into your chair and tell your fellow astronauts about your thoughts . . . about what you hope to see when the vehicle lands . . . about what you might touch and hear as you explore the destination. Finally, you drift off to sleep . . . picturing yourself returning to earth . . . seeing once again your friends and relations. You are back where you started . . . tell your muscles to move . . . open your eyes.

You may wish to have students discuss their "trips" which, of course, parallel in some way the content of the reading selection to be assigned. In the classroom where this example was devised, students in a literature class participated in the imagery discussion prior to reading a short story on space travel. Discussion questions included: "How did you feel just before entering the space capsule?" "What were the reactions of your companions?" "Where did your exploration take you?" "Were there things that surprised you on the trip? Colors? Sounds?"

Samples et al. (1977) provided these tips as they explained the imagery strategy:

Relaxed positions are helpful. . . . As few distractions as possible will make the first few experiences easier. A soothing but audible voice is best. For those who can't get themselves to participate, an alternative quiet activity will cut down on embarrassed giggles. Leave lots of "empty" space both in terms of specific content and time to visualize. . . . *(p. 188)*

Guided imagery isn't for everyone. Some teachers will find themselves uncomfortable using it; others will not. As a prereading alternative, however, it gives you an additional option that will help students connect, in this case, what they "see" to what they will read.

Making Predictions

Prediction is a sure aid to reading comprehension. For one thing, strategies and materials for prediction activate thought about the content before reading. Students must rely on what they know through previous study and experience to make educated guesses about the material to be read.

Why an educated guess? Smith (1978) defined prediction as the prior elimination of unlikely alternatives. He suggested that

Readers do not normally attend to print with their minds blank, with no prior purpose and with no expectation of what they might find in the text. . . . The way readers look for meaning is not to consider all possibilities, nor to make reckless guesses about just one, but rather to predict within the most likely range of alternatives. . . . Readers can derive meaning from text because they bring expectations about meaning to text. *(p. 163)*

You can facilitate student-centered purposes by creating anticipation about the meaning of what will be read.

Anticipation Guides

An anticipation guide is a series of statements to which students must respond individually before reading the text. Their value lies in the discussion that takes place after the exercise. The teacher's role during discussion is to activate and agitate thought. As students connect their knowledge of the world to the prediction task, you must remain open to a wide range of responses. Draw upon what students bring to the task, but remain nondirective in order to keep the discussion moving.

An Anticipation Guide Demonstration

Sidney Harris wrote an article for his *Strictly Personal* column concerning an air crash that killed seventy-five persons returning from a college football game. Complete the anticipation guide Box 4.5 and then read the article.

Box 4.5

ANTICIPATION GUIDE DEMONSTRATION: "CRASH WAS NO TRAGEDY"

Directions: Before you read Harris's article, check those incidents you think Harris will classify as tragedies in the column headed You. Discuss your responses with class members, providing reasons for your choices. After reading the article, check in the column headed Harris those incidents that Harris could label as tragedy.

You   Harris

_____ _____   1. In his desire to remain in office, a law and order president authorizes breaking the law (for political and national security reasons) and is ultimately driven from office.

_____ _____   2. During the Master's Tournament, a golfer leading by ten strokes on the sixteenth hole of the last round is struck and killed by lightning.

_____ _____   3. In Guatemala, an earthquake kills 16,000 persons and leaves five times as many homeless.

_____ _____   4. A mass murderer slips and falls to his death as police close in on him.

_____ _____   5. A community spends one million dollars to upgrade its football program instead of its airport, and then its football team dies in a crash at that airport.

_____ _____   6. An understudy for an ill leading lady breaks her leg hurrying to meet her cue in her debut in a leading role.

_____ _____   7. A father and mother of three die in a head-on auto accident on the way home from a New Year's Eve party. The father was heard to brag about his capacity for alcohol and his ability to drive after drinking heavily.

         _____   8. A soccer team crashes in the Andes and those who are left are forced to eat the flesh of the victims in order to have a chance to live. Only seven of thirty-six survive.

_____ _____   9. As his defenses crumble before the onslaught of the allies, a ruthless dictator shoots and kills himself and has his body cremated.

_____ _____   10. The week before the Master's Tournament, the golfer in statement 2 laughed at a near miss and asserted that as long as he wore a band-aid on his arm, nothing could happen to him. He refused to get off the course during a violent thunderstorm.

Crash Was No Tragedy
Sydney J. Harris

We say that differences in words are "just semantical" and so we fail to understand the important distinctions between words that we use interchangeably. But if we use the wrong word, it is hard to think properly.

For a few days last November, the newspapers were filled with the story of "the Marshall University air tragedy" that killed 75 persons returning from a football game to Huntington, W. Va.

If I said it was not a *tragedy* but a *catastrophe,* you would retort that I was quibbling about words, or that I am being shallow and unfeeling. I think I can show you that you would be wrong on both counts.

An airplane crash is a catastrophe (literally, from the Greek, an "overturning"), like a sudden flood, a fire, a falling girder. Such accidents are part of the natural order and of the human condition; they result from the contingency of things, and are sad or shocking or pitiful—but they are not tragic.

There was, however, a tragic element in the Marshall University air crash; and we can recognize it only if we comprehend the difference between the two words. The tragedy lay in the community's frantic effort to have a winning football team, coupled with its indifference to an unsafe airport.

The school's and the city's hunger for football fame prompted the formation of a booster organization, the Big Green Club, made up of wealthy local business and professional men, who collected funds to help pay for the college's athletic program.

Two years ago, the athletic department's budget began to boom. A new coach was hired, players were recruited from other states, and the college's president resigned under pressure from sports buffs. Vigorous lobbying attempts were made in the state legislature to obtain $1 million for the building of an athletic field and facilities.

Meanwhile, the president of the Tri-State Airport Board confessed the day after the crash: "I've been sleeping with this possibility for the last eight years."

He blamed the lack of funds for the airport failure to have either radar or a warning light system—which would cost about $1 million, the price of the proposed athletic field.

In the classic Greek conception of tragedy, *hubris,* or false pride, is followed by *hamartia,* or sin, and this in turn is followed by *nemesis,* the fate that catches up with human pride and folly.

When having a victorious football team means more to the citizens than having a safe airport, then community *hubris* is riding for a terrible fall.

The players paid with their lives for this sin, but only if we understand the true nature of their "tragedy" will they not have died in vain.

SOURCE: Strictly Personal, by Sydney J. Harris © 1970 Field Enterprises, Inc. Courtesy of Field Newspaper Syndicate.

This demonstration shows how strongly anticipation is founded on what the reader brings to the reading selection. Your response to each statement reflects what you know and believe already about the two concepts tragedy and catastrophe. Notice that the opportunity to discuss your responses with other class members may have broadened your conceptual base or helped to further articulate and clarify the difference between the two terms.

By contrasting You and Harris, you probably read the selection more attentively, with purpose, to determine how accurate your predictions were and how similar or different your choices were from those of the author.

If there are differences between your choices for tragedy and Harris's, you have the opportunity to justify the reasons for your choices against those Harris provided. What better critical reading experience could you have?

Anticipation guides may vary in format but not in purpose. In each case, the reader's expectations about meaning are raised prior to reading the text. Keep these guidelines in mind in constructing and using an anticipation guide:

1. Analyze the material to be read. Determine the major ideas—implicit and explicit—with which students will interact.

2. Write those ideas in short, clear declarative statements. These statements should in some way reflect the world that the students live in or know about. Therefore, avoid abstractions whenever possible.

3. Put these statements into a format that will elicit anticipation and prediction making.

4. Discuss readers' predictions and anticipations prior to reading the text selection.

5. Assign the text selection. Have students evaluate the statements in light of the author's intent and purpose.

6. Contrast readers' predictions with author's intended meaning.

Classroom Examples

A junior high social studies teacher prepared students for a reading assignment which contrasted the characteristics of Northern and Southern soldiers in the Civil War. She began by writing *Johnny Reb* and *Billy Yank* in two columns on the chalkboard. She asked students to think about what they already knew about the two groups of soldiers. How do you think they were alike? How were they different? After some discussion, the teacher directed the students as follows:

> Johnny Reb and Billy Yank were common soldiers of the Civil War. You will be reading about some of their basic differences in your textbook. What do you think those differences will be? Before reading your assignment, place the initials JR in front of the phrases that you think best describe Johnny Reb. Place initials BY in front of those statements which best describe Billy Yank. Do not mark those statements common to both sides.

The anticipation guide for the above activity included ten statements:

    ____ 1. more likely to be able to read and write

    ____ 2. best able to adjust to living in the open areas

    ____ 3. more likely to be from a rural setting

    ____ 4. took a greater interest in politics

___ 5. more deeply religious

___ 6. often not able to sign his name

___ 7. disliked regimentation of army life

___ 8. more likely to speak more slowly and with an accent

___ 9. more probably a native American

___ 10. common man in the social order

Of course, each of the points highlighted in the statements was developed in the text selection. Not only did the students get a sense of the major ideas they would encounter in the text selection, but they also read to see how well they predicted which statements more accurately represented soldiers from the South and the North during the Civil War.

A science teacher began a weather unit by introducing a series of popular clichés about the weather. He asked students to anticipate whether or not the clichés had a scientific basis. See Box 4.6.

Box 4.6

ANTICIPATION GUIDE FOR CLICHÉS ABOUT WEATHER

Directions: Put a check under "Likely" if you feel that the weather saying has any scientific basis; put a check mark under "Unlikely" if you feel that it has no scientific basis. Be ready to explain your choice.

Likely	Unlikely	
_____	_____	1. Red sky at night, sailors delight; red sky at morning sailors take warning.
_____	_____	2. If you see a sunspot there is going to be bad weather.
_____	_____	3. When the leaves turn under it is going to storm.
_____	_____	4. If you see a hornet's nest high in a tree a harsh winter is coming.
_____	_____	5. Aching bones mean a cold and rainy forecast.
_____	_____	6. Ground hog sees his shadow—six more weeks of winter.
_____	_____	7. Rain before seven, sun by eleven.
_____	_____	8. If a cow lies down in a pasture, it means that it is going to rain soon.
_____	_____	9. Sea gull, sea gull sitting on the sand; it's never good weather while you're on land.

The prereading discussion led students to review and expand their concepts of "scientific truth." Throughout different parts of the unit, the teacher returned to one or two of the clichés on the anticipation guide and suggested to the class that the textbook assignment would explain whether or not there was a scientific basis for each saying. Students were then directed to read to find out what the explanations were.

A final example of how an anticipation guide may be used as a prereading strategy is evident in a high school English teacher's presentation of Richard Brautigan's poem "It's Raining in Love." The poem is a good example of a contemporary poem that discusses love in a not so typical way. It is the kind of poem that captures the way many high school students feel. Note the format used for the teacher's anticipation activity in Box 4.7.

Box 4.7

ANTICIPATION GUIDE FOR "IT'S RAINING IN LOVE"

Directions: We have already read several poems by Richard Brautigan. Before reading "It's Raining in Love," place a check in the You column next to each statement that you think expresses a feeling the poet will deal with in the poem. Discuss your choices in small groups and explain why you checked the statements you did. Then I'll assign the poem. After reading the poem, check the statements in the Poet column that express the feelings that the poet did deal with in his poem.

You   Poet

_____ _____ Being in love is a painful experience.

_____ _____ Boys can be just as nervous as girls when they like a member of the opposite sex.

_____ _____ It is OK for a girl to call a boy and ask him out.

_____ _____ It's better to be friends with members of the opposite sex than to be in love with them.

_____ _____ Poetry about love must be mushy to be effective.

_____ _____ Once a person has been in love, he's much more sensitive to another person's feelings when he finds out that person likes him.

Student-Generated Questions

Teaching students to generate their own questions about material to be read is one of the major instructional goals of prereading preparation. Two of the most important questions that students can ask in approaching a reading task are: What do I think this selection is about? Why do I think so? The first question invites prediction; the second demands that students examine their background knowledge or preview material in relation to the predictions that they have made. When students begin to ask questions about upcoming reading, their purposes for the reading task become more clear and focused.

Expectation Outline

Spiegal (1981) suggested the development of an Expectation Outline to help students ask questions about text. She recommended the Expectation Outline for factual material, but the strategy can be adapted to narrative stories as well. The Expectation Outline is developed on the chalkboard or an overhead projector transparency as students simply tell what they expect to learn from a reading selection.

If students are reading a factual selection, you may have them first take several minutes to preview and skim the material. Then ask, "What do you think your assignment is going to be about?" Ask students to state their expectations in the form of questions. As they suggest questions, the teacher groups related questions on the chalkboard or transparency. You also have the opportunity to ask students what prompted them to ask these questions in the first place. At this point, students may be encouraged to refer back to the text to support questions.

Once questions have been asked and grouped, the class labels each set of questions. Through discussion, students begin to see the major topics which will emerge from the reading. Lead them to recognize that gaps might exist in the Expectation Outline for the assignment. For example, you may add a topic or two to the outline for which there were no questions raised. Upon completion of the Expectation Outline, students read to answer the questions generated.

For narrative materials, students may use the title of the selection, pictures, or key words and phrases from the selection to ask their questions. For example, direct students to preview a story by skimming through it quickly, studying the pictures and illustrations (if any) and jotting down five to ten key words or phrases that appear to indicate the main direction of the story. As students suggest key words and phrases, write these on the board and categorize them. Then ask students to state what they expect to find out from the story. Have them raise questions about its title, setting and characters, plot and theme. As an alternative to questions, students may summarize their expectations by writing a paragraph about the story using the key words and phrases that were jotted down and categorized.

Your Own Questions

A variation on the Expectation Outline is a strategy called *Your Own Questions*. Here's how it works:

1. Have students listen to or read a portion of text from the beginning of a selection.

2. Ask students to write five to ten questions that they think will be answered by reading the remainder of the selection.

3. Discuss some of the questions asked by the students before reading. Write the questions on the board.

4. Students then read to see if questions are answered.

5. After reading, which questions were answered? Which weren't? Why not?

To get a feel for *Your Own Questions*, read the opening paragraphs from a selection entitled "The Guest Lecturer." Then use the space below to write at least five questions you expect to be answered from the remainder of the selection:

Guest Lecturer

The tension in the air could be sliced with a knife. The hearing had lasted nearly five hours. More than two hundred people, many of them students, were in the meeting room where the session was held. Bob Herring and Ray Weatherman, the two American history teachers, sat attentively. They didn't blink an eyelash at the verdict: letters of reprimand were to be written for the two teachers and their department head.

The Hard Rock School Committee had concluded that the teachers made an error in judgment but didn't deserve to be suspended. Little did Bob and Ray realize the community turmoil that would be created when they invited a guest lecturer, a young prostitute, to speak to their high school class.

Questions to be Answered in
"The Guest Lecturer"

1. _____
2. _____
3. _____
4. _____
5. _____

Now turn to Chapter 6, page 179 and read the remainder of the selection. Which of your questions were answered? Which weren't? Of those questions not directly answered by the reading selection, which can be answered by inference and critical evaluation on your part?

Strategies such as an Expectation Outline or Your Own Questions teach children how to approach reading material with an inquisitive mind. These instructional strategies, and the others presented in this chapter, form a bridge between teacher-initiated guidance and independent learning behavior on the part of students.

Looking Back, Looking Forward

Teachers can reduce the uncertainty that students bring to reading material by helping them raise questions and anticipate meaning. The reader's background knowledge or schema is the given in any kind of a classroom situation that requires reading. The teacher must make full use of this given by showing students how to connect what they know already to the new—the ideas presented in the content material. When students exhibit "schema inadequacies," the instructional goal is to build and activate schema for reading in advance of assignment-making.

In addition to background-building activities which rely on lecture, demonstration, or audio-visual aids, teachers should remember that reading itself makes a major contribution to the knowledge that is at the command of students. Participating in conceptually related reading, i.e., multiple readings on the same topic, can be a powerful way of helping readers generate background information and knowledge. Furthermore, teacher-initiated instructional activities involving advance organizers, analogies, previews, structured overviews, and brainstorming can also help to generate and activate schema for reading.

A teacher arouses curiosity for reading material by creating conceptual conflict. Students will read to resolve conflicts arising from problem situations, taking a perspective, examining values and attitudes, and guiding imagery of important ideas to be encountered during reading.

The questions students raise as a result of predicting will feed them into the reading material and keep them on course. Anticipation guides, expectation outlines, self-questioning, and previewing techniques are strategies for stimulating predictions and anticipation about the content under study.

Asking questions and sustaining discussion are two of the bread-and-butter issues involved in helping students to learn from texts. Although we highlighted the raising of questions before reading in this chapter we will extend and elaborate on the role of questions and questioning in the next chapter.

Suggested Readings

Anderson, R. C., & Pearson, P. D. (1984). A schema-theoretic view of basic processes in reading comprehension. In P. D. Pearson (ed.), *Handbook of Reading Research*. New York: Longmans, Green.

Ausubel, D. P., Novak, J. D., & Hanesian, H. (1978). *Educational Psychology: A Cognitive View* (2nd ed.). New York: Holt, Rinehart and Winston.

Bransford, J. (1983). Schema activation–schema acquisition. In R. C. Anderson, J. Osborn, and R. Tierney (eds.), *Learning to Read in American Schools*. Hillsdale, N.J.: Erlbaum.

Estes, T., & Vaughan, J., Jr. (1985). Prereading anticipation (Chapter 9). *Reading and Learning in the Content Classroom* (2nd ed.). Boston: Allyn and Bacon.

Herber, H. (1978). Prediction as motivation and an aid to comprehension (Chapter 7). *Teaching Reading in Content Areas* (2nd ed.). Englewood Cliffs, N. J.: Prentice Hall.

Langer, J. (1982). Facilitating text processing: The elaboration of prior knowledge. In J. Langer and M. T. Smith-Burke (eds.), *Reader Meets Author/Bridging the Gap*. Newark, Del.: International Reading Association.

Macklin, M. (1978). Content area reading is a process of finding personal meaning. *Journal of Reading,* **22**, 212–213.

Moore, D. W. Readence, J., & Rickelman, R. (1982). *Prereading Activities for Content Area Reading*. Newark, Del.: International Reading Association.

Thelen, J. (1984). Prereading strategies for teaching science (Chapter 3). *Improving Reading in Science* (2nd ed.). Newark, Del.: International Reading Association.

Vacca, R. T. (1977). Readiness to read content area assignments. *Journal of Reading,* **20**, 387–392.

CHAPTER FIVE

Questions and Questioning

Always the beautiful answer who asks a more beautiful question.
—E. E. CUMMINGS

Organizing Principle

Questions are the tools of our trade. They dominate instructional time in most classes. Reflect for a moment on the number of times you have asked students to respond to questions. If you have yet to teach, recall the number of times that you have been asked questions by instructors. Questions are important. When used effectively in lessons that require reading, questions promote thinking and light the way to productive learning and retention of content material. But questions can also be counterproductive when used habitually in the classroom with little forethought or preparation. The success or failure of classroom discussion often rests with the quality of the questions asked during question-answer exchanges.

It has been said that a good question is half the answer. What, then, is a bad question? Probably a question in and of itself is neither good nor bad. Questions are tools in the hands of the teacher, but they are only as good as the context in which they are asked. The organizing principle of this chapter says this to teachers: *How, when, and where a question is used to guide reading determines its effectiveness.*

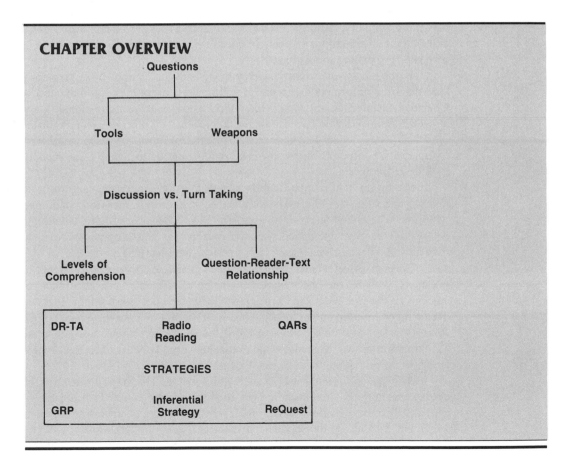

CHAPTER OVERVIEW

Study the Chapter Overview before reading. What do you already know about the concepts that are on the overview? What do you need to know more about? When you finish reading you should be able to respond fully to the questions below:

1. When do questions become tools? When do they become weapons?

2. How is discussion different from turn taking?

3. What are levels of comprehension?

4. What is the three-way relationship among a question, the text to which it refers, and the reader's background knowledge? How does knowledge of this relationship help the teacher pose questions?

5. Which strategies for questioning and discussion seem most appropriate for your content area? Why?

Asking questions in classrooms is part of the American way. Imagine a classroom without questions. It is no exaggeration to suggest that in instructional situations teachers talk to students in questions most of the time. And students respond by speaking in answers.

At their best, questions trigger inquiry and application. They transform students from information seekers to information users. As we intimated in Chapter 4, an information seeker is the student who asks, "What do I already know about the topic? What do I need to find out more about?" Information users, on the other hand, are students who know how to integrate information and put it to work for them—to solve problems, to make judgments, or to invent new ways of looking at the world.

The bright side of questions is that they work. The issue, according to Pearson and Johnson (1978), "is not whether or not to use questions, but how, when and where they ought to be used" (p. 154). The issue of how, when, and where is all the more intensified when we consider that questions can be tools, but they can also become weapons which interfere with learning.

Consider three related scenarios which illustrate the negative effects of questions. We label the first scenario "On the Spot." Questions can sometimes put students on the spot and make them defensive. On the Spot questioning freezes up a learning opportunity rather than making the most of it. Within the context of the classroom, students are socially constrained to answer questions. During On the Spot question-answer exchanges, the classroom very likely assumes a quiz show atmosphere, pitting student against student.

Most students, young and old alike, know that On The Spot questions can be used menacingly by the teacher, even though they are posed in the name of learning objectives. Samples et al. (1977) went so far as to characterize questions which put students on the spot as conversational acts of aggression.

Do you recall ever being put on the spot by a question? In that interminable second or two between question and response, between pounding heart and short gasps for air, do you remember asking yourself, "What's *the* right answer—the one this instructor expects?"

When questions are used to foster a "right answer only" atmosphere in class they will not focus thinking about what has been read, nor will they prompt the processes by which students construct knowledge from text material. Instead they make the response—the correct answer—the all-important concern. Some students even become the classroom "answer machines." (An "answer machine" is easily recognizable. Usually one arm is several inches longer than the other— from constantly shooting the arm skyward in a quick, jerky motion to gain attention during a question-answer interchange.) The danger of putting students On The Spot is that we run the risk of losing most of the class during discussion by actively seeking responses from students who will give us what we want to hear—the right answer.

Closely related to the On The Spot scenario is the sometimes familiar routine labeled by Pearson and Johnson (1978) "Guess What's in My Head." Guess What's in My Head unfolds in classrooms from primary through graduate instruction. The game is often initiated unwittingly by the teacher. The ground rules, nevertheless, are easy to figure out: ". . . the teacher has a specific response in mind. And each time a student fails to give the desired response, the teacher says, 'uh huh,' or 'okay?' and calls on another volunteer until finally someone has accurately guessed what is in the teacher's head" (Pearson and Johnson, p. 186).

Unfortunately, some students soon learn to play Guess What's in My Head with consummate skill. They will read everything but the material to answer "correctly." They scrutinize the teacher's gestures for the slightest of indications that they are on the right track. As they respond to body language and facial gestures, these students skillfully verbalize under, over, and around a question until they strike the responsive chord they seek—a nod of approval.

Questioning becomes another form of weaponry in classrooms when it turns into an "Interrogation Session." In this scenario questions are used to check on whether or not students have read the material. When questioning becomes interrogating, the teacher's goal usually is veridicality ("the truth, the whole truth, and nothing but the truth"). The teacher fires one question after another, typically pausing no more than a second or two between queries. The questions are mostly low level in that they require verbatim text responses from students. Interrogation questions will test comprehension rather than guide its development.

The three scenarios are each tied to what some authorities on teacher behavior and effectiveness consider the prevalent instructional model in American schooling, *turn taking* (Duffy, 1983). Turn taking occurs whenever the teacher asks a question or assigns a turn, the student responds, and the teacher gives feedback by correcting or reinforcing the response. Teachers often depend on turn taking to "discuss" the content of textbook assignments. Yet what results is hardly a discussion at all. During turn taking routines, questions usually forestall or frustrate discussion. Question-answer exchanges are brief, usually three to five seconds in duration, sometimes less, sometimes more. Rather than characterize these question-answer exchanges as discussion, it is more appropriate to view them as recitation.

Turn Taking vs. Discussion

Turn taking almost always involves some form of recitation. The striking feature of recitation is that the teacher's speech consists of questions. Dillon (1983) noted that during a recitation, "we might judge that *too many* questions are being asked at *too fast* a pace. But the exchanges take the form they do because the teacher speaks in question-form, not because of the number of questions he asks in a brief time" (p. 11). To illustrate this point, Dillon (1983, pp. 10–11) provided a transcript from a typical recitation conducted by a high school teacher of United States history:

> T: OK, so we've kind of covered leadership and some of the things that Washington brought with it. Why else did they win? Leadership is important, that's one.
>
> S: France gave 'em help.
>
> T: OK, so France giving aid is an example of what? France is an example of it, obviously.
>
> S: Aid from allies.
>
> T: Aid from allies, very good. Were there any other allies who gave aid to us?
>
> S: Spain.
>
> T: Spain. Now, when you say aid, can you define that?
>
> S: Help.
>
> T: Define "help." Spell it out for me.
>
> S: Assistance.
>
> T: Spell it out for me.
>
> S: They taught the men how to fight the right way.
>
> T: Who taught?
>
> S: The allies.
>
> T: Where? When?
>
> S: In the battlefield.
>
> T: In the battlefield?

In the exchanges above the students take turns answering questions about the success of Washington's revolutionary army. The eight question-answer exchanges lasted a little more than thirty seconds, or four to five seconds per exchange. Each student addressed a response to the teacher, not other students. The nature of turn taking is such that it is *verboten* for another student to "jump in" to the exchange, unless first recognized by the teacher to take a turn.

In turn-taking situations, as you can infer, certain "rules" accompany class-room discourse. One was alluded to earlier: the teacher speaks in questions; the students speak in answers. And the form of their answers indicate another rule of turn taking: give just enough information specified by the question to satisfy the teacher. No wonder question-answer exchanges are brief. Interestingly, as part of the exchange, students invariably address their responses to the teacher. The implicit rule is never address other students because only the teacher gives feedback. Each respondent, thus, awaits his or her turn to answer further questions. Any attempts at conversation or discussion are stifled.

While recitation serves several legitimate educational purposes (quizzing, drilling, reviewing), it may produce negative effects on students' cognitive, affective, and expressive processes. Given the rules that operate during turn taking, teachers may very well increase student passivity and dependence. Furthermore, turn taking leads to limited construction of meaning from text. Because the pace of questions is often rapid, readers hardly have the time to think, clarify, or explore their understanding of the text material undergoing questioning.

Asking Questions Within the Context of Discussion

To guide comprehension of text material, questions need to be posed within the framework of discussions. If you were to observe in a content area classroom over several days, you would be apt to notice text selections assigned along with several questions for "discussion" the next day. However, the next day's discussion may never surface. In its place you might witness quizzing, interrogating, or other forms of recitation. Whereas turn taking centers on one-to-one question-answer exchanges between the teacher and a student, discussion involves a much different kind of classroom discourse.

Discussion can best be described as conversational interactions between teacher and students as well as students and other students. The teacher doesn't speak in questions over long stretches of time, although questions are used judiciously throughout most discussions. As a result, discussion signifies an exchange of ideas and a high degree of participation among all parties involved.

Even the most effective teachers on occasion turn a question into a weapon, or discussion into recitation.

The scenarios described above illustrated the negative effects of questions which work against discussion. They obviously must be avoided whenever the teacher's goal is to help students think and discuss.

Asking questions, even those designed to get students to "open up" and share their understanding of text, doesn't always result in a good discussion or, for that matter, a bad discussion; just nondiscussion. It is important to recognize that many students have become used to tuning out. Because of the preponderance of noise in their daily lives, school included, they have grown accustomed to turning a deaf ear. The equivalent of noise in a classroom instructional situation occurs whenever students do not make sense out of what they are doing or what is happening (Smith, 1979). Students stand a better chance of participating attentively in discussion when they have a clear sense of purpose, understand the discussion task, and are given explicit directions and clear explanations. Moreover, they are keenly aware of when teachers are more preoccupied with the questions they ask than with the responses students give.

In Chapter 10, we elaborate on ways to promote positive small group behavior for discussion. Discussion is one of the major process strategies in the content area classroom; many of the reading strategies in this text revolve around discussion of some sort. However, we conclude this section with several suggestions for creating an environment in which discussion takes place, whether in small group or whole class situations.

1. Arrange the room in such a way that students can see each other and huddle in conversational groupings when they need to share ideas.

A good way to judge how functional a classroom is for discussion purposes is to select a discussion strategy which does not require much question asking. For example, in the previous chapter we saw how brainstorming involves a good mixture of whole class and small group discussion. Students need to alternate their attention from the chalkboard (where the teacher or another student is writing down all the ideas offered within a specified time) to their small groups (where they might categorize the ideas) back to the "front" of the room (for comparison of group categories and summarization). If students are able to participate in the various "stages" of brainstorming with a minimum of chair moving or other time-consuming movements, to see the board and to converse with other students without undue disruption, then the room arrangements are adequate or conducive to discussion.

2. Encourage a climate in which everyone is expected to be a good listener, including the teacher.

Let each student-speaker know that you are listening. As the teacher begins to talk less, students will talk more. Intervene either to determine why some students might not be listening to each other or who are unusually good role models for others. Accept all responses of students in a positive way.

Try starting out with very small groups of no more than three students. Again, rather than use questions, have students react to a teacher-read statement ("Political primaries are a waste of time and money"). In the beginning, students may feel constrained to produce answers to questions to satisfy the teacher. A statement, however, serves as a possible answer and invites reaction and justification. Once a statement is given, set a timer or call time by your watch at two-minute intervals. During each interval one student in the group may agree or disagree *without interruption*. After each group member has an opportunity to respond, the group summarizes all dialogue and one person presents this to the class (Gold and Yellin, 1982, pp. 550–552).

3. Establish the meaning of the topic and the goal of discussion: "Why are we talking about railroad routes and how do they relate to our unit on the Civil War?"

Explain directions explicitly and don't assume that students will know what to do.

Many of the content area reading strategies in this book involve some group discussion. Frequently, strategies progress from independent, written responses to sharing, comparing those responses in small groups, then to pooling small-group reactions in a whole-class discussion. Without the guidance of a teacher who is aware of this process, group discussion tends to disintegrate. With the guidance of a teacher who explains both the content (topic) and the process (directions), group discussions can occur smoothly. (See Chapter 11 for a more detailed discussion.)

4. Keep the focus of the discussion on the central topic or core question or problem to be solved.

One way to begin discussion is by asking a question about a perplexing situation or establishing a problem to be solved. Many of the strategies and suggestions in Chapter 4 are useful for this purpose. From time to time, it may be necessary to refocus attention on the topic by piggybacking on comments made by particular students. "Terry brought out an excellent point about the underground railroad in northern Ohio. Does anyone else want to talk about this?" During small group discussions, a tactic that keeps groups on task is to remind them of time remaining in the discussion.

Keeping the focus is one time when teachers may legitimately question to "clarify the question." They may also want to make sure that they understood a particular student's comment, "Excuse me, would you repeat that?" Often, keeping the discussion focused will prevent the class from straying away from the task.

5. Avoid ineffective behavior that is bound to squelch discussion.

Try, for example, not to repeat questions, whether they are your own or the students'. Give students enough "think time" to reflect on possible answers before calling on someone or rephrasing your question. Moreover, try to avoid repeating answers or answering your own question. (One way to prevent yourself from doing the latter is to resist having a preset or "correct" answer in your own mind when you ask a question beyond a literal level of comprehension.) Finally, do not interrupt students' responses or permit others to interrupt students' responses. Do, however, take a minute or two to summarize and bring closure to a group discussion just as you would with any instructional strategy.

A good discussion helps students to clarify relationships, integrate, and use information from the text. Discussion allows students to explore and construct meaning. The questions and comments raised during discussion are particularly important. However, the type of questions formulated must take into consideration the three-way relationship that exists among the question, the text to which it refers, and the reader's background knowledge. We examine this relationship further in the next section.

Levels of Comprehension and Types of Questions

Because reading is a thoughtful process, it embraces the idea of levels of comprehension. Readers respond to meaning at various levels of abstraction and conceptual difficulty. Herber (1978) argued that the levels construct is a simple treatment of comprehension. Content area reading is not complicated by teaching snippets of comprehension skills separately. This is precisely the reason why so many content area teachers with minimal training (or interest) in the detailed aspects of reading instruction find the three-level process useful. Although skills are assumed to operate in each level, the emphasis is clearly on how comprehension skills interact within and among the three levels. Figure 5.1 shows the major aspects of levels of comprehension.

Figure 5.1

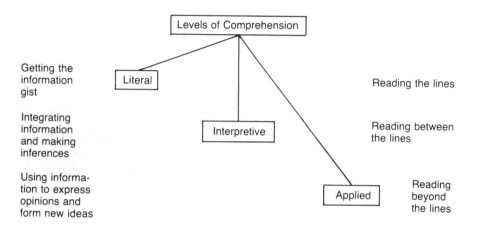

Getting the information gist

Integrating information and making inferences

Using information to express opinions and form new ideas

Literal Level: Getting the Gist

The literal level is another way of saying students can "read the lines" of your content material. They can stay with print sufficiently to get the gist of the author's message. In simple terms, a literal recognition of that message determines what the author says.

Try to recall your freshman year in college when you probably learned the universal strategy of coping with the literal level of your first five-pound text. Probably after careful observation of a "model," that stoic sophomore or junior struggling with a textbook in a library carrel, you rushed to the nearest bookstore and purchased your first felt-tip marker. Its ink was pink or yellow, wasn't it? Then you began to get the gist as you underlined the essential information in your text readings.

If you were like us, your yellow felt-tip pen soon became as comfortable as Linus's blanket. The only trouble, of course, is that soon into the business of underlining, you moved from selective markings to full-scale assaults on the printed page. You probably began to change entire pages of white background to yellow background as your marker ran amuck with indiscriminate frenzy. You were learning. Or so you thought.

The trouble is that searching for important literal information isn't an easy chore, particularly if readers haven't matured enough to know how to make the search, or even worse, haven't determined why they are making it in the first place. Most students can and will profit handsomely from being shown how to recognize the essential information in text.

Interpretive Level: Integrating Information

Knowing what the author says is necessary but not sufficient in constructing meaning from print. Good readers search for conceptual complexity in material. They "read between the lines." They focus not only on what authors say, but also on what authors mean by what they say. Herber (1978) clarified the difference between literal and interpretive levels this way: "At the literal level readers identify the important information. At the interpretive level readers perceive the relationships that exist in that information, conceptualizing the ideas formulated by those relationships. . . ." *(p. 45)*

The interpretive level is laced with inferences about the author's intended meaning. How the reader conceptualizes implied ideas by integrating information is part and parcel of the interpretive process.

As we stated in Chapter 2, the ability to perceive and use text organization is essential to learning from the text. Recognizing the structure of relationships that the author weaves together helps the reader to make inferences that are implicit in the material.

For example, study the passage below, which is organized according to cause-effect relationships. Figure 5.2 shows how a cause combines with several effects to form a logical inference that is implicit in the text passage.

> As part of an experiment, young monkeys were taken away from their mothers when they were born and each was raised in complete isolation. When these monkeys were brought together for the first time, they didn't want to play with each other as monkeys usually do. They showed no love for each other. And in fact they never learned to live together. It seemed that living apart from their mothers and from each other from the very beginning had some unusual side effects on these growing monkeys.

Applied Level: Constructing Knowledge

From time to time throughout the book you have probably been trying to read us—not our words but us. And, in the process of reconstructing our messages, you probably raised questions similar to these: So what? What does this information

Figure 5.2

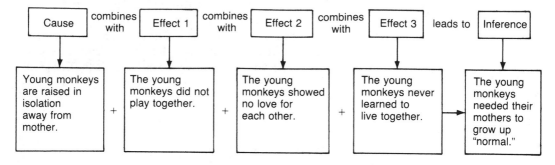

mean to me? Does it make sense? Can I use these ideas for content instruction? Your attempt to seek significance or relevance in what we say and mean is one signal that you are reading at the applied level. You are reading beyond our lines. You are essentially constructing knowledge.

Reading at the applied level is undoubtedly akin to the act of discovery. It underscores the constructive nature of reading comprehension. Bruner (1961) explained that discovery "is in its essence a matter of rearranging or transforming evidence in such a way that one is enabled to go beyond the evidence so reassembled to additional new insights" (p. 21). When students function at the applied level they know how to synthesize information—lay that synthesis alongside what they know already—to express opinions about and to draw additional insights and fresh ideas from content material.

Reader-Text-Question Relationship

Questioning taxonomies identify and classify the types of questions which can be asked to stimulate a thoughtful response, Bloom's (1956) *Taxonomy of Educational Objectives: Cognitive Domain* represents the seminal work done in this area. Bloom identified six levels of cognitive performance.

Cognitive Processes	*Student Behaviors*
1. Knowledge	The student recalls or recognizes information.
2. Comprehension	The student changes information into a different symbolic form of language and discovers relationships among facts, generalizations, definitions, values, and skills.
3. Application	The student solves a lifelike problem that requires the identification of the issue and the selection and use of appropriate generalizations and skills.

4. Analysis   The student solves a problem through conscious knowledge of the parts and forms of thinking.

5. Synthesis   The student solves a problem that requires original, creative thinking.

6. Evaluation   The student makes a judgment of good or bad, or right and wrong, according to designated standards.

Taxonomies such as Bloom's underscore the complexity of intellectual activity. They have also led to a greater study and emphasis on the role of questions and question-asking strategies. While these earlier classifications categorized questions apart from the reader and the text, the emphasis today is on posing questions within the context of both the reader's knowledge base and the text.

Herber (1978) reported that positive relationships existed between the Levels of Comprehension construct and Bloom's taxonomy. Moreover, Pearson and Johnson (1978) proposed that the type of question asked to guide comprehension should be based on the *information readers need to answer the question*. As a result, teachers must help students become aware of likely sources of information as they respond to questions. For example, some questions have answers which can be found directly in the text. These questions are *textually explicit* and lead to answers which are "right there." Other questions have answers that require students to search the text and think about the information. These questions are *textually implicit* and lead to "think and search" responses. A third type of question requires students to rely mainly on background knowledge and experience. In other words, responses to these questions are more inside the reader's head than from the text itself. These questions are schema-based and lead to "on your own" answers (Raphael, 1982). "Right There," "Think and Search," and "On Your Own" are mnemonics for responses made at the three levels of comprehension just discussed.

A comparison is made in Table 5.1 between Herber's Levels of Comprehension construct, Bloom's taxonomy, and Pearson and Johnson's question-answer classification.

If students "learn best the things they are asked about" (Wixson, 1983), then text questions deliberately designed to elicit responses at three levels of comprehension are powerful teaching aids. They can presumably stimulate a full range of cognitive activity among students. Many kinds of responses can be agitated at the literal level by textually explicit questions, at the interpretive level by textually implicit questions, and at the applied level by schema-based questions.

Text questions posed at the three levels of comprehension reinforce reading performance. As Herber and Nelson (1975) indicated, "Good questions, accompanied by reinforcing feedback on the nature and quality of the response, can raise the students' level of sophistication in their use of reading skills implicit in those questions" (p. 514). In the next section, we examine how to incorporate questions

Table 5.1 A Comparison of Herber, Pearson and Johnson, and Bloom

Herber's Levels of Comprehension	Pearson and Johnson's Question-Answer Relationships	Bloom's Cognitive Operations
Literal level	Textually explicit questions	Knowledge
Interpretive level	Textually implicit questions	Comprehension
Applied level	Schema-based questions	Application
		Analysis
		Synthesis
		Evaluation

into strategies which facilitate comprehension and class discussion of text material.

Questioning Strategies

Questions are sometimes calculated, sometimes spontaneous. They dominate the teaching strategies observed in classrooms from kindergarten through college. Taba's (1967) work illustrated quite clearly that "the most marked single influence" on thinking seemed to rest with the impact of questioning in the classroom. In this section we describe several question and discussion strategies which influence thinking during reading. These strategies are equally at home with narrative or expository prose, depending on how each is adapted to specific types of texts in different content areas and at different grade levels. They are (1) the Question-Answer Relationship (QAR) Strategy, (2) the Directed Reading-Thinking Activity (DR-TA), (3) the Inferential Strategy, (4) the Guided Reading Procedure (GRP), (5) Reciprocal Questioning (ReQuest), and (6) Radio Reading.

As you study these strategies in detail, note the differences as well as the commonalities among them. Each strategy can be adapted to meet the demands inherent in any subject matter material, narrative or expository. Think about the kinds of adaptations you will have to make to meet particular needs.

Question-Answer Relationship (QAR)

The QAR strategy enhances students' abilities to answer comprehension questions. The strategy is based on the Pearson and Johnson classification noted earlier. It teaches students (1) the three-way relationship that exists among question-text-reader's knowledge, and (2) three specific learning strategies to find information they need to answer questions.

Procedures related to learning QARs can be taught directly to students by reading teachers and reinforced by content area specialists. Keep in mind, however, that students may come to your class totally unaware of what information sources are available for seeking an answer; or they may not know when to use different sources. If this is the case, then it is worth the effort over several days to directly instruct students in the relationship between questions and answers.

Direct instruction involves training. It may take up to three days to show students how to identify the information sources necessary to answer questions. Raphael (1982, 1984) suggested the following steps, which we have adapted for content area situations.

1. Introduce the concept of QARs by showing students a chart or an overhead transparency containing a description of the three basic question-answer relationships. (We recommend a chart that can be positioned in a prominent place in the classroom. Students may then refer to the chart whenever needed during training sessions or actual content area lessons.) Figure 5.3 is adapted from a chart recommended by Raphael.

2. Begin the first training session by assigning students three short passages from the textbook (no more than two to five sentences in length). Follow each reading with one question from each of the QAR categories on the chart. Then discuss the differences between a "Right There" question and answer, a "Think and Search" question and answer, and an "On Your Own" question and answer. Explanations should be clear and complete. Reinforce the discussion by assigning several more short text passages and asking a question for each. Students will soon begin to "catch on" to the differences among the three QAR categories.

3. Continue the second day of training by practicing with short passages — with one question for each QAR category per passage. First, give students a passage to read with questions *and* answers *and* identified QARs. Why do the questions and answers represent one QAR and not another? Second, give students a passage with questions and answers; this time they have to identify the QAR for each. Finally, give students passages, decide together which strategy to use, and have them write their responses.

4. Review briefly on the third day. Then assign a longer passage (75–200 words) with up to five questions (at least one each from the three QAR categories). First have students work in groups to decide the QAR category for each question and the answers for each. Next, assign a second passage, comparable in length, with five questions for students to work on individually. Discuss responses either in small groups or with the whole class.

5. Apply the QAR strategy to actual content area assignments. For each question asked, students decide on the appropriate QAR strategy and write out their answers, i.e.,

Figure 5.3 Introducing QARs

Where Are Answers To
Questions Found?

In the Text:

Right There!

The answer is in the text. The words
used in the question and words used
for the answer can usually be found
in the same sentence.

Or

Think and Search!

The answer is in the text but the
words used in the question and those
used for an answer would not be in
the same sentence. You need to think
a lot about the sentences before you
can answer the question.

Or

On Your Own

The text got you thinking, but the answer
is inside your head. So think about it
and use what you know already to answer
the questions.

What is nationalism?
__ Right There
__ Think and Search
__ On My Own
Answer:_____
(Discussion follows.)

    Once students are sensitive to different information sources for different
types of questions and know how to use these sources to respond to questions,
variations can be made in the QAR strategy. For example, you might consider
having students generate their own questions to text assignments—perhaps two
for each QAR category. They then write down the answers to the questions as they
understand them, except that they leave one question unanswered from the Think

and Search category and one from the On Your Own category. These are questions on which the student would like to hear the views of others. During the discussion students can volunteer to ask their unanswered questions. The class is invited first to identify the question by QAR category and then contribute answers, comments, or related questions about the material (Dillon, 1983).

A second variation involves discussions of text. During question-answer exchanges, consider prefacing a question by saying, "This question is *right there* in the text." Or, "You'll have to *think and search* the text to answer." Or, "You're *on your own* with this one." Make sure that for Think and Search and On Your Own questions you pause several seconds or more for "think time." Think time or "wait time" is critical to responding to questions at interpretive or applied levels of comprehension. Gambrell (1980) found that by increasing think time to five seconds or longer, the length of student responses increases as well as the quality of their speculative thinking.

Directed Reading-Thinking Activity (DR-TA)

The DR-TA fosters critical awareness by moving students through a process that involves prediction, verification, judgment, and ultimately extension of thought. The teacher directs reading and agitates thinking; therefore, the teacher should pose open-ended and/or directive questions which prompt interpretation and application.

The atmosphere created during a DR-TA questioning episode is paramount to the strategy's success. You must be supportive and encouraging so as not to inhibit students' free participation. Never refute any predictions that students offer—to do so is comparable to pulling the rug out from under them.

"Think time" is again important. When you pose an open-ended question, is it reasonable to pause no more than two, three, five, or even ten seconds for a response? If silence pervades the room for the several seconds or more that have lapsed from the time a question has been asked, simply wait a few more seconds. Too often, the tendency is to slice the original question into smaller parts. Sometimes a teacher starts slicing too quickly out of a sense of frustration or anxiousness (after all, three seconds of lapsed time can seem an eternity in the midst of a questioning foray) rather than the students' inability to respond. Silence may very well be an indication that hypothesis formation or other cognitive activities are taking place in the readers' heads. So, wait—and see what happens.

To prepare for a DR-TA with narrative or expository text, analyze the narrative material for its story structure or the expository material for its super-ordinate and subordinate concepts. For expository texts, what do you see as relevant concepts, ideas, relationships, information in the material? The content analysis will help you decide on logical stopping points as you direct students through the reading.

For short stories and other narrative material, it is best to develop a *story map* as suggested in Chapter 2. You may recall that a story map defines what most stories have in common. It allows the teacher to determine the key elements of a story: *the setting* (time and place, major characters) and *the events within the plot* [the initiating event or problem-generating situation, the protagonist's reaction to the event and his/her goal to resolve the problem, the set of attempts to achieve the goal, outcome(s) related to the protagonist's attempts to achieve the goal and resolve the problem, the character's reaction].

Once these elements have been identified, the teacher has a framework for deciding on logical stopping points within the story. In Figure 5.4, we indicate a general plan which may be followed or adapted for specific story lines.

Figure 5.4 Potential Stopping Points in a DR-TA for a Story Line with One Episode

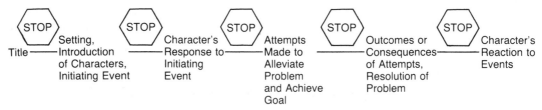

As you examine Figure 5.4, notice that the suggested stopping points come at key junctures in a causal chain of events in the story line. Each juncture suggests a logical stopping point in that it assumes that the reader has enough information from a preceding event(s) to predict a future happening or event.

Steps in the DR-TA

Set the climate and direct the DR-TA by the frequent use of three questions:

What do you think? or What do you think will happen next?

Why do you think so? or What part of the story gave you a clue?

Can you prove it? or What else might happen?

The following may be considered general steps in the DR-TA:

1. Begin with the title of a narrative or with a quick survey of the title, subheads, illustrations, and so forth in expository material. Ask: "What do you think this story (or section) will be about?" Encourage predictions. Ask: "Why do you think so?"

2. Ask students to read silently to a predetermined logical stopping point in the text. A 5″ by 8″ index card or blank sheet of paper placed on the page will guide students and slow down those who want to read on before answering the questions.

3. Repeat questions as suggested in step 1. Some predictions will be refined; new ones will be formulated. Ask: "How do you know?" to encourage verification. Redirect questions.

4. Continue silent reading to another suitable point. Ask similar questions.

5. Continue this way to the end of the material. A note of caution: too frequent interruption of reading may detract from the focus of attention, which needs to be on larger concepts rather than details.

How do you apply the DR-TA to expository test situations? This is precisely the question that Homer (1979) asked. Her plan specifies the following procedures:

1. *Identifying purposes for reading.* Individual or group purposes set by students based on some limited clues in material and their own background of experience.
   a. "From only reading the chapter title (subtitles, charts, maps, etc.) what do you think the author(s) will present in this chapter (passage, next pages, etc.)?"
   b. Record speculations on chalkboard and augment by the query, "Why do you think so?"
   c. Encourge discussion. If speculations and statements of proof yield an inaccurate or weak knowledge base, review through discussion. Frequently terminology will be introduced by students in their predictions (especially from those more knowledgeable). The teacher may choose to capitalize on such situations by further clarifying significant concepts, etc. If done, this should be accomplished in a way that enhances pupil discussion and inquiry through discovery techniques.
   d. A poll can be taken to further intensify the predictive process. A debatelike setting may naturally ensue at this point pending the outcome of the poll count. Additional proof may be needed from available reference books.

2. *Adjustment of rate to purposes and material.* Teacher adjusts amount of reading depending upon the purposes, nature, and difficulty of the reading material; skimming, scanning, and studying are involved.
   a. "Read to find out if your predictions were correct." The reading task may be several pages within a chapter, an entire chapter, a few passages, etc. If the teacher designates numerous stopping points within the reading task, then the same steps for "identifying purposes" should be executed at each stopping point.

3. *Observing the reading.* The teacher observes the reading by assisting students who request help and noting abilities to adjust rate to purpose and material, to comprehend material, and to use word recognition strategies.

4. *Developing comprehension.* Students check purposes by accepting, rejecting, or redefining purposes. This can be accomplished by providing discussion time after having read a predetermined number of pages or by encouraging students to rework predictions as they read. Revised predictions and hypotheses can be written on paper by the students during the reading.

5. *Followup activities: Discussion, further reading, additional study, writing.* Students and teacher are identifying these needs throughout the strategy.

a. After the reading students should be asked (1) if their predictions were inaccurate, (2) if they needed to revise or reject predictions during the reading, (3) how they know revision was necessary, (4) what were their newly created predictions.

b. Discussion in small groups is most constructive for this step. A recorder can be appointed by the group. It is this person's responsibility to share the groups' reading-thinking processes with the total class. These should be compared with original predictions.

c. The teacher should ask open-ended questions that encourage generalization and application relevant to students' predictions and significant concepts presented. In any followup discussion or questioning the demand for proof should always prevail. "How do you know that?" "Why did you think so?" "What made you think that way?" Encourage students to share passages, sentences, etc., for further proof.

A DR-TA Transcript of an Actual Lesson

Greenslade (1980) illustrated a DR-TA in action with a transcript of an actual social studies lesson. Note the interactions among teacher and students as they walk through a text assignment on a unit entitled "The Great Depression of the 1930s."*

Looking at the title and thinking about what you might already know about the subject, what do you think this unit will be about?

Something that happened back in the twenties.

What kinds of things about the twenties?

Troubles in the twenties.
Prosperity means troubles.

(Students read silently.)

Now what do you think?

People were paid during the war and they could buy more goods.
They could buy now and pay later.

Have you changed your mind about the meaning of the word prosperity?

Yes, it means good things.

*Source: Bonnie Greenslade, "Awareness and Anticipation: Utilizing the DR-TA in the Content Classroom," *Journal of Language Experience* 2 (1980): 21–28. Used with permission of the author.

Why have you changed your mind?

Well, I read the book and it means a different thing. The people are having good things happen.

What kinds of good things?

Food was cheaper.
Gas was cheaper.

Why do you think things were cheaper?

Well, they really weren't, because the people didn't have as much money to buy them.
You could buy now and pay later.

Why do you think that buy now, pay later is important here?

Well, you wouldn't have to pay for the food or goods all at once. You could pay a little each month.

Do you think that is a good thing or a bad thing?

Good. *(All)*

Why?

If you need something now but don't have the money you could get it anyway and pay for it by the month.

Do you think the prosperity will continue?

Probably.
No.

Why?

I don't know.
Well, the way things are today, it couldn't have continued.
Prices went way up.

Are we prosperous today?

No.
Things started going down when prices started going up.

What do you expect to read next?

That prices start to go up.
And keep going up.
Rising prices will ruin the prosperity.

(Students read silently.)

Now what do you think?

We were right, because it says that wages went from $13.00 in 1925 to about $25.00.
The prices are rising.

What makes you think prices are rising?

It's the wages that are rising, not prices.
Well, when pay goes up, prices go up too.

What do you expect to find next?

There will be more things to buy.

Why?

Because if factories hire more workers then they're able to make more of the products they're manufacturing.

Where will this lead?

To more inflation.

Why?

Prices will rise higher and higher.
That's what happens today.
It's been going up since then.

(Students read silently.)

Based on new information, what do you think now?

I was wrong. Everybody needs jobs now.
Everybody is bankrupt.
The banks tried to get their money from the investors and they didn't have it. They couldn't get their money back.

What happened?

They started closing.
They were losing all their money.
By 1932 the banks were closing.
People had borrowed money and couldn't pay it back so they had to close up.

What is going to happen next?

Inflation is going to go higher.

Why?

Because the production went down and they need more money.
They'll have to raise the prices.
Stores need more money to stay open.

Where will the money come from?

Not from the banks. They're all closed.
They can fire workers and save money.
But the factories are already bankrupt.
You can't save money you don't have.

What else will happen?

The people will be in trouble.

How?

They won't have the products the factories make.
They won't have money to buy the goods because they won't have jobs.
They won't have money to buy food.

(Students read silently.)

Have any of your predictions been confirmed?

It says children had torn clothes at school.
Children were asking for food from the schools.
Stores offered to give away food and so many people wanted some that there
was a riot.
The government should have given everybody enough to live on.

Why do you think that?

Nobody should have to starve.
It was the government's fault that the problem started.

Why do you say that?

Because they were involved in a war and the depression started because of changes after the war.

Did you find that information in the text?

No, but I thought it implied it. It said people had lots of money to spend after the war and began to overbuy.
It says that American factories produced huge amounts of supplies for our troops and our allies during World War I. Everybody had jobs.
Everybody saved their money during the war because there really wasn't much to buy. It was all going to the war. After the war, they were so happy they began to buy just for the heck of it.
They started to buy on credit and then they got in trouble.
When the bills came they couldn't pay.
Then the banks went bankrupt. They lost all their money because nobody could pay them.

The DR-TA begins with very open-ended or divergent responses and moves toward more accurate predictions and text-based inferences as students acquire additional information revealed in the reading. Compare the DR-TA to the Inferential Strategy, which makes substantial use of students' ability to activate background knowledge and make predictions.

Inferential Strategy

Hansen (1981) proposed the Inferential Strategy for elementary children. Yet with some adaptation it can be used in secondary content area instructional situations. Note that the use of questions in a DR-TA puts the spotlight on students' background experiences and their ability to make predictions. This is precisely the case with the Inferential Strategy as well. The strategy is based on the notion that students comprehend better when they possess appropriate background knowledge about a topic and can relate new text information from their readings to familiar experiences. According to Hansen, "Young children seldom draw inferences spontaneously," but need to be taught the process at an early age. Older readers also benefit handsomely from instruction that shows them how to connect previous experience and knowledge to new information from the material.
Unlike the DR-TA, the Inferential Strategy does not require stopping points throughout the reading selection. Instead, it relies on a line of questions *prior* to reading and discussion afterwards.

Consider the following steps in the Inferential Strategy:

1. Analyze the content selection for important ideas central to the material. Before assigning the class to read the material, select *three* or *four* ideas that are important or might be difficult to understand.

2. Plan prereading questions. Develop *two* questions for *each idea* identified in the content analysis. One question is posed to tap background knowledge relative to the idea; the other, prediction. For example:
   Background Question: How do you react when you feel uncomfortable in a social situation?
   Prediction Question: In the selection you are about to read, Tim feels unsure of himself on his first blind date. How do you think Tim will react when he meets his date? Ask students to write predictions before discussion takes place.

3. Discuss responses to background and prediction questions *before* reading. Discuss both students' previous experience with the topic and their predictions for the selection.

4. Upon finishing the prereading discussion, assign selection to read.

5. After reading, relate predictions to what actually happened in the selection. Evaluate the three or four ideas which motivated background and prediction questions.

An eighth-grade English teacher implemented the Inferential Strategy for a short story called "August Heat" by W. F. Harvey. A story map prepared by the teacher outlined the key elements in the story that students would need to perceive. Figure 5.5 depicts the story map.

Given the story line, the teacher decided on the following ideas which she felt were important enough or difficult enough for students to warrant close attention:

1. Not everything that happens can be explained by reason and logic.

2. In many cases, the way an incident or event is reported depends on who is doing the reporting.

3. Some stories are "open-ended." The reader's imagination will determine the outcome.

The class explored each of these ideas through prereading discussion which focused on (a) a background question and (b) a prediction question for each idea:

Idea 1: (a) Have you ever had anything happen to you that seemed like an unusual coincidence or a case of ESP?
(b) "August Heat" is about an artist who draws a picture of a man he has never seen who is on trial in a courtroom. Knowing just this much information and the title of the story, can anyone predict what this story is going to be about?

Figure 5.5 *Story Map for "August Heat"*

The Setting

Time and Place: A hot, oppressive, steamy day in an English city on
                  August 20, 190___ .
Character: James Withencroft, an artist

The Problem

    On impulse, Withencroft draws a picture of a sweaty, guilty-looking fat
man who is on trial and sitting in the defendant's box. The artist doesn't
know what possessed him to draw the work, but he feels it is his best work
ever.

The Goal

To figure out why he, the artist, drew the picture.

Event 1:	The artist goes for a walk and encounters Atkinson, the very man whose picture he has drawn.

Event 2:	The artist discovers that Atkinson, a tombstone engraver, has had an impulse to carve a name unknown to him on a tombstone.

Event 3:	The name on the tombstone is revealed to be that of the artist, with the date of death being August 20, 190___ .

Event 4:	The artist is persuaded to stay the evening at the engraver's house, lest he meet his demise on the way home.

Event 5:	The artist suspects that the tombstone engraver is fated to murder him.

The Resolution

The story ends with the reader left to resolve the outcome.

Idea 2: (a) Have you ever talked with two people, both of whom witnessed the same incident, and found that their versions of the same event were different?

(b) This story is told to you by the main character himself. How do you think this might influence the way you read the story?

Idea 3: (a) Can you think of any movies you have seen that left you totally "hanging" at the end? You never did find out what happened. Did this leave you frustrated and disappointed, or do you prefer to decide for yourself what happens?

(b) This story is also a cliff-hanger. You will have to decide for yourself what happens. Knowing this ahead of time, what might you be looking for as you read that will help you to determine your own conclusion?

Class members wrote down their predictions about the story before reading. Several students volunteered to share theirs with the class. The predictions were later contrasted with inferences derived from the story during a postreading discussion. As a follow-up to the discussion, the students formed pairs to decide on a possible ending. Each pairing's first task was to skim through the story and list clues that would support their ending. If enough pairs of students believed that the engraver killed the artist, they could opt to set up a mock trial to try the engraver. Other pairs of students had the option of collaboratively writing the ending of the story.

The DR-TA and Inferential Strategy share several common premises. The next strategy, however, is founded on a different set of assumptions. As you read about the GRP, contrast it with the DR-TA and Inferential Strategy.

Guided Reading Procedure (GRP)

The GRP emphasizes close reading. It requires that students gather information and organize it around important ideas, and it places a premium on accuracy as students reconstruct the author's message. With a strong factual base, students will work from a common and clearer frame of reference. They will then be in a position to elaborate thoughtfully on the text and its implications.

Steps in the GRP

The GRP is a highly structured activity and therefore should be used sparingly as a training strategy—perhaps once a week at most. These steps are suggested:

1. Prepare students for reading: clarify key concepts; determine what students know and don't know about particular content to be studied; build appropriate background; give direction to reading.

2. Assign a reading selection: 500–900 words in middle grades (approximately five to seven minutes of silent reading); 1000–2000 words for

high school (approximately ten minutes). Provide general purpose to direct reading behavior. Direction: read to remember all you can.

3. As students finish reading, have them turn books face down. Ask them to tell what they remember. Record it on the chalkboard in the fashion in which it is remembered.

4. Help students recognize that there is much that they have not remembered or have represented incorrectly. Simply, there are implicit inconsistencies which need correction and further information to be considered.

5. Redirect students into their books and review the selection to correct inconsistencies and add further information.

6. Organize recorded remembrances into some kind of an outline. Ask guiding, nonspecific questions: "What were the important ideas in the assigned reading?" "Which came first?" "What facts on the board support it?" "What important point was brought up next?" "What details followed?"

7. Extend questioning to stimulate an analysis of the material and a synthesis of the ideas with previous learnings.

8. Provide immediate feedback, such as a short quiz, as a reinforcement of short-term memory.

A GRP Illustration

Eighth graders were assigned a reading selection from the music education magazine *Pipeline*. The selection, "Percussion—Solid as Rock," concerns the development and uses of percussion instruments from ancient to modern times.

The teacher introduced the selection by giving some background. She then asked students to remember as much as they could as they read the assignment silently. The teacher recorded the collective memories of her students on a transparency, projecting responses onto an overhead screen. Then she asked, "Did you leave out any information that might be important to know about?" Students were directed to review the selection to determine if essential information was missing from the list on the screen. The teacher also asked, "Did you mix up some of the facts on the list? Did you misrepresent any of the information in the author's message?"

These two questions are extremely important to the overall GRP procedure. The first question—"Did you leave out any information that might be important?"—encourages a review of the material. Students sense that some facts are more important than others. Further questioning at this point will help them distinguish essential from nonessential information. The second question—"Did you misrepresent any facts?"–reinforces the importance of selective rereading and rehearsal because of the limitations imposed by short-term memory.

Next the teacher asked the class to study the information recorded on the screen. The teacher requested the students to form pairs and then assigned the following task: "Which facts on the overhead can be grouped together? Organize the information around the important ideas in the selection. You have five minutes to complete the task."

Upon completion of the task the teacher encouraged students to share their work in whole-group discussion. Their groupings of facts were compared, refined, and extended. The teacher served as a facilitator, keeping the discussion moving, asking clarifying questions, provoking thought. She then initiated the next task: "Let's organize the important ideas and related information. Let's make a web."

Figure 5.6 shows what the students produced.

Figure 5.6
Semantic Web of "Percussion—Solid as Rock"

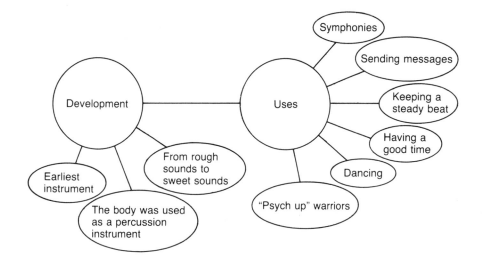

Outlining the mass of information will make students aware of the text relationships developed by the author. Producing the author's organizational structure leads to more efficient recall at a later time and lays the groundwork for interpreting and applying the author's message. Once this common framework is developed, your questioning should lead to more divergent and abstract responding by the students.

The discussion "took off" after the outline was completed. The teacher asked several applied questions that helped students associate their previous experiences and beliefs about drumming to the content under discussion. Cognitive performance centered on evaluation and application as students linked what they knew to what they were studying.

The final suggested step in the GRP is a short quiz—mainly to demonstrate in a dramatic way how successful the students can be with the reading material. The quiz should be viewed as positive reinforcement, not an interrogation check. Most of the students in this class earned perfect or near-perfect scores on the quiz—and this is as it should be.

Reciprocal Questioning (ReQuest)

ReQuest was originally devised as a "one-on-one" remedial procedure involving the student and teacher. Yet this strategy can easily be adapted to content class-rooms to help students think as they read. ReQuest encourages students to ask their own questions about the content material under study. Self-declared questions are forceful. They help students establish reasonable purposes for their reading. Betts (1950) described a "highly desirable learning situation" as one in which the student does the questioning: "That is, the learner asks the questions, and sets up the problems to be solved during the reading activity" (p. 450).

ReQuest fosters an active search for meaning. The rules for ReQuest, as described by Manzo (1969), follow:

> The purpose of this lesson is to improve your understanding of what you read. We will each read silently the first sentence. Then we will take turns asking questions about the sentence and what it means. You will ask questions first, then I will ask questions. Try to ask the kind of questions a teacher might ask, in the way a teacher might ask them. You may ask me as many questions as you wish. When you are asking me questions, I will close my book (or pass the book to you if there is only one between us). When I ask questions, you close your book. . . . Any question asked deserves to be answered as fully and honestly as possible. It is cheating for a teacher to withhold information or play dumb to draw out the student. It is unacceptable for a student to answer with "I don't know," since he can at least attempt to explain why he cannot answer. If questions are unclear to either party, requests for rephrasing or clarification are in order. The responder should be ready (and make it a practice) to justify his answer by reference back to the text or to expand on background that was used to build or to limit an answer. Whenever possible, if there is uncertainty about an answer, the respondent should check his answer against the text. *(pp. 124–125)*

Steps in ReQuest

Although the rules for ReQuest were devised for one-on-one instruction, they can be adapted for the content classroom. If you decide to use ReQuest in your class, consider these steps:

1. Both the students and the teacher silently read a common segment of the text selection. Manzo recommends one sentence at a time for poor comprehenders. However, text passages of varying length are suitable in applications to a classroom. For example, both teacher and students begin by reading a paragraph or two.

2. The teacher closes the book and is questioned about the passage by the students.

3. Next there is an exchange of roles. The teacher now queries the students about the material.

4. Upon completion of the student-teacher exchange, the next segment of text is read. Steps 2 and 3 are repeated.

5. At a suitable point in the text, when students have processed enough information to make predictions about the remainder of the assignment, the exchange of questions stops. The teacher then asks DR-TA-type questions: "What do you think the rest of the assignment is about?" "Why do you think so?" Speculations are encouraged.

6. Students are then assigned the remaining portion of the selection to read silently.

7. The teacher facilitates follow-up discussion of the material.

You can modify the ReQuest procedure to good advantage. For example, consider alternating the role of questioner after each question. By doing so you will probably involve more students in the activity. Once students sense the types of questions that can be asked about a text passage, you may also try forming ReQuest teams. A ReQuest team composed of three or four students is pitted against another ReQuest team. Your role is to facilitate the multiple action resulting from the small-group formations.

Our own experiences with ReQuest suggest that students may consistently ask factual questions to "stump" the teacher. Such questions succeed brilliantly, because you are subject to the same restrictions imposed by short-term memory as the students. That you "miss" an answer or two is actually healthy—after all, to err is human.

However, when students ask only verbatim questions because they don't know how to ask any others, then the situation is unhealthy. The sad fact is that many students don't know how to ask questions that will stimulate interpretive or applied levels of thinking. Therefore, your role as a good questioner during ReQuest is to provide a model that students will learn from. Over time you will notice the difference in the quality of student questions formulated.

Radio Reading

Does oral reading have a place in content areas? The answer is, "Sometimes, if . . ."

When students are required to read orally in content area classes, the result is often a tortured and senseless rendition—an extended version of round-robin reading, still commonly practiced in elementary classes. Try to recall this scenario as you probably lived it as a secondary school student a few years ago:

Your teacher directs you to turn to a particular page in the textbook. "We're going to read orally. Tony, please begin." Tony gulps, then starts. Bill, who sits behind Tony, figures he'll be asked to read next. He starts rehearsing the paragraph after Tony's. Meanwhile, Pauline sits in the third row, second seat. She resourcefully counts off eight paragraphs; her lips move visibly as she also rehearses. And who in the class is listening to Tony read? The teacher, of course, along with about ten students, is ready to come to Tony's rescue when he falters on a word too difficult to pronounce.

In round-robin reading each class member follows along with the reader until his or her part comes up. Because of the stress and storm that oral reading creates in most adolescents, few students actually listen to the reader except to correct mispronounced words. Most class members have determined quite cleverly which part of the text to be responsible for when their turn comes to read. Didn't you hate it when the teacher upset the usual routine for calling on readers?

Round robin literally is sense*less* at any level of instruction. It lacks sense because hardly anyone pays attention to the author's message when engaged in the activity. A legitimate purpose for oral reading, as a result, is destroyed.

The main instructional objective for oral reading in a content area class is to communicate ideas to others. Artley (1972) noted that oral reading has a worthwhile function if it is used "to interpret what the writer says or feels to concerned listeners" (p. 47). To this end, radio reading is a powerful alternative to round-robin methods. Furthermore, radio reading will promote good questioning behaviors because reading orally will be viewed as a communication process by students rather than a tedious exercise in frustration.

Radio reading maximizes communication between the reader and class members who must listen attentively. The ground rules are quite simple: the reader reads and the listeners listen. When the reader completes reading, the listeners respond by discussing what was comprehended. Therein lies the potential of radio reading as a questioning strategy.

Vacca (1976) recommended that the reader initiate discussion by asking questions of the audience. Typically, questions will be literal. Vacca, therefore, suggested that the teacher also take part as a radio reader "to model higher level questioning techniques when it is her (or his) turn" (p. 29).

Steps in Radio Reading

Radio reading works smoothly when used in small groups with four to six members. An instructional sequence which has proved successful follows:

1. Assign the text selection to be read. Provide prereading preparation as needed.

2. Form small groups. Each group member selects a segment of text to read. Several minutes are given for rehearsal and the formulation of questions for discussion.

3. Begin radio reading. As the reader reads, listeners have their books closed.

4. Initiate discussion of what was read. The radio reader asks each member of the group a question or two to prompt the discussion. If a question is unclear, the listener can ask for a restatement.

5. Each listener takes a turn as reader.

When small groups are used, charting responses to the reader's questions sustains the process, especially among middle school students. Box 5.1 shows

Box 5.1

Radio Reading   Secretary_____

                                   Date _____

List the names of those in the group. Mark a + or − in columns for each question. Mark an R in the box for the reader.

	Names	Questions						
		1	2	3	4	5	6	7
1.	Tony	R	−	+	+	−		
2.	Bill	+	R	−	−	+		
3.	Pauline	+	+	R	+	+		
4.	Patricia	−	+	+	R	−		
5.	Fred	+	+	−	+	R		

The secretary will fill in this sheet correctly and hand it to the teacher before the end of the period.

---

a score sheet that was devised for this purpose. A "secretary" in each group marks a plus or minus beside each person's name on the score sheet to indicate a satisfactory response to the reader's question. It is the reader's prerogative to decide whether or not an answer is satisfactory.

Radio reading has been used also as a whole-class activity. Unfortunately, active participation by most of the class members is drastically reduced, particularly during discussion. If you decide, nevertheless, to use radio reading with the whole class, plan it in advance. Designate your radio readers ahead of time so that they will have an opportunity to rehearse their portion of text and to give thought to the questions they will ask. Make sure that each student has the chance to read—don't always choose the best oral readers. In fact, a great motivational technique is to set up a microphone to amplify the reader's message to his or her listeners—thus adding a touch of authenticity to the radio motif.

There are several predictable student responses to difficult words while reading orally. First, many readers will respond to radio reading smoothly, requesting pronunciation help only when it appears absolutely necessary to do so. Other students, however, will request help for a difficult word even though the teacher believes they have the word attack skills to decode it. Greene (1979) suggested there is only one legitimate behavior in this situation: tell the reader the requested word.

It is not appropriate for the listener to play games with the reader. All responses such as "look at it again," "look at the first letter," "sound it

out," "you had it yesterday," "see if you remember it," "it rhymes with
___," are strictly forbidden. Radio reading involves a contract between
the reader and the listener. If the reader asks for a word it is
immediately supplied. *(p. 106)*

The contract between reader and listeners is built on the premise that oral reading is
a communication process. Therefore any attempts to short-circuit communication
through word attack games should be avoided.

A third response is for the reader not to request help when assistance is
actually needed. If the reader produces a reasonable substitute for a difficult word,
this is acceptable and highly desirable behavior. If the reader attempts to pronounce the word but botches it terribly, this should be accepted by the listeners if it
does not hinder communication of an important idea. During questioning, a
listener can request a rereading of that point in the text where mispronunication
took place. The correct pronunciation is then supplied by one of the listeners or the
teacher.

A final comment: Activities such as radio reading or ReQuest help students
to develop questioning competencies. As emphasized earlier, your model as a
good questioner is important to the development of these competencies. You might
also consider setting aside a few minutes periodically to teach students about
question asking. Begin with questions which prompt responses at a literal level and
progress gradually to applied-level questions. Contrasting examples work nicely.
For instance, a typical student question may be on the literal level: "What was the
name of the ship?" You may want to contrast the question with one that is posed at a
higher level: "Why do you think the ship was named *Dark Horizon?*" Sharing a
little insight on the art of questioning will go a long way.

Looking Back, Looking Forward

Questioning is a predominant technique used in content classrooms; its major
purpose is to promote thinking. When used effectively, the questions teachers ask
serve as guides for reading. Teachers need to know how, when, and where to use
questions and which questioning strategies are most appropriate for their content
area.

Questioning can also become counterproductive in the classroom. Teachers
who unwittingly use questions as weapons actually produce negative effects. They
may, for instance, put one student on the spot as they seek the right answer. This
creates an atmosphere more like a quiz show than a learning environment. Or,
teachers convey a "guess what's in my head" tone. They allow students to continue
guessing until—finally—someone has accurately guessed. A third counterproductive situation arises when teachers ask low-level questions of the interrogation
variety. They're trying to find out whether or not students have read the material.

These questioning scenarios belong to a widely used instructional model,
turn taking. In turn taking, one-to-one question-answer exchanges between
teacher and student occur too quickly to give readers time to think. We suggested

an alternative model in this chapter, discussion. In discussion, conversational interactions between teacher and students and students and other students take place. Discussion is of special importance because many of the content area reading strategies in this book involve some group discussion. We offered suggestions for creating an environment conducive to classroom discussion.

Positive relationships among the Levels of Comprehension construct and Bloom's taxonomy and Pearson and Johnson's question-answer classification were explained. When designing questions, teachers should pay attention to the strong relation among questions, reader, and text. Likewise, in choosing questioning strategies, teachers should look for those which facilitate comprehension and class discussion of text material.

To this end, we shared six questioning strategies in this chapter. The first, QAR, calls for direct instruction in the relationship between questions and answers. The DR-TA and the GRP are complete lesson procedures which help guide and extend student reading performance. The IS involves teaching students the process of relating new text information from their readings to familiar experiences. The remaining two strategies, ReQuest and Radio Reading, develop student questioning competencies through silent and oral performance, respectively.

Although questioning is an integral part of content area reading instruction, there are times when students will need additional guidance to handle difficult text assignments. In the chapter that follows, we explain the development and use of reading and study guides. These guides bridge the gap between difficult material in textbooks and the ability of students to comprehend the material independently. Guides provide the immediate support students need to learn from text as they are learning how to take charge of their own learning.

Suggested Readings

Andre, T. (1979). Does answering higher level questions while reading facilitate productive reading? *Review of Educational Research,* **49,** 280–318.

Dillon, J. (1983). *Teaching and the Art of Questioning.* Bloomington, Ind.: Phi Delta Kappa.

Guthrie, J. (ed.). (1977). *Cognition, Curriculum and Comprehension.* Newark, Del.: International Reading Association.

Hunkins, F. (1972). *Questioning Strategies and Techniques.* Boston: Allyn and Bacon.

Pennock, C. (ed.). (1979). *Reading Comprehension at Four Linguistic Levels.* Newark, Del.: International Reading Association.

Raphael, T., & Pearson, P. D. (1982). *The Effect of Metacognitive Awareness Training on Children's Question Answering Behavior.* Urbana, Ill.: University of Illinois Center for the Study of Reading, Technical Report No. 238.

Sanders, N. (1966). *Classroom Questions; What Kinds?* New York: Harper & Row.

Singer, H., & Donlan, D. (1982). Active comprehension: Problem-solving schema with question generation for comprehension of complex short stories. *Reading Research Quarterly,* **17,** 166–186.

Smith, C. (1978). Evaluating answers to comprehension questions. *Reading Teacher,* **31**, 896–900.

Stauffer, R. (1969). *Directing Reading Maturity as a Cognitive Process.* New York: Harper & Row.

Vacca, R. T. (1978). Questions and advance organizers as adjunct aids. In C. Smith and L. Mikulecky (eds.), *Secondary Reading: Theory and Application.* Bloomington, Ind.: School of Education, Indiana University.

CHAPTER SIX

Reading and Study Guides

The dear people do not know how long it takes to read. I have been at it all my life and cannot say that I have reached my goal.
—GOETHE

Organizing Principle

Goethe, in his eighties when he made the statement quoted opposite, captured the essence of learning to read. Reading is an act of maturity. From the very first day we pick up books, we are reading to learn and learning to read. We grow *in* reading. We grow *through* reading. And our development as readers continues throughout life. Teachers can contribute to the reading maturity of students within the context of subject matter instruction. While the raison d'être of content area reading is to show students how to learn from texts independently, many students may have trouble handling the conceptual demands inherent in difficult texts. Teacher-prepared adjunct instructional materials, commonly called reading or study guides, provide the support that students need to read *difficult* text material. As you study the role of reading and study guides in content area instruction, keep in mind the main idea behind this chapter: *Teacher-made adjunct instructional materials which accompany reading assignments help students experience the satisfaction of learning content from texts.*

CHAPTER OVERVIEW

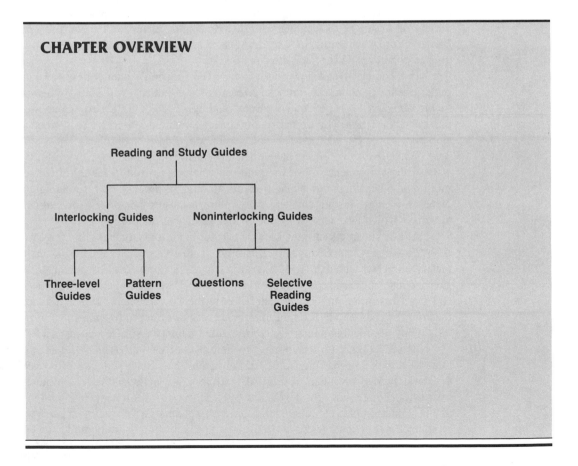

Through the use of adjunct instructional materials such as reading and study guides, a teacher builds in the structure students need to handle difficult reading materials. Consider the following questions as you study the Chapter Overview and prepare to read:

1. Why develop and use adjunct instructional materials?
2. What is the purpose and value of reading and study guides?
3. How do interlocking guides differ from noninterlocking guides?
4. How might the different types of interlocking and noninterlocking guides be adapted to different content area texts?

Good readers know *why* they read. They also know *when* and *how* to read differently at different times, because they know that they read different texts for different reasons. Such readers are said to be "skilled" or "mature" because they are in control of their own cognitive processes as they read. They're in the driver's seat. Gibson and Levin (1975) maintained that mature readers develop and use a variety of strategies for dealing with different kinds of texts. A mature reader knows the value of "sizing up" a reading task at hand, setting purposes, and asking questions before, during, and after reading.

In Chapters 4 and 5 we built a case for showing students how to read purposely and thoughtfully. Purpose determines how students will adapt strategies to the text and keep on course during reading. There's little new about this particular revelation. The Roman writer Seneca remarked centuries ago, "When a ship does not know what port to sail toward, no wind is favorable."

When *maturing* readers have difficulty raising questions before, during, or after reading, teachers, as we suggested in Chapter 5, need to model effective questioning behavior and guide students through a process of responding to meaning in text. In this chapter, we explore the use of *adjunct instructional materials* which also serve a modeling and guidance function.

Adjunct instructional materials are teacher-made tools for learning. They are designed with three broad objectives in mind: (1) to give students a feel for what it means to interact with a difficult text selection; (2) to stimulate classroom discussion about the ideas and concepts under study; and (3) to help students comprehend and study text more effectively than if left to their own devices. Hence adjunct materials are commonly referred to as *reading guides* or *study guides*.

Why are reading and study guides called adjunct instructional materials?

Frase (1971), an instructional psychologist, defined an *adjunct aid* as any kind of stimulation that facilitates learning from text. Since aids are often not a natural part of an author's original text, they are called *adjuncts*. Adjunct instructional materials are developed by teachers to accompany text assignments. For example, the anticipation guides explained in Chapter 4 are a type of adjunct instructional material. In this chapter, a reading or study guide can be placed beside the text while students are reading. According to Tutolo (1977), "The student refers to the guide, then the text, or vice versa. Or, the student may refer back and forth to guide and text while reading the associated text" (p. 504).

Reading and study guides simplify difficult text for students (Herber, 1978). As a result, guides make textbook life in the classroom easier for students. Don't think by "easier" that we mean "less challenging" or "less productive." Just the opposite is intended. Reading and study guides are used in content classes primarily because the text material is difficult and important enough to warrant guidance. The judicious use of these adjunct materials will make learning easier.

The conceptual load of content area textbooks is often greater than the levels of reading maturity that students bring to the task. As a result, students experience difficulty comprehending what they read. They simply do not know what ideas are important enough to merit concentrated study. The whole idea of adjunct guide materials is to provide enough instructional support and direction for students to learn successfully from text. In the process of doing so, they will gain confidence. Over time, reading guides help to contribute to the development of strategies which lead to independent reading.

To some teachers the use of guides is tantamount to spoon-feeding. Maybe it is. However, spoon-feeding doesn't necessarily mean that you are "giving the content away." It means that you care enough to simplify the tough sledding that is ahead for students when the information in text appears too overwhelming to read on their own. Without some simplification, students' only alternative is often to avoid textbooks altogether.

In this chapter, two types of guides are examined—those which are *interlocking* and those which are *noninterlocking* (Tutolo, 1977). Interlocking guides are devised in such a way as to provide a framework for responding to text material at three levels of comprehension. These levels were described in Chapter 5 as *literal, interpretive,* and *applied* levels of cognitive functioning. When using an interlocking guide, students proceed from the literal level to the interpretive level to the applied level. All literal-level tasks are grouped together, as are all interpretive and applied tasks.

Noninterlocking guides, on the other hand, do not assume or imply a hierarchical relationship among levels of comprehension. Instead, a noninterlocking guide provides a framework which directs students to seek information and search for relationships as they interact with text. As Tutolo (1977) put it, "The thinking necessary for understanding (a text selection) might vary from literal to application and back to literal as the reader moves through the connected discourse" (p. 504).

Interlocking and noninterlocking guides give teachers and students more flexibility in dealing with textbooks. Guides increase your instructional repertoire. You are able to use a variety of instructional formats for specific instructional purposes. These purposes will become clear as we examine different types of interlocking and noninterlocking adjunct materials. For students, guides provide a means for becoming successful with textbooks. Rather than avoid textbook reading altogether, students will begin to use text as a vehicle for learning.

Reading and study guides have immediate and long-term payoffs. They are firmly grounded in the here and now, working to aid students to understand the text material better than they would if left to their own resources. But guides also pay handsome dividends over time. A guide *stimulates* learning and *simulates* processes required for independent reading. It shows students how to handle material effectively and efficiently over time so that they will develop the maturity to eventually read on their own.

Three-Level Reading Guides

A three-level reading guide directs readers through interlocking levels of comprehension. One of the best ways to become familiar with the three-level guide as an instructional tool is to experience one. Therefore, we invite your participation in the following demonstration.

Several years ago we came across an article in the newspaper with some significance about teachers' actions. First preview the three-level guide in Box 6.1 and then read the fictitious selection that we developed based on the newspaper item. After reading the selection, complete the guide.

Box 6.1

THREE-LEVEL GUIDE TO "GUEST LECTURER"

I. *Directions:* Check the items you believe say what the author says. Sometimes the exact words will be used; other times other words may be used.
___ 1. Letters of reprimand were to be written for two teachers and their department head.
___ 2. The school committee decided the teachers made an error in judgment.
___ 3. The teachers were finally suspended for three days.
___ 4. Students and parents generally felt the "lecture" was a mistake.
___ 5. School officials approved the prostitute's visit beforehand.
___ 6. Control over the program will be tightened in the future.

II. *Directions:* Put a check on the line beside any of the statements below which you think are reasonable interpretations of the author's meaning.
___ 1. Emotion rather than reason prevailed among some members of the community.
___ 2. Parents and students seemed to view the controversy differently.
___ 3. A few vocal parents led the attack against the teachers.
___ 4. The prostitute's lecture is another example of teachers and students trying to take over the schools.
___ 5. The teachers involved in the controversy were glad to be reprimanded and not suspended.

III. *Directions:* To apply what you read means to take information and ideas from what you have read and connect them to what you know. Place a check in the blank beside any statements below which are supported by statements in level II and by previous experience or study. Be sure you can defend your answers.
___ 1. A prostitute can contribute to one's formal education.

___ 2. Schools should be run more *for* students than *by* them.

___ 3. Ends justify means.

___ 4. Ideas and actions alien to the status quo usually precipitate aggressive reaction and restrictive requirements.

Guest Lecturer

The tension in the air could be sliced with a knife. The hearing had lasted nearly five hours. More than two hundred people, many of them students, were in the meeting room where the session was held. Bob Herring and Ray Weatherman, the two American history teachers, sat attentively. They didn't blink an eyelash at the verdict: letters of reprimand were to be written for the two teachers and their department head.

The Hard Rock School Committee had concluded that the teachers made an error in judgment but didn't deserve to be suspended. Little did Bob and Ray realize the community turmoil that would be created when they invited a guest lecturer, a young prostitute, to speak to their high school class. The class was an innovative social studies elective, "Economics and Politics in the Community." The teachers didn't suspect that their guest lecturer would get some residents of Hard Rock so "bent out of shape."

"I want them suspended," bellowed Anton Slipman to the cheers of some of the parents in the room. "What does a teacher have to do to get suspended?" Slipman wondered. As a member of the school committee, he continued his tirade against the teachers. "This is the most outrageous thing to happen in Hard Rock since I can remember." More cheers. Slipman was hot. "At least forty, maybe fifty, people in the community have contacted me. They're as upset as I am." And they all must have been in the room.

One parent stood up and shouted, "I'm going to send my children to a private school if things keep up the way they have been going." Another added, "I want to know who's running the schools. The students? The teachers? What's going on?"

Mr. Prufrock, the department head of social studies, squirmed restlessly in his chair during the entire session. He was the teachers' supervisor. Why didn't he stop them from inviting the prostitute? Although he had listened to part of the guest lecturer's talk, he claimed that he and the principal had not sanctioned the lecture beforehand.

Bob Herring and Ray Weatherman explained in detail the objectives of the controversial course. Weatherman, the more vocal of the two, said, "Prostitution is a victimless crime, just like bookmaking and homosexuality. The only victim is the law that is broken." Some gasps were heard in the room.

Dr. Picasso, the school superintendent, acknowledged that students in the class had talked to alcoholics and drug addicts as part of the program, and they even saw an X-rated movie called "Without a Stitch." But he said, "Having a prostitute speak to students overstepped the bounds and contradicted the mission of the school."

Most of the students who testified at the hearing agreed that the guest lecturer had provided them with a good learning experience. One girl accused the school committee of being overprotective. "If we don't learn about these things in school, where are we going to learn about them—on the street?" Slipman, however, warned the girl, "These schools aren't going to be run for what you want."

In the end, Slipman lost the fight for suspension of the two teachers and the department head. The attorney for the teachers promised to fight the reprimand. The superintendent of schools indicated in a memorandum to the school committee that controls over the controversial course would be tightened.

And the students? They attended school the next day.

Several comments are in order on your participation in the three-level guide demonstration. First of all, note that the three-level format gave you what Herber (1970) has described as a "conscious experience" with comprehension levels as a process. Consider also that as you walked through the process you responded to and manipulated the important explicit and implicit ideas in the material. You may have sensed the relatedness of ideas as you moved within and among the levels.

Why did we direct you to first preview the guide and then read the material? Because previewing helps create a predisposition for reading the material. As you recall from Chapter 4, previewing helps to reduce the reader's uncertainty about the material to be read. You know what is coming. When we asked you to read the guide first, we hoped to raise your expectations about the author's message. In a sense, previewing the reading guide fulfills the same purpose as the materials and strategies suggested in Chapter 4. By encountering some of the ideas before reading you are in a more flexible and adaptive position to direct the search for information that may be relevant in the reading material.

You probably noted also that the declarative statements did not require you to produce answers to questions. Rather, you had to make decisions among likely alternatives. Herber and Nelson (1975) supported the notion that it's easier to recognize possible answers than to produce them.

Notice too that in a very positive way the statements can serve as springboards for discussion and conversation about the content. Were students to react to guides without the opportunity to discuss and debate responses, the adjunct material would soon deteriorate into busy work and paper shuffling.

A final comment: your maturity as a reader probably is such that you didn't need structured guidance for this selection, particularly at levels I and II. If you make the decision that certain segments of your text can be handled without reading guidance, then don't construct guide material. A three-level guide is a means to growth in reading and growth through reading. It is not an end in itself. Were we to use "Guest Lecturer" in a class for adult learners, we probably would provide prereading instruction to activate interest in and thinking about the content before reading and then follow with a guide at level III—thus providing just enough structure to suit our purposes.

Using and Constructing Three-Level Guides

Don't be misled by the apparent discreteness of comprehension levels. Don't, as Dale (1969) pronounced, suffer from "hardening of the categories." The term *levels* implies a cognitive hierarchy that may be more apocryphal than real. A reader doesn't necessarily read first for literal recognition, then interpretation, and finally application—although that may appear to be a logical sequence. Many readers, for example, read text for overarching concepts and generalizations first and then search for evidence to support their inferences.

Most important is that you recognize that in reading, levels are probably interactive and inseparable (just as skills are within levels). Nevertheless, the classroom teacher attempts to have students experience each aspect of the comprehension process as they read content material. In doing so, students adapt skills and strategies as they interact with the material. They get a feel for the component processes within reading comprehension. They come to sense in an instructional setting what it means to make inferences; what it means to use information as the basis for those inferences; and what it means to rearrange or transform acquired understandings into what they know already in order to construct knowledge.

The reading guide is not meant to be used with every text assignment every day. If it were to be, it would soon be counterproductive. One math teacher's evaluation of a three-level guide crystallizes this point: "The students said the guide actually helped them organize in their minds the author's ideas and helped them to understand the material. I think the guide was successful but I would not use it all the time because many of the assignments don't lend themselves to this type of activity." The three-level reading guide is but one instructional aid which helps students grow toward mature reading and independent learning.

Merlin the magician doesn't wave his magic wand to ensure the effectiveness of three-level guides. They can be facilitative only when students know how to work in groups and know how to apply techniques that have been taught clearly. The heart of the matter is what the teacher does to make guided reading work.

Finally, we urge you also to consider guides as tools, not tests. Their real value ultimately lies in providing for the adaptation and application of skills to subject material. But we hasten to emphasize one more time that individual skills and levels are likely to be interactive and inseparable from one another. Think of each statement in a reading guide as a prompt that will initiate that interaction and reinforce the quality of the reader's response to meaning in text material.

There are no set procedures for constructing three-level reading guides. Before constructing a guide, however, the teacher has to make at least two important decisions. First, you should examine content material to decide what information to emphasize. Given your content objectives, what are the important ideas that should be emphasized? Second, Earle (1969) suggested you decide how much assistance students will need to succeed. What are the students' competencies? The depth of understanding that you expect them to achieve? The difficulty of the material?

Having made these decisions you may wish to consider these guidelines:

1. Begin construction of the guide at level II, the interpretive level. Analyze the text selection, asking yourself, "What does the author mean?" Write down in your own words those inferences that make sense to you and fit your content objectives. Make sure your statements are written simply and clearly. (After all, you don't want to construct a guide to read the guide.)

2. Next, search the text for propositions, explicit pieces of information, needed to support the inferences you have chosen for level II. Put these into statement form. You now have level I, the literal level.

3. Decide whether you want to add a distractor or two to levels I and II. There is some debate whether distractors detract from the guided experience (Herber, 1978). My suggestion is that you follow your instincts. We

have found that a distractor can maintain an active response to the information search, mainly because students sense that they cannot indiscriminately check every item and therefore focus the information search more carefully. Others, however, feel that a distractor reinforces a "right-wrong" mentality and should not be used.

4. Develop statements for level III, the applied level. Such statements represent additional insights or principles that can be drawn when relationships established by the author are combined with other ideas outside the text selection itself but inside the heads of your students. In other words, help students connect what they know already to what they have read.

5. Be flexible and adaptive. Develop a format that will appeal to you and your students. Try to avoid crowding too much print on the reading guide.

Examining Guides from Different Content Areas

The format of the guide should vary. The classroom examples that follow serve only as models. As you study these illustrations, think of ways that you will be able to adapt and apply the three-level construct to your content materials.

Literature

Reading guides are extremely useful adjuncts in the study of literature. A three-level guide can easily be adapted to dramatic, narrative, and poetic forms of literature. For example, note in Box 6.2 how a ninth-grade English teacher used a three-level guide for Shakespeare's *Romeo and Juliet*. The class was at the tail-end of its study of the play, and the guide helped students to pull together some of the important points related to the climatic action of the final act. Moreover, the statements in levels II and III of the guide helped students reflect on possible inferences and themes that emerge from the action.

Box 6.2

THREE-LEVEL GUIDE FOR ROMEO AND JULIET

I. *Literal Level:* Check the items that explicitly represent some of the important details and actions in the last part of the play.

___ 1. The reason Friar Laurence married Romeo and Juliet was to bring the families of Montague and Capulet together.

___ 2. Friar Laurence believed words of wisdom would help Romeo deal with his banishment.

___ 3. Juliet gave the ring to the Nurse to give to Romeo as a sign of her love.

___ 4. Lady Capulet believed marriage to Paris would take care of all of Juliet's sorrows.

___ 5. Paris was going to Juliet's grave nightly to place flowers.

___ 6. Prince Escalus said that he was the one to blame for the deaths because he had not acted decisively enough.

II. *Interpretive Level:* Several statements are listed below which may represent what the play-wright means. If you think any of the statements are reasonable inferences and conclusions, put a check on the line provided. Be prepared to support your answers using parts of the play.

__ 1. Romeo would be alive if the apothecary had obeyed the law.

__ 2. Lord and Lady Capulet are to blame for Juliet's death because they forced her into marriage.

__ 3. If Prince Escalus had punished the Montagues and Capulets earlier, the entire tragedy would not have happened.

__ 4. Romeo's impulsiveness, rashness, immaturity, and emotionalism caused him problems.

__ 5. A fourteen-year-old is not capable of true love.

__ 6. Romeo did not want to kill Paris.

III. *Applied Level:* To apply what you read means to take information and ideas from what you have read and connect it to what you already know. If you think the statements below are supported by statements in Section II and by previous experience or study, place a check in the blank provided. Be sure you have good reasons to justify your answers if called upon to do so.

__ 1. Those who live by the sword, die by the sword.

__ 2. Those in positions of power must take responsibility for the actions of those under them.

__ 3. A person cannot change the role that fate has ordained for him.

__ 4. The most important thing in life is love. It is even worth dying for.

__ 5. No person has the right to take his/her own life.

__ 6. Nothing is worth dying for.

__ 7. Our own personalities shape our lives, and we can shape our personalities by the choices we make.

__ 8. Events outside our control shape our lives.

Three-level guides can be used not only with drama, but also with short stories and novels. A seventh-grade language arts teacher developed a sequence of reading guides for different sections from the novel *Flowers for Algernon*. The teacher introduced *Flowers for Algernon* as part of a unit on values. He had given the students a great deal of preparation—simulation games and values clarification exercises—before introducing the novel. He developed the reading guides to initiate discussion and extend the students' thinking about their own values. In the novel, the main character, Charlie Gordon, gets a chance to live in two worlds—one in which he is a mentally retarded individual and one in which he is intellectually superior. The teacher wanted his students to recognize changes in people's values as Charlie goes through his changes and moves from one world to another. As you study one of the guides, notice the following: (1) the teacher's use of simple, declarative statements, and (2) the use of Right There, Think and Search, and On Your Own mnemonics to signal different levels of question-answer relationships as presented in Chapter 5.

Box 6.3

READING GUIDE FROM FLOWERS FOR ALGERNON

Directions: Charlie Gordon's values should be easy to identify, but as the text says, Charlie gets a chance to live in two worlds. Watch for changes in people's values as Charlie goes through his changes. Follow the directions for each part of the reading guide after or while reading each of the four sections.

Pages 172–176

A. *Right There:* Check those statements that can be found directly in the reading assignment. They may or may not be in exact words.

—— 1. Charlie wants to be smart.

—— 2. Charlie sees nothing in the ink blots.

—— 3. Miss Kinnian recommends Charlie to the doctors.

—— 4. Charlie beats Algernon in every maze test.

—— 5. Charlie has good motivation.

—— 6. Charlie likes his friends at the factory

B. *Think and Search:* Check the statements which are reasonable inferences and conclusions from the reading assignment.

—— 1. Charlie has no imagination.

—— 2. Charlie is honest.

—— 3. Drs. Nemur and Strauss hope to create a new breed of intellectual supermen through their surgical techniques.

—— 4. The doctors triple Algernon's intelligence through surgery.

—— 5. The hospital people are very patient with Charlie.

—— 6. Charlie's friends at the factory really like him.

—— 7. To "pull a Charlie Gordon" is to do something really stupid.

C. *On Your Own:* Check statements that might apply to your own experience in real life.

—— 1. Some people make fun of the mentally retarded.

—— 2. It is possible to surgically increase intelligence.

—— 3. Some people have the patience and desire to help the mentally retarded.

—— 4. Motivation is important to learning.

The three-level guide in Box 6.4 was designed for eleventh graders as part of a Modern American Poetry unit. The purpose of the guide was to have students experience an e. e. Cummings poem at different levels of complexity. Although the English teacher considered the class to be able readers, he felt that his students needed assistance to deal effectively with the poet's unusual style as well as his explicit and implicit meanings.

Preview the three-level guide for Cummings's poem, read through the

Box 6.4

THREE-LEVEL GUIDE
FOR CUMMINGS POEM

l(a
e. e. cummings*

l(a
le
af
fa
ll
s)
one
l
iness

I. *Directions:* Check the statements that say what the poet said.
___ 1. Fall has arrived.
___ 2. Loneliness
___ 3. A leaf falls.
___ 4. Oneliness

II. *Directions:* Check each statement below that you believe represents what the poet meant by what he said.
___ 1. Loneliness is like the falling of a leaf.
___ 2. Loneliness is a quiet time.
___ 3. To be one is to be lonely.
___ 4. An occurrence in nature is similar to what occurs in humankind.
___ 5. (Other) _____

III. *Directions:* Check those statements which you believe express ideas you can support based on what you know and your interpretation of the poem.
___ 1. Oneliness is not a human characteristic.
___ 2. Loneliness can be a beautiful time.
___ 3. No man is an island.
___ 4. Loneliness is a slow death.
___ 5. Nature teaches us about ourselves.
___ 6. (Other) _____

poem, and then complete the guide. Where an alternative choice says "other," develop a statement that reflects an idea within the specified level of comprehension. If possible, compare your statements with others' statements.

A poem presents a problem at the interpretive and applied levels. Is it possible, or even desirable, to separate the poet's intended meaning from your personal response to that meaning? In some reading situations you may wish to consider combining levels II and III when developing a reading guide. The guide will then prompt two levels of thinking—explicit and implicit responses to meaning.

Mathematics

Consider how mathematics teachers might adapt the reading guide to suit their purposes. The nature of the mathematical content should determine the form of the guide. Word problems in particular illustrate this point. For example, Riley and Pachtman (1978) explained: "Mathematical word problems constitute a new area of difficulty for the student. Unlike the language of narrative material, the language of word problems is compact. Mathematic concepts and relationships are often 'hidden' or assumed and therefore not readily apparent to the student" (p. 531). Riley and Pachtman suggested how the three-level guide can be adapted to meet the reading demands implicit in solving word problems. The procedure is as follows: (1) level I = the facts of the problem; (2) level II = the mathematical ideas or concepts underlying the problem; (3) level III = the numerical depictions related to the problem. Study Box 6.5, which illustrates the adaptations which can be made when reading word problems in math.

Box 6.5

WORD PROBLEM READING GUIDE

Problem: Tom has collected 239 empty cans for recycling. He puts 107 into a big box. How many must he put in each of two smaller boxes if he uses the rest of the cans and puts the same number in each box?

I. Facts of the Problem
Directions: Read the word problem above. Then under column A check those statements that contain the important facts of the problem. Look back at the problem to check your answers. Under column B check those statements you think will help you solve the problem.

A (Facts)	B (Will help)	
_____	_____	107 cans went into the big box.
_____	_____	The cans were for recycling.
_____	_____	Tom had collected 239 empty cans.
_____	_____	Tom had one big box and two smaller ones.
_____	_____	Tom put the cans into three boxes.
_____	_____	The cans were empty.
_____	_____	107 cans had to be put into two smaller boxes.

II. Math Ideas
Directions: Check the statements that contain math ideas about this problem. Look back to column B of part I to prove your answers. (You may change your answers in part I if you wish to.)
___ Division is putting an amount into equal groups.
___ To find the total amount of a group we add the parts.
___ When we take an amount away we subtract to find the amount left.
___ Adding groups with the same amount in each group is multiplying.
___ Subtracting is separating a group into two parts.
___ When we put an amount into groups of the same size we divide the amount by the number of groups.

III. Numbers
Directions: Below are possible ways of getting an answer. Check those that will work in this problem. Look back to Column B of part I and to part II to prove your answers. (You may change some of your answers in parts I and II if you wish to.)
_____ (239 ÷ 2) + 107
_____ (239 − 107) ÷ 2
_____ 107 ÷ 2
_____ 239 ÷ 2
_____ 239 − 107
_____ 107 + 239
Now that you have responded to each part of the guide, you may compute the answer to the problem.

Box 6.6 exhibits a reading guide used with junior high school students who were in a "below average class" class. Again, observe the reinforcement of QARs as well as the way the statements are written to meet the competencies of the students.

Box 6.6

FRACTIONS

I. *Right There:* What did the material say?
Directions: Check each statement below that you can find on the pages you just read.
___ 1. 49/52 is a fraction.
___ 2. A fraction has two numbers.
___ 3. A fraction is a whole of a part.
___ 4. 50¢ = half a dollar.
___ 5. $\dfrac{0 \quad 0 \quad 0}{O \quad \frac{1}{3} \quad 1}$

___ 6. Fraction = $\dfrac{\text{parts used}}{\text{total parts}}$

___ 7. You must use two numbers to write a fraction.

II. *Think and Search:* What does the material mean?
Directions: Check each statement below that you think is true and can defend.
___ 1. Fractions are important in your life.
___ 2. You can make a fraction by putting the number 3 inside the circle: $\dfrac{O}{4}$

___ 3. You can make a fraction by putting the number 8 inside the circle: $\dfrac{O}{8}$

___ 4. $O = \frac{1}{3}$
___ 5. $\frac{3}{5}$ means ●●●○○.

III. *On Your Own:* How can you use fractions?
Directions: Check each item you agree with.
___ 1. You are on an elevator with seven persons. Two out of the seven are men; $\frac{2}{7}$ of the people are men.
___ 2. Start with 8. Take half of it. Take half of the answer, then half of the last answer. Keep on doing this. Pretty soon you will reach zero (0).
___ 3. Pete Rose had three hits in five at bats. You can say this by writing a fraction.

Social Studies. A ninth-grade teacher developed the three-level guide in Box 6.7 to show students how to read a textbook section entitled "Building the First Cities." He directed the students to complete the three-level guide *as* they read the assignment. Examine the variation at the literal level. Completing the guide as you read helps you read selectively and focus on essential information.

Box 6.7

THREE-LEVEL GUIDE: BUILDING FIRST CITIES

I. *Directions:* For the statements below, tell which of the four cities listed is being described exactly by the author. Use this letter code:

B = Boston
C = Charleston
N = New York
P = Philadelphia
____ 1. the first seaport to be settled
____ 2. rice the main crop
____ 3. many settlers businessmen
____ 4. a busy and beautiful city
____ 5. planned streets
____ 6. theaters here
____ 7. much fishing here
____ 8. a library here built by Ben Franklin
____ 9. the first public schools here
____ 10. planters as leaders here
____ 11. the University of Pennsylvania and religious freedom here
____ 12. many dinners and dances for rich people
____ 13. the largest city for 150 years
____ 14. a hot, humid city

II. *Directions:* On the basis of what you've read, check each of the statements below about our first four major cities with which the author would agree:
____ 1. Early American cities had some paved streets.
____ 2. Cities were places where news and ideas were exchanged.
____ 3. Minorities were rarely seen in the cities.
____ 4. People of all religions were welcomed everywhere.
____ 5. The common people were allowed a voice in controlling all of the earliest cities.
____ 6. Trade was necessary for the survival of the cities.
____ 7. Entertainment was available in some cities.
____ 8. The early cities were inhabited by different national groups.

III. *Directions:* Check the statements below that you agree with:
____ 1. The early cities were like people: to be healthy they had to be busy with work to do.
____ 2. The early city could be pictured as "a strong young man wearing work clothes."
____ 3. The early city could be pictured as "a middle-aged man wearing a clean, pressed suit."
____ 4. Transportation + money = city problems.

Business

A teacher in a general business course used the reading guide in Box 6.8 as part of concept extension for a chapter on "Evaluating Our Economic System." To reinforce basic ideas presented in the textbook, she had students study a newspaper article entitled, "The Downscaling of The American Dream." Prior to reading, preparatory discussion centered around the students' knowledge of the expression, "The American Dream." The teacher then distributed the article with the reading guide, reviewed the construct of different levels of comprehension, and directed students to read and complete the guide.

Box 6.8

THREE-LEVEL GUIDE FOR DOWNSCALING OF THE AMERICAN DREAM

I. *Right There!* What did the news reporter say? Check the items you believe say what the author says.
___ 1. America's standard of living is the world's highest.
___ 2. Today, the middle class is lowering its expectations.
___ 3. In families with incomes over $25,000 a year, two-thirds combine the earning power of two full-time paychecks.
___ 4. Inflation means having more money to spend.
___ 5. More young people are moving back home and giving up their independence.
___ 6. In times of inflation, the debtor benefits more than the creditor.
___ 7. In a 1980 poll of college freshmen, more than 60% rated "being very well off financially" as a top goal in life.
___ 8. People with large incomes never have large debts.
___ 9. Many middle-class Americans see the rich getting richer.

II. *Think and Search!* What did the news reporter mean? Check the items which you think are possible inferences and conclusions from the article.
___ 1. The American Dream is now beyond the reach of many Americans.
___ 2. One full-time income can easily support a comfortable middle-class lifestyle.
___ 3. In inflationary times, borrowing money may be a wise decision.
___ 4. Inflation usually results in decreased purchasing power.
___ 5. Today's young people cannot make it on their own because they are just plain lazy.
___ 6. Even people with large incomes need to handle their finances carefully.
___ 7. America's vast wealth is divided equally among the poor, the middle class, and the rich.

III. *On Your Own!* How can you use these ideas? To use what you read means to take information and ideas from what you have read and connect them to what you know. Place a check by statements you can support from the article.
___ 1. The American Dream is alive and well.
___ 2. Bankruptcy knows no bounds—it can affect anyone.
___ 3. For women, marriage is a ticket to a life of leisure.
___ 4. A dollar saved is a dollar earned.
___ 5. Life with Mom and Dad does not necessarily end at age 18.
___ 6. A college degree equals money in the bank.

Science and Health

The simplicity of Box 6.9 speaks for itself. A fifth-grade teacher constructed it as part of a health unit. Students completed the guide individually and then discussed their responses in small groups.

Box 6.9

HEALTH AND GROWTH: "HOW DO YOU GROW UP?"

I. What did the author say?

Directions: Place a check on the line in front of the number if you think a statement can be found in the pages you read.

___ 1. Every human being has feelings, or emotions.

___ 2. Research workers are studying the effects of repeated use of marijuana on the body.

___ 3. You should try hard to hide your strong emotions such as fear or anger.

___ 4. Your feelings affect the way the body works.

___ 5. You are likely to get angry at your parents or brothers or sisters more often than at other people.

II. What did the author mean?

Directions: Check the statements below that state what the author was trying to say in the pages you read.

___ 1. Sometimes you act in a different way because of the mood you are in.

___ 2. Emotional growth has been a continuing process since the day you were born.

___ 3. The fact that marijuana hasn't been proven to be harmful means that it is safe to use.

___ 4. Each time you successfully control angry or upset feelings you grow a little.

III. Do you agree with these statements?

Directions: Check those statements that you can defend.

___ 1. Escaping from problems does not solve them.

___ 2. Decisions should be made on facts, not fantasies.

___ 3. Getting drunk is a good way to have fun.

Study the adaptations made on Box 6.10, a three-level guide for a relatively sophisticated group of seniors, as compared to those in Box 6.9. This new guide is difficult and different. It requires the students to manipulate information and participate actively in the reading assignment.

Box 6.10

DIFFUSION THROUGH A MEMBRANE

I. Observations

Directions: Check all items below which you observed through the lab experiment.

___ 1. When you add Lugol (iodine) to starch solution the solution turns black.

___ 2. When you add Lugol to a glucose solution the solution turns orange.

___ 3. When you add Benedict to a glucose solution the solution turns black.

___ 4. When you add Benedict to a glucose solution the solution turns orange.

___ 5. The bag containing the glucose and starch solution is slightly fuller.

___ 6. Glucose molecules passed through the semipermeable membrane.

___ 7. Starch molecules can pass through the semipermeable membrane.

___ 8. Iodine molecules (Lugol solution) can pass through the semipermeable membrane.

___ 9. Benedict molecules can pass through the semipermeable membrane.

___ 10. The purpose of using the two test tubes containing the water-Benedict solution and the water-Lugol solution is to see and compare the difference in color of the solutions in other test tubes.

II. Interpretations

Directions: Fill in the blanks to make the following interpretations of the previous experiment correct.

1. Benedict solution is used to indicate the presence of _____ in a solution.
2. Lugol is used to indicate the presence of _____ in a solution.
3. _____ molecules and _____ molecules can pass through a semipermeable membrane.
4. _____ molecules cannot pass through a semipermeable membrane because they are too big.
5. The two test tubes containing a _____ solution and a _____ solution were used as controls for this experiment.
6. The bag containing the glucose and starch solution is fuller because more _____ diffused in than diffused out.

III. Implications

Directions: Using information from the previous experiment and from principles A, B, or C below, check the situations described below which you feel could occur. Be ready to explain your answers in terms of the principles and what you observed in the lab.

Principles

A. A substance moves from a region of greater concentration to a region of lesser concentration until there is an equal distribution of molecules on both sides (diffusion).
B. Smaller particles go through the cell membranes more easily and thus faster than do large particles.
C. A solution similar in nature to a solution lost by a cell will be absorbed faster than a dissimilar solution.

___ 1. Road construction causes a landscaper's tree farm once composed of dry fields to become swampy. Within a few weeks several of the trees die.
___ 2. An industrious gardener overfertilizes his plants. As a result he has a very productive garden and is able to share a lot of his produce with his neighbors.
___ 3. The body responds faster to medicine taken orally than it does to medicine taken intravenously.
___ 4. A person with only a slight case of diabetes may take insulin orally, whereas a person with a severe case of diabetes must inject insulin.
___ 5. It is impossible for a doctor to determine through a blood test whether a person has been drinking excessively, because alcohol molecules do not permeate blood cells.
___ 6. When a surgeon is transplanting an organ, it is important to keep the organ being transplanted in an isotonic solution.
___ 7. After an athlete has been working out for an extended period of time, her body cells respond faster to Gator-Ade than water.

And, as a concluding classroom example, you can see how foreign language students will also experience the process of levels of comprehension. The Spanish teacher who constructed Box 6.11 marveled at how well the guide helped to focus attention on the reading selection.

Box 6.11

THREE-LEVEL READING GUIDE

I. Leer paginas 183 y 184, "A un colegio."

Instrucciónes: Ponga una marca en cada una de las frases que usted cree que el autor de esta lectura dice. A veces las frases son iguales; en otros casos algunas palabras diferentes se pueden usar.

___ 1. Todas las escuelas de Hispanoamerica son públicas.

___ 2. Jaime y Carmen son hermanos.

___ 3. Carmen va a una escuela pública.

___ 4. La escuela de Carmen está en una antigua residencia.

___ 5. El colegio se llama Colegio San Martín.

___ 6. Carmen y Jaime van a la escuela en tren.

___ 7. En Hispanoamerica todos los muchachos y las muchachas van a la escuela juntos.

___ 8. El ambiente de las escuelas es bastante informal.

___ 9. Jaime se levanta temprano.

___ 10. La familia de Carmen y Jaime desayunan juntas.

___ 11. En Sur America el colegio es lo mismo que nuestro "high school."

___ 12. En muchos paises hispanoamericanos, si las familias tienen dinero, suelen mandar a sus hijos a escuelas particulares.

___ 13. En muchos colegios, los alumnos no van de un aula a otro.

II. *Direcciónes:* Varias frases están escritas en seguida que representan lo que quiere decir el autor y que son interpretaciónes con razón de la lectura. Ponga los numeros de las frases de la primera parte que usted cree son combinados a formar las ideas de la segunda parte:

___ a. En Sur America hay escuelas públicas y particulares.

___ b. Las familias que tienen los fondos mandan a sus hijos a escuelas particulares.

___ c. Las escuelas de casi todas las partes de Hispanoamerica son mas formales que las de los EEUU.

___ d. En muchos paises de Hispanoamerica los alumnos solo van a las escuelas los años primarios.

___ e. En algunos paises hay más alumnos que escuelas donde pueden asistir.

III. *Direcciónes:* Ponga una marca en las frases que usted cree pueden ser soportadas por las ideas del autor o por otras ideas de información que usted tiene.

___ a. Las escuelas en Sur America son más difíciles que las nuestras.

___ b. La educación de los pueblos es menos que en los EEUU.

___ c. La populación de Sur America es mucha, y no hay escuelas para todos.

___ d. Si la gente tiene buena educación, hay mejor gobierno en el pais.

As we have shown, one important way to guide comprehension is through three-level reading guides, which a teacher constructs to bridge the gap between students' competencies and the difficulty of text material. As you consider adapting three-level reading guides to content area materials, keep these summarizing points in mind. First, the three-level guide stimulates an active response to meaning at the literal, interpretive, and applied levels. It helps readers to acquire and construct knowledge from content material that might otherwise be too difficult for them to read. Second, levels of comprehension interact with one another during reading; in all probability levels are inseparable among mature readers. Nevertheless, for instructional purposes, it is beneficial to have students experience each level in order to get a feel for the component processes involved in comprehending. And third, three-level guides will help students develop a good sense of the conceptual complexity of text material.

In the next section, another type of reading guide is considered: *the pattern guide*. Pattern guides give the teacher additional options for guiding comprehension through teacher-prepared materials.

Pattern Guides

In Chapter 2, we examined how authors organize information in text. An expository text may be organized according to several major patterns or organizational structures: *cause-effect, comparison-contrast, time order, enumeration,* and problem-solution. These patterns are difficult for maturing readers to discern, but once students become aware of the importance of text organization and learn how to search for relationships in text, they are in a better position to retain information more efficiently and effectively and to comprehend material more thoroughly (Meyer, Brandt, and Bluth, 1979).

The pattern guide creates an experience for students similar to that of the three-level guide. But you can see the difference between the two guide materials at the literal level. A pattern guide helps students perceive and use the major text relationships that predominate in the reading material. Although the three-level guide focuses on a recognition of the relevant information in the material, text organization is implicit.

How, then, might you simplify the search for structure in reading materials as you teach your content? First, you should try to keep to a minimum the number of patterns that students identify and use. Second, your goal should be to guide students to recognize a single pattern that predominates over long stretches of print, even though you recognize that individual paragraphs and sentences are apt to reflect different thought relationships within the text selection.

Using and Constructing Pattern Guides

A pattern guide is a variation of the three-level guide. The difference between the two lies in the literal level: rather than have students respond to relevant information per se, you can create guide material which allows them to experience how the information fits together. Research and experience (Vacca, 1975, 1977; Herber, 1978) indicate that the following teaching sequence works well in content classes:

1. Examine a reading selection and decide upon the predominant pattern used by the author.

2. Make students aware of the pattern and how to interpret the author's meaning as part of the total lesson.

3. Provide guidance in the process of perceiving organization through a pattern guide followed by small-group or whole-class discussion.

4. Provide assistance in cases where students have unresolved problems concerning either the process and/or the content under discussion.

This sequence is deductive. Once you decide that a particular text selection has a predominant pattern, share your insights with the class. Perceiving text organization is undoubtedly one of the most sophisticated activities that a reader engages in. Chances are that most readers will have trouble recognizing text organization independently. By discussing the pattern before they read, students will develop a frame of reference which they can apply during reading. From a metacognitive point of view, discussing the pattern and why the reader should search for relationships is a crucial part of the lesson.

The pattern guide itself tears the text organization apart. The students' task, then, is really that of piecing together the relationships that exist within the predominant pattern. Interaction among class members as they discuss the guide heightens their awareness of the pattern and how the author uses it to structure information. Students learn from one another as they share their perceptions of the relationships in the reading selection.

The final step in the teaching sequence should not be neglected. As students work on or discuss a pattern guide, provide feedback that will keep them going, that will clarify and aid in rethinking the structure of the material, that will get students back into the material. Combining information is an important intellectual act requiring analysis followed by synthesis. It isn't enough, in most cases, to exhort students to "read for cause-effect" or "study the sequence." You must show them how to perceive organization over long stretches of print. Pattern guides will help you do this.

As you consider developing a pattern guide you may find it useful to follow these three steps:

1. Read through the text selection, identifying a predominant pattern.

2. Develop an exercise in which students can react to the structure of the relationships represented by the pattern.

3. Decide on how much guidance you want to provide in the pattern guide. If it suits your purposes you may develop sections of the guide for the interpretive and applied levels. Or you may decide that these levels can be handled adequately through questioning and discussion once students have sensed the author's organization through the guided reading activity.

Pattern guides help students to follow relationships among ideas. They are most suitable for expository materials, where a predominant pattern of organization is likely to be apparent.

Examining Pattern Guides from Different Content Areas

Note the variations in the first two classroom examples of pattern guides. Each was developed by a teacher to help students recognize the cause-effect pattern. In presenting the guides to their classes, the teachers followed the four-step teaching sequence just outlined. Study each illustration as a model for preparing your own guides based on causes and effects.

Auto Mechanics

The students in an auto mechanics class—part of a high school vocational arts program—were described by the teacher as "nonreaders." Most activities in the course are "hands on," as you might expect, and although the student have a textbook, it's seldom used.

But the auto mechanics teacher felt that the textbook section on transmissions warranted reading because of the relevance of the material. To help the students follow the author's ideas, the teacher constructed the pattern guide in Box 6.12.

The students worked in pairs to complete the guide. When some had trouble locating certain effects in the assignment, the teacher told them what page to study. As a result of the guided recognition of cause-effect, the teacher felt that students would better be able to handle interpretation and application through class discussion followed by a hands-on activity.

Box 6.12

POWER MECHANICS

Directions: In your reading assignment on transmissions find the causes that led to the effects listed. Write each cause in the space provided.
1. Cause: _____
   Effect: Grinding occurs when shifting gears.
2. Cause: _____
   Effect: Car speed increases but engine speed remains constant while torque is decreasing.
3. Cause: _____
   Effect: Car makers changed over to synchronizing mechanisms.
4. Cause: _____
   Effect: Helical gears are superior to spur gears.
5. Cause: _____
   Effect: Some cars cannot operate correctly with three-speed transmissions and require extra speeds.
6. Cause: _____
   Effect: Most manuals have an idler gear.
7. Cause: _____
   Effect: All cars require some type of transmission.

Social Studies

A junior high school teacher prepared a matching activity to illustrate the cause-effect pattern for students who were studying a unit entitled "The American Indian: A Search for Identity." One reading selection from the unit material dealt with Jenny, an adolescent member of the Blackfoot tribe, who commits suicide.

The teacher asked, "Why did Jenny take her life?" The question led to prereading discussion. The students offered several predictions. The teacher than suggested that the reading assignment was written in a predominantly cause-effect pattern. He discussed this type of pattern, and students contributed several examples. Then he gave them the pattern guide to complete as they read the selection—Box 6.13.

The class read for two purposes: to see whether their predictions were accurate and to follow the cause-and-effect relationships in the material. Notice that the social studies teacher included page numbers after most of the causes listed on the guide. This helped students focus their attention on the relevant portions of the text. First the students read the selection silently, then worked in groups of four to complete the pattern guide.

Box 6.13

JENNY

Directions: Select from the causes column at the left the cause which led to each effect in the effects column at the right. Put the number of the cause in the proper space in the answer box.

Causes	Effects
___ 1. Jenny took an overdose of pills (p. 9).	a. Unemployment rate for the Blackfeet is about fifty percent.
___ 2. The buffalo herds were destroyed and hunger threatened (p. 10).	b. The first victim of this life is pride.
___ 3. Indians remained untrained for skilled jobs (p. 10).	c. Blackfeet became dependent on the white man's help for survival.
___ 4. The temperature reaches 50 degrees below zero (p. 10).	d. Blackfeet turn to liquor.
___ 5. There are terrible living conditions (no jobs, poor homes, and so on) (p. 10).	e. The Indian is robbed of his self-confidence.
___ 6. Pride and hope vanish from the Black-feet (p. 11).	f. They are always downgraded.
___ 7. Because we're Indians (p. 12).	g. Eighty percent of the Blackfeet must have government help.
___ 8. The old world of the Indians is crumb-ling, and the new world of the white rejects them.	h. Hope is a word that has little meaning.
___ 9. The attitude of the Bureau of Indian Affairs (p.13).	i. She killed herself.

The examples in Boxes 6.12 and 6.13 reflect noninterlocking formats for a pattern guide. In each case the teachers were working within the literal level to facilitate students' search for text relationships in the assigned text. Pattern guides may also utilize an interlocking format, as the next example shows.

Do you recall the passage from Chapter 4 on how a Pigmy hunter kills an elephant? Notice how part I of the next guide, Box 6.14, aids you to recognize the sequence of events associated with the Pigmy's hunt. The sequence then forms the basis for the interpretive and applied levels of comprehension. Refer to the passage on page 122–123 as you work through the pattern guide.

Box 6.14

TODAY'S STONE AGE ELEPHANT HUNTERS

I. Recognizing the Sequence
Directions: The Pigmy hunter follows ten steps in hunting and killing an elephant. Some of the steps are given to you. Decide which steps are missing and write them in the spaces provided. The Pigmy hunter:

1. takes the trail of an elephant herd.
2. _____
3. selects the elephant he will kill.
4. _____
5. moves in for the kill.
6. _____
7. _____
8. pulls out the spear.
9. _____
10. cuts off _____

II. What Did the Author Mean?

Directions: Check the statements you think suggest what the author is trying to say.

___ 1. The Pigmy hunter is smart.
___ 2. The Pigmy hunter uses instinct much as an animal does.
___ 3. The Pigmy hunter is a coward.

III. How Can We Use Meanings?

Directions: Based on what you read and what you know, check the statements you agree with.

___ 1. A persons' ingenuity ensures survival.
___ 2. Where there's a will there's a way.
___ 3. There are little differences between primitive and civilized people.

Literature

A final example, the comparison-contrast pattern guide in Box 6.15, shows how the format of a guide will differ with the nature of the material (in this case, narrative) and the teacher's objectives. In Box 6.15 juniors in an English class use the pattern guide to discuss changes in character from the story "A Split Cherry Tree."

Box 6.15

"SPLIT CHERRY TREE": CHARACTER CHANGE

Directions: Consider Pa's attitude (how he feels) toward the following characters and concepts. Note that the columns ask you to consider his attitudes to these things (twice—the way he is at the beginning of the story (pp. 147–152) and the way you think he is at the end of the story. Whenever possible, note the page numbers where this attitude is described or hinted at.

At the beginning of the story what is Pa's attitude toward:		At the end of the story what is Pa's attitude toward:
	Punishment	
	Dave	
	Professor Herbert	
	School	

(continued)

His own work

His son's future

Himself

Adapt pattern guide formats to match the major organizational structures in your content materials. In doing so, students will begin to develop the habit of searching for organization in everything they read.

Selective Reading Guides

The three-level reading guide and pattern guide are mainly composed of declarative statements or matching and completion tasks. However, study guides in general have traditionally been constructed from written questions. Nearly twenty years of research on written questions have provided insights into how to ask and position questions in relation to important parts of text assignments. Selective reading guides can be devised for practical application, making full use of the knowledge gained from research. Selective reading guides use noninterlocking formats to show students how to think with print. The effective use of questions combined with "signaling" techniques help to model the way readers interact with text when reading and studying.

Using Questions Effectively

Written questions direct the readers' attention as they study content materials. What you do to guide students through the myriad relationships woven by the author will mean the difference between students who get bogged down on every word of text and students who read actively and selectively.

Teachers must come to grips with the fallacy that every word in a chapter is important to read. In most cases, this just isn't so. Some sections of a text are more important than others. Other sections may be superfluous to your instructional purposes. The instructional problem is one of helping students concentrate on relevant, essential information worth reading.

One solution to this problem is to take into account three characteristics of questions which appear to dominate textbook learning: (1) the position of a question in text, (2) the contiguity or proximity of a question to the content being questioned, and (3) the type of question asked. These characteristics are so interrelated that it is difficult to separate their influence.

Rothkopf (1966) developed an ingenious albeit simple plan to examine what happens when questions are positioned near portions of the text material. He interspersed one or two questions either before or after every one or two pages of a text selection. Questions positioned before each one- or two-page passage were called *prequestions*. Questions inserted after each passage were called *postquestions*.

Upon completing the entire reading selection, which ranged in length from 1000 to 5000 words depending on the experiment, readers were tested on the amount of specific and incidental information they had retained. Specific information included only those facts directly questioned. Incidental information referred to nonquestioned content.

Several things should be kept in mind about most of the research that Rothkopf and subsequent researchers conducted: (1) the questions usually required readers to produce factual bits of information; (2) during the reading of the selection, students were not permitted to turn back to a page once it had been read nor could they take notes while reading; (3) the questions and the text passages were written on separate sheets of paper; (4) "mostly adult"—i.e., college students—participated in the research.

In general here is what was found about the "position effect" of questions interspersed in text material. First, readers receiving factual prequestions retained just about the same amount of information *on questioned material* as those that were given factual postquestions. Second, readers given either prequestions or postquestions demonstrated greater retention of *questioned material* than groups who just read the text selection without the benefit of questions. Of most significance is the third consistent finding of the researchers: readers receiving factual postquestions interspersed in text produced greater recall of incidental information not directly questioned than readers receiving prequestions or none at all.

Rothkopf has characterized this third finding as the "indirect instructive effect" of questions. Postquestions positioned after the passages evidently "shape" the way students study the text. This shaping effect leads to both specific and incidental recall of explicit information in the reading material.

If the crossover from research to real life instruction is to be made, classroom teachers must ask, "So what?" Agreed, factual postquestions do result in greater recall of specific and incidental material than prequestions. But asking questions which direct readers to respond to isolated facts can become a superficial activity in and of itself.

Rickards (1976) predicted that a prequestion which requires a response at the interpretive level will prompt readers to perceive relationships in text in the course of deriving generalizations about the material. His prediction held true. "Conceptual prequestions" interspersed in text helped readers to better organize information and to retain it over longer periods of time than factual postquestions. Rickards's research is encouraging. Yet, what basic research on written questions tells teachers is what they have intuitively or artfully known all along: purpose makes the difference.

If your instructional purpose is to help students acquire as many facts as possible, then consider interspersing factual postquestions throughout the reading assignment. If your instructional purpose is to help students interrelate information and derive generalizations, then consider using prequestions that require an interpretive level of response.

Keep in mind the fact that prequestions as they have been discussed do not suggest a batch of questions positioned before the entire reading selection. And postquestions do not imply responding to a batch of questions after the assigned selection. One of the real contributions made by adjunct question researchers is the recognition that a written question is highly effective if it is next to the content being probed. The closer the question is to the informative material, the better it is as a stimulant.

Instructional purpose is inextricably tied to the type of questions posed. Most of the written questions devised in the adjunct question research tested readers on their accuracy to repeat factual bits of information. As Anderson and Biddle (1975) asserted: "Of practical interest is the fact that adjunct questions can do more than increase the accuracy with which people are able to repeat strings of words . . . adjunct questions which entail paraphrase and application of principles and concepts to new situations may be especially facilitative" (p. 103). Anderson and Biddle's contention reinforces what teachers witness whenever they ask questions to provoke interpretive and applied levels of thinking.

Planning Questions for Selective Guides

One way to intersperse questions throughout a text assignment is to write questions on a separate sheet of paper, providing directions which signal where and when to respond to the questions. The Planning Chart—Table 6.1—synthesizes the information on written questions presented above. The chart provides a quick and easy reference for designing study guides which rely heavily on the use of questions.

Table 6.1 Planning Chart

Instructional Purpose	Type of Question	Position of Question
1. Recall specific and incidental information during reading	Literal	After the informative text passage
2. Recall specific information during reading	Literal	Before or after the informative text passage
3. Interrelate information and derive inferences during reading	Interpretive	Before the informative text passage
4. Evaluate or elaborate upon information during reading	Applied	Before or after the informative text passage

The guide in Box 6.16 was developed for a genetics unit in a high school biology course. The teacher's purpose for developing the guide was to allow students who needed assistance with the process of mitosis to utilize text material productively. The questions excerpted from the guide give you the flavor of its format.

Note that some questions in the guide are posed before a section of text is read because they require that students clarify relationships and organize information (the questions for paragraph 3, on page 91 and paragraphs 13–16, on pages

97–98). Those questions posed after reading are to direct attention to incidental information as well as information keyed by the question. And finally, several of the reading directions do not signal either prequestion or postquestion inspection. The instructor is after questioned material only, and therefore the position of the questions isn't crucial.

Box 6.16

SELECTIVE READING GUIDE: MITOSIS

The primary objective of this assignment is to enable you to isolate the most significant events in the process of mitosis and at the same time to gain an appreciation of the fact that mitosis is a continuous process. You should also gain some appreciation of the rate and control of the process of cell division.

Directions: Read only those parts of the chapter that are listed in the reading directions. Then respond as best you can.

Reading Directions	*Questions*
1. Page 90, paragraphs 1 and 2. First read the paragraphs, then answer the questions.	Do all body cells in mammals constantly divide to produce new cells? What are the four basic activities of cells? 1. 2. 3. 4.
2. Page 91, paragraph 3. Study the questions first, then read page 91, paragraph 3.	As you read about cell division, look for indications that this process does occur in a series of steps. What does the word "morphological" mean as it is used in the passage?
3. Page 91, paragraph 5.	List as many specific events of interphase as you can.
4. Page 94, paragraphs 6 and 7.	List the specific events of prophase.
5. Pages 97–98, paragraphs 13–16. Study the question first, then read these paragraphs.	List below as many differences as you can find between the process of mitosis as it occurs in plant and animal cells: *Animal Cells* *Plant Cells*

Guiding Reading Selectively

Cunningham and Shablak (1975) discussed the importance of guiding students to respond selectively to text. They indicated that content area teachers can impart tremendous insight into how to acquire text information through a selective reading guide or in their words, a "Guide-O-Rama:"

> The teacher begins the Guide-O-Rama by determining the overall purpose for a particular reading assignment. Second, he selects those sections of the reading which are necessary to achieve this purpose.

Most important . . . he eliminates from the assignment any and all sections that are irrelevant to the purpose. Third, for those relevant sections that remain, the teacher determines, *based on his own model reading behaviors,* what a student must operationally do to achieve the purpose—step by step, section by section. *(p. 318, italics ours)*

The premise behind the selective reading guide or Guide-O-Rama rests with the notion that teachers best understand how to process information from their own subject matter. According to Cunningham and Shablak (1975), the teachers' task becomes "the creation of a step-by-step format for modeling their own appropriate behaviors" (p. 381).

Study in Box 6.17 the generic examples provided by Cunningham and Shablak to illustrate the types of reading behavior that can be signaled in the Guide-O-Rama.

Box 6.17

SIGNALING READING BEHAVIOR IN A GUIDE-O-RAMA*

Page 257, par. 3.
The last sentence of this paragraph states the main idea of the entire chapter. Change the main idea into a question.

Page 61, par. 3 and 4.
These two paragraphs describe (a) what the people of this area were up to, and (b) why they chose this particular spot. Do not read further until you are sure of these two points.

Page 42, par. 1.
The question that is raised at the end of paragraph 1 will be answered in the remainder of this reading. State this question in your own words before reading further.

Page 65, par. 2.
Before attempting to read this paragraph, turn back to page 63 and reread the last paragraph. Does what you read on page 65 give you the facts necessary to solve the problem raised back on page 63? Work with your lab partner to solve the problem. When you think you have the answer, come to me and explain what you did.

Page 61, par. 1.
Read this paragraph quickly in order to get a sense of what is going on.

Page 69, par. 3.
Before reading this paragraph, write down in two sentences what you did in Chapter 1 (don't look back—remember!). Now look at Figure 4.8 and then back to Figure 1.1. Now, do not bother to read the paragraph.

Page 44, par. 3 and 4.
This material is interesting but not essential for understanding. You may read quickly or skip entirely if you wish.

Page 66.
Slow down and read this entire page *very* carefully. It describes the living area in detail. When you have finished the reading, draw the living space as you imagine it in the space provided below.

Page 75, par. 3.
This paragraph summarizes the entire reading selection. Read it slowly. If there is anything you do not understand in this paragraph, go back to the reading and check it over carefully. Ask me if anything still bothers you.

---

*Source: Richard Cunningham and Scott Shablak, "Selective Reading Guide-o-rama: The Content Teacher's Best Friend." *Journal of Reading* 18 (1975): 380–382. Reprinted with permission of Richard Cunningham and Scott Shablak and the International Reading Association.

Box 6.18 illustrates how a junior high school social studies teacher developed a selective reading guide which mixes written questions with appropriate signals for processing the material.

Box 6.18

Selective Reading Guide for "ADVERTISING: THE PERMISSIBLE LIE"

Page 128. Read the title. Write a definition of a permissible lie. Give an example of this type of lie.

Page 128, par. 1. Do you agree with this quotation? Why or why not?

Pages 128–129. Read paragraphs 2–6 slowly and carefully. What aspects of TV were "borrowed" from radio? Write them down. From personal experience, do you think TV reflects reality? Jot an answer down, then continue reading.

Pages 129–130. Read paragraphs 7–15 quickly. What specific types of commercials are being discussed?

Pages 130–131. Read paragraphs 16–26 to find out the author's opinion of this type of commercial.

Page 131. Read paragraph 7. The author gives an opinion here. Do you agree?

Pages 131–133. Read to page 133, paragraph 45. You can skim this section, slowing down to read parts that are especially interesting to you. What are some current popular phrases or ideas in modern advertising? Think of some commercials you've seen on TV. List another word or idea or fad that's used in a lot of advertising.

Pages 133–134. Read paragraphs 45–50 quickly. Give your own example of a "sex-based" advertisement.

Page 134, par. 51. According to the author, what is a good test for an advertisement? Do you agree? Would most advertisements pass or fail the test? Try out a few.

Page 134, par. 52. Restate Comant's quote in your own words.

After reading the assignment, summarize what you read in one hundred words or less.

Numerous examples were presented of different types of reading and study guides. Space limitations prohibit us from including at least one example of the different reading and study guides for each content area. However, enough varied instructional formats were presented to model how guides might be used and developed for different instructional purposes across a wide range of texts. The ball is now in your court. We encourage you to develop and experiment with several reading and study guides for potentially difficult text assignments in your content area.

Looking Back, Looking Forward

Reading and study guides show students how to acquire information during reading. Guides can be interlocking or noninterlocking in nature. That is to say, a reading guide can be designed to have students experience what it means to respond to a text at different levels of comprehension. Such a guide is interlocking because students first respond to literal-level tasks, then to interpretive-level tasks, and then to applied-level tasks. A noninterlocking guide, on the other hand, does not assume or imply that there is a hierarchical relationship among levels of comprehension. In a noninterlocking guide students are directed to respond to portions of text according to the cognitive processes necessary to comprehend the material fully.

Various types of interlocking and noninterlocking formats were examined. The three-level reading guide is a clear example of an interlocking guide. The three-level guide stimulates an active response to meaning at the literal, interpretive, and applied levels. A pattern guide is similar to a three-level guide, except that it gives students a feel for what it means to recognize and use patterns of organization in content materials. Students begin to develop the habit of searching for organization in everything they read when they have the opportunity to perceive patterns that predominate over long stretches of print.

Questions in selective reading guides are illustrative of noninterlocking guides. These guides should be predicated on the effective use of questions interspersed throughout a text assignment. Nearly twenty years of research on written questions have provided insights into how to position questions in relation to important parts of the text material. A selective reading guide models appropriate reading behavior by illustrating how a mature reader might interact with a text assignment. Students walk through the assignment by responding to various directions, signals, and questions which direct their reading behavior.

In the next chapter we explore the role of writing in content area learning. The information presented in this chapter is intended to show how writing activity can go beyond "mechanical uses" in the content classroom.

Suggested Readings

Gray, W. (1960). The major aspects of reading. In H. Robinson (ed.), *Development of Reading Abilities. Supplementary Educational Monographs Series, no. 90.* Chicago: University of Chicago Press.

Herber, H. (1978). Levels of comprehension (Chapter 3). *Teaching Reading in Content Areas.* Englewood Cliffs, N.J.: Prentice-Hall.

Horowitz, R. (1985). Text patterns: Part I. *Journal of Reading,* **28**, 448–454.

Horowitz, R. (1985). Text patterns: Part II. *Journal of Reading,* **28**, 534–539.

Niles, O. (1965). Organization perceived. In H. Herber (ed.), *Developing Study Skills.* Newark, Del.: International Reading Association.

Olson, M., & Longnion, B. (1982). Pattern guides: A workable alternative for content teachers. *Journal of Reading,* **25**, 736–741.

Robinson, H. A. (1983). *Teaching Reading, Writing, and Study Strategies: The Content Areas* (3rd ed.). Boston: Allyn and Bacon.

Vacca, R. T. (1975). Development of a functional reading strategy: Implications for content area instruction. *Journal of Educational Research,* **69**, 108–112.

CHAPTER 7

Writing to Learn

*We do not write in order to be understood; we write in
order to understand.*
—C. DAY LEWIS

Organizing Principle

Writing is not without its rewards or surprises. The surprises are discovering what you want to say about a subject; the rewards lie in knowing that you crafted to satisfaction that which you wanted to say. C. Day Lewis didn't sit down at his desk to write about things that were already clear in his mind. If he did, there would have been little incentive to write. Lewis used writing first to discover and clarify meaning—*to understand*—and second, to communicate meaning to others—*to be understood*.

Reading and writing have been taught in most classrooms as if they bear little relationship to one another. The result has often been to sever the powerful bonds for meaning making that exist between reading and writing. From our vantage point, there's little to be gained from teaching reading apart from writing. The organizing principle reflects this notion: *Writing to learn is a catalyst for reading and studying course material.*

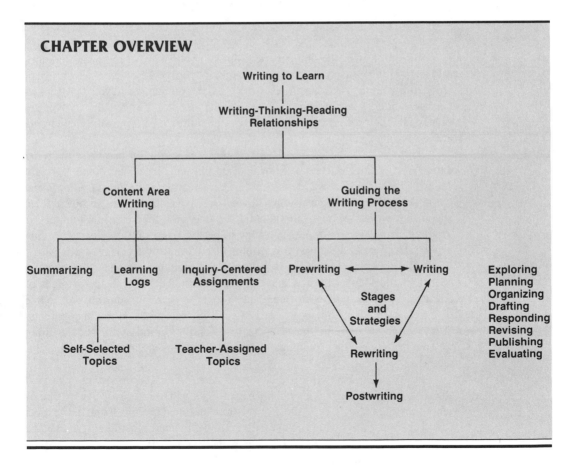

CHAPTER OVERVIEW

Study the relationships depicted in the Chapter Overview. The questions below are pivotal to your understanding of the material presented in the chapter. When you finish reading, you should be able to answer these questions fully.

1. Why emphasize writing to learn in content area subjects?

2. How does writing influence thinking? What is the relationship between writing and reading?

3. Why and how should writing be extended in content area classrooms?

4. Why is summarizing information a potentially useful learning activity? What do students need to know about writing a summary?

5. Explain the uses of learning logs.

6. How can teachers guide inquiry-centered writing through student-selected topics and teacher-made assignments?

7. Why should writing be thought of and taught as a process? Explain various strategies that are integral to each stage of the writing process.

Sinclair Lewis, the first American author to win a Nobel prize for literature, said that writing is just work. It doesn't matter if "you dictate or use a pen or type or write with your toes—it is still just work." Microcomputers and word processors notwithstanding, writing isn't easy for most people. Yet for those who are successful, the process of writing—sweat and all—is enormously challenging and rewarding.

Perhaps for this reason Allyse's mother was a little bit perplexed with her daughter's writing. Allyse is thirteen years old and, by all accounts, a bright student. Yet her mother was bewildered by her daughter's writing activities *in* and *out* of school. "She'll spend hours slaving over pages to mail to an out-of-state friend, but writes skimpy, simple-minded paragraphs for school assignments." When questioned about the discrepancy in her writing, Allyse's gut-level reply was all the more confusing. "But, Mom, that's what my teachers want."

Allyse may never win a Nobel prize for literature. But she does have a need to write. Most children and adolescents do. Often, just out of sight of teachers, students will write continually to other students during the course of a school day—about boys, girls, teachers, intrigues, problems, parents, or on just about anything that happens to be on their mind at a particular time. The topics may not be academically oriented, but they are all quite real and immediate to students.

In Allyse's case, writing to an out-of-state friend is so important to her that she is willing to struggle with a blank page to "keep in touch." However, as far as school writing is concerned, she probably has "psyched out" what teachers expect from her. She knows what she needs to do to get by and, most likely, to even be successful. Allyse intuitively understands the role of writing in her classes and operates within that context.

Although writing occupies a big chunk of lesson time in secondary schools, we believe that it is rarely given much instructional attention by most content area specialists other than perhaps English teachers. While students are often observed engaging in some form of writing, we wager that few teachers make conscious decisions or plans related to the uses of writing in the content classroom. Just as we argued in Chapter 1 that reading infrequently enters the plans of many content area teachers (other than to assign students textbook pages), writing also happens in classrooms, but its uses have been limited in scope.

One important aspect of a major study of writing was to observe writing taking place throughout the academic year in various content area classrooms in two midwestern high schools (Applebee, 1981). In order to describe the writing observed in the classrooms, Arthur Applebee looked at the ways in which teachers used writing to achieve their content objectives. He classified their uses of writing into four categories based on the kinds of writing activity observed.

One category of writing activity was described by Applebee as the *mechanical uses of writing;* that is, "writing without composing" in which students were not required to generate ideas, explore meaning, or communicate to others. A second category was classified as the *informational uses of writing*. The focus of this type of writing was on the information students convey about course-related material through the production of text. A third category, *personal uses,* involved activities such as keeping a journal or letter writing, where the writing focused on the interests and activities of the writer. The *imaginative uses of writing* was the fourth category and it was characterized by story writing, poems, play scripts, or other literary forms.

Within the framework of these four categories of writing, Applebee's findings were revealing. He noted:

> Pooling all observations, *an average of 44 percent of the observed lesson time involved writing activities of one type or another*. These activities were dominated by mechanical and informational uses of writing (occurring during an average of 24 and 20 percent of observed time, respectively). Informational writing was dominated by note-taking (17 percent of observed time). . . . *On average only 3 percent of lesson time was devoted to longer writing requiring the student to produce at least a paragraph of coherent text.* (italics ours)

Allyse's response to her mother's question begins to make sense. It reflects what researchers such as Applebee have consistently observed to be the role of writing in content classrooms; namely, that it is mainly restricted to mechanical uses, one- or two-sentence responses to study questions, or note taking. While the purposes behind these uses may be legitimate, students must have varied and broader experiences with writing. Three good reasons compel teachers to take a second look at the role of writing in their classrooms. First, writing improves thinking. Second, it is a valuable tool for learning. Third, writing is intimately related to reading. One vital way to help students study and comprehend what they read is through the act of composing.

There is no better way to think clearly about a subject than to have the occasion to write about it. Clear thinking and clear writing go together. Little wonder that Edward Albee, the contemporary playwright, once said, "I write to find out what I'm thinking about." However, the mere act of writing doesn't necessarily guarantee improved thinking or learning. Teachers, through what they say and do, can give students a choice. On the one hand, a teacher can create situations where students more or less go through the motions, often producing lifeless writing lacking purpose or commitment. On the other hand, a teacher can create an environment for writing in which students work hard to discover what they have to say about a subject and how best to say it. The classroom environment for writing lends encouragement to inexperienced student writers and provides instructional support so that students can play with ideas, explore concepts, and synthesize what they are learning in a content class.

Albeit writing can be a powerful force in thinking and learning, but why include a chapter on it in a content area reading textbook? Our reason is simple enough: students who write, read more. Or as Moffett and Wagner (1983) put it, "The best way . . . to learn to comprehend is to compose" (p. 10). A good way to think about reading and writing is that they are two sides of the same coin. Both the reader and the writer are involved in meaning making. While the writer works to make a text sensible, the reader works to make sense out of text.

There's gold to be mined in extending the uses of writing in the content classroom. Writing to learn can be a springboard for reading and studying course material. Conversely, reading can be a catalyst for writing to learn.

Writing in Content Classrooms

Creating occasions to write regularly is a powerful strategy for learning subject matter. Myers (1983) put it best: "Students who participate in a writing to learn program are likely to learn more content, understand it better, and retain it longer" (p. 7). This is the case because writing activities promote thinking and learning, *but in different ways*. Writing a summary of a reading selection, for example, is likely to result in greater understanding and retention of important information. However, another type of writing task—let's say an essay—may trigger analysis and synthesis when the task calls for the application of ideas to a new situation.

Because writing promotes different types of learning, a broad spectrum of writing experiences should be integrated into content area instruction. As we noted in the beginning of this chapter, Arthur Applebee's research, which has included The National Study of Writing in the Secondary School, funded by the National Institute of Education, examined the instructional contexts in which students are asked to write (Applebee, 1984). The National Study has provided a comprehensive look into school-based writing activities. It includes reports of case studies of individual schools, nationally conducted school surveys, analyses of popular textbooks, and longitudinal studies of the writing activities of individual students. In general, the National Study has affirmed that writing plays a paltry role in school learning. Instructional activities have focused almost exclusively on paragraph-or-less answers to study questions or on note taking.

We do not deny the usefulness of study questions (a topic that was examined in Chapter 5) or taking good reading and listening notes (a topic of discussion in the next chapter). Yet we deplore instructional situations which miss the boat by not engaging students in writing to learn through activities such as summaries, learning logs, and other inquiry-centered writing assignments emphasizing the process of manipulating and extending ideas. So let's look at some ways that the context for writing in content classrooms can be improved and broadened.

Writing to Summarize Information

Summarizing information from textbook selections can be a valuable writing to learn activity but it has been too infrequently used in content area classrooms. In fact, only in the past several years has summarization received its due as a potentially important learning activity. Much of the recent attention is the result of text-based research which has shown that summary writing helps students to understand and retain important ideas (Kintch and vanDijk, 1978; Brown, Compione, and Day, 1981; Brown, Day, and Jones, 1983).

Writing a summary involves reducing text to its gist—to its main points. To become adept at summary writing, students must be able to discern and analyze text structure. If they are insensitive to the organization of ideas and events in expository or narrative writing, students will find it difficult to distinguish important from less important information. Good summarizers, therefore, guard against including information that is not important to the text passage being condensed. Immature text learners, on the other hand, tend to *retell* rather than condense information, often including interesting but inessential tidbits from the passage in their summaries. Good summarizers write in their own words but are careful to maintain the author's point of view and stick closely to the sequence of ideas or events as presented in the reading selection. When important ideas are not explicitly stated in the material, good summary writers create their own topic sentences to reflect textually implicit main ideas.

The recent work of educators and psychologists leads us to conclude that most students experience some level of difficulty in summarizing information. However, the older the students, the more skilled they appear to be at planning ahead and writing summaries (Brown and Day, 1983; Brown, Day, and Jones, 1983). As might be expected, good readers are better summarizers than poor readers. Winograd (1984), for example, compared good and poor readers in the eighth grade on their ability to write summaries. First, through interviews, Winograd found that most of the eighth graders, regardless of reading ability, knew that a summary included the most important ideas from a passage. However, in actual summary writing performance, poor readers had difficulty identifying what adults judged to be the important ideas in a passage. They also had trouble using the rules and steps associated with the task of summarizing.

In various parts of this book, Chapters 5 and 6 in particular, we have explored how to help text learners identify and infer important ideas. In Chapter 8, we examine outlining strategies that show students how to organize and relate ideas to one another. Sensitivity to textually important ideas and relationships is the first step in learning how to summarize effectively. However, students must also understand and become aware of the *task demands* inherent in summarization. That is to say, they must learn the rules or procedures necessary to reduce text to its bare essence.

Learning How to Summarize

Kintch and vanDijk (1978) were among the first to formulate a set of basic rules for summarization based on analyses of how people summarize effectively. Others have modified and adapted these rules, but generally students must become cognizant of the following procedures:

1. *Include no unnecessary detail.* In preparing a summary, students must learn to delete trivial and repetitious information from a text passage.

2. *Collapse lists.* When a text passage includes examples, details, actions, or traits, students must learn how to compact these into broader categories of information. With frequent exposure to instructional strategies such as structured overviews, vocabulary categorization exercises (explained in Chapter 9), and outlining strategies (explained in Chapter 8), students will soon become aware that similar items of information can be subsumed within more inclusive concepts. They must learn to summarize information by collapsing a list of details and thinking of a key word or phrase that names its concept. Study the examples that Hare and Borchardt (1984) gave: ". . . if you saw a list like eyes, ears, neck, arms, and legs, you could say 'body parts.' Or, if you saw a list like ice skating, skiing or sledding, you could say 'winter sports' " (p. 66).

3. *Use topic sentence.* Expository text sometimes contains explicit topic sentences which tell what a paragraph is about. However, if a paragraph doesn't have a topic sentence, students must learn to create their own for a summary. This is probably the most difficult task demand placed on maturing learners.

4. *Integrate information.* Summarizers must learn how to use key words, phrases, and explicit and invented topic sentences to compose a summary. The first three rules help students to do the "leg work" for summarizing. In other words, the rules *prepare* students for writing the summary. Yet when they actually put ideas into words on paper, they must integrate the information into a coherent piece of writing.

5. *Polish the summary.* Because writing to learn often follows a composing process, students must learn to revise a *draft* of a summary into a more organized, natural-sounding piece of writing. While "rethinking" a summary, students will get a firmer grasp on the main points of the material and state them clearly.

Hare and Borchardt (1984) used essentially the same rules above for an experimental instructional program for minority high school students. They utilized direct, explicit instructional techniques to show the students how to use the rules to write a summary. The instructional sessions included knowledge building to ensure that the students knew what a summary was and were aware of the rules. Once cognizant of how procedures worked, the students were given practice, feedback, and review in how to write a summary. Also, the teachers used modeling techniques to demonstrate the steps. Culminating activities led to writing summaries on their own. The students made significant progress in their efficiency and utilization of rules to write a summary, especially when compared to students who did not receive such training. In Chapter 8, we explain an instructional framework for teaching study strategies which uses explicit training procedures similar to those developed by Hare and Borchardt.

Using the GRP to Write a Summary

Teachers can show students how to write a summary not only through explicit, direct training but also through strategies such as the Guided Reading Procedure (GRP). The GRP has already been explained in Chapter 5, pages 163–165. As you may recall, after students have read a text passage, they turn their books face down and try to remember everything that was important in the passage. Their recalls are recorded by the teacher on the chalkboard. Seize this opportune moment to show students how to delete trivial and repetitious information from the list of ideas on the board. As part of the procedure, the students are given a "second chance" to return to the passage, review it, and make sure that the list contains all of the information germane to the text.

When this step is completed, the teacher then guides students to organize the information in outline form. Here is where students can be shown how to collapse individual pieces of information from a list into conceptual categories. These categories can be the bases for identifying or creating topic sentences. The students can then integrate the main points into a summary.

The Hierarchical Summary Procedure.

The rules and procedures for writing a summary are complicated. Nevertheless, Taylor (1982) showed that with extensive teacher guidance, middle grade students can improve their ability to summarize information.

Taylor proposed a "hierarchical summary procedure" that directs students' attention to the organization of ideas in expository textbook selections. She found that the procedure increases the amount of information students recall after reading textbook material. In addition, it improves the overall quality of students' expository compositions (Taylor, 1983). Here's how the hierarchical summary procedure works:

1. Assign students to *preview* a three- to five-page textbook selection. The selection must have main headings and subheadings. Then show students how to create a *skeletal outline* for the selection. On the board, write a Roman numeral for every major section in the selection that is designated

by a main heading, and a capital letter for every subsection designated by a subheading. Leave about five or six spaces between capital letters. An example of a skeletal outline follows:

In the example above, the text selection has one major section with four subsections. (Chapter 8 contains additional information on strategies for previewing and using different kinds of outlining formats.)

2. Direct the students to use the outlines *as a study guide*. As they read the material the students should do the following:

— With the help of the teacher, the students write *in their own words* a main idea statement for each subsection as they read the selection.

— When the main idea is written for the first subsection, the students should list several important details to support the main idea in the space provided on the outline.

— As a class, the students discuss their main idea statement and the supporting details. Make sure that the students are on the right track. You may have to demonstrate and explain this aspect of the procedure until students fully understand the task.

— The students repeat the procedure with the remaining subsections contained within the first major section of the outline. Once the subsections are completed, students now generate *in their own words* a topic sentence for the major section they have just read. They write the topic sentence in the space designated by the appropriate Roman numeral on their outlines.

— Then, in the left margin of their outlines, the students write key words or phases for any subsections which appear to go together. They should draw lines between the key phrases and corresponding subsections. This is similar to collapsing a list of ideas into its main point or concept.

— Next, class discussion centers on students' topic sentences and key phrases.

— When students have been walked through the first section of the summary outline, they work, if necessary, on finishing each remaining section until the outline is completed.

Box 7.1 depicts a summary outline that was completed for a social studies text selection with one major heading and five subheadings.

Box 7.1

AN EXAMPLE OF A HIERARCHICAL SUMMARY FOR SOCIAL STUDIES TEXT SELECTION CONTAINING ONE HEADING AND SIX SUBHEADINGS*

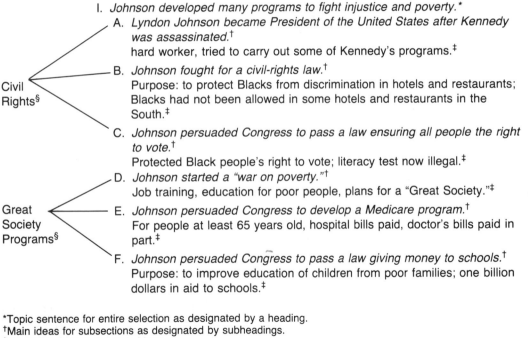

I. *Johnson developed many programs to fight injustice and poverty.**

A. *Lyndon Johnson became President of the United States after Kennedy was assassinated.*[†]
hard worker, tried to carry out some of Kennedy's programs.[‡]

Civil Rights[§]

B. *Johnson fought for a civil-rights law.*[†]
Purpose: to protect Blacks from discrimination in hotels and restaurants; Blacks had not been allowed in some hotels and restaurants in the South.[‡]

C. *Johnson persuaded Congress to pass a law ensuring all people the right to vote.*[†]
Protected Black people's right to vote; literacy test now illegal.[‡]

D. *Johnson started a "war on poverty."*[†]
Job training, education for poor people, plans for a "Great Society."[‡]

Great Society Programs[§]

E. *Johnson persuaded Congress to develop a Medicare program.*[†]
For people at least 65 years old, hospital bills paid, doctor's bills paid in part.[‡]

F. *Johnson persuaded Congress to pass a law giving money to schools.*[†]
Purpose: to improve education of children from poor families; one billion dollars in aid to schools.[‡]

*Topic sentence for entire selection as designated by a heading.
[†]Main ideas for subsections as designated by subheadings.
[‡]Supporting details for main ideas.
[§]Key phrases connecting subsections.

*Reprinted with permission from the International Reading Association and Barbara Taylor, "A Summarizing Strategy to Improve Middle Grade Students Reading and Writing Skills," *The Reading Teacher,* November 1982, p. 203.

Students should participate in structured class discussions with plenty of feedback and modeling for the first *three* summary outlines. According to Taylor, after completing three summaries, students should be able to do their own with minimal teacher help. By the *sixth* application of the procedure, they should be able to work completely on their own.

3. Use the summary outline for a variety of study and writing activities. One of its real benefits is in providing *rehearsal* situations for studying text. For example, a summary outline is excellent for review purposes, especially if a student is paired with a classmate, in which case they can alternate telling each other everything they know and remember about each subsection of a reading selection. In addition, the summary outline can be a springboard for writing. It can be the basis for assigning students to compose a written summary of the reading selection. Or the outline can be used for more extensive writing assignments. In this case, students must extend and synthesize what they have learned from the reading selection. The summary outline, then, serves as a planning tool for the prewriting stage of the composing process. Guiding the writing process through stages such as prewriting is explained in more depth later in the chapter.

The hierarchical summary procedure makes provisions for close reading which can become tedious. Therefore, we recommend using it intermittently so that students do not get bored with the procedure. However, the first six applications of the strategy should proceed on a steady basis over a several-week span so that students build knowledge and awareness of the step in the procedure.

Polishing a Summary

A good summary often reflects a process of writing *and* rewriting. Learning how to write a "polished" summary is often a neglected aspect of instruction. When students reduce large segments of text, the condensation often is stilted. It sounds unnatural. We are convinced that students will learn and understand the main points better and retain them longer when they attempt to create a more natural-sounding summary which communicates the selection's main ideas to an audience, i.e., a reader such as the teacher and/or other students. Rewriting in a classroom situation is often preceded by *response* to a draft—by peers and the teacher. We deal in much more detail with responding and revising situations in a later section of this chapter. For now, however, let us suggest the following:

— Compare a well-developed summary that the teacher has written with the summaries written by the students. Contrasting the teacher's version with the student productions leads to valuable "process" discussions such as the use of introductory and concluding statements, the value of connectives like *and* and *because* to show how ideas can be linked, and the need to paraphrase, i.e., "putting ideas into your own words" to convey the author's main points.

— Present the class with three summaries: One is good in that it contains all of the main points and "flows" smoothly. The second is OK: it contains most of the main points but is somewhat stilted in its writing; the third is poor in content and form. Let the class rate and discuss the three summaries.

— Team students in pairs or triads and let them read their summaries to one another. "Student response groups" are one of the most effective ways to create feedback for writing in progress.

— In lieu of response groups, use the whole class for responding. With prior permission from several students, discuss their summaries. What were the merits of each one and how could they be improved for content and form?

The real learning potential for summary writing lies in students using their own language to convey the author's main ideas. Often, they will find it difficult to put content ideas into their own words. This is one of the reasons why learning logs can be an important learning activity. Logs serve several functions in writing to learn. In Chapter 3, for example, we recommended their use for evaluative purposes. In the next subsection, we expand on the instructional uses of logs in the content classroom.

Using Learning Logs

Learning logs add a new dimension to personal learning in content area classrooms. Also referred to as *journals* or *thought books,* learning logs are probably one of the most versatile writing to learn strategies available to students and teachers in any subject area. And one of the most productive.

The strategy is simple to implement but must be used regularly to be effective. Students keep an ongoing record of learning *as* it happens in a notebook or looseleaf binder. They write in their own language, not necessarily for others to read but to themselves, about what they are learning. Entries in logs influence learning by revealing problems, clarifying thinking, and generating ideas and questions.

There is no one way to use learning logs, although teachers often prefer allowing five or ten minutes at the end of a period for students to respond to "process questions" such as the following: "What did I understand about the work we did in class today? What didn't I understand? At what point in the lesson did I get confused? What did I like or dislike about class today?" The logs can be kept in a box and stored in the classroom. The teacher then reviews them during or after school to see what students are learning and to better understand their concerns and problems. Let's take a look at how two teachers integrate logs into their instructional contents.

Two Math Teachers

Two math teachers have reported using learning logs with much success in their classrooms. Mr. Kennedy, a middle school teacher, has designed what he calls a "writing in math" program where learning logs are a key feature (Kennedy, 1985). In addition to the process questions above, he likes to ask students what they're wondering about. What specific questions do they have about material being studied? He also finds that logs are effective for "making notes." According to Kennedy, the distinction between taking and making notes is central to the use of learning logs: "Taking notes is copying someone else's information; *making* notes is writing interpretive comments and personal reminders such as 'Ask about this' or just 'Why?' " (p. 61).

And then there's Ms. Church, a high school Algebra II teacher. She introduces learning logs to her class this way:

> From time to time, I'll be asking you to write down in your logs how you went about learning a particular topic in this class. In other words, can you capture that moment when things finally made sense to you and how you felt? And can you express the frustration that might have preceded this moment? *(Pradl and Mayher, 1985, p. 5)*

Students at first might be tentative about writing and unsure of what to say or reveal—after all, this type of writing is reflexive and personal. It takes a trusting atmosphere to "open up to the teacher." However, to win the trust of students, teachers like Ms. Church refrain from making judgmental or evaluative comments when students admit a lack of understanding about what's happening in class. If a trusting relationship exists, students will soon recognize the value of logs, although perhaps not as enthusiastically as one high school student:

> This journal has got to be the best thing that's hit this chemistry class. For once the teacher has direct communication with every member of the class. No matter how shy the student is they can get their lack of understanding across the teacher. . . . These journals act as a "hot line" to and from the teacher. I feel this journal has helped me and everyone that I know in class. The only thing wrong is we should have started these on the first day of school!! In every class! *(Pradl and Mayher, 1985, p. 8)*.

Ms. Church's students probably feel the same way about their Algebra II class. Here are some of the things that they do in their logs. For starters, Ms. Church likes to start a new topic by asking students to jot down their predictions and expectations of what the topic might involve. She also has her students write down their understanding of any new theorem that is introduced. After students feel that they have learned a theorem well, they use their logs to imagine how they might explain the theorem to another person, less well informed, like a younger sister or brother.

Both Ms. Church and Mr. Kennedy use logs to have students create word problems that are then used to challenge other members of the class. Kennedy likes to have students write different kinds of word problems in their learning logs: "Sometimes I have them supply the data (for example, 'Write a problem involving the use of percent'); other times I supply the data (for example, 'Write a problem using the numbers 200, 400, and 600')" (Kennedy, 1985, p. 51).

Most learning log activities require thinking but do not demand a "finished product." Students soon learn to write without the fear of making errors involving spelling, punctuation, capitalization, or grammar. Emphasis is on communicating content ideas or problems with content, not with the surface level of the writing.

However, there are times when students should know in advance that learning log entries will be read aloud in class. According to Levine (1985), this is when students often produce their best writing, because they are composing for an audience of peers. Josh, for example, an eighth grader, wrote about a lab experiment this way:

> Today in class we did a demo to try and find effective ways of recovering the solute from a solution.
>
> Several people came up with ideas as to how we could do this. A few people suggested filtering the solution, and others thought heating the solution so it evaporated would bring the solute back.
>
> First we tried filtering a copper sulfate solution but found that process didn't work. Evidently the crystals had dissolved to such an extent, that they were too small to be gathered by the filter paper.
>
> We then heated the solution and found we were far more successful than in our first try. Approximately thirteen minutes after we began heating the solution, a ring of copper sulfate crystals appeared in the bowl where the solution was. Eventually all the liquid evaporated leaving only the crystals.
>
> Quite obviously I learned that to recover the solute from a solution you can heat the solution. I also learned not to bother trying to filter the solution. *(Levine, 1985, p. 45)*

Jeremy's "letter" to the President, after studying the effects of nuclear war in his social studies class, reflects both personal and informative writing:

> November 7, 1983
>
> Dear Mr. President,
>
> How is life in the White House? In school we have been studying the horrible effects of a nuclear war. The United States alone has enough nuclear weapons to wipe out 1 million Hiroshimas. The earth doesn't even have that many cities that big.
>
> In a nuclear war 1.1 billion people would be killed outright, and they are the lucky ones. Another 1.1 billion would suffer from burns and radiation sickness.
>
> 1 nuclear warhead or 2 megatons is 2 million tons of TNT, imagine 15 megatons . . .
>
> During a nuclear war buildings and people would be instantly vaporized. The remaining people would starve to death. The radiation would be 250 rads or 1,000 medical x-rays which is enough to kill you.
>
> After all this I hope you have learned some of the terrible facts about nuclear war. *(Levine, 1985, p. 44)*

Learning log writing is often called "free" writing because students like

Jeremy are able to express what's on their minds honestly—without pretense. *Freewriting* in logs has several advantages. One is to use freewriting to generate and discover ideas.

Freewriting

Use learning logs to engage students in sustained, spontaneous writing as a way of generating ideas. When asked to freewrite, students shouldn't be concerned with form or correctness. As Draper (1982) stated:

> The instructor emphasizes that the purpose of the free writing is to generate a flow of words and thoughts without concern for polished phrases or mechanics. The writer is not to worry about spelling, punctuation, grammar, complete sentences, or paragraphs. He is to write, keep writing, and if a block occurs, to repeat the last written word again and again until another thought comes.   *(p. 153)*

To write freely, students must look within themselves. The writing they produce mirrors personal knowledge and is often loosely structured. For this reason, freewriting has also been called *expressive writing* (Britton, 1975).

Ken Macrorie (1970) and Peter Elbow (1973)—strong advocates of freewriting—recognized the writer's need to remove the often self-imposed pressure of "getting it right" the first time. Such pressure usually leads to "writer's block"—the inability to get started or come to grips with a writing task. However, as the name implies, freewriting places no restriction on the writer's thinking. The writer, sticking close to self, puts into words whatever comes to mind. The result over time is often twofold: (1) improved fluency (the volume and quantity of writing increases) and (2) the emergence of the writer's attitude toward the subject (his stance or voice). Here's where the learning log enters the picture.

Teachers should direct students to write freely in their logs on topics they are studying in class. "Focused freewriting" leads to an exploration of important concepts and content-related objectives. It allows students to write as much as they can *about the given topic* within a specified period of time (usually five to ten minutes) without the pressure of competing or being evaluated.

Students should be encouraged to react to one another's freewritings. Whole-class or small-group discussions can focus on whether the writer told an audience everything it needed to know. Class members can make suggestions as to what ideas need to be developed. What advice do they have to help the writer focus on a topic or clarify his or her purpose? Is the writer attempting to do too much or too little?

The learning log is a versatile and productive writing to learn strategy. Students can write about anything that is pertinent to learning a subject—from making notes to telling what they have accomplished, or they can participate in more elaborate tasks like freewriting.

The act of discovery is integral to freewriting. Inquiry-centered writing tasks also promote discovery.

Inquiry-Centered Writing

The backbone of any unit of study should be individual and/or group inquiry. The inquiry process "opens the self" for the reading of many different kinds of materials. Developing inquiry-centered writing assignments helps students to understand and synthesize what they're learning.

Inquiry-centered writing must be carefully planned, giving just the right amount of direction to allow students to explore and discover ideas on their own. The inquiry process isn't a "do your own thing" proposition, for budding researchers need structure. Many an inquiry project has been wrecked on the shoals of nondirection. The trick is to strike a balance between teacher guidance and student self-reliance. An inquiry activity must have just enough structure to give students (1) a problem focus, (2) physical and intellectual freedom, (3) an environment where they can obtain data, and (4) feedback situations to share the results of their writing.

Box 7.2 outlines various aspects of the procedures for guiding an inquiry-centered writing project.

Box 7.2
_____

PROCEDURES FOR GUIDING INQUIRY-CENTERED WRITING PROJECTS

I. Raise Questions, Identify Interests, Organize Information
   A. Discuss interest areas related to the unit of study
   B. Engage in goal setting
      1. arouse curiosities
      2. create awareness of present level of knowledge
   C. Pose questions relating to each area and/or subarea
      1. "what do you want to find out?"
      2. "what do you want to know about _____ ?"
      3. record the questions or topics.
      4. "what do you already know about _____ ?"
   D. Organize information; have students make predictions about likely answers to gaps in knowledge
      1. accept all predictions as possible answers
      2. encourage thoughtful speculations in a nonthreatening way

II. Select Materials
   A. Use visual materials
      1. books and encyclopedias
      2. magazines, catalogues, directories
      3. newspapers and comics
      4. indexes, atlases, almanacs, dictionaries, readers' guides, card catalog
      5. films, filmstrips, slides
      6. videotapes, television programs
   B. Use nonvisual materials
      1. audiotapes
      2. records

3. radio programs
4. field trips
C. Use human resources
1. interviews
2. letters
3. on-site visitations
D. Encourage self-selection of materials
1. "what can I understand?"
2. "what gives me the best answers?"
III. Guide the Information Search
A. Encourage active research through
1. reading
2. listening
3. observing
4. talking
5. writing
B. Facilitate with questions
1. "how are you doing?"
2. "can I help you?"
3. "do you have all the materials you need?"
4. "can I help you with ideas you don't understand?"
IV. Have Students Keep Records
A. Keep a learning log which includes plans, procedures, notes, rough drafts, etc.
B. Keep book-record cards
C. Keep a record of conferences with the teacher
V. Consider Different Forms of Writing
A. Initiate a discussion of sharing techniques
B. Encourage a variety of writing forms:
1. an essay or paper
2. a "lecture" to a specific audience
3. a case study
4. story, adventure, science fiction, etc.
5. dialogue, conversation, interview
6. dramatization through scripts
7. commentary or editorial
8. thumbnail sketch
VI. Guide the Writing Process
A. Help students organize information
B. Guide first-draft writing
C. Encourage responding, revising, and rewriting
D. "Publish" finished products
1. individual presentations
2. classroom arrangement
3. allow for class interaction

Finding and Investigating Problems

Ideally, an inquiry arises out of the questions that students raise about the subject under study. A puzzling situation may arouse curiosity and interest. Or perhaps the teacher will provoke puzzlement through a discussion of differences in opinion, a reaction to inconsistencies in information in content material, or a response to an emotional issue. Joyce, Weil, and Wald (1972) recommended using questions to initiate an inquiry such as the following:

How is _____ different from _____? How are they alike?
What has changed from the way it used to be?
What can we learn from the past?
What caused _____ to happen? Why did it turn out that way?
What will happen next? How will it end?
How can we find out?
Which way is best?
What does this mean to you? How does this idea apply to other
  situations?

As a result of questioning, students should become aware of their present level of knowledge and the gaps that exist in what they know. They can use the questioning session to identify a problem. You might ask, "What do you want to find out?" During the planning stage of an inquiry the emphasis should be on further analysis of each individual or group problem, breaking it down into a sequence of manageable parts and activities. The teacher facilitates by helping students to clarify problems. As students progress in their research, data collection and interpretation become integral stages of the inquiry. Students will need the physical and intellectual freedom to investigate their problems. They will also need an environment—a library or media center—where they will have access to a variety of information sources including (1) printed materials (books and encyclopedias; magazines, catalogues, directories; newspapers), (2) nonprinted materials (audiotapes; records; films, filmstrips, slides; videotapes, television programs), and (3) human resources (interviews; letters; on-site visitations).

The teacher's role during data collection and interpretation is that of a resource. Your questions will help the student interpret data or perhaps raise new questions, reorganize ideas, or modify plans. "How are you doing?" "How can I help?" "Are you finding it difficult to obtain materials?" "Which ideas are giving you trouble?"

Using the Library and Reference Materials

In addition to textbooks, three sources of information are basic to learning and instruction in content area subjects. They are (1) reference sources which contain specialized information, (2) books and pamphlets pertinent to the content area, and (3) periodical sources of information dealing with a specific subject. Gaining access to these sources means that students need a working knowledge of *where to go and how to use information* not usually housed in their classrooms.

For this reason we endorse in principle the need for systematic, organized instruction in the use of the library.

Knowing what the sources of information are and how to use those sources become the main goals for instruction. To put these goals into practice, teachers should provide preliminary or review activities such as the following:

1. *Introduce students to the ways libraries work.* Plan an informal tour to take a class to the library. Locate the loan desk, reference desk, and magazines; point out posted regulations and physical arrangements. The students will get a look at others using the library; later have a discussion about their observations. Also, invite a librarian to speak to the class (in the library if possible) about his or her job responsibilities. Encourage students to ask the librarian about procedures. Have them guess what kinds of questions are usually asked of librarians.

2. *Provide brief "search encounters" in the library.* Ask students to think of questions they personally want answered about the subject they are studying. Subsequent introductory instruction on library use can then be built naturally around helping students answer their own questions. Act as a resource person while the students learn to use reference books, periodical indexes, and card catalogs. After two or three individual, personal "search encounters," students should be ready to use the library for larger inquiry tests.

3. *Reinforce library skills that are truly basic.* Once students acquire the basic concepts behind the library as a learning resource, it's time for some direct advice on how to become "library-wise." The basic approach to "intelligent library use at all levels" centers around how to locate (1) general information through general reference books; (2) specific information through periodical indexes; (3) ideas and information in greater depth through books from card catalogs (Devine, 1981). Locate and explain encyclopedias, dictionaries, almanacs, periodical indexes, and the card catalog (divided according to author, title, and subject). Also explain and distinguish between the Dewey Decimal and Library of Congress call number systems.

Systematic instruction in using the library and reference materials pays off. This becomes apparent when you observe students in the library who have had this instruction. Instead of simply going "to the same shelves" continually, they are now able to locate sources of information for specific purposes.

Procedures for guiding the writing process and sharing students' writing are discussed in the next major section. However, before proceeding to this discussion, we acknowledge that not all inquiry-based writing tasks involve self-selected topics. There are many occasions when teachers will assign topics to investigate. These assignments involve students in the writing process and may or may not include extensive library and field work.

Teacher-Assigned Topics

The key to good student writing on teacher-assigned topics is to design good writing assignments. The teacher's primary concern should be with how to make an assignment *explicit* without stifling interest or the spirit of inquiry. An assignment should provide more than a subject to write on. Topic-only assignments can quickly turn students off. The ambiguity of a topic-only situation is often too much to overcome.

Suppose you were assigned one of the topics below to research and write on:

— the arms race,

— batiking,

— the role of the laser beam in the future,

— victims of crime.

No doubt, some of you would probably begin writing on one of the topics without hesitation. Perhaps you already know a great deal about the subject, have strong feelings on it, and can shape the direction of the discourse without much of a problem. Others, however, might resist or even resent the activity. Your questions might echo the following concerns: "Why do I want to write about any of these topics in the first place? For whom am I writing? Will I write a paragraph? an essay? a book?" The most experienced writer must come to grips with questions such as these, and even more complicated ones, "How will I treat my subject? What stance will I take?" If anything, the questions raise to a level of awareness the *rhetorical context*—the *purpose, audience,* and *form* of the writing, and the writer's *stance*—that most writing assignments should provide. A rhetorical context for writing allows students to assess the writer's relationship to the subject of the writing (the topic) and the reader (the audience for whom the writing is intended). Lindemann (1982) suggested a *communications triangle* to show how the context can be defined. Some of the questions raised by the relationships among writer-subject-reader within the communications triangle are depicted in Figure 7.1. The writer plans a response to the writing assignment by asking questions such as: "Who am I writing this for? What do I know about my subject? How do I feel about it? What stance can I take in treating the topic?" A good assignment, then, *situates* students in the writing task by giving them a purpose for writing and an intended audience. It may also allude to the form of the writing and the stance the writer will take toward his or her topic.

Creating Lifelike Contexts for Writing

Students need to know why they are composing and for whom. One of the ways to characterize discourse, oral or written, is through its aims or purposes. As students approach a writing assignment, let them know its purpose. Is the writing aiming at personal expression? Is it to persuade? describe? explain? Or is it to create a text

Figure 7.1 A Communications Triangle: Defining a Rhetorical Problem for Writing*

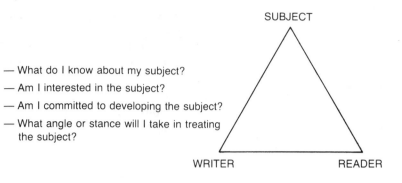

— What do I know about my subject?
— Am I interested in the subject?
— Am I committed to developing the subject?
— What angle or stance will I take in treating the subject?

— Who am I writing this for?
— What kind of response am I looking for?
— What does the reader need to know to understand the subject?

which can be appreciated in its own right for its literary or imaginative quality? These purposes are broad, to be sure, but each underscores an important aim of discourse (Kinneavy, 1971).

Some writing assignments will stimulate inquiry when they create lifelike situations in which the purpose for writing is directly tied to the audience. Instead of assigning an essay on "how to batik," give students a situation to ponder:

> To show that you understand how batiking works, imagine that you are giving a demonstration at an arts and crafts show. Describe the steps and procedures involved in the process of batiking to a group of on-lookers, recognizing that they know little about the process, but are curious enough to find out more.

— What do I know about my subject?

— Am I interested in the subject?

— Am I committed to developing the subject?

— What angle or stance will I take in treating the subject?

— Who am I writing this for?

— What kind of response am I looking for?

— What does the reader need to know to understand the subject?

Or take, as another example, "the arms race" topic:

> The debate over the arms race has people taking different sides of the argument. There are some who argue that the arms race will lead to a nuclear holocaust. There are others who contend the arms race is the only way to maintain peace in the world.

*Adapted from Erika Lindemann, *A Rhetoric for Writing Teachers*. New York: Oxford University Press, 1982.

You have been selected to write a "position paper" for the class in which you debate your side of the argument. Another student has been selected to defend an opposing position. The class will then vote on the most persuasive of the two positions.

Once you have investigated the issue thoroughly, convince as many classmates as possible that your position is the best one. Your paper should be long enough to persuade the class effectively.

As you can see from the two examples, each creates a lifelike context, identifies a purpose, an audience, and suggests the writer's stance and a form of discourse, i.e., a "position paper" or "demonstration." In each case, students will not necessarily make the assumption that the teacher is the audience, even though ultimately the teacher will evaluate the written product. McAndrew (1983) portrayed the reality of classroom audiences this way:

The real audience in the classroom is the teacher. Let's admit that up front. The teacher in his/her role as teacher-as-grader — is always and inescapably the audience for class assignments. But if we are to improve our students' writing skills, we must . . . try to create situations that allow students to experience writing to a variety of audiences even though we know, and the students know, that somewhere down the line the teacher will be the audience. *(p. 49)*

Additional Examples

Writing assignments can be designed to create lifelike contexts for a variety of instructional purposes. Daigon (1979, p. 118) showed how assignments can direct students to write to an audience other than the teacher:

— Write to Hercules. After telling him which of the 12 tasks he handled best, describe a task that needs to be done in your town that only he could do.

— Tell Cinderella about your troubles with sisters or brothers and how you handled it. Or, tell Cinderella's fairy godmother how you would use her magic powers to have the very best day or night of your life.

— Write to the author and suggest changes or additions you would like to see in the story.

Daigon further suggested that assignments should be addressed to any appropriate reader — other students, real or fictional characters, people, alive or dead — who might be interested in the subject.

In addition to activities which address an audience other than the teacher, assign students to assume the roles or identities of others in situations that specify an audience. Notice how Daigon (1979, p. 119) adapted the activities above so that student writers would have the opportunity to take a stance by writing in a voice other than their own:

— You are Hercules. Tell Jupiter, your father, about the task you found most difficult to do and how you managed to do it.

— Make believe you are Cinderella. Write what is going through your mind as you see your sisters preparing for the ball.

— Pretend you are the villain and write to the author of the story giving reasons why he/she should change the ending so that YOU win the contest instead of the main character.

Assignments such as these contrive situations and audiences in the context of what is being read or studied. However, they are far from trivial, nonacademic, or inconsequential. Instead, when students "become" someone else they must look at situations in a nontraditional way. After writing, they can compare different stances on the same issue and examine the validity of the viewpoints that were taken.

Although some writing assignments may contrive situations and audiences, others should reflect real situations and audiences outside the classroom. For example, letters to the editor of the local newspaper, to political leaders, authors, and scientists can be an important part of classroom study. We will have more to say on audience identification later in this chapter when we examine the role of "publication" in the writing process.

Discourse Forms

A write to learn program recognizes that content ideas can be expressed through a variety of writing forms. These discourse forms can be easily incorporated into the context of writing assignments. Tchudi and Yates (1983) provided a representative listing of some of these forms for content area writing. See Figure 7.2.

Figure 7.2 Some Discourse Forms for Content Area Writing*

Journals and diaries (real or imaginary)	observations
Biographical sketches	public/informational
Anecdotes and stories:	persuasive:
from experience	to the editor
as told by others	to public officials
Thumbnail sketches:	to imaginary people
of famous people	from imaginary places
of places	Requests
of content ideas	Applications
of historical events	Memos
Guess who/what descriptions	Resumés and summaries
Letters:	Poems
personal reactions	Plays
	Stories

*Reprinted from Stephen Tchudi and JoAnne Yates, *Teaching Writing in the Content Areas: High School*. Washington, D.C.: National Education Association, 1983, p. 12.

Fantasy
Adventure
Science fiction
Historical stories
Dialogues and conversations
Children's books
Telegrams
Editorials
Commentaries
Responses and rebuttals
Newspaper "fillers"
Fact books or fact sheets
School newspaper stories
Stories or essays for local papers
Proposals
Case studies:
  school problems
  local issues
  national concerns
  historical problems
  scientific issues
Songs and ballads
Demonstrations
Poster displays
Reviews:
  books (including textbooks)
  films
  outside reading
  television programs
  documentaries
Historical "you are there" scenes
Science notes:
  observations
  science notebook
  reading reports
  lab reports
Math:
  story problems

solutions to problems
record books
notes and observations
Responses to literature
Utopian proposals
Practical proposals
Interviews:
  actual
  imaginary
Directions:
  how-to
  school or neighborhood guide
  survival manual
Dictionaries and lexicons
Technical reports
Future options, notes on:
  careers, employment
  school and training
  military/public service
Written debates
Taking a stand:
  school issues
  family problems
  state or national issues
  moral questions
Books and booklets
Informational monographs
Radio scripts
TV scenarios and scripts
Dramatic scripts
Notes for improvised drama
Cartoons and cartoon strips
Slide show scripts
Puzzles and word searches
Prophecy and predictions
Photos and captions
Collage, montage, mobile,
  sculpture

When students write in a particular discourse form, the work bears a stamp of authenticity.

Although a good assignment doesn't fully prepare students to engage in writing, it does give them a framework for planning and drafting. How teachers guide students through "stages" of the writing process ensures successful writing.

Guiding the Writing Process

A blank page is the writer's call to battle. Getting started can be difficult, even terrifying. However, a good writer recognizes the difficulty of the undertaking and finds it stimulating. Writing is motivating.

Some writers come to grips with the blank page by performing one or more "starting rituals." Pencils are sharpened, the desk top cleared of clutter. Eventually, the first words are put on paper and everything which has occurred to this point — all of the mental and physical gymnastics a writer goes through — and everything that will happen toward completion of the writing task — can best be described as a process.

One of the teacher's first tasks is to make students aware that the writing process occurs in stages. It's the exceptional student who leaps in a single bound from a "finished product" in his or her head to a "finished product" on paper. In this book, the stages of writing are defined broadly as *prewriting, rewriting,* and *postwriting.* Figure 7.3 overviews these stages.

Figure 7.3 Stages in the Writing Process*

Prewriting	
"getting it out"	Exploring and generating ideas
	Finding a topic
	Making plans
	audience?
	form?
	voice?
	Getting started
Writing	
"getting it down"	Drafting
	Sticking to the task
	Developing fluency and coherence
Rewriting	
"getting it 'right' "	Revising for meaning
	Responding to the writing
	Organizing for clarity
	Editing and proofreading for
	the conventions of writing,
	word choice, syntax
	Polishing
Postwriting	
"going public"	Publishing and displaying
	finished products
	Evaluating and grading

*Adapted from Dan Kirby and Tom Liner, *Inside Out: Developmental Strategies for Teaching.* Montclair, N.J.: Boynton/Cook Publishers, Inc., 1981.

By no means are the stages in the writing process neat and orderly. Few writers proceed from stage to stage in a linear sequence of events. Instead, writing is a "back-and-forth" activity. Exploring and generating ideas before writing may lead to plans for a piece of writing, but once engaged in the physical act of composing, writers often discover new ideas, reformulate plans, write, and revise.

Lindemann (1982) described stages in the writing process as recurring or *recursive*. In other words, writing is

> . . . a messy business, rarely in real life as tidy as textbook descriptions portray it. We don't begin at step one, "find a topic," and follow an orderly sequence of events to "proofreading the paper." Certainly, we plan what we want to say before we begin drafting, but the act of writing generates new ideas and shapes new plans. In other words, prewriting and writing occur at the same time. So can writing (drafting) and rewriting, for we never commit words to paper without changing at least one or two here and there. *(p. 23)*

Figure 7.4 depicts the "back-and-forth" nature of writing as different steps or procedures that recur as writers move toward completion of a composition.

Figure 7.4 The Recursive Nature of the Writing Process

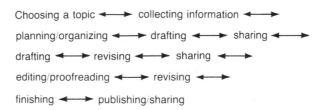

Exploring, Planning, and Organizing

What students do before writing is as important as what they do before reading. Prewriting activity, like the prereading strategies discussed in Chapter 4, involves planning, building and activating background knowledge, setting goals, and getting ready for the task at hand. In other words, prewriting refers to everything that students do before the physical act of putting words on paper for a first draft. Actually, the term *prewriting* is somewhat misleading because students often engage in some form of writing before working on a draft. As we have shown, freewriting in learning logs is a good strategy for the student writer.

The time and energy spent before writing might best be described as rehearsing (Graves, 1978). Rehearsal is what the writer consciously or unconsciously does to get "energized" — to get ideas out in the open, to explore what to say and how to say it. What will I include? What's a good way to start? What is my audience? What form should my writing take? Prewriting instruction involves any activity or experience that motivates a student to write, generates ideas for writing, or focuses attention on a particular subject. Through prewriting preparation, students can be guided to think about a topic in relation to a perceived audience and the form that a piece of writing will take. A teacher who recognizes that the writing process must slow down at the beginning will help students to discover that they have something to say and that they want to say it.

Getting started on the right foot is what prewriting is all about. Generating discussion about an assignment before writing buys time for students to gather ideas and organize them for writing. Discussion prior to writing is as crucial to success as discussion prior to reading. In preparing seniors to write letters to the editor concerning the legal age for drinking in Ohio, a "Problems in Democracy" teacher asked students for their opinions: "At what age do you think people in Ohio should be permitted to drink alcoholic beverages?" The discussion among the senior students, as you might anticipate, was animated. The teacher followed the discussion by assigning a newspaper article on the legal age issue. Further discussion generated more ideas and helped students formulate a stand on the issue.

Many of the reading strategies in Chapter 4, with some modification, can be used effectively for writing situations. Several strategies in particular will help students to rehearse for writing by gathering and organizing ideas: *brainstorming, clustering,* and *jot-charting*.

Brainstorming

A frequently used prewriting strategy is brainstorming. Brainstorming permits students to examine ideas from content area lessons as rehearsal for reading or writing. In doing so, it helps them to set purposes for reading or writing, because it gives students problems to solve. Examine how the following two variations on brainstorming can easily be adapted to writing situations:

1. Present a concept or problem to students based on some aspect of what they have been studying. Set a time limit for brainstorming ideas or solutions. The teacher calls "Stop" but allows *one more minute* for thinking to continue. Creative ideas are often produced under time pressure.

   In a high school special education class for students with "learning problems," several weeks had been spent on a unit dealing with the Civil War Era. As part of their study of the Reconstruction period, students explored issues such as the rebuilding of the South and the dilemma presented by freed slaves. One of the culminating learning experiences for the chapter on freed slaves concerned a writing activity designed to help students synthesize some of the important ideas that they had studied. As part of her introduction of the writing assignment, the teacher began the prewriting phase of the lesson with the lead-in: "Using any information that you can recall from your text or class discussion, what might have been some of the problems or concerns of a freed slave immediately following the Civil War? "Let's do some brainstorming." As students offered ideas related to prejudice, lack of money, homes, and food, the teacher listed them on the board. Getting ideas out in the open in this manner was the first step in her prewriting strategy. In the next subsection on *clustering*, we'll discuss how the teacher used brainstorming as a stepping stone for students to organize ideas and make decisions about the writing assignment.

2. Engage students in "brainwriting" (Rodrigues, 1983). Here's how it works. Divide the class into small groups of four or five students. Each group member is directed to jot down ideas about the writing assignment's topic on a sheet of paper. Each student then places his or her paper in the center of the group, chooses another's list of ideas, and adds to it. The group compiles the best ideas into a single list and shares them with the class. The advantages of brainwriting include: (1) the contribution of every student, and (2) the time to consider ideas.

Brainstorming techniques allow students to become familiar with a topic and, therefore, to approach writing with purpose and confidence. Often teachers combine brainstorming with another prewriting strategy — *clustering*.

Clustering

Clustering is similar to *semantic webbing (mapping)*, which is explained in the next chapter as a strategy for outlining information. To introduce the concept of clustering, the teacher should write a key word on the chalkboard and then surround it with other associated words that are offered by the students. In this way students not only gather ideas for writing but also connect the ideas within categories of information. Teacher-led clustering provides students with an awareness of how to use the prewriting strategy independently. Once they are aware of how to cluster ideas around a topic, students should be encouraged to create their own clusters for writing.

A cluster can take many different forms but essentially student writers must connect supporting ideas to a key concept word by drawing lines and arrows to show the relationships that exist:

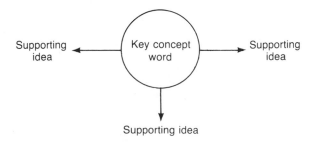

For each supporting idea, students can generate additional ideas (examples, details) which are connected by lines to extend the cluster:

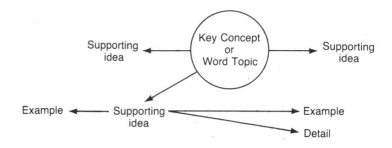

In one of the earlier brainstorming examples, we described how a special education teacher used the list of ideas generated by her students to explore the concerns of freed slaves during the post–civil war period. This was a first step in the pre-writing phase of the writing activity. The second step was to cluster the words into meaningful associations based on student suggestions. The teacher modeled the activity by choosing as the key word the concept of "Freed Slaves." She then drew a line to the upper right-hand corner of the chalk board and connected the key word to the word *problems*. She connected some of the words generated by students during brainstorming to the cluster. The teacher then asked what some of the results of the freed slave's problems would be. One student volunteered the word *suffering*. The teacher wrote *suffering* in the upper left-hand corner of the cluster and asked students to brainstorm some examples. These examples were then connected to the cluster.

The remainder of the prewriting experience centered on discussion related to the *aid* freed slaves received and the *opportunities* that resulted from the Reconstruction years. Examine Box 7.3, which depicts the completed cluster that the teacher and students produced on the chalkboard.

With the cluster as a frame of reference, students were assigned to write what it would have been like to be a freed slave in the 1860s and '70s. They were asked to consider what the form of the writing should be. Since the textbook presented a variety of primary sources (diary entries, newspaper clippings, death notices), the students could, if they decided, write in one of those forms. Or, they could approach the writing activity as a historian would and write an account that might be read by other students as a secondary source of information. One member of the class became so involved in the activity that he wanted his historical document to appear authentic "by aging" the paper. This he did by burning the edges so that it would look "historic." (See Figure 7.5.)

Students should begin to develop their own clusters for writing as soon as they understand how to use the strategy effectively. They should feel comfortable enough to start with a basic concept or topic—written in the center of a sheet of paper—and then to "let go" by making as many connections as possible on the paper. Connections should develop rapidly, "radiating outward from the center in any direction they want to go" (Rico, 1983, p. 35). Since there is no right or wrong

Box 7.3

Free slaves immediately after Civil War

way to develop a cluster, students should be encouraged to play with ideas based on what they are studying and learning in class.

The value of clustering in writing shouldn't be sold short. Gabriele Rico (1983), a leading proponent of this prewriting strategy, maintained that it not only "unblocks and releases" information stored in the student writer's mind, but it also generates inspiration for writing. Moreover, clustering becomes a self-organizing process. According to Rico (1983), "As you spill out seemingly random words and phrases around a center, you will be surprised to see patterns forming until a moment comes—characterized by an 'Aha!' feeling—when you suddenly sense a focus for writing" (p. 35). Students can discuss their clusters in small groups and share their plans for writing. Or, as Rico recommended, they can begin to write immediately after clustering.

Jot-charting

Like clustering, jot-charting provides a way for students to organize information. However, it doesn't rely on freely associating ideas to a key concept word. Instead, jot-charting helps students to collect and connect ideas by outlining them on a matrix. The strategy is especially appropriate for writing that relies on explanation and description of ideas, people, events, characters, or processes.

Figure 7.5
Student's Writing Sample on What it would be like to be a Freed Slave

> May 3, 1866
>
> My mane is Toby and I had been a slave for eight years before we were freed. It was good at fist But them we realizied there were problems.
>
> We had great prolblems. Prejudice kept us from doing what we wanted to do. Black Codes which were suppose to help Didnt help us at all. We werent allowed to be out after dark. We werent allowed to Carry a gun. We werent allowed to go out without a pass.
>
> We had mo food. my famly had mo food. my kids were all sick and there was mothing I could do nothing to help them. We had mo money to buy any medicine to help them.
>
> But there was some mice people. They were the army and Quakers helped my kids get better and they helped us get some land and food for my famly. then we started a farm we grew crops and got money.
>
> We had some opertumites. We could move to anther state for a Job. We could also get an Education. Some Blacks even gained Gooerment positions.

Across the top of the matrix, list some of the main ideas that are to be analyzed or described in the writing assignment. Along the side of the matrix, list some of the areas by which these ideas are to be considered. As part of the prewriting preparation, students complete the chart by jotting notes and ideas from course material, class lectures, etc., in the spaces created by the matrix.

A language arts teacher used jot-charting as a planning tool for a writing activity that compared famous heroes from the stories that the class had read. The activity directed students to write about how the heroes (David, Hercules, Beowulf) approached and handled challenges. The jot-chart in Box 7.4 helped students to reread selectively and to take notes in preparation for the writing assignment.

Box 7.4

JOT-CHART FOR "STORIES ABOUT HEROES"

	David	Hercules	Beowulf
Each hero's feelings when confronted with his challenge.			
How did each hero handle his challenge?			
How did each hero react after conquering his challenge?			

Students in the language arts class discussed their jot-charts before engaging in writing. Jot-charting can be an effective outlining tool for writing and also has value as a study strategy in that it provides a framework upon which students can organize and relate information.

Guiding the First Draft

The writing stage involves getting ideas down on paper in a fluent and coherent fashion. The writer drafts a text with an audience (readers) in mind.

If students are well rehearsed for writing, first drafts should develop without undue struggle. The use of in-class time for first-draft writing is as important as alotting in-class time for reading. In both cases, teachers can regulate and monitor the process much more effectively. For example, while students are writing, a teacher's time shouldn't be occupied grading papers or attending to other unrelated chores. As Tchudi and Yates (1983) explained in *Writing in the Content Areas,* teachers can do much to influence the quality of writing and learning *as* students are writing:

When students are writing during class time, the teacher can take an active role. For example, monitor facial expressions—they often tell when a student is starting to get in a jam and needs help. Float around the class during a writing assignment, glancing at first paragraphs and rough beginnings, offering advice if it seems needed—In other words, help students get it right *while* they are writing and encourage them to solve problems the first time around.   *(pp. 12–17)*

The writing stage, then, should be a time to confer individually with students who are having trouble using what they know to tackle the writing task. Serve as a sounding board or play devil's advocate: "How does what we studied in class for the past few days relate to your topic?" or "I don't quite understand what you're getting at. Let's talk about what you're trying to say." Students should also have the opportunity to confer with one another: "There are great benefits from such forms of peer collaboration as encouraging writers to bounce ideas off one another, reading draft paragraphs aloud to seek advice, pumping their friends for new advice" (Tchudi and Yates, 1983, p. 17). Teacher feedback and peer collaboration underscore the importance of *response* in the writing process.

Responding and Revising

Rewriting helps students to "take another look"—to rethink a paper. This is why good writing often reflects good rewriting. From a content area learning perspective, rewriting is the catalyst for clarifying and extending concepts under study. Rewriting text hinges on the feedback students receive between first and second drafts.

Teacher feedback is always important, but it's often too demanding and time consuming to be the sole vehicle for response. It may also lack the *immediacy* that student writers need to "try out" their ideas on an audience—especially if teachers are accustomed to taking home a stack of papers and writing comments on each one. The "paper load" soon becomes unmanageable and self-defeating. An alternative is to have students respond to the writing of other students. By working together in "response groups," students can give reactions, ask questions, and make suggestions to their peers. These responses to writing-in-progress lead to revision and refinement during rewriting.

Student Response Groups

The purpose of peer response groups is to provide a testing ground for students to see how their writing influences a group of readers. Writers need response to sense the kinds of changes they need to make.

Healy (1982) made an important distinction between *response* and *evaluation*. Response involves an initial reaction to a first draft. The reaction is usually in the form of questions to the writer about the content and organization of the writing. Both teacher and student share responsibility for responding. Evaluation, on the other hand, involves a final assessment of a piece of writing that has progressed through drafts. The teacher has primary responsibility for evaluating a finished product.

Learning to respond to writing in peer groups requires training. Response groups must be "phased in" gradually—students can't be expected to handle response tasks in groups without extensive modeling and coaching. Moreover, response groups shouldn't be initiated too early in the school year. After a month or two of regular writing activity, students will be more confident in their writing ability and will, in all probability, have developed some fluency in their writing. It is at this point that they are ready to be introduced to responding and rewriting situations.

The following steps, adapted from Healy (1982) and Camp (1982), provide enough structure to shift the burden of feedback from teacher to students:

Step 1. Discuss students' attitudes toward school writing and attempt "to shape new ones if existing attitudes are constricting or counterproductive" (Healy, 1982, p. 268). For example, talk about writing as a process that occurs in stages. When students are engaged in an important writing task that will be presented to others ("published"), they shouldn't expect a finished product in one sitting. A first draft is often rough around the edges. It usually needs focus and clarity. Let students know what you value in their writing. Moreover, emphasize the importance of "trying out" writing on an audience before tackling a final draft. Tryouts are a time to react as readers to writing, not nitpick over errors or correct writing as evaluators.

Step 2. Use the whole class as a response group to demonstrate how to give feedback to a writer. On an overhead transparency, show a paper what was written by an "anonymous" student from a different class. Read the paper aloud and talk about it. The goal is to practice talking about writing without posing a threat to any of the students. Camp (1982) suggested kicking off discussion with the question: "If you were the teacher of this student, and you received this paper, what would you decide to teach the student *next,* so that the next paper he or she writes will be better than this one?" (p. 21). Let the class brainstorm responses. List their suggestions on the chalkboard, and then ask the students to reach a consensus as to the most important points for improvement. Conclude the discussion by acknowledging that responses to content and organization have a higher priority than to mechanics. Writers-in-progress need feedback on how to set their content and organize it before attending to concerns related to spelling, capitalization, punctuation, and grammar.

Step 3. On an overhead transparency, project another paper from a different class and ask students to respond to the writing by making comments or raising questions. Write these on the transparency next to the appropriate section of the paper. You may find that students have difficulty with this task, so demonstrate several responses that tell what is positive about the paper. What do you as a reader like about it? What is done well?

Note the differences between *useful* and *useless* feedback. The response, "This section is confusing," is of little help to the writer because it isn't specific enough. A useful response, however, is one in which the writers learn what information a reader needs: "I was confused about the Bay of Pigs invasion. Did Kennedy fail to give backup support to the commandos?" Students will soon catch on to the idea that a response gives information which helps the writer to better understand the needs of an audience.

Step 4. Form small groups of three or four students. Distribute dittoes of a paper that was written in a different class. Also pass out a "response sheet" to guide the group discussions. The response sheet contains several questions which pattern what to look for in the writing. In Figure 7.6 Camp (1982) used a response sheet to guide response to a paper based on a personal experience.

Figure 7.6 Example of a Response Sheet*

RESPONSE SHEET: PERSONAL EXPERIENCE WRITING

WRITER _____

RESPONDER _____

A. What did you like best about this paper? What worked really well?

_____

_____

_____

_____

B. What questions would you ask the writer about things in this paper that were confusing or unclear to you?

_____

_____

_____

_____

C. Where in the paper would you like more detail? Where could the writer show instead of telling?

_____

_____

_____

_____

D. Rate each of the following on a scale from 1 to 4. 4 is tops.
  1. Beginning _____   3. Ending _____
  2. Use of conversation _____   4. Title _____

*From Gerald Camp, *A Success Curriculum for Remedial Writers*. Berkeley, Calif.: The National Writing Project, University of California, Berkeley, 1982, p. 28.

E. For each item you scored low, make a suggestion for improvement.

_____

_____

_____

_____

Tchudi and Yates (1983) provided categories of questions to ask in response groups. The questions relate to *purpose, content, organization, audience, language,* and *style* and are presented in Figure 7.7. Note that students shouldn't respond to more than three or four questions in any one response group session. Choose or devise questions that are the most appropriate to the writing assignment.

Figure 7.7 Questions for Response Groups*

Note: Do not have students ask *all* these questions (or similar ones) at every revising session. Rather, pick some questions that seem most appropriate to your assignment and have the students work on two or three each time.

PURPOSE
- Where is this writing headed? Can readers clearly tell?
- Is it on one track, or does it shoot off in new directions?
- Is the writer trying to do too much? Too little?
- Does the author seem to *care* about his/her writing?

CONTENT
- When you're through, can you easily summarize this piece or retell it in your own words?
- Can a reader understand it easily?
- Are there parts that you found confusing?
- Are there parts that need more explanation or evidence?
- Are there places where the writer said too much, or overexplained the subject?
- Can the reader visualize the subject?
- Does it hold your interest all the way through?
- Did you learn something new from this paper?

ORGANIZATION
- Do the main points seem to be in the right order?
- Does the writer give you enough information so that you know what he/she is trying to accomplish?
- Does the writing begin smoothly? Does the writer take too long to get started?
- What about the ending? Does it end crisply and excitingly?

*From Stephen Tchudi and JoAnne Yates, *Teaching Writing in the Content Areas: Senior High School.* Washington, D.C.: National Education Association, 1983, p. 20.

AUDIENCE

- Who are the readers for this writing? Does the writer seem to have them clearly in mind? Will they understand him/her?
- Does the writer assume too much from the audience? Too little?
- What changes does the writer need to make to better communicate with the audience?

LANGUAGE AND STYLE

- Is the paper interesting and readable? Does it get stuffy or dull?
- Can you hear the writer's voice and personality in it?
- Are all difficult words explained or defined?
- Does the writer use natural, lively language throughout?
- Are the grammar, spelling, and punctuation OK?

Once students have completed the response sheets have them share their comments with one another. Return to a whole-class format to draw conclusions about the activity.

Step 5. Form response groups to discuss first drafts that the students have written. Healy (1982, p. 274) recommended the following conditions for working in small groups:

— Keep the groups small — two to five at first.

— Sit as far away as possible from other groups for noise control.

— Write the names of your response partners on the top of your original draft.

— After hearing a paper read, ask the writer any comments or questions which occur to you. The writer will note the questions on the paper.

— Encourage the writer to ask for help with different sections of his/her paper.

— Make all revisions on your original draft before doing the final. Staple both copies together.

A variation on these conditions is to use response sheets to guide the group discussions. They are particularly useful in the beginning when the task of responding is still new to students. However, with enough modeling and practice, response sheets will probably not be necessary.

One additional point: during the revision of the original draft, encourage students to be messy. For example, show them how to use carets to make insertions, and allow them to cross out or to cut and paste sections of text, if necessary. The use of arrows will help students show changes in the position of words, phrases, or sentences within the text.

Once feedback is given on the content and organization of a draft, response group members should work together to edit and proofread their texts for spelling, punctuation, capitalization, word choice, and syntax. Accuracy counts. "Cleaning up" a text shouldn't be neglected, but students must recognize that concern for proofreading and editing comes toward the end of the process.

Revising a text is hard work. Some students even think that *rewriting* is a dirty word. They mistake it for recopying—emphasizing neatness as they painstakingly transcribe from pencil to ink. They need a good rationale for "going the extra mile." One solid reason is the recognition that their work will be presented to others. Publishing is an incentive for revising. As Camp explained, ". . . the final draft of all major writing assignments are published in some way. This final step is . . . just as essential as any of the others" (p. 41). If writing is for reading—and indeed it is—then teachers must find ways to value students' finished products.

Publishing

Kirby and Liner (1981, p. 215) gave four good reasons for publishing students' written products:

1. Publishing gives the writer an audience, and the writing task becomes a real effort at communication—not just writing to please the teacher.

2. Publishing is the only reason for the writing to be important enough for the hard work of editing and proofreading.

3. Publishing involves the ego, which is the strongest incentive for the student writer to keep writing.

4. Publishing is fun.

Most students realize early in their school experience that the teacher is their only audience for writing. When the audience is not described in a writing assignment, students typically assume that the teacher will be the sole reader. Topic-only assignments reinforce this assumption:

— How does the Soviet government squelch dissidents?

— Argue for or against smoking in public places.

— What causes "acid rain"?

We do not deny or denigrate the importance of the teacher as an audience. Neither do students. We agree with Purves (1983) that ". . . schools, real institutions that they are . . . should teach writing for general audiences represented by the real teacher" (p. 44).

However, when the classroom context for writing encourages a range of possible audiences for assignments (including the teacher), the purposes for and the quality of writing often change for the better. This is why we called for audience-specific writing assignments early in the chapter.

When students know that their written products will be presented publicly for others to read, they develop a heightened awareness of audience. Teachers need to mine the audience resources that exist in and out of the classroom. As we just showed, response groups are one way to share writing-in-progress. Here are some ways to share finished products.

Oral Presentations to the Class

Reading finished papers aloud is a natural extension of peer responding for work-in-progress. When the writing is tied directly to content objectives, students not only have fun sharing their products, but they also learn a great deal from their colleagues. We recommend the frequent use of read-aloud sessions as a way of publishing so that all students will at one time or another have an opportunity to present.

Teachers should establish a tone of acceptance during oral presentations of original writing. The writer reads; the listeners react and respond. One variation is to establish a "professional conference" atmosphere wherein student "scientists," "historians," "literary critics," "mathematicians," "business executives," etc., convene to share knowledge with one another. Several students who have written on a related topic might even present a symposium—in which case one or two of their classmates should serve as discussants. Opportunities for learning abound when the focal point for class reaction and discussion centers around student-developed texts.

Class Publications. Class-produced newspapers, magazines, anthologies, and class books are excellent ways to publish student writing. These vehicles for publication fit in effectively with the culmination of a unit of study. Identify a title for a class publication that reflects the theme or objective or the unit. For example, *The Civil War Chronicle,* a magazine produced by an eleventh-grade American History class, was patterned after the formats found in *Time* and *Newsweek.* A ninth-grade English class studying *To Kill a Mockingbird* put together *The Maycomb Register.* The students researched events associated with the time period (1936) set in the novel and wrote a variety of local (related to the story), national, and international news items. The teacher had students involved in all phases of the newspaper's production, including typesetting and layout. She even had the paper professionally printed. To pay for the printing, the students sold the newspaper to schoolmates, parents, and neighbors.

Producing a newspaper or a magazine requires teamwork and task differentiation. We suggest that students participate not only as writers, but also work in groups to assume responsibility for editing, proofreading, design, and production. Production of a class publication need not be as elaborate or expensive an activity as *The Maycomb Register.* Dittoed publications have the same effect on student writers when they see their work in print.

Room Displays

Display student writing. As Kirby and Liner (1981) found, ". . . a display of finished products attracts attention and stimulates talk and thinking about writing" (p. 217). Establish a reading fair in which students circulate quietly around the room reading as many papers as they can. Judy and Judy (1981) suggested that student writers provide blank sheets of paper to accompany their finished products so that readers can comment. They also recommended "one-of-a-kind" publications for display. These publications "preserve" the writing in a variety of forms (folding books, leaflets, scrolls, quartos, and folios). In their book, *Gifts of Writing* (1980), the Judys have outlined numerous formats for one-of-kind publications.

Publishing for Real World Audiences

Letters, community publications, commercial magazines, and national and state contests are all vehicles for "real world" publishing outside of the classroom and school. Letters, in particular, are valuable because there are so many audience possibilities:

> Students can write everyone from school officials to administrators of policies in education, industry, and business. They can write to artists, musicians, poets and actors to offer adulation or criticism. They can write on issues of immediate concern or long range interest. *(Judy and Judy, 1981, p. 119)*

In addition to letters, the local newspaper, PTA bulletin, or school district newsletter sometimes provide an outlet for class-related writing activity. Commercial magazines (see Appendix D for a list of addresses compiled by Teachers and Writers Collaborative) and national and state writing contests also offer opportunities for publication. Commercial magazines and writing contests, of course, are highly competitive. However, the real value of writing for commerical publication lies in the authenticity of the task and the audience-specification it provides.

Guiding the writing process leads to products which eventually must be evaluated. How do teachers assign grades to writing which has progressed through drafts?

Evaluating and Grading

The paperload in classrooms where writing happens regularly is a persistent matter of concern for teachers. They often blanch at the prospect of grading 125 or more papers. A science teacher reacted to us in a workshop this way: "The quickest way to squelch my interest in writing to learn is to sock me with six sets of papers to correct at once." We couldn't agree more—weekends weren't made for drowning in a sea of red ink.

Yet the notion of what it means to evaluate written work must be examined. Evaluating "to correct" papers is an inappropriate concept in a "process approach" to writing. It suggests that the teacher's role is primarily one of detecting errors and making corrections or revisions in papers. Overemphasis on error detection often telegraphs to students that correctness rather than the discovery and communication of meaning is what writing is all about. Content area teachers who view their job as an error hunt soon become, and understandably so, reluctant to devote hours to reading and "correcting" papers.

The types of errors that often take the most time to detect and correct are those which involve various elements of language such as punctuation, spelling, and grammar. These elements, sometimes referred to as the *mechanics* or *form* of writing, must take a back seat to other features of writing, mainly *content* and *organization*. It's not that linguistic elements should be ignored or left unattended. However, they must be put into perspective. As Pearce (1983) explained, "If writing is to serve as a catalyst for gaining insight into course material, then content—not form—needs to be emphasized. . . . If a paper has poor content, then no amount of correcting elements of form will transform it into a good piece of writing" (p. 214). Ideas, and how they are logically and coherently developed in a paper, must receive top priority when one is evaluating and grading writing in content area classrooms.

Once writing is thought of and taught as a process, teachers can begin to deal effectively with the paperload. While the volume of papers will inevitably increase, it is likely to become more manageable. For one thing, when provisions are made for active student response to writing, much of the feedback that a student writer needs will come *while* writing is still going on. Guiding and channeling feedback as students progress with their drafts is a type of *formative* evaluation. In contrast, a *summative* evaluation takes place during the postwriting stage, usually after students have shared their finished products with one another.

Summative evaluations are often *holistic* in nature so that a teacher can quickly and accurately judge a piece of writing based on an impression of its overall effectiveness. Thus, a holistic evaluation permits teachers to sort, rank, and grade written pieces rather efficiently and effectively. Holistic scoring is organized around the principle that a written composition is judged on how successfully it communicates a message, rather than on the strengths and weaknesses of its individual features. The "whole" of a composition, if you will, is greater than the sum of its "parts." In other words, teachers don't have to spend inordinate amounts of time enumerating and counting errors in a paper. Instead, the paper is judged for its total effect on a rater.

Primary Trait Scoring

One type of holistic measure, *primary trait scoring,* is of particular value in content area writing situations. Primary trait scoring is tied directly to a specific writing assignment. An effective assignment, as you recall, provides a rhetorical context. The student writer's task is to respond to the special blend of purpose, audience, subject, and role specified in the assignment. Primary trait scoring helps the teacher to decide how well students completed the writing task.

As a result, primary trait scoring focuses on those characteristics in a paper which are crucial for task completion. How successfully did students handle the assignment in relation to purpose, audience, subject, or role? For example, reread the "arms race" assignment on page 226. Given the rhetorical context of that assignment, papers should be evaluated for these primary traits or characteristics:

(1) accurate content in support of a position; (2) a logical and coherent set of ideas in support of a position; and (3) a position statement that is convincing and persuasive when aimed at an audience of fellow students.

Pearce (1983) recommended that teachers develop a *rubric* based on the primary traits exhibited in student papers. A rubric is a scoring guide. It provides a summary listing of the characteristics that distinguish high-quality from low-quality compositions. Study the rubric in Box 7.5 that Pearce developed for the assignment below:

Box 7.5

---

*A RUBRIC FOR GRADING**

Paper topic: 1960s approaches to civil rights in the United States

High-quality papers contain:
An overview of civil rights or their lack during the 1960s, with three specific examples.
A statement defining civil disobedience, with three examples of how it was used and Martin Luther King's role.
At least one other approach to civil rights, with specific examples, and a comparison of this approach with King's civil disobedience that illustrates differences or similarities in at least two ways.
Good organization, well-developed arguments, few mechanical errors (sentence fragments, grammatical errors, spelling errors).

Medium-quality papers contain:
An overview of Black civil rights during the 1960s, with two specific examples.
A statement defining civil disobedience, with two examples of its use and Martin Luther King's involvement.
One other approach to civil rights, with examples, and a comparison of it with King's civil disobedience by their differences.
Good organization, few mechanical errors, moderately developed arguments.

Lower-quality papers contain:
A general statement defining civil disobedience with reference to Martin Luther King's involvement and at least one example.
One other approach to civil rights and how it differed from civil disobedience.
Fair organization, some mechanical errors.

Lowest-quality papers contain:
A general statement on who Martin Luther King was or a general statement on civil disobedience.
A general statement that not all Blacks agreed with civil disobedience.
A list of points, poor organization, many mechanical errors.

*Reprinted with permission from the International Reading Association and Daniel Pearce, "Guidelines for the Use and Evaluation of Writing," *Journal of Reading*, December 1983, p. 215.

> Write a time capsule document analyzing Martin Luther King's approach to civil rights during the 1960's. Compare this approach to one taken by other Black leaders. *(p. 214)*

For this assignment, papers were evaluated for the following traits: (1) accurate and adequate content about civil disobedience; (2) a comparison of King's approach to civil disobedience with at least one other Black leader's approach; and (3) a logical and organized presentation which provides evidence for any generalization made.

There are other types of holistic scoring procedures that can be used to evaluate and grade papers. For example, *analytical scales* and *checklists* can be developed to judge the quality of a piece of writing. These are explained in detail in an excellent monograph, *Evaluating Writing,* published by the National Council of Teachers of English (Cooper and Odell, 1977).

Looking Back, Looking Forward

When students write to learn in content area classrooms, they are involved in a process of manipulating, clarifying, discovering, and synthesizing ideas. The writing process can be a powerful strategy for helping students gain insight into course material. The value of writing, therefore, lies in its use as a tool for comprehending. What's more, writing and reading often are interwoven. Students who write more, read more.

Unfortunately, the uses of writing have been noticeably limited in content area classrooms. These uses have been restricted to noncomposing activities such as filling in the blanks on worksheets and practice exercises, writing paragraph-or-less responses to study questions, or taking notes. Because of its potentially powerful effect on thinking and learning, the role of writing in content areas should be broadened. Writing can be expanded along several fronts across the curriculum.

One important writing activity involves showing students how to summarize information from course material. Summary writing often results in greater understanding and retention of main ideas in text. Students need to become aware of summarization rules, and receive explicit instruction in how to use these rules to write and polish a summary. Also, students will profit from keeping a learning log. Learning logs can be used to record learning as it occurs. That is to say, students can write about their accomplishments or their lack of understanding about a concept being studied. Freewriting in learning logs encourages the discovery of ideas. It helps to recognize what they know about a subject they're studying. In addition, content area writing should be expanded to include inquiry-centered activities. Teachers can guide students to find topics to investigate. Such an inquiry is based on interests, curiosity arousal, and self-selection. Students can also be assigned topics for inquiry-centered writing. These topics should be introduced in assignments that make the writing task explicit. An explicit assignment helps students to assess the purpose, audience, and form of the writing as well as the writer's role.

Writing should be thought of and taught as a process. When students are guided through a process for writing they will be in a better position to generate ideas, set goals, organize, draft, and revise. The writing process occurs in steps or stages. The stages of writing, as presented in this chapter, included prewriting, writing, rewriting, and postwriting. Prewriting activities such as brainstorming, clustering, jot-charting, and discussion help students to explore ideas, set purposes, and organize for writing. Prewriting situations get students ready to write—to transcribe ideas into words on paper. This step—writing—leads to an initial draft. Rewriting activities include a response by students or teacher to drafts. Feedback *while* writing is in progress is essential for revision to occur. Postwriting activities involve a sharing of finished products and a summative evaluation. Holistic scoring was recommended as a means of evaluating completed drafts.

Writing to learn is a springboard for reading course material. In a very real sense, writing is a productive strategy for studying, the topic of the next chapter. In this chapter, we examine the use of study strategies in content area classrooms. What does it mean to study? How can study strategies lead to independence in learning? Let's read to find out.

Suggested Readings

Applebee, A. N. (1981). *Writing in the Secondary School: English and the Content Areas*. Urbana, Ill.: National Council of Teachers of English.

Camp, G. (1982). *A Success Curriculum for Remedial Writers*. Berkeley, Calif.: The National Writing Project, University of California.

Camp, G. (ed.). (1982). *Teaching Writing: Essays from the Bay Area Writing Project*. Montclair, N.J.: Boyton/Cook.

Jensen, J. (ed.). (1984). *Composing and Comprehending*. Urbana, Ill.: National Council of Teachers of English.

Kirby, D., & Liner, T. (1981). *Inside Out: Developmental Strategies for Teaching Writing*. Montclair, N.J.: Boyton/Cook.

Lindemann, E. (1982). *A Rhetoric for Writing Teachers*. New York: Oxford University Press.

Macrorie, K. (1980). *Searching Writing*. Rochelle Park, N.J.: Hayden.

Martin, N., D'Arcy, P., Newton, B., & Parker, R. (1976). *Writing and Learning Across the Curriculum*. Montclair, N.J.: Boyton/Cook.

Murray, D. (1982). *Learning by Teaching*. Montclair, N.J.: Boyton/Cook.

Myers, J. (1984). *Writing to Learn Across the Curriculum*. Bloomington, Ind.: Phi Delta Kappa.

Tchudi, S., & Huerta, M. (1983). *Teaching Writing in the Content Areas: Middle School/Junior High*. Washington, D.C.: National Education Association.

Tchudi, S., & Tchudi, S. (1983). *Teaching Writing in the Content Areas: Elementary School*. Washington, D.C.: National Education Association.

Tchudi, S., & Yates, J. (1983). *Teaching Writing in the Content Areas: Senior High School*. Washington, D.C.: National Education Association.

CHAPTER EIGHT

Study Strategies

But I tried though—I sure as hell did that much.
—McMurphy in KEN KESEY's *One Flew over the Cuckoo's Nest*

Organizing Principle

Studying text is hard work. It takes deliberate effort. Concentration. Discipline. Patience with print. Students need reasons for studying, whether their purposes involve acquiring, organizing, synthesizing, recalling, or using information and ideas. The good reader develops strategies for studying. Although these strategies may vary from learner to learner, they are often put to effective use when needed for specific reading tasks. Skilled readers, for example, know how to approach text and make plans for reading. They also know how to locate and summarize important points, organize information, and even get out of jams when they run into trouble with a difficult text. Other students, less skilled, often flounder with tasks that require studying. These students lack knowledge of and control over the strategies necessary for effective textbook learning.

The use of study strategies is directly related to a student's knowledge and awareness. The organizing principle of this chapter underscores this relationship: *As students become more aware of reading processes—for example, how to*

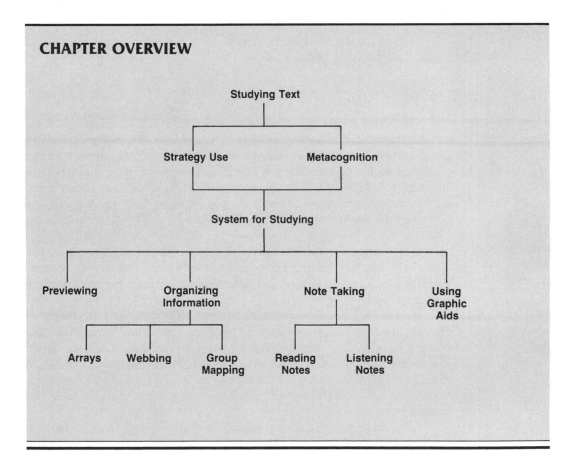

CHAPTER OVERVIEW

identify important ideas in text—they become better able to use and monitor strategies for studying. Content area teachers can show maturing readers how to study text purposefully and deliberately. In turn, students will learn to adapt study strategies to their own needs.

The Overview will help you approach the major ideas in this chapter. As you study the Overview, begin to make plans for reading. What major ideas do you anticipate encountering? When you finish reading the chapter, you should be able to answer these questions:

1. What is the relationship between students' metacognition and use of strategies for studying?

2. How do students learn to develop a system for studying? What is the importance of strategies for previewing text material, organizing and relating information, taking notes, and using graphic aids?

3. Explain several strategies for organizing and relating information. What do these strategies have in common? How do they differ?

4. What is the role of listening in note taking? How can students become aware of and use different types of reading notes?

5. How can students become more aware of and use strategies for studying graphic materials?

The poster caught our attention immediately. It had just gone up on the bulletin board in Julie Meyer's classroom. "School Daze: From A to Z" defined significant school activities in the lives of students, each beginning with a letter of the alphabet. The entry for the letter *S* just happened to be the subject of this chapter. It read, "STUDY: *Those precious moments between soap operas, movies, sports, video games, food, personal grooming, and general lollygagging when one opens one's school books—and falls asleep*" (Hallmark Cards, 1982).

While some students might agree that study is a quick cure for insomnia, few of us would deny that studying textbooks is one of the most frequent and predominant activities in schools today. The older students become, the more they are expected to learn from textbooks.

It's not uncommon to find a teacher prefacing textbook assignments by urging students to "study the material." And some do. They are able to study effectively because they know what it means to *approach* a text assignment: to *analyze* the reading task at hand, to *make plans* for reading, and then to *use* strategies to suit their purposes for studying. Students who approach text in this manner achieve a level of independence because they are in charge of their own learning.

Other students, less skilled in reading and studying, wage a continual struggle with text. Some probably wonder why teachers make a big fuss out of studying in the first place. For them, the exhortation to "study the material" goes in one ear and out the other. Others try to cope with the demands of study. Yet they are prone to equate studying text with rote memorization—cramming "meaningless" material into short-term memory.

Whenever a teacher urges students to study, he or she probably has something definite in mind. Whatever that "something" is, it shouldn't remain an ambiguous or unattainable classroom goal. The problem all too often for maturing readers is that they aren't *aware* of what it means to study, let alone use and orchestrate various learning activities and strategies.

Content area teachers are in a strategic position to make a difference. What better context than the content area classroom to teach learners what it means to be a *student*. The term *student,* derived from Latin, literally means "one who studies." A person who studies knows how to learn. In some respects an alternative title for this chapter might be, "Learning How to Learn."

The Meaning of Study

Because the bulk of studying is spent reading and rereading, the term "reading-study skills" was probably invented to serve as an umbrella concept. At one time or another, almost all the so-called reading skills have been included under the rubric of studying. Defining study by lists of skills which include everything but the proverbial kitchen sink isn't too helpful in actual practice. Marksheffel (1966) observed the folly of such lists: "A complete tabulation of all the specific skills . . . would be a wearisome, never-ending cataloguing of limited value" (p. 215).

Nila B. Smith's (1959) straightforward definition of study is a simple and practical way of conceptualizing what it means to study. She explained studying as strategies we use when our purpose is to do something with the content we have read. At least two characteristics of studying are implicit in "doing something" with the content: intention and deliberation.

Studying is an intentional act. Students need to have a reason for studying as much as they need to have a reason for reading. Doing something means putting strategies to good use by applying them toward purposeful ends. No wonder, then, that study is often characterized by deliberate, diligent work.

The extrinsic reason that most students give for studying is to cover the material or do well in a course. Students will tell you that they study to pass tests. Fair enough. They are quick to associate studying with memorizing information. A concept of study which includes retention has merit. But students run the risk of committing a reductionist fallacy by believing that one part equals the whole, or simply that memorizing is study. Too many students spend too much time using up too much energy on what often becomes their only means of study—rote memorization. Rote memorizing leads to short-lived recall of unrelated bits and pieces of information. Alternatives to rote memorization should be taught and reinforced when and where they count the most—in a content classroom.

Studying is an unhurried and reflective process. The lack of discipline and patience with print is probably one reason why so few adolescents and young adults study effectively on their own in secondary schools or in college. A sociology instructor once met with students who were doing poorly in his class during their first semester in college. The purpose of the meeting was to discuss ways to study sociology. The students, however, soon turned the meeting into a battleground, venting their own frustrations with the course. The sociologist finally reached his own boiling point: "Listen, the bottom line is this: studying is hard work. You can't read sociological material once and expect to 'get it' through osmosis. You should 'work' the material. Read it. And reread it. First, get the facts straight in your head. And eventually you will make them a part of you."

We find ourselves agreeing with the college instructor's analysis of the "bottom line." Studying text is hard work. Cultivating the right habits and attitudes toward studying is essential. And this is where teachers can help the most. But teaching students how to study has to go beyond the "you should" stage or a litany of imperatives. A learner needs exhortation but also a good model or two.

A teacher has the right to expect students to study a subject—and a responsibility to show them how to do this. We read once that *effective* means doing the right thing and *efficient* means doing the thing right. When it comes to studying, it's easy to do the wrong things well. In order for students to use study strategies effectively and efficiently, a content area teacher must first help them connect what they know already about their own reading strategies to the act of studying.

Metacognition and Study Strategies

Metacognition, as it applies to reading, has been described throughout this book as the *knowledge* learners have about reading strategies *and* the ability to capitalize upon such knowledge to *monitor* their own reading. Self-knowledge and self-monitoring are tandem concepts. The former is a prerequisite for the latter. Together self-knowledge and self-monitoring help to explain how maturing readers can begin to assume the lion's share of responsibility for their own learning.

Students who are independent learners know *how, why,* and *when* to use study strategies for specific reading tasks or assignments. They know enough about knowing to recognize the importance of (1) analyzing the reading task that confronts them; (2) reflecting upon what they know or don't know about the material to be read; (3) devising plans for successfully completing the reading, and evaluating and checking their progress in accomplishing the task (Brown, 1978).

A teacher needs to know if students *know* enough about their own reading and study strategies to approach content area text assignments flexibly and adaptively. How students *approach* reading is the key. Different text assignments may pose different problems for the reader to solve. This is why students must be aware of the nature of a particular reading task and how to handle it when assigned text material. Is the student sophisticated enough to ask questions about the reading task? Make plans for reading? Use and adapt strategies to meet the demands inherent in the particular text assignment? Or, does a student approach every text assignment in the same manner—"plowing through" or "slugging along," whichever the case may be—with little notion of why, when, or how to read the text material? Plowing through cumbersome text material just once is more than most students can cope with. The prospect of rereading or reviewing seems downright dreadful. However, teachers are in a position to show students that "working" with the material doesn't necessarily mean twice inflicting upon one-self the agony of slow, tedious reading.

To be in command of their own reading, students must know what to do when they run into trouble. This is what self-monitoring is all about. Do students have a repertoire of strategies within reach to get out of trouble if they stumble into a state of confusion and misunderstanding?

The experienced reader responds to situations in text in much the same manner that the experienced driver responds to situations on the road. Reading and driving become fairly automatic processes until something happens. As Milton (1982) noted, "Everything is fine for experienced drivers as long as they are in familiar territory, the car operates smoothly, they encounter no threat from other drivers, weather, road conditions, or traffic. . . . But, let even one factor become problematic, and drivers shift more attention to the process of driving" (p. 23).

And so it goes for the reader who suddenly gets into trouble with a text assignment. Attention shifts from automatic processing to strategies which will help work the reader out of the jam that has arisen. The problem encountered may parallel the driver's—unfamiliar territory or getting temporarily lost. Only in the reader's case the text is unfamiliar and difficult—and it doesn't take much to get "lost" in the author's line of reasoning or text organization.

Other problems which may disrupt smooth reading might involve a concept too difficult to grasp, word identification, or the inability to identify the important ideas in the text. These problems represent major roadblocks which, if left unattended, could hamper the reader's attempts to get the gist of the text passage or construct knowledge and build meaning. It is in situations such as these that metacognitive processes play an important role in learning from text.

Factors Influencing Study

Metacognitive knowledge and the ability to use study strategies are closely linked together. Perhaps the linkage helps to explain why many students have difficulty studying effectively. As Armbruster, Echols, and Brown (1982) so aptly put it: ". . . before the learner can use effective studying strategies, he/she must be aware of *text, task* and *self,* and how they interact to effect learning" (p. 22, italics added). Students in content area learning situations need to consider four factors which undergird effective studying: (1) the characteristics each learner brings to studying, (2) the nature of the materials being studied, (3) the strategies to be used, and (4) the reading task that is the purpose of studying.

Characteristics of the Learner

Students need to take into account and deal with their perceptions of themselves as readers. Do they have an image of themselves as competent comprehenders? How do they deal with negative feelings toward reading? Do they lack confidence? Do they lack interest in the subject? Do they procrastinate? Do students approach a text assignment with a sense of purpose? Do they pause to consider what they know or don't know about the material to be read? Have they settled into a state of "learned helplessness" in which they perceive themselves as unable to overcome failure?

Questions such as these can be posed in brief "self-awareness" sessions that teachers conduct for students. The instructional strategies presented in previous chapters are powerful tools which give students a sense of accomplishment and self-confidence as readers. In addition, the results of the assessment procedures in Chapter 3 provide an avenue for teachers to share with students what they will need to do to be successful with print. An assessment of study strategy use is an initial step in explicit instruction for effective studying. Assessment of study strategies is discussed in greater detail later in this chapter.

The Nature of the Materials

As students prepare to study they must consider the text material that has been assigned. How well is it organized? Is a predominant pattern of organization recognizable? Do the headings and subheadings signal the main and subordinate ideas in the material? Do the chapter's introduction and summary help the reader predict the author's main points? Is the text poorly written?

Brown and Smiley (1977) found that older students (junior high through college) become increasingly better able to make use of extended study time than children below seventh grade. The key to Brown and Smiley's finding lies in the older student's greater sensitivity to the way texts are organized. Given extended study time, older students are able to predict in advance the important elements of a text and then use the study time effectively to identify the author's main ideas and supporting information. In short, they are able to capitalize on their knowledge of textual importance and its role in comprehending.

Reading and Study Strategies

Sharon Smith (1982) suggested several major categories of text activities in which mature readers engage at the college level. These categories are indeed applicable to students in junior and senior high content area classrooms: *cursory text activities, constructive text activities,* and *monitoring activities.*

Cursory text activities help students to analyze the reading task at hand and devise plans for reading. These strategies involve inspectional reading. Do students know how to preview an assignment? Do they skim for main points, predict and anticipate content? Cursory text strategies enable readers to focus on decisions: What is important? What is especially difficult? What are the key terms and concepts? What shall I skip? How should I begin? In Chapter 4 many instructional techniques and procedures were suggested for the very purpose of helping students build a general framework for learning. In this chapter we'll explore previewing as a study strategy which accomplishes a similar purpose.

Constructive text activities help students build meaning and process information in depth. Strategies for summarizing text, outlining, and note taking help students to discriminate the essential from the inessential as well as to synthesize and organize information. What is the text about? What does it mean? What is the significance of the material? How can I use these meanings? The instructional strategies in Chapters 4, 5, 6, and 7 demonstrate for students how to engage in constructive meaning building activities.

The monitoring strategies students should consider are directly related to metacognitive awareness and experiences with text. Do students recognize reading obstacles and make conscious decisions to do something about them? Do they, for example, *ignore* certain problems and *read on* because the problem is not critical to understanding? Do students *change the rate of reading* — slowing down or speeding up — depending upon the purpose for reading and the difficulty of the material? Do they *reread* selectively? Do they monitor comprehension by checking with other students or the teacher to see if they are on the right track?

The Reading Task

The fourth factor that students must take into consideration is the reading task itself. Do they understand the assignment? Are the teacher's expectations clear? Are they aware that different tasks require different strategies?

Invariably a teacher will complain that students read text assignments superficially — just enough to parrot back answers to questions that accompany the text. So students search for the portions of the text which satisfy the questions and skip everything else. Alternatives to this scenario lie in the critical tasks that teachers ascribe to reading. If, for example, students view "homework" as little more than answering a set of questions which will be turned in to the teacher, then their actions are probably justifiable. However, students must recognize and understand that studying text means more than answering homework questions. And that's where teachers can help.

An Instructional Framework for Teaching Study Strategies

Explicit instruction helps students become aware of, use, and develop control over study strategies (Archer, 1979; Brown and Palincsar, 1982). Explicit methods provide an alternative to "blind" instruction. In blind instructional situations, students are taught what to do, but this is where instruction usually ends. Although directed to make use of a set of procedures which will improve studying, students seldom grasp the rationale or "payoff" underlying a particular study strategy. As a result, they attempt to use the strategy with little basis for evaluating its success or monitoring its effectiveness. Explicit instruction, however, attempts not only to show students *what* to do, but also *why, how,* and *when.* Pearson (1982b) concluded that such instruction helps "students develop independent strategies for coping with the kinds of comprehension problems they are asked to solve in their lives in schools" (p. 22).

The instructional framework which follows combines explicit teaching of study strategies with content area materials. The framework for lessons has four components: *assessment, awareness, modeling and demonstration,* and *application.*

By way of analogy, the instructional framework provides experiences similar to those needed by athletes and other performers who are "in training." To "perform" well with texts, students must understand the rules, rehearse, work on technique, practice. A coach (the teacher) is needed to provide feedback, guide, inspire, and share the knowledge and experiences that she or he possesses.

Let's take a closer look at each component in the instructional framework.

Assessment

The assessment component of the instructional model is "tryout" time. It gives the teacher an opportunity to determine the degree of knowledge the students have about a study strategy under discussion. Moreover, assessment yields insight into how well the students use a strategy to handle a reading task. For these reasons, assessing the use of a strategy should occur in as natural a context as possible.

Assessment usually can be accomplished within a single class period, following the steps outlined below:

1. Assign students a text passage of approximately 1000–1500 words. The selection should take most students ten to fifteen minutes to read.

2. Direct students to use a particular study strategy. For example, suppose that the strategy students are to develop involves outlining a text selection. Simply ask students to do the things they normally do to read a passage and then develop an outline of it. Allow about twenty additional minutes to complete the task.

3. Observe the use of the strategy. Note what students do. Do they underline or mark important ideas as they read? Do they appear to skim the material first to get a general idea of what to expect? In the case of outlining, what do they do when actually constructing the outline?

4. Ask students to respond in writing to several key questions about the use of the study strategy. For example, What did you do to outline the passage? What did you do to find the main ideas? Did you find outlining easy or difficult? Why?

Awareness

Assessment is a springboard to making students aware of the *why* and *how* of a study strategy. During the awareness step, a give-and-take exchange of ideas takes place between teacher and students. As a result, students should recognize the *rationale* and *process* behind the use of a study strategy. To make students more aware of a study strategy, consider the following activities:

1. Discuss the assessment. Use your observations and students' reflective responses to the written questions.
2. "Set" the stage by leading a discussion of *why* the strategy is useful. What is the payoff for students? How does it improve learning?
3. Engage in activities which define the rules or procedures necessary to be successful with the study strategy.
4. Have students experience the use of the study strategy by practicing the rules or procedures on a short selection from the textbook.

Awareness provides students with a clear picture of the study strategy: the *why* and *how* are solidly introduced. The road has been paved for more intensive modeling and demonstration of the strategy.

Modeling and Demonstration

Once the "why" and a beginning sense of "how" are established, the students should receive careful follow-up in the use of the study strategy. "Training sessions" are characterized by demonstration through teacher modeling, explanations, practice, reinforcement of the rules or procedures, and more practice. The students progress from easy to harder practice situations, and from shorter to longer text selections. The following activities are recommended:

1. Use an overhead transparency to review the rules or steps that students should follow.
2. Have students keep a "learning log" as discussed in Chapter 7. Each section of the log reflects a study strategy that students are learning to control. Direct the students to the section of the learning log that deals with the study strategy under development. Each student should have a copy of the rules and/or steps in the log to review. The log is also used by students to make entries toward the end of a demonstration session. The entries may include their progress and struggles as well as their thoughts and reflections on the use of the strategy. As Hoffman (1983) explained, "They can write about their participation or lack of it; their difficulty in paying attention, or in understanding the teacher; what they learn . . ." (p. 345). Collect the journals periodically and respond to entries accordingly. The entries are also quite useful in planning additional sessions to help reinforce the use of the strategy.
3. Demonstrate the study strategy. Walk students through the steps. Provide explanations. Raise questions about the procedures.

4. As part of a demonstration, initiate the "think aloud" procedure to model how to use the study strategy. By thinking aloud, the teacher shares with students the thinking processes he or she uses in applying the study strategy. Thinking aloud is often accomplished by reading a passage out loud, stopping at key points in the text to ask questions and/or provide prompts. The questions and prompts mirror the critical thinking required to apply the study strategy. Once students are familiar with the think aloud procedure encourage them to demonstrate and use it during practice sessions.

5. Reinforce and practice the study strategy with "trial runs" using short selections from the textbook. Debrief with questions after each trial run. Did the students follow the steps? How successful were they? What caused them difficulty? Have them make journal entries. Often a short quiz following a trial run shows students how much they learned and remembered as a result of using the study strategy.

The demonstration sessions are designed to provide experience with the study strategy. Students should reach a point where they have internalized the steps and feel in control of the strategy.

Application

The preceding components of the instructional framework should provide enough training for students to know *why, how,* and *when* to use study strategies which have been targeted by the teacher for emphasis. Once students have made generalizations about strategy use, regular class assignments should encourage application. Rather than assign for homework a text selection accompanied by questions to be answered, frame the assignment so that students will have to apply certain study strategies. For example, students might be required to summarize, outline, or take notes on the assigned material.

Developing a System for Studying

When students know how, why, and when to study, they will use and orchestrate strategies into a system of learning. Students will approach a text assignment differently, choosing the study strategies best suited to themselves and the subject they're studying (Moore, 1981).

In the past, systems for study have been readily taught to students with the expectation that once a formula is learned it will be applied in independent learning situations. Numerous "study systems," often identified by acronyms, have presented a complex set of steps for students to follow. Perhaps the most widely recommended study system is SQ3R (Robinson, 1961).

SQ3R stands for

Survey. The reader previews the material to develop a general outline for organizing information.

Question. The reader raises questions with the expectation of finding answers in the material to be studied.

Read. The reader next attempts to answer the questions formulated in the previous step.

Recite. The reader then deliberately attempts to answer out loud or in writing the questions formulated in the second step.

Review. The reader finally reviews the material by rereading portions of the assignment in order to verify the answers given during the previous step.

Although originated as an independent study procedure for college-level students, most junior high and high school learners who are exposed to SQ3R find it difficult to use on their own. They are easily frustrated, if not overwhelmed, by strict adherence to the number of steps in the procedure. Each step has its own built-in level of complexity.

We suspect that a study system such as SQ3R is not used by most students because it is taught as a formula. Memorize the steps. Practice the procedures several times. Now use it for life. In other words, students are often taught what to do without enough explicit instruction to lead to self-control. The key to any system's effectiveness may very well lie in how students learn to control it through selective and flexible use.

In the final analysis students need to learn how to become "text-smart." Being text-smart is comparable to being "street-smart." It's knowing how to stay out of trouble; it's knowing when to and when not to take short-cuts; it's knowing how to survive the everyday cognitive demands that are a natural part of classroom life.

A system for studying evolves gradually within each learner. Maturing readers need to make the transition from teacher-centered guidance to self-control and regulation of their own reading and studying. How students become text-smart is the focus of the remaining sections of the chapter.

Previewing: Laying the Groundwork for Independent Study

Previewing text material lays the groundwork for studying effectively. Students who know how to preview text are in a strategic position to take charge of their own learning. Previewing is the pinnacle skill in what we have already described as inspectional reading. It is the type of cursory learning activity that helps readers to analyze the task at hand and make plans for reading.

To analyze the reading task and make plans, a student must ask questions such as these:

—What kind of reading is this?

—What is my primary goal or purpose?

—Should I try to remember details or read for the main ideas only?

—How much time will I devote to the reading assignment?

—What do I already know about the topic? What do I need to know?

In essence, questions such as these will make students aware of the purposes for a reading assignment so that they can adapt their reading and study to the task.

A strategy such as previewing gives students some idea of what a text selection is about before reading it. It prepares them for what is coming. Students' tendency, of course, is to jump right into an assignment, often without rhyme or reason, and plow through it. Not so, however, when they learn how to preview material. This prereading technique helps them to raise questions and set purposes which will lead to more efficient processing of information.

When students raise questions about content material that they preview, they are likely to examine the extent of their own uncertainty and to find out what they don't know about the information they will acquire during reading. As a result of previewing and questioning, students become involved in a search for answers during reading. However, previewing and questioning require active participation by students; this is why high-powered as well as low-powered readers have trouble previewing on their own. They need teachers who will provide explicit instruction in how to preview and activate questions. Where does the teacher start?

Teaching for Self-Control

Start the way a Harvard professor did (Perry, 1959). William Perry conducted an experiment with 1500 freshmen who were probably among the "finest readers in the country." He assigned a chapter from a history book, instructing the students to use their best strategies to read and study it. After approximately twenty minutes he asked them to stop reading and answer multiple-choice questions on the details of the chapter. Not surprisingly, the vast majority of the students scored high on the test. Yet, when they were asked to write a short essay summarizing the main idea of the chapter, only fifteen students did so successfully. Why? Because these fifteen freshmen, about one percent of the students in the experiment, took the time to preview the chapter before plunging into the details of the material.

Use this anecdote, as well as observations from an assessment of how students actually approach a text selection, to drive home the importance of "sizing up" the material before reading it. Discuss the reasons why most readers just plow through the material. And through give-and-take exchanges, begin to develop a rationale for previewing.

Previewing works well when content materials contain textbook aids which are organizational, typographic, or visual in nature. Textbook writers use these aids as guideposts for readers.

Certain organizational aids such as the table of contents, preface, chapter introductions and/or summaries, and chapter questions give readers valuable clues about the overall structure of a textbook or the important ideas in a unit or chapter. Previewing a table of contents, for example, not only creates a general impression, but also helps readers to distinguish the forest from the trees. The table of contents gives students a feel for the overall theme or structure of the course material so that they may get a sense of the scope and sequence of ideas at the very beginning of the course. The teacher can also use the table of contents to build background and discuss the relatedness of each of the parts of the book. Model for students the kinds of questions which should be raised. "Why did the authors sequence the material this way?" "Why do the authors begin with _____ in Part One?" "If you were the author, would you have arranged the major parts in the text differently? Why?"

The table of contents can also be used to introduce a chapter or unit. The teacher might ask students to refer to Part One on the table of contents. "What do you think this part of the book is about?" "Why do you think so?" Key words can also be highlighted for discussion. For example, key terms in the table of contents of a business textbook may lead to questions such as these: "What do you think the author means by *values*?" "What does *budgeting* mean? What does it have to do with *financial planning*?" Open-ended questions such as these help readers to focus attention on the material and also illustrate the value of predicting and anticipating content.

As students zero in on a particular chapter, they can make use of additional organizational aids such as the introduction, summary, or questions at the end of the chapter. These aids often create a frame of reference for the important ideas in the chapter.

Typographical and visual aids within a chapter are also invaluable devices for previewing. Students can survey chapter titles; headings and subheadings; words, phrases, or sentences in special type; and pictures, diagrams, illustrations, charts, and graphs in advance of reading to get a general outline—an agenda, so to speak—of what to expect.

In general, students should learn and follow these steps or "rules" when previewing:

1. Read the title. Convert it to a question.

2. Read the introduction, summary, and questions. What seem to be the author's main points?

3. Read the heads and subheads. Convert them to questions.

4. Read print in special type. Why are certain words, phrases, or sentences highlighted?

5. Study visual materials such as pictures, maps, diagrams. What do the graphics tell you about the chapter's content?

The teacher demonstrates the preview and then models effective previewing/ questioning behaviors. This entails walking students through the process. Select several pages from the assigned reading and develop transparencies in which you annotate the type of questions which students should ask while previewing. Then share the overhead transparencies with the class, explaining the reasons for your annotations. You might then have students open their textbooks to another section of the chapter. Take turns asking the kind of questions that you modeled, paying attention to the organizational, typographical, and visual aids in the assigned material. Finally, as students develop metacognitive awareness, have them raise their own questions while previewing.

Skimming: Intensive Previewing

A natural part of previewing is to learn how to skim content material effectively. Skimming involves intensive previewing of the material to see what the reading assignment will be about. One recommendation is to show students the importance of reading the first sentence (usually a topic statement or important idea) of every paragraph. In this way, they will get a good sense of what is coming.

In addition, an effective motivator for raising students' expectations about the material is to have them skim an entire reading selection rapidly—in no more than one or two minutes. Encourage students to zip through every page and not to get bogged down on any one section or subsection. The class must then reconstruct what they have skimmed. Ask them to recall everything that they have read. You and they will be amazed at the quantity and quality of the recalls.

> Sherer (1975) pointed out the value of skimming to one of his students: She could skim . . . read titles, summaries, topic sentences and headings, first and last paragraphs, or search for major concepts and premises—on her way to locating information. . . . Once she had selected the most pertinent part of a reading assignment, she could slow down the pace and read more intensively, secure in knowing she was reading this material to meet a specific goal. *(p. 25)*

Previewing and skimming are similar techniques for getting general understanding through selective reading. They should be used to "size up" the material, to judge its relevance to a discussion or a topic, or to gain some notion of what a passage is about. However, other study strategies such as outlining, note taking, and summarizing demand that students organize and integrate information. These strategies require in-depth processing and the ability to distinguish important top-level ideas from supportive points and details.

Outlining and Relating Information

Perceiving the organization of ideas is an integral part of reading comprehension. Producing that organization is an integral part of studying.

Good readers follow the way an author relates ideas. They look for organization in everything they read. Producing the relationships that exist among ideas in a passage is one of the most sophisticated study activities that secondary students will attempt. Why? Because they must recognize not only that ideas are connected to one another but that some ideas are more important than others. Throughout this book we have argued that the hierarchy of concepts in content material must be analyzed and used to good advantage by readers. We have shown in Chapter 2 how some ideas are subordinate to others. Main ideas, however, are always in a superordinate or top-level position in the hierarchy. Facts and details are always subordinate to high-level concepts.

The problem of distinguishing important ideas from supportive points and details is complicated by at least three factors. First, instruction in reading classes rarely transcends the level of the paragraph when it comes to finding main ideas. Students who are responsible for content area assignments must perceive main ideas over long stretches of text material, yet they are rarely shown how to do this in reading class. Second, some content material is too difficult or just poorly written. If the ideas in a reading selection lack cohesion, are too abstract, or go beyond the experiential grasp of the reader, the reader will not discern relationships. And third, many important ideas in a reading passage are not actually stated but rather implied. When left to their own devices, some students will have trouble making inferences about implied main ideas.

Outlining helps students clarify relationships. An outline is a product. After readers have sensed or identified relationships, they can produce organization as a means of study through outlining. Developing an outline is analogous to fitting together pieces in a puzzle. In the case of outlining, Hansell (1978) suggested, "The completed puzzle shows the separate identity of each idea as well as the part each idea plays in the total picture" (p. 248). As a study technique, outlining strategies can be used effectively to facilitate a careful analysis and synthesis of the relationships in content material. They can form the basis for critical discussion and evaluation of the author's points.

Problems arise when students are restricted by the means in which they must depict relationships spatially on paper. The word *outlining* for most of us immediately conjures up an image of the "correct" or "classic" format that we have all learned at one time or another but have probably failed to use regularly in real-life study situations. The classic form of outlining has the student represent the relatedness of information in linear form:

I. Main Idea
    A. Idea supporting I
        1. detail supporting A
        2. detail supporting A
            a. detail supporting 2
            b. detail supporting 2
    B. Idea supporting I
        1. detail supporting B
        2. detail supporting B
II. Main Idea

This conventional format represents a hierarchical ordering of ideas at different levels of subordination. Roman numerals signal the major or superordinate concepts in a text section, upper-case letters the supporting or coordinate concepts, Arabic numbers the supporting or subordinate details, and lower-case letters sub-subordinate details.

Maturing readers have trouble using a restricted form of outlining. Initially at least, they need a more visual display than the one offered by the conventional format. Several "free-form" outlining strategies permit students a certain degree of freedom and latitude in making connections among ideas presented in text. *Arrays* and *semantic webs* (sometimes referred to as *semantic maps*) are quite useful for narrative or expository texts. *Group mapping* activities stimulate student-centered organizational structures and are particularly worthwhile for clarifying relationships in narrative material.

The Array Procedure

In presenting outlining strategies to students, make sure that they fit into the instructional framework previously discussed. For example, begin by assessing how students normally outline material. Do they have a sense of subordination among ideas? Do they have strategies for connecting major and minor concepts? Do they use alternatives to the conventional format? Make them aware of the rationale for organizing information through outlining. The jigsaw puzzle analogy — fitting pieces of information together into a coherent whole — works well for this purpose. With assessment and awareness building thoroughly accomplished, the stage is set for illustrating, modeling, and applying the strategies.

According to Hansell (1978), students use the array technique to decide how to arrange key words and phrases to produce the relationships in reading material. The student can use words, lines, and arrows as symbols to show the nature of the relationships. The only rule in a free-form outline such as an array is that students must attempt to create a logical spatial arrangement among key words and phrases which connect important ideas to supporting information. This can best be done with straight and uncrossed connecting lines.

Hansell illustrated, using the story of Adam and Eve, how the visual display in an array might be arranged in two different ways depending on one's interpretation of text relationships. See Figure 8.1 for depictions of how two arrays might differ when students position key words around a central idea, such as "apple." The "correct" form of an array, as you can see, is relative. The extent to which students can justify a visual display will indicate its appropriateness.

You can introduce the array-outlining procedure to students following these steps:

1. Divide the class into heterogeneous groups of three or four members each.

2. Give each group strips of paper and ask them to copy the key words and phrases that you have previously identified as representing the important and supporting ideas in a text selection.

Figure 8.1.
Two Array Depictions*

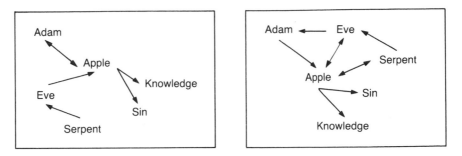

*SOURCE: T. Stevenson Hansell, "Stepping up to Outlining," *Journal of Reading* 22 (1978): 248–252. Reprinted with permission of T. Stevenson Hansell and the International Reading Association.

3. Pronounce each word or phrase; if necessary discuss its meaning. Next, feed students into reading by asking several questions in which they must hypothesize answers. Then assign the reading.

4. Have each group create an array after they have finished reading by laying out the strips of paper and selecting the most important idea, and then arranging the remaining slips around it.

5. Have one member of each group copy the layout on a larger piece of paper and draw lines to show connected ideas and arrows to show the direction of the relationship.

6. Have the groups share their arrays and discuss their reasons for placement and connection.

Once students become familiar with constructing the array, they can move toward more independent production. For example, without help from the teacher small groups can generate their own lists of words and phrases to represent the important and supporting ideas in a text selection. Eventually, making an array can be an individual rather than a group activity.

Semantic Webbing

A semantic web (or semantic map) is similar to an array in that students learn to identify important ideas and show how they fit together. Teachers are not faced with the problem of teaching a restricted, conventional outline format, but instead, of helping students understand what is read.

As with all free-form outlines the main rule to drive home is that the students are responsible for creating a logical arrangement among key words or phrases which connect main ideas to subordinate information. And, like the array, instruction should proceed from teacher-guided modeling and illustration to student-generated productions.

A semantic web has four components (Freedman and Reynolds, 1980):

1. *A core question or concept.* The question or concept (stated as a key word or phrase) establishes the main focus of the web. All of the ideas generated for the web by the students are related in some way to the core question/concept.

2. *Web strands.* The subordinate ideas generated by the students which help to clarify the question or explain the concept.

3. *Strand supports.* The details, inferences, and generalizations which are related to each web strand. These supports help to clarify and distinguish one strand from another.

4. *Strand ties.* The conections which students make between or among the strands; in other words, strand ties depict the relationships strands have with one another.

Students use the semantic web as an organizational tool to visually illustrate categories and relationships associated with a core question or superordinate concept under study. To model and illustrate the use of a semantic web, a junior high social studies teacher walked students through the process. The class began a unit on Ohio's early settlements. As part of prereading discussion three questions were raised for the class to ponder: What do you think were the three most important early settlements in Ohio? What do you think these settlements had in common? How were they different? In what ways might the location of a settlement be important to the survival of the settlers? Predictions were made and discussed and lead naturally to the text assignment.

The teacher assigned the material, directing students to read with the purpose of confirming or modifying their predictions and remembering everything they could about the early settlements.

After reading, the students formed small groups. Each group listed everything they could remember about the settlements on index cards — with one piece of information per card.

In the center of the chalkboard, the teacher wrote "The First Ohio Settlements" and circled the phrase. She then asked students to provide the main web strands that helped answer the question and clarify the concept, "What were Ohio's most important early settlements?" The students responded by contrasting their predictions to the explanations in the text assignment. The teacher began to build

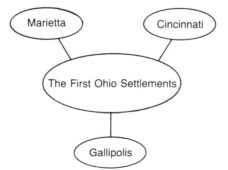

the semantic web on the board by explaining how web strands help students answer the questions and understand the main concept.

Next, she asked the students to work in their groups to sort the cards that were compiled according to each of the settlements depicted in the web. Through discussion, questioning, and think-aloud probes, the class completed the semantic web depicted in Figure 8.2.

Figure 8.2
Semantic Web: The First Ohio Settlements

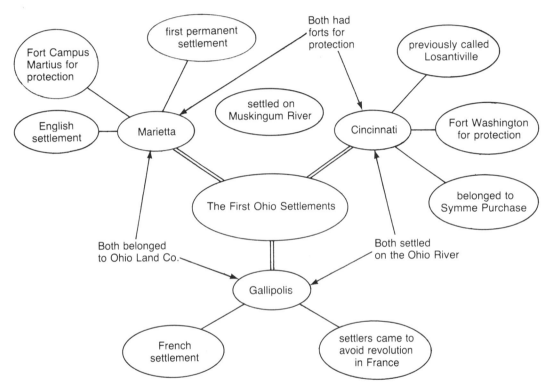

Some teachers prefer to distinguish web strands from strand supports through the use of lines. Notice that in Figure 8.2, a double line connects the web strands to the core concept. Strand supports are linked to each web strand by single lines. With younger students, some teachers also recommend using different colored chalk to distinguish one strand from another. Finally, notice that strands are tied together by lines with arrows. In Figure 8.2, the strand ties were initiated by teacher probes, i.e., "What did Marietta and Gallipolis have in common?"

With appropriate modeling, explanation, and experience, students soon understand the why, what, and how of semantic webbing and can begin to develop individual webs. We suggest that the teacher begin by providing the core question or concept. Students can then compare and contrast their individual productions in follow-up discussion. Of course, text assignments should also be given in which students identify the core concept on their own and then generate the structures which support and explain it.

The semantic web is easily adapted to different content area texts. For example, Figure 8.3 depicts a web for a science selection dealing with "The Crystals of Earth."

In addition to being referred to as *maps,* semantic webs have also been called *radial outlines* because key concepts and supporting information are included in the graphic representation.

Figure 8.3
Science Example of Semantic Web*

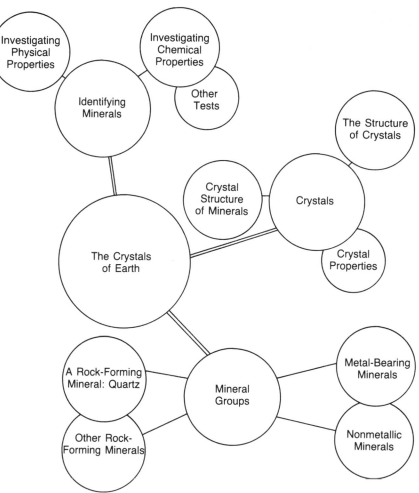

*Source: James Walker, "Squeezing Study Skills (into, out of) Content Areas," in R. T. Vacca and J. A. Meagher, *Reading Through Content,* Storrs, Conn.: University Publications and the Reading-Language Arts Center, University of Connecticut, 1979, pp. 77–92. Used with permission of the author.

The disadvantage of using free-form formats such as the semantic web or radial outline is that subordinate details are difficult to organize in the visual display. However, when the teacher's purpose is to show how to distinguish superordinate from supporting or coordinate ideas, the free-form outline is a fitting alternative to the conventional style.

The Group Mapping Activity

The Group Mapping Activity is another free-form outlining strategy that is especially appropriate for narrative text. We recommend it as an individual and small-group study strategy because it leads to dynamic interaction through discussion. As with the array and semantic web, students are responsible for generating a diagram showing the interrelationships among ideas. The diagram is a graphic representation of each student's interpretations of the text or his or her personal responses to the narrative material.

Once students have read a selection, Jane Davidson, an originator of the strategy, suggested the following instructions: " 'Map your perceptions of the passage on a sheet of paper. There is no right way to map. Elements, ideas, or concepts are simply put in diagram form. You might choose to use boxes or circles. You may also wish to draw lines to show relationships. Your map will represent your interpretations or perceptions of information for the passage. Do not look back at the passage at this time' " (Davidson, 1982, p. 52).

Upon completion of their maps, students form discussion groups to share their structures. In the short story called "All the Years of Her Life" by Morley Callaghan, a boy was caught stealing articles from a drugstore where he worked. His mother calmly convinces the owner of the shop that her son should not be turned over to the police. Later, the boy realized his mother was tired, alone, and frightened. He felt he understood her for the first time in his life. In response to the story, here's a glimpse of the discussion generated by the group mapping activity:

> "I drew two diagonal lines intersecting each other shortly after the beginning and then moving away from each other—never to touch again. I lettered in the word 'sadness' because I feel it is sad that these two individuals will never really know and understand each other. The intersection of the lines represents their brief moment of communication, but I don't think they'll ever communicate again."
>
> "That's really interesting—I never thought of it that way. What are you basing that on?"
>
> "It says in the passage—that although he wants to talk to his mother, he doesn't say a word."
>
> "But, I drew my map showing that he finally grew up—here on my map is the point at which he understands his mother, so he doesn't need to talk to her at that point; I think they *will* communicate after this." *(Davidson and Bayliss, 1979, p. 6)*
>
> Mapping is learned by trying out and then experiencing the maps of others.

Davidson stressed the importance of letting students generate their own individual structures, even though they may become frustrated with their first mapping experience. She warned that initially they will need encouragement and some modeling. A teacher may wish to illustrate the mapping activity by showing how students from previous classes produced maps for a particular story. Contrast the maps. Talk through how each student visualized the relationships and responded in a personal way to the material. Another tactic is to have the class read a short passage, and then use an overhead projector and transparency to generate a map. As the teacher develops the map, he or she can think aloud, ask questions, explain connections, and give rationale for specific text interpretations and personal responses. According to Davidson (1982), "Students' initial frustration at their first Group Mapping Activity is rarely repeated in subsequent experiences. . . . After they have been involved in discussions following mapping and have had an opportunity to see and analyze others' maps, their frustrations subside" (p. 55).

Conventional Outlining Procedures

The conventional outline has a great deal of value and shouldn't be misinterpreted in light of the previous discussions. For although the conventional form restricts students to a definite format, they can use it effectively once they become comfortable with the process of organizing and relating ideas in text. Sufficient application of free-form outlining should precede introduction of the restricted format.

The transition from free-form to restricted outlining should be gradual and guided. Many reading authorities recommend a progression of restricted outlining assignments. The first assignment provides students with a "skeleton" outline partially completed by the teacher as illustrated in Figure 8.4.

Figure 8.4
Partial Outline from Chapter on "Evaluating Our Economic System"

    I.   The Gross National Product
        A.   Definition and Uses of GNP
            1.
            2.
            3.
        B.   Explanations: Real Dollars, Base Year
            1.
            2.
   II.   Circles and Cycles
        A.
        B.   Business Cycles
            1.
            2.
            3.
            4.

III. Inflation
   A.
      1.
      2.
      3.
      4.
   B. Causes of Inflation
      1.
      2.
      3.
      4.
   C. Effects of Inflation
      1.
      2.
      3.
      4.

The second assignment might provide a partial outline less filled out than the first. By the third assignment the teacher may present a blank skeletal framework for the outline, but with the main and subordinate information on a separate sheet of paper. Students then match the phrases at the appropriate levels within the skeletal hierarchy. By the fourth assignment the teacher provides the skeletal outline alone. In subsequent assignments, students generate their own outlines using a conventional format.

The level of difficulty of each of these assignments can be set to meet the needs of students in a particular class. The combination of free-form outlining with a gradual progression into restricted outlines should give students enough experience to produce organization in text.

Taking Notes

Walter Pauk's response to the question, "Why take notes?" is profound in its simplicity—because we forget (Pauk, 1978). Over fifty percent of the material read or heard in class is often forgotten in a matter of a few minutes. Strategies which trigger recall and overcome forgetting are essential. Nevertheless, note taking ranks among the most neglected areas of study instruction. Palmatier and Bennett (1974) observed that note taking is an "accepted phenomenon," particularly of the American college scene. Yet when Palmatier and Bennett surveyed the note-taking habits of college students,

> Only thirty-seven of the 223 students surveyed (17 percent) reported having received any formal instruction in the skills of notetaking. Further, in most cases the instruction was of extremely short duration, thirty minutes or less, and *was in effect more warning as to the necessity for taking notes rather than instruction on how to do so.* [p. 217, italics ours]

If instruction is to be meaningful, students need to be shown how to take notes in actual situations that require taking notes—during reading and listening.

Strategies for Taking Reading Notes

An effective study activity for acting upon and remembering material is to annotate what is read in the form of reading notes. Reading notes can be put on "study cards" (index cards), in the study journal previously mentioned or a "thought book" which is kept expressly for the purpose of compiling written reactions, reflections, and annotations on text readings.

Reading notes should avoid verbatim text reproductions. Instead, notes can be used to paraphrase, summarize, react critically, question, or respond personally to what is read. Whatever the form that reading notes take, students need to become aware of the different types of notes that can be written and then be shown how to write them.

In a complex study system called REAP (Read, Encode, Annotate, Ponder), Eanet and Manzo (1976) underscored the importance of writing notes as a means of helping students learn from what they read. The originators of REAP described the different kinds of annotations that students can write. Several of the annotations are particularly appropriate for middle grade and secondary school students. For example, read the passage on "Wild Cargo: The Business of Smuggling Animals" in Box 8.1. Then study each of the annotations made by a high school student.

Box 8.1

WILD CARGO: THE BUSINESS OF SMUGGLING ANIMALS*

Unpleasantness for those trading illegally in wild animals and their products is escalating around the world. Within the past decade government after government has passed laws to restrict or prohibit the sale of wildlife seriously depleted by hunting and habitat destruction. With legal channels pinched, animal dealers have resorted to nefarious schemes to continue the flow.

Wildlife is big business. Exotic-bird collectors will pay $10,000 for a hyacinth macaw . . . in New York I tried on a pair of trendy western boots trimmed in lizard skin. The price? "Two-hundred thirty-five," the clerk said, with an archness suggesting that most of his customers didn't bother to ask. . . .

These items are being sold legally. But somewhere in the dim beginnings of their trail through commerce, they may have been acquired illegally. . . .

This fascination with wildlife within the affluent nations of the world adds to the disappearance of animals in the less developed countries. In between stand the illegal traders willing to circumvent the wildlife-protection laws to satisfy the demand and their own pocketbooks. . . .

Wildlife smuggling is costing the U.S. millions of dollars to control and is denying income to the treasury of any nation that would otherwise receive duty from legal imports. It has spread diseases that would have been detected in legal quarantine periods . . . an irreversible effect of illegal trade could be the extinction of animal species that are finding fewer and fewer places to hide. *(pp. 290–294)*

*Source: Noel Grove, "Wild Cargo: The Business of Smuggling Animals." National Geographic, 159 (March 1981): 287–315.

The summary annotation condenses the main ideas of a text selection into a concise statement as discussed in the previous chapter. Summary notes are characterized by their brevity, clarity, and conciseness. When a note summarizes expository material, it should clearly distinguish the important ideas in the author's presentation from supporting information and detail. When the summary note involves narrative material such as a story, it should include a synopsis containing the major story elements that were described in Chapter 2. Examine below an example of a summary notation from a student's notecard:

> Summary Note
>
> The illegal trading of wildlife and their products is a profitable business in affluent countries around the world. The continuation of such trade threatens both developed and undeveloped nations economically and ecologically. More recent laws are making this illegal trade much more difficult to carry out.

The thesis annotation answers the question, "What is the main point that the author has tried to get across to the reader?" The thesis annotation has a telegramlike character. It is incisively stated, yet unambiguous in its identification of the author's main proposition. The thesis note for a story identifies its theme. Study the example below.

> Thesis Note
>
> Illegal wild animal trade is a very profitable business. Illegal wildlife trade is a threat to man and his environment. More laws throughout the world can restrict this activity

The critical annotation captures the reader's reaction or response to the author's thesis. It answers the question, "So what?" In writing critical notes, the reader should first state the author's thesis, then state his or her position in relation to the thesis, and finally defend or expand upon the position taken.

Critical Note

The trading of wildlife for high profits is something all men will pay for ultimately. Countries are being cheated out of needed revenues. But more importantly, the future of species of animals is being threatened. The money-minded traders also give little thought to the spread of disease that could be avoided by legal quarantines. All nations need to cooperate to pass stricter laws to control or prohibit the trade of life and survival for temporary luxury.

The question annotation raises a significant issue in the form of a question. The question is the result of what the reader thinks is the most germane or significant aspect of what he or she has read (see page 277 for example).

Using the Instructional Framework to Teach Reading Notes

Showing students how to write different types of notes begins with assessment, leads to awareness and knowledge building, modeling and practice, and culminates with application. First, assign a text selection and ask students to write whatever reading notes they wish on a separate sheet of paper. Then have the class analyze the assessment, share student notes, and discuss difficulties in taking notes. Use the assessment analysis to orient students to the importance of reading notes as a strategy for learning and retention.

Teaching students how to actually write different types of notes from their readings begins first with awareness and knowledge building. They should be able to recognize and define the various kinds of reading notes that can be written. Eanet and Manzo recommended the following strategy: first, assign a short

> Question Note
>
> [Should illegal wildlife trade be allowed to continue or, at least, be ignored, after unsuccessful attempts to stop it] The author says that it is becoming more unpleasant for illegal trades of wildlife and their products due to more laws instituted by governments around the world. He also cites serious economic and ecological reasons not to give up the fight.

selection to be read in class, then write a certain type of annotation on the board. Ask students how what they read on the board relates to the passage that was just assigned. Through discussion, formulate the definition and concept for the annotation under discussion.

As part of a growing understanding of the different annotations, students should be able to discriminate a well-written note from a poorly written one. Have the class read a short passage, followed by several examples of a certain type of annotation. One is well written; the others are flawed in some way. For example, a discussion of critical annotations may include one illustration of a good critical note, one which lacks the annotator's position, another which fails to defend or develop the position taken.

Modeling and practice should follow naturally from awareness and knowledge building. The teacher should walk students through the process of writing different types of notes by sharing his or her thought processes. Show how a note is written and revised to satisfaction through think-aloud procedures. Then have students practice writing notes individually and in peer groups of two or three. Eanet and Manzo suggested that peer-group interaction is nonthreatening and leads to productions which can be duplicated or put on the board, compared, and evaluated by the class with teacher direction.

To facilitate application to real classroom reading tasks, we suggest that students write regularly in a thought book or compile study cards.

Keeping a Thought Book

As part of taking reading notes on a regular basis, students should keep a "thought book" to share with others (Eanet and Manzo, 1976). The thought book can be a section of the study journal or a separate looseleaf notebook for writing reading notes on text material. The students should be directed to write certain types of notes in the thought book depending on the teacher's objectives. For example, they may be directed to summarize, react critically, pose questions based on what they have read, or state the author's thesis.

It may be wise to save note writing in the thought book for the latter half of a class period. The next class period then begins with a review or a sharing of notes, followed by discussion and clarification of the text material based on the annotations.

Using Study Cards

Notes written on index cards are an alternative to the thought book. Require students to compile "study cards" based on text readings. One tactic is to write question annotations formulated during previewing on one side of the cards, and responses to the questions on the other side. For example, ask students to convert the major subheadings of a text selection to questions, writing one question per card. The responses probably will lend themselves to summary or critical annotations depending on the questions posed. Later, students can use the study cards to prepare for a test. As part of test preparation a student can read the question, recite outloud the response and then review the written annotation which was previously compiled.

Lester (1984) offered the following tips for recording note card information:

1. *Use ink*. Penciled notes blur easily with repeated shuffling of the cards.

2. *Use index cards*. Four-by-six or three-by-five inch index cards for taking notes are more durable and can be rearranged and organized more easily than large sheets of paper.

3. *Jot down only one item per card*. Don't overload a card with more than one type of annotation or one piece of information.

4. *Write on one side of card*. Material on the back of a card may be overlooked when studying.

Listening: A Prerequisite to Note Taking

Consider a very typical classroom scene. The setting is an eleventh-grade business education class. The teacher has prepared a lecture on consumerism. How will she be able to tell whether class members are active or inactive participants in the lecture? Let's take a closer look at the dynamics operating in her room.

A student in the back row next to the window glances briefly toward the football field outside. Yet with pen in hand he seems to be listening. Another student just under the teacher's nose sits back in her chair with arms folded and eyes staring straight ahead. Both students display the two most obvious criteria for active listeners: eye contact and body cues. So do most of the remaining twenty-seven students. The teacher, however, isn't satisfied that the whole class is actively participating. Why? She knows that active listening involves more than physical attentiveness. Active participation involves the productive use of the time in each student's head between hearing the teacher's words and hearing the next words she will utter.

The circle in Figure 8.5 represents each student's total "thinking space" for listening.

A wedge equal to about one-tenth of the total thinking space is reserved for simply hearing the teacher's words. What comprises the remaining nine-tenths of the listener's thinking space? Obviously, the student's thinking speed far outstrips the teacher's (or any speaker's) talking speed. What students do with this leftover time determines how active and productive their participation will be in the whole-class presentation.

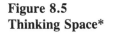

**Figure 8.5
Thinking Space***

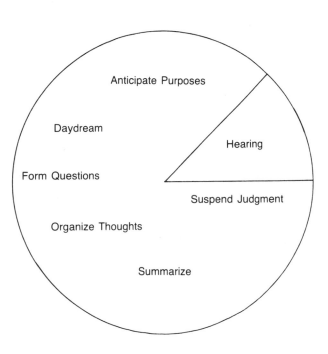

*Source: Sarah Lundsteen, *Children Learn to Communicate*, © 1976, p. 79. Adapted by permission of Prentice-Hall, Inc., Englewood Cliffs, N.J.

Let's hypothesize that the student in the back row and perhaps fifteen other students in the class were using their thinking space productively. They might be doing some of the following things to enhance learning:

1. taking notes and responding to questions raised,

2. anticipating the teacher's next point,

3. establishing continuous purposes for listening,

4. forming some questions that zero in on what's been said,

5. organizing their thoughts into categories of some kind,

6. suspending making judgments until more information is received,

7. summarizing the bits of information the teacher has presented.

Let's assume that the remaining students were not making the best academic use of their thinking space during the lecture. They may have been doing some of these things to impede participation in the presentation:

1. faking attention (staring at the teacher, for example) while daydreaming,

2. planning some private activity (such as the next weekend at the beach),

3. jotting down notes to pass along to a friend in the next row,

4. failing to screen out irrelevant details and distractions such as the intermittent noise of hallway footsteps or the untied shoe one row over.

This scene occurs in every lecture situation, no matter how dynamic a speaker is.

Active listening is the first step toward effective notetaking. The teacher can prime students to listen actively, as the *listening guide* and the *guided lecture procedure* show.

Listening Guide

Castallo (1976) maintained that note taking is a two-step process which involves (1) listening for main points in a lecture and (2) writing those points in an organized manner for later use. He suggested that teachers can use a listening guide as the first step in teaching successful note taking.

To develop a listening guide the teacher must be prepared to give an organized lecture. Or to put it another way, you must know what you're going to say before you say it. This means reviewing lecture notes and deciding what the main and supporting ideas will be and the order in which you will present them. When you accomplish this you should develop a skeletal outline of the lecture, leaving empty spaces for students to fill in during the presentation. The outline in effect becomes the listening guide.

Castallo (1976) provided an illustration of a listening guide from a junior high science class. The science teacher's lecture dealt with two types of learning. His introduction went like this:

> Today's topic is learning. We will be discussing how people learn in two different ways. The first type we shall discuss will be learning through *positive reinforcement*. The second type of learning we shall discuss will be learning through *negative reinforcement*. We shall list at least *three examples* of each type and discuss how they are related. When we finish we shall also discuss how they are related. When we finish we shall also discuss how learning takes place through another method which is related to negative reinforcement *(ignoring)*. *(Castallo, 1976, p. 290)*

The introduction provided a conceptual overview for the students. The teacher then expanded on the main points of the lecture. Students completed their listening guides as the lecture progressed. The teacher completed the same guide on an overhead projector to "alleviate any possible misunderstandings."

Guided Lecture Procedure

Another strategy which promotes active listening and the productive use of thinking space is the Guided Lecture Procedure (GLP). The GLP is the listening counterpart to the Guided Reading Procedure, which was explained in Chapter 7.

Here's how the GLP works:

1. Students are told not to take notes during the lecture and are encouraged instead to listen with the intent of retaining all information presented.

2. The teacher writes on the chalkboard the three or four main objectives of the lecture. The students read and copy the objectives. Next to each objective, the teacher writes technical terms new to the students which will be used during the lecture.

3. The teacher then lectures for approximately half the class period.

4. After the lecture the teacher directs students to write down individually and quickly everything they recall. They may abbreviate and annotate. The teacher encourages students to use "visual thinking" in order to "see" what interrelationships and categories of knowledge they can form.

5. Students then form small groups to review and discuss the lecture. This is the crux of the activity. They outline their notes in sequential order, identifying major ideas, relating these to pertinent details, and checking to make sure their outline fits with the objectives and new vocabulary the teacher listed.

The GLP provides the structure students need to participate in active listening and study. If questions arise during small-group interaction, the teacher should be ready to help students resolve them.

The originators of the GLP recommended that a writing assignment be given as a follow-up to the class activity: ". . . the student writes in narrative form, independently of her/his notes, the lecture's major concepts, pertinent details, and conclusions. This activity helps the student retain the information and provides an immediate self-appraisal regarding areas that should be studied in more detail" (Kelley and Holmes, 1979, p. 603).

The listening guide and the GLP aren't so much methods for note taking as they are stimulants for active, intensive listening. In the next section, we will examine a note-taking method that can be learned easily.

A Strategy for Taking Listening Notes

Every study skills textbook recommends a "classic" note-taking method, but Palmatier's (1973) procedure is one of the few that has been tested empirically and found to be easier to learn than other methods. The *note-taking system for learning* (NSL) is labeled as such because it not only provides for organizing information but also forms the basis for studying for tests.

The NSL makes several provisos for effective note taking. First, a student should use only one side of an 8½-by-11 inch sheet of looseleaf paper with a legal-width margin (if necessary, the student should add a margin line three inches from the left side of the paper). Second, the student should take lecture notes to the right of the margin. Although no specific format for recording notes is required, Palmatier (1973) suggested that students "develop a format which uses subordination and space to illustrate the organization of the material. Subordination of items may be achieved through indentation to show continuation of ideas or through enumeration to show series of details" (p. 38). Third, the student is to put labels in the left-hand margin that correspond with units of information recorded in the notes. The labels help to organize the welter of information in the right-hand column and give students the chance to fill in gaps in the notes. The labeling process should be completed as quickly as possible following the original taking of notes.

Finally, the student takes *reading notes* on separate sheets of paper and inserts them into appropriate positions in the lecture notes. According to Palmatier (1973), "This putting together of both reading and lecture notes into a single sequence is one reason for limiting notes to only one side of the paper . . . if the student has taken complete lecture and reading notes, he now has all material organized into a single system for learning" (pp. 37–38).

Once notes are taken and the labeling task is completed, the system can be used by students to study for exams. For example, in preparing for a test, the student can spread out the note pages for review. One excellent strategy is to show students how to spread the pages, in order, in such a way that the lecture notes are hidden by succeeding pages and only the left-margin labels show. The labels can then be used as question stems to recall information—for example, "What do I need to know about *(label)*?" Accuracy of recall, of course, can be checked by referring to the original notes which were concealed by overlapping the pages.

Using Graphic Aids

It's not at all surprising to find five hundred or more graphic aids in a single secondary textbook. These graphics are there for a reason. They represent more than icing on the cake; as Robinson (1975) pointed out, publishing costs are too high to sustain mere embellishment. The fact is that graphic materials enhance understanding and interpretation.

A writer has definite purposes in mind in using graphic aids to enhance text material. In some cases an aid is used to expand upon a concept developed in the main text. In other cases a graphic might be inserted to serve as an example or an illustration of an idea the writer has introduced. Such aids support points which are sometimes buried in the text. Graphic aids, particularly charts and tables, also help readers by summarizing and organizing information. Moreover, aids such as pictures, cartoons, and maps are "experience builders"; they add a "reality dimension" to the connected discourse. For example, the text description of the points in the arrangement of the entries in the *Reader's Guide to Periodical Literature* is more meaningful and concrete because of the graphic aid the authors provide (see Box 8.2).

Box 8.2*

ADVERTISING
Art director who has a way with words also has a book coming from Abrams; publication of The art of advertising; interview, ed by R. Dahlin. G. Lois. Pub W 211:55+ Ja 17 '77

Giving impact to ideas; address, October 11, 1977. L. T. Hagopian. Vital Speeches 44:154-7 D 15 '77

News behind the ads. See alternate issues of Changing times

Preaching in the marketplace. America 136:457 My 21 '77

Selling it. Consumer Rep 42:385, 458, 635 Jl-Ag, N '77
   See also
Photography in advertising
Religious advertising
Television advertising
Women in advertising
   also subhead Advertising under various subjects, e.g. Books—Advertising

Here are some important points to notice about the arrangement of the entries in the *Readers' Guide:*

1. Articles are entered under the author's last name and also under the subject with which the article deals.
2. Author and subject entries are arranged in alphabetical order.
3. The author's name in an author entry is in boldface type, the last name first, in capital letters. Subject headings are also in boldface capitals.
4. The numbers at the end of the entry indicate the volume number of the periodical and, following the colon, the pages on which the article appears. A plus sign (+) means that the article is continued on a later page in the magazine.
5. The issue in which the article appears is shown by the month of publication, abbreviated, the day of the month if the magazine is published more than once a month, and the year.

Students tend to skip over graphic aids entirely or pay only cursory attention to them. Perhaps the sheer number of graphics in a text provides a visual overkill which diverts students from studying any of them seriously. And study skills instruction in a reading class, isolated from real curricular need, doesn't transfer to content area reading assignments as much as we would like to believe. Although students learn the terminology and mechanics of reading graphic aids, they may see little relation between a "reading lesson" and the application of skills in a "content lesson." Studying graphic aids is often a matter of demand and purpose in a meaningful reading situation.

It's a difficult task to read graphic material in conjunction with written text. Students must be shown how to engage in back-and-forth reading, going from print to visual and visual to print. The example of the arrangement of entries in the *Reader's Guide* nicely illustrates how students must study an illustration as they read the corresponding text section.

Teachers can assist students to use graphic aids productively through planned guidance. Summers (1965) recommended four conditions that would "maximize" learning from graphic aids in a content area. Students should be taught to (1) recognize and interpret separate elements presented in graphic aids, (2) analyze and understand the relationships between elements contained in graphic aids, (3) pose questions and seek answers through the use of graphic aids, and (4) make inferences and draw conclusions from graphic aids in light of the problem at hand. The processes involved in reading visual material are basically the same as those tapped while reading connected discourse.

Open-book discussions are good times for the teacher to provide the direction that students need to study graphic aids successfully. You in effect say to students, "OK, let's take a few minutes to look closely at how the author(s) of our textbook used the (name the graphic) on page 67."

An open-book discussion walks students through an analysis of a graphic aid. The teacher models the types of questions students themselves should raise when they encounter a graphic in a reading assignment. "Focus questions" will prod students into isolating and identifying important elements in the graphic. A good starting point is always a discussion of the title or caption. "Clarifying questions" will prompt students into analyzing the relationships among the elements and making inferences.

The overhead projector can be put to good use during an analysis of graphic aids. Use color markings for emphasis to show relationships and also to show students the inferential connections that they must make to draw conclusions. Participation in several demonstrations will have a positive effect on students' studying.

By way of illustration, let's turn our attention to specific examples which spotlight and extend the points just made.

Charts, Graphs, and Tables

Pictorial representations are common fixtures in most content area material. The complexity of graphic material varies. Yet even the most uncomplicated-looking chart, graph, or table can challenge the student's ability to interpret meaning. Consider, for example, the following illustrations.

Middle-grade youngsters must make many inferential decisions to interpret and understand the "stream" chart illustrated in Figure 8.6.

Figure 8.6
Stages in the Development of Money*

1. barter

2. objects used as a measure of value

3. valuable items used as a medium of exchange

4. money coined from precious metals

5. paper money printed

*source:Robert Carter and John Richards, *Of, By and For the People.* Westchester, Ill.: Benefic Press, 1972, p. 360.

They must infer that:

1. The "stages" represent a time sequence with early times depicted in stage 1 and modern times depicted in stage 5.

2. The evolution of money is based on hundreds of years of elapsed time.

3. The contents of the bushels in stages 1, 2, and 3 represent a farmer's grain (or a reasonable alternative).

4. A bushel of grain is a valued item.

5. Bartered "objects" are animate or inanimate.

6. Different objects (such as the steer) have more value than other objects.

7. The equal sign in stage 2 suggests the comparable value of different objects.

8. The contents of the box being held in stage 3 must be of substantial value.

9. Paper money is a substitute for precious metals (gold or silver).

The students must also learn the technical terms *barter, medium of exchange, precious metals,* and even *measure of value.* You must translate them into language the students can understand.

The "path of a check" schematic in Figure 8.7 is quite concrete. It illustrates pictorially what may be a difficult sequence of ideas to grasp in the text explanation. Senior high business students can actually "see" the process and the forms used to make the transaction. The chart is an effective experience builder. Nevertheless, in order to make interpretations students must sense the implied chain reaction—the cause-effect pattern. They must know that the arrows indicate the direction of the relationships. In addition, they must read the "fine print" between pictured items.

The general purpose of charts, graphs, and tables is to present and summarize information. Questions or statements should be developed, if none already accompanies a graphic, to help students interpret such information. For example, the table in Box 8.3 shows how American history teachers from the Louisville, Kentucky, school system developed a three-level question guide to help students respond to numerical information which summarizes the breakdown of Electoral College votes in the 1960 presidential race in key states.

Since bar and pie graphs are used mainly to make comparisons between sets of relationships, they can be used to identify trends and make generalizations. Notice that in the pie graph in Box 8.4 students must decide whether certain generalizations are correct. The statements serve as springboards to interpretation by helping students identify trends emerging from the comparative data.

In contrast to a bar graph or pie graph, a textbook might also use a line graph to compare how two or more sets of data whose relationships are proportional change over time in order to give students a graphic aid to help them predict information. Study the line graph in Figure 8.8, from *Life Science: A Problem-Solving Approach.*

Figure 8.7
The Path of a Check*

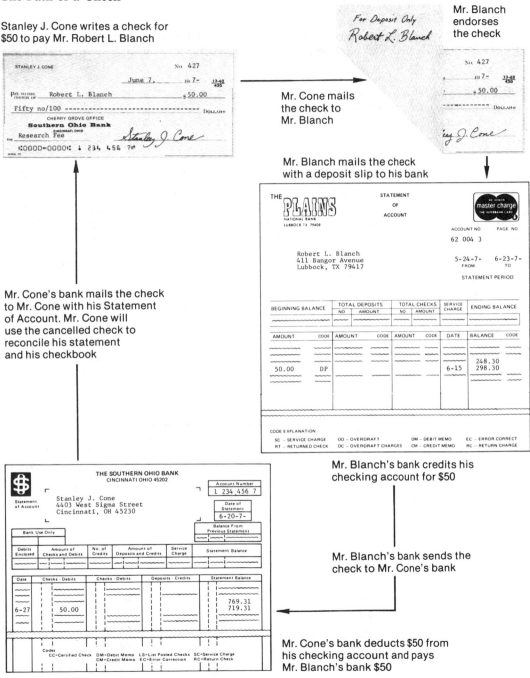

Stanley J. Cone writes a check for
$50 to pay Mr. Robert L. Blanch

Mr. Blanch
endorses
the check

Mr. Cone mails
the check to
Mr. Blanch

Mr. Blanch mails the check
with a deposit slip to his bank

Mr. Cone's bank mails the check
to Mr. Cone with his Statement
of Account. Mr. Cone will
use the cancelled check to
reconcile his statement
and his checkbook

Mr. Blanch's bank credits his
checking account for $50

Mr. Blanch's bank sends the
check to Mr. Cone's bank

Mr. Cone's bank deducts $50 from
his checking account and pays
Mr. Blanch's bank $50

*SOURCE: James Meehan, William Pasework, and Mary Ellen Oliverio, *Clerical Office Procedures,* 5th ed. Cincinnati: South-Western Publishing Company, 1973, p. 521.

Box 8.3

THE ELECTORAL COLLEGE*

The Electoral College System suffers several shortcomings. The most serious is that it can produce a President who has won a majority of the electoral votes even though he did not receive a
majority of the popular vote.

From the table below:
1. Determine the total number of popular votes cast.
2. Determine the total number of electoral votes each candidate received.

State	Electoral Votes	Kennedy	Nixon	Kennedy	Nixon
California	32	3,224,099	3,249,722		32
Illinois	27	2,377,846	2,368,988	27	
Kentucky	10	521,855	602,607		10
Ohio	25	1,944,248	2,217,611		25
Pennsylvania	32	2,556,282	2,439,956	32	
Texas	24	1,167,932	1,121,699	24	
Total					

Answer the following questions using the chart.
I. Literal Level
    1. In what state did Nixon receive the largest number of electoral votes?
    2. In what state did Kennedy get the largest number of popular votes?
    3. Which candidate received more popular votes?
II. Interpretive Level
    4. Why may the Electoral College be described as a "winner take all" system?
III. Applied Level
    5. Do you think there should be an alternative to the Electoral College System? If so, what?

**Source: *Study Guides for Skill Development.* Louisville, Ky: Jefferson County Board of Education, 1978.*

The authors of the text did a fine job of asking questions to help students interpret and apply information from the population graph. Here's a sampling of their questions:

1. In what year was the grasshopper population greatest?

2. In what year was the frog population greatest?

3. Why did the grasshopper population reach a peak immediately after the rye grass?

4. Why was the frog population never as great as the grasshopper population?

5. The population of which organism seems to control all of the populations in this food chain?

6. Why were all three populations nearly constant during the last five years?

Box 8.4

PIE GRAPH: BUDGET OF A LARGE AMERICAN CITY*

Examine this graph of the budget of a large American city for the years 1969–1970.

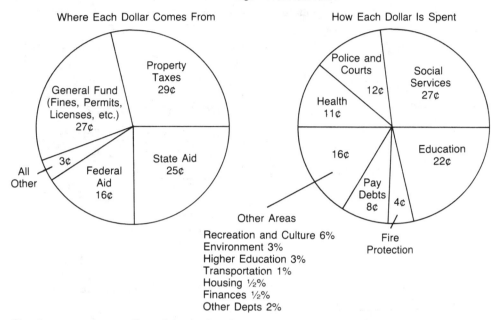

Total Budget: $6,600,000,000

Where Each Dollar Comes From

Property Taxes 29¢

General Fund (Fines, Permits, Licenses, etc.) 27¢

All Other 3¢

Federal Aid 16¢

State Aid 25¢

How Each Dollar Is Spent

Police and Courts 12¢

Social Services 27¢

Health 11¢

16¢

Education 22¢

Pay Debts 8¢   4¢

Fire Protection

Other Areas

Recreation and Culture 6%
Environment 3%
Higher Education 3%
Transportation 1%
Housing ½%
Finances ½%
Other Depts 2%

Check your understanding of the budget by telling whether or not the following are correct generalizations.

1. The city depended heavily upon help from the state and federal government to carry out its services.

2. The greatest expense was for aid to the poor and programs to help the poor.

3. Programs for housing and recreation cost more than expenses for health sevices.

4. Transportation costs were one of the largest of city expenses.

5. The greatest source of money for the city was the tax on property.

6. Without federal help, some city services would have had to be cut.

7. Planning for the future of the city was a big expense item.

8. All the money collected from taxes on property could not pay for all the cost of police and fire protection.

*SOURCE: John O'Connor, Morris Gall, and Robert Goldberg, *Exploring the Urban World.* New York: Globe Book Company, 1972, p. 403. Used with permission.

7. What population would have to be increased first in order to have an increase in the frog population?

8. Which of the three populations will probably show an increase next year?

9. Which population will probably be the last to show an increase due to the addition of the fertilizer?

10. What populations would be affected if an insect-killing chemical were applied to the grass around the pond? Explain your answer.

Figure 8.8
Population Graph: The Growth in Population of Three Organisms in a Pond Community*

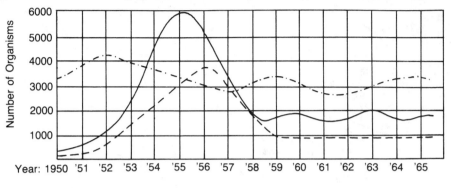

Key: Rye Grass: –·–·–   Grasshopper: ——   Frog: – – –
*Source: Joseph L. Carter et al., *Life Science: A Problem Solving Approach*. Lexington, Mass.: Ginn and Company, 1971, pp. 361–363. © 1979, 1971 by Ginn and Company (Xerox Corporation). Used with permission.

A steady progression of thought-provoking questions such as these leads students from interpretation to prediction to application. Where questions do not accompany a graphic, content teachers have little recourse other than to develop their own.

Maps, Pictures, and Cartoons

Students need a great deal of interpretive skill to use maps, pictures, and cartoons effectively. Inferences from these aids must be made in relation to the text material.

Pictures in a textbook are invaluable. They can be used to reduce uncertainty, arouse interest, and stimulate questions. A well-timed picture breathes life and adds clarity to the printed word. Through their realism, pictures can expand experience and help avoid misunderstanding. They are particularly effective in showing step-by-step developments, contrasts and comparisons, and the status of things, processes, and events.

Cartoons are fraught with implications based on symbolic representations. Students may lack the background experience or prior knowledge to interpret adequately the symbols and implied meanings in a cartoon. Questions such as those for the cartoons in Box 8.5 will lead students to identify elements and relationships in cartoons. These relationships then will form the basis for interpretation and application. Of course, teachers also should consider the use of declarative statements in a three-level-guide format as another option available for helping students to respond to meaning in cartoons.

Because they are compact and devoid of redundancy, maps also require a great deal of student and teacher attention. A valuable chapter by Summers (1965) contains excellent background material on the nature, complexity, and diversity of maps. It is a "must" resource for content instructors. Summers pointed out the irony that teachers face when working with fairly decent "map readers" who happen to be poor "map thinkers." These students can locate information adequately, for they know terminology. Yet they cannot make the cognitive leap into interpretation. They need to engage in activities similar to those which have already been illustrated in this section.

According to Summers (1965), a map thinker should be aware of the following elements when studying a map*:

1. *Map Title*—A map title is similar to a book title; it gives the name of the area the map is depicting or the type of information to be shown. Map titles should be read carefully for a brief, succinct introduction to the map and its features.

2. *Legend*—The legend or key is often compared to the table of contents of a book. Just as the table of contents tells you what the book is about the legend or key indicates what the symbols on the map stand for, the scale of the map, and other data. A symbol may be a drawing, pattern, or color used to indicate map facts, usually a class of objects rather than a specific object. A variety of symbols may be found on maps although there is a tendency to use standard symbols from map to map. The legend or key is most often found in a separate box on the map. It is extremely helpful for students to visualize the things for which map symbols stand. Looking at the green of a map, one should actually "see" the rugged mountains.

3. *Direction*—Cardinal direction is indicated or can be inferred in some fashion on all maps. The top of the map usually, but not always, indicates North. It is important that students realize that North is not just a direction but that it is also a concept with the related understandings of true and magnetic North, intermediate distances, and the polar regions.

4. *Distance—Scale*—Any representation of earth on a map or globe is actually a graphic reduction from actual size. The scale of a map indicates what a unit of distance on the map is equal to on the earth itself. Three types of scale are in common use: graphic scale, statement scale, and fractional scale. The type of scale is relatively unimportant but the major

*E. G. Summers, "Utilizing Visual Aids in Reading Materials for Effective Reading," in Harold L. Herber, ed., *Developing Study Skills in Secondary Schools*. Newark, Del.: International Reading Association, 1965, pp. 113–114. Reprinted with the permission of E. G. Summers and the International Reading Association.

Box 8.5

INTERPRETING POLITICAL CARTOONS

Musical Chairs[†]

"We can get it for you wholesale."

[†]Redrawn with permission of the McNaught Syndicate.

Directions: Study the cartoons and then complete the exercise below. Put answers on a separate piece of paper.

Identification

    1. List three words which best describe what each cartoon shows.

    2. What is happening in each cartoon? Who is involved?

    3. What issues do these cartoons raise?

Relationships

    4. What two things do these cartoons have in common?

    5. How is the main character portrayed in each cartoon?

Interpretation

    6. Select one cartoon and identify the main character or item portrayed. Identify the other characters or items included in that cartoon.

    7. Describe how the main character or item is related to the other character or items portrayed.

    8. What observations or conclusions can you make about the problem, based on the information provided by these cartoons?

Application

    9. Select two cartoons and describe several of the ideas each cartoon illustrates.

   10. Given what you know about the energy problem, what might happen if Congress, the oil companies, or the public reacted as some of these cartoons indicate?

†Redrawn with permission of the McNaught Syndicate.

*SOURCE: *Study Guides for Skill Development.* Louisville, Ky.: Jefferson County Board of Education, 1978.

---

point to remember is that scale enables you to tell how far something is or how big something is. A small-scale map depicts a large area made smaller while a large-scale map depicts a small area made larger.

    5. *Location*—Grid systems are useful in locating places on maps. Grids section maps into smaller segments by use of horizontal or vertical lines. Special grids such as township range lines and those used on city maps and Atlases section by use of marginal letters and numbers. Parallels and meridians provide a means of locating places by latitude and longitude from agreed-upon fixed points. Projections are devices used to depict a curved area of surface on a flat map and involve distortions. Various projections have been developed and each has advantages and disadvantages.

    6. *Types of Maps*—The major map types are land, elevation, climate, natural vegetation and water features, political, economic, and population. Each type provides a different kind of information about an area. Often, combinations of several types appear on one map.

    A teacher shouldn't assume that students will attend to these elements independently. Students need to be made aware of the relevant pieces of information such as those described above that are contained in map elements. Nevertheless, a map thinker is not only aware of important information but knows how to use it to make inferences and draw conclusions.

Looking Back, Looking Forward

Study was described in terms of showing students how to do something with what they have read. To be successful at studying, learners must develop knowledge and awareness of reading strategies as well as the ability to monitor their own reading. Self-knowledge and self-monitoring are the cornerstones of independent learning from text. Through explicit instructional methods, a teacher can show students how to use study strategies to their advantage.

We explored four areas of study strategy instruction: previewing text, organizing and relating information, taking notes, and using graphic aids. Previewing involves cursory reading activities which build for the reader a general outline of what to expect in a text assignment. Previewing leads to questioning, predicting, and goal setting.

Outlining and note taking help students to produce organization in the reading material as well as content lecture. Free-form and restricted outlining procedures were discussed. We advised that free-form outlining should precede attempts to have students use the conventional, restricted format. Listening is the essential process in taking class notes. Students can be taught to be active listeners. The note-taking learning system is a method that students can learn easily to help them take and study lecture and reading notes. Graphics are used in content materials to support and enhance the written text. Students easily overlook visual material when they study. Therefore we examined several instructional procedures that would help readers study graphic aids. The questions that content teachers ask to help students focus on and clarify the important points in charts, graphs, tables, pictures, maps, and the like will make a difference.

The next chapter deals with an integral part of content area reading. Content area vocabulary terms—the special and technical words of a subject—are labels for concepts. Vocabulary instruction reading can lay the groundwork for concept development. Many suggestions for vocabulary study lie ahead. As you read the chapter be prepared to classify information under three major categories: vocabulary reinforcement, vocabulary building, and vocabulary awareness.

How does the content teacher extend students' knowledge and use of special and technical terms? The chapter presentation of vocabulary instruction is straightforward. It relies heavily, as you will see, on example.

Suggested Readings

Algier, A., & Algier, K. (eds.). (1982). *Improving Reading and Study Skills*. San Francisco: Jossey-Bass.

Anderson, T., & Armbruster, B. (1984). Studying. In P. D. Pearson (ed.), *Handbook of Reading Research*. New York: Longman.

Baker, L., & Brown, A. (1984). Metacognitive skills and reading. In P. D. Pearson (ed.), *Handbook of Reading Research*. New York: Longman.

Bragstad, B., & Stumpf, S. (1982). *A Guidebook for Teaching Study Skills and Motivation*. Boston: Allyn and Bacon.

Devine, T. (1981). *Teaching Study Skills*. Boston: Allyn and Bacon.

Eanet, M., & Manzo, A. (1976). REAP—a strategy for improving reading/writing/ study skills. *Journal of Reading,* **19**, 647–652.

Pearson, P. D. (1984). Direct explicit teaching of reading comprehension. In G. Duffy, L. Roehler, and J. Mason (eds.), *Comprehension Instruction*. New York: Longman.

Thomas, E., & Robinson, H. A. (1981). *Improving Reading in Every Class* (3rd ed.). Boston: Allyn and Bacon.

CHAPTER NINE

Vocabulary and Concept Development

I am a Bear of Very Little Brain
and long words Bother me.
—A. A. MILNE, from *Winnie-the-Pooh*

Organizing Principle

There is a strong relationship between vocabulary knowledge and reading comprehension. Teachers capitalize on this relationship when they recognize that words must be taught *well enough* to enhance students' comprehension of content materials. Yet the predominant approach to vocabulary study in content areas often is limited to some form of looking up, defining, memorizing, and using words in sentences. While these activities may have some value, they cannot represent the breadth or depth of vocabulary learning in a content area. To teach words well enough to enhance comprehension, teachers must provide students with multiple opportunities to build conceptual and contextual knowledge of technical and special words. That is to say, students must understand how terms relate to one another conceptually and how terms are defined contextually in sentences and passages. Content area terminology must be developed systematically and functionally through the ongoing study of text materials. The organizing principle of the chapter suggests why this is important: *Vocabulary taught and reinforced*

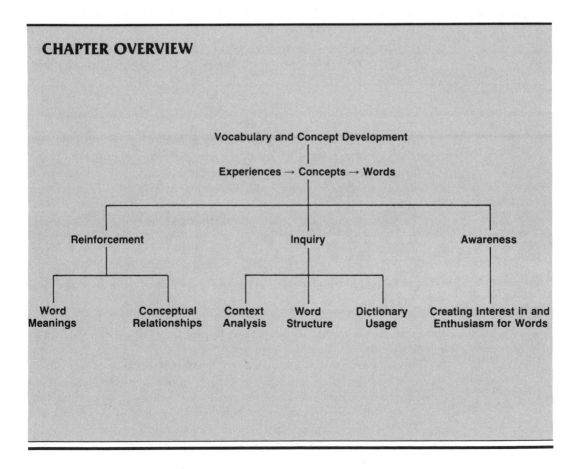

CHAPTER OVERVIEW

Vocabulary and Concept Development

Experiences → Concepts → Words

Reinforcement · Inquiry · Awareness

Word Meanings · Conceptual Relationships · Context Analysis · Word Structure · Dictionary Usage · Creating Interest in and Enthusiasm for Words *within the framework of concept development enhances reading comprehension.*

In order to develop knowledge of content area vocabulary, instructional emphasis must be placed on (1) reinforcement of word meanings and conceptual relationships, (2) development of inquiry skills to help students identify the meanings of unfamiliar words encountered during reading, and (3) an awareness of and sense of excitement for learning new words. As you begin to study the major relationships that exist among key concepts in this chapter, ask yourself these questions:

1. Why should vocabulary be taught within the context of concept development? What is the relationship between experiences, concepts, and words?

2. How do strategies for vocabulary reinforcement help students grasp word meanings and understand conceptual relationships among content area terms?

3. What is meant by vocabulary inquiry? How do the development of inquiry skills help students to use the context of passages, the structure of words, and the dictionary to identify the meaning of unfamiliar words encountered while reading?

4. Why should content area teachers create excitement for learning new words? How do teachers spark interest and create enthusiasm for word study?

Fridays always seemed to be set aside for quizzes when we were students. And one of the quizzes most frequently given was the vocabulary test.

"Look up these words for the week. Write out their definitions and memorize them. And then use each one in a complete sentence. You'll be tested on these terms on Friday."

The extent of vocabulary study for us seemed to consistently revolve around the dull routines associated with looking up, defining, memorizing, and using words in sentences.

Such an instructional pattern soon became a meaningless, purposeless activity—an end in itself, rather than a means to an end. Although there was nothing inherently wrong with looking up, defining, memorizing and using words in sentences, the approach in and of itself was too narrow for us to learn words in depth. Instead, we memorized definitions to pass the Friday quiz—and forgot them on Saturday.

Providing lists of words for students to learn sometimes leads to the ill-found conclusion that vocabulary instruction is separate from concept development in a content area. For classroom teachers, vocabulary instruction often means teaching a corpus of words rather than word meanings that contribute to the development of concepts. The distinction is subtle but important. Once teachers clarify the relationship between vocabulary and concept development, they are receptive to instructional options and alternatives.

Vocabulary is as unique to a content area as fingerprints are to a human being. A content area is distinguishable by its language, particularly the special and technical terms which label the underlying concepts of its subject matter. No wonder Dale (1975) noted that to master a content area "is to learn its key concepts; that is, its language" (p. 12). To illustrate Dale's point, imagine that you are once again a sophomore in high school. For the most part you can still recall how middle school teachers seemed to do more "fun things" in class. But now that you're in high school, you can't help but feel that more is expected from you in the way of schoolwork. The ninth grade was a transition year. You learned the ropes. And now that you're in the tenth grade, you know how to cope with academic demands — at least sometimes.

Your biology teacher assigns a lot of reading from your text — let's say it's *Modern Biology* (1973). The textbook shows its age: the cloth cover of your copy is frayed on the corners. Some sections of the textbook are interesting; some are dull. This particular passage is in between:

*Darwin's Theory of Natural Selection**

In 1859, Charles Darwin, an English scientist, published his *On the Origin of Species by Means of Natural Selection*. His theory of natural selection, while confined to biology, has also influenced other branches of science. According to Darwin, the chief factors that account for the development of new species from a common ancestry can be summarized as follows:

(1) All organisms produce more offspring than can actually survive.

(2) Because of overproduction, there is constant struggle for existence among individuals.

(3) The individuals of a given species vary.

(4) The fittest, or the best adapted, individuals of a species survive.

(5) Surviving organisms transmit variations to offspring.

Overproduction

A fern plant may produce 50 million spores each year. If all the spores resulting from this overproduction matured, in the second year they would nearly cover North America. A mustard plant produces about 730,000 seeds annually. If they all took root and matured, in two years they would occupy an area 2,000 times that of the land surface of the earth. The dandelion would do the same in ten years.

At a single spawning, an oyster may shed 114,000,000 eggs. If all these eggs survived, the ocean would be literally filled with oysters. Within five generations, there would be more oysters then the estimated number of electrons in the visible universe! There is, however, no such actual increase.

*SOURCE: James H. Otto and Albert Towle, *Modern Biology*. New York: Holt, Rinehart and Winston, 1973, pp. 206–207. © 1973.

The elephant is considered to have a slow rate of reproduction. An average elephant lives to be 100 years old, breeds over a span of from 30 to 90 years, and bears about 6 young. Yet if all the young from one pair of elephants survived, in 750 years the descendants would number 19,000,000.

Struggle for Existence

We know that in actuality the number of individuals of a species usually changes little in its native environment. In other words, regardless of the rate of reproduction, only a small minority of the original number of offspring reaches maturity.

Each organism seeks food, water, air, warmth, and space but only a few can obtain these needs in struggling to survive. This struggle for existence is most intense between members of the same species, because they compete for the same necessities.

As you read the passage several of the authors' examples capture your interest and hold your attention. You even form mental images of a world overrun with oysters and mustard plants and begin to get a feel for some of Darwin's ideas.

In retrospect you can give the authors credit for trying to relate some of the abstract concepts in the passage to concrete or familiar examples. But overall, you and your classmates find the material somewhat difficult to read. The words get in your way.

Three types of vocabulary are evident in the biology passage.

The first type, *general vocabulary,* consists of everyday words having widely acknowledged meanings in common usage. The second, *special vocabulary,* is made up of words from everyday, general vocabulary which take on specialized meanings when adapted to a particular content area. The third type, *technical vocabulary,* consists of words which have usage and application only in a particular subject matter field.

In this short passage alone there are at least twenty terms of a special or technical nature:

natural selection	visible universe
organism	species
survival of the fittest	transmit
overpopulation	overproduction
variations	descendants
theory	reproduction
offspring	ancestors
competition	spawn
necessities	maturity
spores	electrons

It would be futile for a biology teacher (or for any content area teacher) to single out for instruction every special and technical term that students will encounter while reading. However, content area terminology can be introduced, developed, and reinforced within the framework of learning concepts. In Chapter 4 we saw how a structured overview can be used to introduce the key concept words in a text assignment, chapter, or unit of study. Moreover, we showed how a teacher can select several words which represent target concepts to carefully teach during the structured overview presentation. In this chapter we explain how to extend and reinforce vocabulary learning as students develop concepts from the course content under study.

Comprehension and Vocabulary Knowledge

If students are not readily familiar with most words they meet in print they will undoubtedly have trouble understanding what they read. The problem is a practical and challenging one for content area teachers: teach vocabulary words well enough to enhance students' comprehension of written language (Beck and McKeown, 1983). Put another way, you must help students develop contextual and conceptual knowledge of words in order to comprehend fully what they read.

The relationship between knowledge of word meanings and comprehension has been well documented by researchers—and acknowledged by students. Intermediate, middle, and high school students have little difficulty recognizing that they don't understand what they're reading when the words get "too hard."

F. B. Davis (1944) and other researchers such as Thurstone (1946) have consistently identified knowledge of word meanings as an important factor in reading comprehension. In studies of text difficulty and readability, whenever passages have been simplified by substituting less difficult words, the passages have been easier to read (Chall, 1958; Wittrock, Marks, and Doctorow, 1975).

Various explanations are used to account for the strong relationship between vocabulary and comprehension. Anderson and Freebody (1981) propose three explanations in the form of hypotheses: the *aptitude, instrumental,* and *knowledge* hypotheses.

The Aptitude Hypothesis

The idea behind the aptitude hypothesis is that both vocabulary and comprehension reflect general intellectual ability. A large vocabulary as measured by test performance is a strong predictor of verbal and mental ability (Wechsler, 1958). As Manzo and Shirk (1972) suggest, "Acquiring a rich vocabulary is everyone's idea. of being learned . . . ." (p. 78). As a result, the relationship between vocabulary and comprehension is explained in this way: The more intellectually able the student, the more he or she will know the meanings of words and, therefore, comprehend better while reading. Students with large vocabularies have a built-in advantage because they often possess superior mental and verbal agility.

However, this does not mean that only "smart" students can acquire words easily. Or that only the most intelligent students profits from vocabulary instruction. Vocabulary knowledge, while a strong correlative of intelligence, is not necessarily hereditary. A student's environment and experiences are crucial in learning concepts and words. A content area classroom environment which promotes wide reading and language experiences influences students' vocabulary growth.

The Instrumental Hypothesis

The instrumental hypothesis can be stated simply: If comprehension depends in part on knowledge of word meanings, then vocabulary instruction ought to influence comprehension. Knowing words plays an instrumental role in students' understanding of text.

The main instructional implication of the instrumental hypothesis is to teach word meanings in depth—and students will find reading material easier to comprehend. Unfortunately, vocabulary instruction research has provided contradictory evidence to this effect. Pany and Jenkins (1977), Schacter (1978), and Tuinman and Brady (1974) show that vocabulary instruction has little effect on comprehension performance. However, more recent studies by Stahl (1983) and Beck, Perfetti, and McKeown (1982) show that when *enough* words from reading selections are taught in *depth,* comprehension is facilitated.

According to Dupuis and Snyder (1983), four outcomes are associated with direct, systematic vocabulary instruction: (1) the more frequently students use words, the easier it is to recall and use them; (2) the more different ways students have used words and seen them used, the easier it is to remember them; (3) the more important, interesting, or experienced-based words are to students, the easier it is to use and remember them; and (4) the more students know about the whole subject, the easier it is to use and remember specific words related to it.

The Knowledge Hypothesis

The knowledge hypothesis has much significance for content area instruction. Unlike the aptitude and instrumental hypotheses, the knowledge explanation suggests that vocabulary and comprehension are a reflection of general knowledge. In other words, *students with large vocabularies related to a given topic also have more knowledge about that topic, which in turn produces better comprehension.* Vocabulary knowledge is viewed more or less as an indicator that a reader is likely to possess more background information and conceptual knowledge to understand a text. Closely tied to a schema view of reading, the knowledge hypothesis proposes that vocabulary words must be taught within a larger framework of concept development.

Students in a content classroom learn new words throughout the year as they learn new information. As Anderson and Freebody (1981) suggest, "Every serious student of reading recognizes that the significant aspect of vocabulary development is in the learning of concepts not just words" (p. 87).

While all three hypotheses have merit in clarifying the relationship between word knowledge and comprehension, the knowledge and instrumental explanations have several valuable implications for vocabulary instruction in content areas: (1) teach word meanings with the context of concept development; (2) teach words in depth through frequent encounters and manipulative activities; and (3) teach words that students need to know to understand what they are reading.

Experiences, Concepts, and Words

Although words are labels for concepts, a single concept represents much more than the meaning of a single word. It might take thousands of words to explain a concept. However, answers to the questions, "What does it mean to know a word?" depend on how well we understand the relationship among personal experiences, concepts, and words.

Concepts are learned through our acting upon and interaction with the environment. Edgar Dale's classic Cone of Experience in Figure 9.1 reminds us how students learn concepts best—through direct, purposeful experiences. Learning is much more intense and meaningful when it is first hand. However, in place of direct experience (which is not always possible), we develop and learn concepts through various levels of contrived or vicarious experience. According to Dale (1969) learning a concept through oral or written language is especially difficult because it is so far removed from direct experience.

Given Dale's Cone of Experience, your participation in the demonstration in Box 9.1 will help illustrate why special and technical terms are good candidates for vocabulary instruction. Before reading further, complete the activity in Box 9.1.

Box 9.1

---

*VOCABULARY DEMONSTRATION: WORDS IN CONTENT AREAS**

Directions: In each of the ten blanks, fill in the name of the content area that includes all the terms in the list below.

1. _____	2. _____	3. _____
nationalism	forestry	metaphor
imperialism	ornithology	allusion
naturalism	zoology	irony
instrumentalism	biology	paradox
isolationist	entomology	symbolism
radicalism	botany	imagery
fundamentalist	bacteriology	simile
anarchy	protista	

4. _____	5. _____	6. _____
prestissimo	centimeter	graffles
adagio	milligram	folutes
larghetto	deciliter	lesnics
presto	millisecond	raptiforms
allegro	kilometer	cresnites

(continued)

largo	decimeter	hygrolated
andante	kilogram	loors
tempo	millimeter	chamlets

7. _____   8. _____   9 _____

polyunsaturated	octagon	auricle
glycogen	hemisphere	ventricle
monosaccharide	decagon	tricuspid
hydrogenation	hexagon	semilunar
enzymes	bisect	apex
lyzine	equilateral	mitral
cellulose	quadrilateral	aorta
	pentagon	myocardium

10. _____

intensity
complementary
hue color neutrals
trial
value
pigments

*SOURCE: Adapted from a workshop exercise developed by Robert Baker at Illinois State University.

If your responses are similar to others we have asked to do this, several predictable outcomes are likely. First of all, it was relatively easy for you to identify the content areas for several of the lists. Your knowledge and experience probably triggered instant recognition. You have a good working concept of many of the terms on these "easy" lists. You can put them to use in everyday situations that require listening, reading, writing, or speaking. They are your words. You own them.

Second, you probably recognized words in a few of the lists even though you may not be sure about the meanings of individual words. In lists 4 and 9, for example, you may be familiar with only one or two terms. Yet you are fairly sure that the terms in lists 4 and 9 exist as words despite the fact that you may not know what they mean. Dale (1975) commented that your attitude toward these kinds of words is analogous to your saying to a stranger, "I think I've met you before but I'm not sure." Several of the words from the lists may be in your "twilight zone": you have some knowledge about them, but "their meanings are a bit foggy, not sharply focussed" (Dale, 1975, p. 24). *Polyunsaturated* in list 7 is a case in point for some of us who have heard the word used in television commercials and may even have consciously sought polyunsaturated foods at the supermarket. Nevertheless, our guess is that we would be hard pressed to define or explain the meaning of *polyunsaturated* with any precision.

Finally, in one or two cases a list may have completely stymied your efforts at identification. There simply was no connection between your existing knowledge and any of the terms. You probably are not even sure whether the terms in one list really exist as words. Perhaps list 6 fell into this category?

Your participation in this activity leads to several points about vocabulary

Figure 9.1
Dale's Cone of Experience*

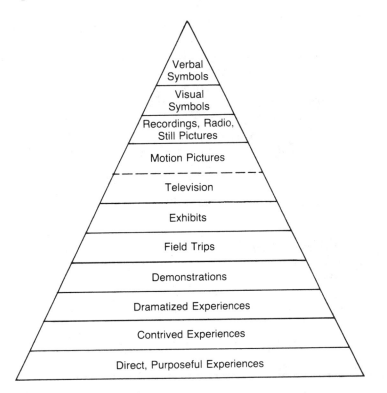

Verbal
Symbols

Visual
Symbols

Recordings, Radio,
Still Pictures

Motion Pictures

Television

Exhibits

Field Trips

Demonstrations

Dramatized Experiences

Contrived Experiences

Direct, Purposeful Experiences

*SOURCE: Edgar Dale, *Audiovisual Methods in Teaching*, 3rd ed. © 1946, 1954, 1969 by Holt, Rinehart and Winston.

instruction and concept development in content areas. The activity is a good reminder that every subject matter field creates a unique language to represent its important concepts. Words are just labels—nothing more or less—for these concepts. All the words on the lists (with the exception of list 6) represent concepts.

The definition of a special or technical term can undoubtedly be learned by rote without approaching a conceptual level of understanding. Gagně (1970) said, "An edge might be defined as a 'region of abrupt change in intensity of the pattern of light waves reflected to the eye from a surface.' It should not be supposed that this kind of verbalizing would be very effective in bringing about the learning of a concept" (p. 177). Retaining a definition of a technical term, however, is often a necessary first step in learning abstract concepts. Although you may have been able to define many of the words on the lists, your ability to conceptualize them, to apply them in a variety of ways, may be limited.

Which content area did you identify for list 6? In truth, the terms in this list represent jabberwocky—nonsense. They are bogus words which were invented to illustrate the point that many of the content terms in textbooks look the same way to students that the nonsense words in list 6 looked to you. You were able to pronounce most of them with little trouble but were stymied when you tried to connect them to your knowledge and experience. Students are stymied this way every day. But they are stymied by real words which represent the key concepts of a content area.

The words in these lists were actually taken from middle and high school textbooks. Just think for a moment about the staggering conceptual demands that we place on adolescent learners daily as they go from class to class. Terminology that they encounter in content material is often outside the scope of their normal speaking, writing, listening, and reading vocabularies. Special and technical terms often do not have concrete referents; they are abstract and must be learned through definition, application, and repeated exposure.

Words and Concepts

Concepts provide mental images. These images may represent anything that can be grouped together by common features or similar criteria—objects, symbols, ideas, processes, or events. In this respect, concepts are similar in nature to schemata. A concept hardly ever stands alone, but, instead, is bound by a hierarchy of relations. As a result, "most concepts do not represent a unique object or event but rather a general class linked by a common element or relationship" (Johnson and Pearson, 1978, p. 33).

Bruner, Goodnow, and Austin (1977) suggest that we would be overwhelmed by the complexity of our environment if we were to respond to each object or event that we encountered as unique. Therefore we invent categories (or form concepts) to reduce the complexity of our environment and the necessity for constant learning. For example, every feline need not have a different name to be known as a cat. Although cats vary greatly, the common characteristics that they share cause them to be referred to by the same general term. Thus, in order to facilitate communication, we invent words to name concepts.

Consider your concept for the word *ostrich*. What mental picture comes to mind? Your image of *ostrich* might differ from ours, depending on your background knowledge of the ostrich or the larger class to which it belongs known as *land birds*. Moreover, your direct or vicarious experiences with birds may differ significantly from someone else's. Nevertheless, for any concept we organize all of our experiences and background knowledge into conceptual hierarchies according to *class*, *example*, and *attribute* relations.

The concept *ostrich* is part of a more inclusive class or category called *land birds*, which in turn are subsumed within an even larger class of animals known as *warm-blooded vertebrates*. These class relations are depicted in Figure 9.2.

In any conceptual network, class relationships are organized in a hierarchy consisting of superordinate and subordinate concepts. In Figure 9.2 the superordinate concept is *animal kingdom*. *Vertebrates* and nonvertebrates are two classes within the animal kingdom; they are in a subordinate position in this hierarchy. *Vertebrates,* however, divided into two classes, *warm-blooded* and *cold-blooded,* is superordinate to *mammals, birds, fish,* and *amphibians*—types or subclasses of vertebrates. The concept *land birds,* subordinate to *birds,* but superordinate to *ostrich,* completes the hierarchy.

For every concept there are examples of that concept. An *example* is a member of any concept being considered. A *nonexample,* conversely, is anything not a member of that concept. Class/example relations are complementary: vertebrates and nonvertebrates are examples within the *animal kingdom. Mammals, birds, fish,* and *amphibians* are examples of *vertebrates. Land birds* is one example of *birds,* and so on.

Figure 9.2
Illustration of Concept Hierarchy Based on Class Relations

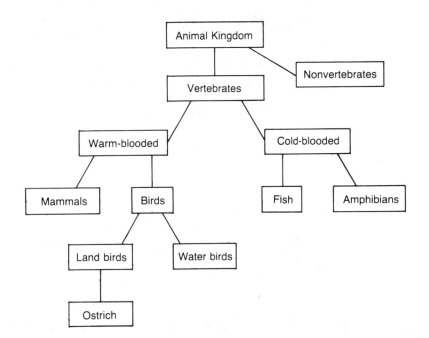

Let's make *land birds* our target concept. What are some other examples of land birds in addition to the ostrich? *Penguin, emu,* and *rhea* are a few which can be shown in relation to one another as in Figure 9.3. We could have listed more examples of land birds. Instead, we now ask, "What do the ostrich, penguin, emu, and rhea have in common?" This allows us to focus on their relevant attributes— those features, traits, properties, or characteristics common to every example of a particular concept. In this case the *relevant attributes* of land birds are the characteristics that determine whether the ostrich, penguin, emu, and rhea belong to the class of birds called *land birds.* An attribute is said to be

Figure 9.3
Class/Example Relations for Concept *Land Birds*

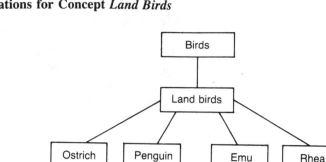

critical if it is a characteristic that is necessary for determining class membership. An attribute is said to be *variable* if it is shared by some but not all examples of the class. An *irrelevant attribute* is any characteristic not shared by any examples of the class.

Thus we recognize that certain physical and social characteristics are shared by all land birds, but not every land bird has each feature. Virtually all land birds have feathers, wings, and beaks. They hatch from an egg and have two legs. They differ in color, size, habitat, and size of feet. Some land birds fly and others, with small wings which cannot support their bodies in the air, do not. In what ways is the ostrich similar to other land birds? How is the ostrich different?

This brief discussion of the concept *ostrich* was designed to illustrate an important principle: *Teachers can help students build conceptual knowledge of content area terms by teaching and reinforcing the concept words in relation to other concept words*. As you study how to devise activities which introduce and reinforce conceptual relations among words, keep in mind Goodman's (1976) proposition that, "Vocabulary is largely a term for the ability of the child to sort out his experiences and concepts in relation to words and phrases in the context of what he is reading" (p. 480).

Vocabulary Reinforcement and Extension

Students need many experiences, real and vicarious, to develop word meanings and concepts. They need to use, text, and manipulate technical terms in instructional situations which capitalize on reading, writing, speaking, and listening activities. In having students do these things, the teacher creates the kind of natural language environment that is needed to reinforce vocabulary and concept development.

Germane to this chapter is the development of vocabulary extension and reinforcement exercises for this purpose. Specifically, we will study how to design materials and activities to increase students' grasp of word meanings and concepts. As they work with these activities and materials, students usually discover an attractive bonus: they are fun to do. The manipulative, gamelike structure of reinforcement activities captivates even the most reluctant student in a classroom.

As a rule of thumb, vocabulary reinforcement exercises should be completed individually by students and then discussed either in small groups or in the class as a whole. The oral interaction in team learning situations gives more students a chance to use terms. The increased volume in participation creates an atmosphere for reinforcement. Students can exchange ideas, share insights, and justify responses in a nonthreatening situation. Barron and Earle (1973) suggested the following procedures for small-group discussion of reinforcement activities:

1. End small-group discussion only after the group has discussed each answer and every member of the group understands the reasons for each answer.

2. Encourage the active participation of all group members. A student who has trouble with a particular exercise can still make a valuable contribution by asking questions or asking someone to explain answers.

3. Limit talk to the particular exercise or to related questions.

4. Make sure that students use the words and their meanings in discussing the answers, rather than using letters and numbers (for example, "I think the answer to number 1 is C, 2 is F").

When to assign vocabulary reinforcement activities is an important consideration. Using them before reading has merit in certain situations. Herber (1978) commented, "Logically, it makes sense to have definitions reinforced before reading the material so that meanings can be developed during reading" (p. 159). On the other hand, teachers may also opt to reinforce vocabulary after reading. The issue is really a question of timing and instructional purpose. Postreading vocabulary exercises extend students' ability to use and manipulate concepts attained from reading. In either situation, before or after reading, reinforcement materials will serve to enhance vocabulary and concept learning.

Vocabulary exercises which prompt students to make simple associations between technical terms and their definitions have some value. These activities fall into two broad categories: matching exercises and word puzzles. Simple associational tasks are particularly useful in cases where the reader "does not know or use the word or phrase in his oral language but can grasp the meaning, particularly in familiar natural language" (Goodman, 1976, p. 283). In other words, a technical term may appear to be unfamiliar and troublesome at a surface level but actually represent a meaning familiar to students. In this situation, associating the new with the known through a matching exercise or word puzzle is useful.

However, a note of caution is in order: The learning of definitions is no sure guarantee that students will be able to use or conceptualize the technical vocabulary of a content area. Teachers should discourage students from merely repeating definitions without attempting to approach a conceptual level of understanding. Making simple associations between technical words and definitions is a beginning step in the development of concepts in text material.

Abstract concepts, such as *square root* or *natural selection,* lack concrete referents. Their meanings often depend on experiences and a level of conceptual development which most maturing learners have not yet attained. Such abstract concepts can be grasped only through a continual process of definition in which students experience words that convey concepts in familiar and meaningful contexts. Good writers know this. Protheroe (1979) observed,

> In regard to presenting unfamiliar or difficult vocabulary, the goal of the author is to use the word in as many familiar contexts as possible or to build an array of familiar contexts into which the word can be placed so that the student will nod his or her head and say, "Yeah, yeah, I know that," or "Oh, is that what that word means?" *(p. 103)*

To the extent that matching exercises and word puzzles can reinforce the "Oh, is that what that word means?" behavior, they have some use. But recognize that students must work with words on more than just a definitional level in order to conceptualize them.

More complex associations involving relationships reinforce an understanding of word meanings and concepts. Vocabulary exercises should be developed not only to reinforce definitions but also to help students manipulate words in relation to other words. *Analogies, word sorts, categorizing activities, concept circles,* and *post structured overviews* are examples of the types of exercises and activities that can be used for this purpose. These conceptual tasks enable students to recognize that pairs of words are related, that is to say, that words can be grouped according to *class, example,* or *attribute* relations we just discussed.

Reinforcing and Extending Conceptual Relationships Among Words

When students manipulate technical terms in relation to other terms, they are thinking critically. Vocabulary activities can be designed to give a class the experience of *thinking about, thinking through,* and *thinking with* the technical vocabulary of a subject. Working with relationships among technical terms provides this opportunity.

Teachers in content areas can capitalize on the four basic cognitive operations associated with learning concepts and words (Henry, 1974). The first involves *the act of joining* or "bringing together." Comparing, classifying, and generalizing are possible through the act of joining. Teachers who ask students to explain how words are related or have them sort through word cards to group words together are involving them in the act of joining.

The *act of excluding* is a second conceptual operation worth considering when teaching words in relation to other words. As the operation implies, students must discriminate, negate, or reject items because they do not belong within the conceptual category. When a student must decide which word does not belong in a set of other words, the process involves exclusion. In this case, students would search through their background knowledge to distinguish examples from nonexamples or relevant attributes from irrelevant attributes as we did with the ostrich example earlier in this chapter.

A third conceptual activity or operation involves the *act of selecting*. Students simply learn to make choices and to explain why based on what they experience, know, or understand. Synonyms, antonyms, and multiple meaning words lend themselves well to the act of selecting.

A fourth aspect of thinking conceptually involves the *act of implying*. Are your students able to make decisions based on if-then, cause-effect relations among concept and words? Dupuis and Snyder (1983) contended that the most common form of vocabulary exercise using implication is the analogy. They suggest that the act of implying is such a complex cognitive activity that it actually requires the use of joining, excluding, and selecting processes.

Through the aid of vocabulary reinforcement and extension activities, students will sense the acts of joining, excluding, selecting, and implying. They will recognize that they can classify and categorize words which label ideas, events, or objects. In short, they study words critically and form generalizations about the shared or common features of concepts in an instructional unit. Word sorting, categorizing, completing concept circles, drawing analogies, and creating structured overviews are activities which get the job done effectively.

Word Sorts

A word sort is a simple yet valuable activity to initiate. Individually or in small groups, students literally sort out technical terms which are written on cards or listed on an exercise sheet. The object of word sorting is to group words into different categories by looking for shared features among their meanings. According to Gillet and Kita (1979), a word sort activity gives students the opportunity "to teach and learn from each other while discussing and examining words together" (pp. 541–542).

Gillet and Kita also explained that there are two types of word sorts—the "open" sort and the "closed" sort. Both are easily adapted to any content area. In the closed sort students know in advance of sorting what the main categories are. In other words, the criterion which the words in a group must share is stated. The closed sort reinforces and extends the ability to classify words and fosters convergent and deductive thinking.

Open sorts, on the other hand, prompt divergent and inductive reasoning. No category or criterion for grouping is known in advance of sorting. Students must search for meanings and discover relationships among technical terms without the benefit of any structure. For example, if you were given the following list of names, how many different arrangements could be made by grouping together two or more names? You must be able to justify the reason or reasons for each arrangement.

Washington	Susan B. Anthony
Alexander the Great	John Kennedy
Rembrandt	Edison
Columbus	De Gaulle
Hitler	Helen Hayes
Caesar	Napoleon
Cleopatra	Einstein
Henry Ford	Margaret Mead

The possibilities are unlimited. Your arrangements probably run the gamut from the obvious (men versus women, modern versus ancient leaders, inventors, artists) to the less obvious (names given to foods and cities, faces on monetary currency worth one American dollar) to the bizarre (suspected of having venereal disease).

Both types of word sorts, open and closed, are useful vocabulary reinforcement activities. Let's take a closer look at each.

Open Sorts. A similar experience to the one you just had awaits students when they are assigned to manipulate a corpus of words in an open-sort activity. Examine how an art teacher reinforced understandings with high school students. She asked students to work in pairs in order to classify the words below by arranging them into logical groups:

jordan	roka	cornwall stone
ball	lead	cone
antimony	chrome	wheel
cobalt	slip	bisque
mortar	scale	stoneware
scrafitto	kaolin	oxidation
	leather	
	hard	

Several categories which students formed included *types of clay, pottery tools,* and *coloring agents.*

Closed Sorts. Closed sorts help students study words critically by requiring them to classify terms in relation to more inclusive concepts. Study how a business teacher helped reinforce concept development from an assignment that students had just read on types of resources. He directed students to classify the list of terms under the three types.

tools	trees	power plants
minerals	wildlife	buildings
water	factories	
labor	tractors	
machinery	typewriters	

Natural Resources	Capital Resources	Human Resources

Categorization

Vocabulary reinforcement exercises involving categorization require students to determine relationships among technical terms in much the same manner as open and closed sorts. The difference, however, lies in the amount of structure students are given to make cognitive decisions. Put another way, students are usually given four to six words per grouping and asked to do something with them. That something depends on the format used in the exercise. For example, you can give students sets of words and ask them to circle the word in each set which includes the others. This exercise demands that students perceive common attributes or examples in relation to a more inclusive concept, to distinguish superordinate from subordinate terms. Study several sample exercises from different content areas:

Social studies
Directions: Circle the word in each group that includes the others.

1. government	2. generals	3. throne
council	troops	coronation
judges	armies	crown
governor	warriors	church

English
Directions: Circle the word that best includes the others.

1. satire	2. irony	3. humor
humor	pun	satire
irony	malapropism	irony
parody	faux pas	tone

Geometry
Directions: Circle the word that includes the others.

1. closure	2. irrational	3. function
distributive	rational	domain
property	real	range
associative	complex	relation
commutative	integers	preimage

Other categorization exercises may direct students to cross out the word that does not belong in each set. This format forces students to manipulate words that convey the meanings of common items. Examine the sample exercises below:

Health/Home Economics
Directions: Cross out the word in each group that doesn't belong.

1. fats	2. meat	3. liver
protein	butter	leafy vegetables
nutrients	oatmeal	fruits
carbohydrates	fish oil	minerals

Biology
Directions: Cross out the word in each group that does not belong.

1. asexual	2. oögenesis	3. polyembryony
conjugation	fragmentation	fertilization
gamete production	budding	parthenogenesis
fertilization	binary fission	spermatogenesis

Language Arts

Directions: Below are words that we have been using while studying the news-paper. Look at each set very carefully. Three words are related in some way. Cross out the one word that does not belong with the other words. Be sure you can defend your answers.

1. AP	2. picture	3. jumpline
wire service	caption	column
UPI	story	caption
ABC	index	page

A variation on this format directs students to cross out the word that does not belong, and then explain in a word or phrase the relationship which exists among the common items.

English

Directions: Cross out the word in each set that does not belong. On the line above the set, write the word or phrase that explains the relationship among the remaining three words.

1. spectacle	2. drama	3. Aristotle	4. time
thought	comedy	Fergusson	character
disclosure	epic	Harris	place
language	tragedy	Marlowe	action

Teachers find that they can construct categorization activities efficiently and effectively when the activities refer back to a previously constructed structured overview. The tie-in between an overview and categories is logical: since structured overviews depict superordinate-subordinate relationships among key terms, it is relatively easy to develop reinforcement exercises involving categorization from them.

For example, turn to the overview on abnormality in Chapter 4, on page 114. Study the relationships shown among the key terms. If you were to construct categories in which students would circle the word in each set that included the others, which possible word groups might be formed? Probably groups similar to these:

1. neurosis	2. paranoia	3. depression
abnormality	schizophrenia	neurosis
mental	catatonia	phobia
retardation	hebephrenia	anxiety
psychosis		

A quick perusal of the abnormality overview would also give you ideas for categories in which students would cross out the word that didn't belong in each set. Examples:

1. depression	2. catatonia	3. neurosis
anxiety	mental	psychosis
antisocial	retardation	personality
phobias	paranoia	disorders
	hebephrenia	schizophrenia

The secret to constructing categories, of course, is to know the superordinate and subordinate relationships among terms in a unit or a chapter.

Concept Circles

One of the more versatile activities we have observed in a wide range of grade levels is the concept circle. Concept circles provide still another format and opportunity to study words critically—for students to relate words conceptually to one another. A concept circle may simply involve putting words or phrases in sections of a circle and directing students to describe or name the concept relationship that exists among the sections. The two examples below are from a fourth-grade class; the circle on the left was part of a geography lesson and the one on the right is from a history lesson:

1. _____   2. _____

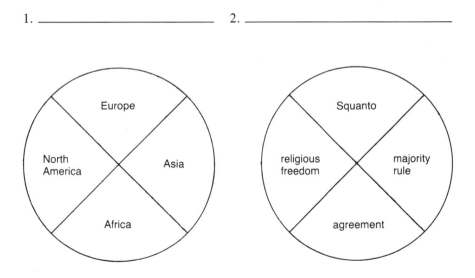

In addition, a teacher might direct students to shade in the section of a concept circle which contains a word or phrase that *does not relate* to words or phrases in the other sections of the circle. Once students shade in the section, they must then identify the concept relationships that exists among the remaining sections. Finally, a concept circle can be modified by leaving one or two sections of the circle empty as in the example on the following page:

Direct students to fill in the empty section with a word or two which relates in someway to the terms of the other sections of the concept circles. Students are then put in the position of justifying their word choice by identifying the overarching concept depicted by the circle.

As you can see, concept circles serve the same function as categorization activities. However, students respond positively to the visual aspect of manipulating sections in a circle. Whereas categorization exercises sometimes appear like "tests" to students, concept circles are "fun" to do.

Word Analogies

In Chapter 4 we explored how an analogy could be used as an "organizer" to help students *relate* a familiar concept to an unfamiliar concept. Word analogies also trigger critical thinking about relationships. Bellows (1980) explained that an analogy is actually a comparison of two similar relationships: "On one side the objects are related. On the other side the objects are related in the same way. Like a mathematical equation, an analogy has equal or balanced sides" (p. 509). Students who are not familiar with the format of an analogy may have trouble reading it successfully. Therefore, teachers should give a short demonstration or two which will walk students through the reading/reasoning process involved in completing an analogy.

For example, a science teacher might write on the chalkboard: "Eating : people :: photosynthesis : ___." The teacher can then point out that the colon (:) stands for *is to* and the double colon (::) stands for *as*. The class reads aloud: "Eating is to people as photosynthesis is to ___." The students should be encouraged to complete the analogy and to explain the relationship between the items in each pair. In doing so, they will transform "Eating is to people as photosynthesis is to plants" into a new thought pattern which may go something like this: People can't survive without eating and plants can't survive without photosynthesis. Or: Both eating and photosynthesis are essential life-sustaining processes for people and plants respectively.

Ignoffo (1980) explained the practical value of analogies this way: "Analogies are practical because they carry an implied context with them. To work the analogy, the learner is forced to attempt various . . . procedures that involve articulation, problem-solving and thinking" (p. 520). To stimulate articulation, problem solving, and thinking, many types of analogies can be constructed. Several of the more useful types for content areas are included in Box 9.2. As you study these, try your hand at completing each analogy by underlining the word which best fits in each blank space.

Box 9.2

COMMON TYPES OF ANALOGIES

1. *Part to whole*
   Clutch : transmission :: key :
   (starter, engine, exhaust)

2. *Person to situation*
   Lincoln : slavery :: _____ : independence
   (Jefferson, Kennedy, Jackson)

3. *Cause and effect*
   CB : radio reception :: television : _____
   (eating, homework, gym)

4. *Synonym*
   Bourgeoisie : middle class :: proletariat : _____
   (upper class, lower class, royalty)

5. *Antonym*
   Pinch : handful :: sip : _____
   (pet, gulp, taste)

6. *Geography*
   Everest : Matterhorn :: _____ : Alps
   (Ozarks, Andes, Himalayas)

7. *Measurement*
   Minutes : clock :: _____ : temperature
   (liters, degrees, gradations)

8. *Time*
   24 hours : rotation :: 365 days : _____
   (Eastern Time, revolution, axis)

Analogies can easily be adapted to the technical terminology in any content area. Examine, for example, an analogy exercise from a junior high geography unit:

DIRECTIONS: Fill in the blank with the word from the list below that best expresses the same relationship with the third word as the second word does with the first.

Example 1. Good : bad :: happy : *sad*. Read the line as follows: Good is to bad as happy is to sad. Both pairs are opposites.

Example 2. Big : small :: large : *little*. Read the line as follows: Big is to small as large is to little. The two pairs express the same idea in different words.

1. Bay : gulf :: cape : _____
2. Latitude : longitude :: Equator : _____
3. Hill : mountain :: sea : _____
4. Tropic of Cancer : Tropic of Capricorn :: Arctic Circle : _____
5. North Pole : South Pole :: prime meridian : _____
6. Water : land :: oceans : _____
7. Tributary : river :: peak : _____

longitude	International Date Line	sea
latitudes	prime meridian	hills
mountain	Antarctic Circle	tropics
Equator	peninsula	continent
river	basin	ocean

Post Structured Overviews

Earlier in the text, we described the structured overview as a technique to introduce students to the important interrelationships among the key concepts they are about to study. Along with semantic mapping, structured overviews provide visual displays of how words are related to other words. Barron and Stone (1973) have also reported the positive effects of what they term *graphic post organizers*—the same as post structured overviews—which students construct after reading.

A graphic post organizer—or post structured overview—allows students to work in groups to relate important content area terms in a spatial arrangement. To do this, students must analyze the relationships among the words.

The post structured overview as a reinforcement activity presumes that students are aware of the idea behind a structured overview. If they are not, you will need to provide them with an example or two. You can then introduce the class to a post structured overview by following these steps from Barron and Stone.

1. Type the key words on a ditto master.
2. Following reading and study of the material to be learned, place students into small groups of about two or three students each.
3. Distribute the list of terms and a packet of three-by-five inch index cards to each group.
4. Students write each word from the list on a card. They then work together to decide upon a spatial arrangement among the cards which depicts the major relationship among the words.
5. As students work, provide assistance as needed.
6. Initiate a discussion of the constructed overviews.

Before actually assigning a post structured overview to students, the teacher should prepare for the activity by carefully analyzing the vocabulary of the material to be learned. List all the terms that are essential for students to understand. Then add relevant terms which you feel the students already understand and which will help them relate what they know to the new material. Finally, construct your own overview.

The form of student-constructed post structured overviews will doubtlessly differ from the teacher's arrangement. However, this difference in and of itself should not be a major source of concern. According to Herber (1978),

> Form is not the issue; substance is, and that is demonstrated by a clear portrayal of the implicit relationships among key words. . . . Students will see things differently than teachers and from one another. It is good . . . for the teacher to have thought through his or her own arrangement of the words for purposes of comparison, clarification and confirmation. *(p. 149)*

What is important, then, is that the post structured overview reinforce students' ability to relate essential ideas to one another through the key vocabulary terms in content materials.

Reinforcing Contextual Knowledge

Artley (1975) captured the role that context plays in vocabulary learning when he said, "It is the context in which the word is embedded rather than the dictionary that gives it its unique flavor" (p. 1072). Readers who build and use contextual knowledge are able to recognize fine shades of meaning in the way words are used. They know the concept behind the word well enough to apply that concept in different contexts. In this section, we suggest several ways to *reinforce* and *extend* a student's contextual knowledge of content area terms. In the next section, techniques are suggested to help students *inquire* into the meaning of an unknown word by using its context.

Modified Cloze Passages

Cloze passages can be created in a similar manner to reinforce technical vocabulary. However, the teacher usually modifies the procedure for teaching purposes. Every *n*th word, for example, needn't be deleted. The modified cloze passage will vary in length. Typically, a 200- to 500-word text segment yields sufficient technical vocabulary to make the activity worthwhile.

Should you consider developing a modified cloze passage on a segment of text from a reading assignment, make sure that the text passage is one of the most important parts of the assignment. Depending upon your objectives, students can supply the missing words either before or after reading the entire assignment. If they work on the cloze activity before reading, use the subsequent discussion to build meaning for key terms and to raise expectations for the assignment as a whole. If you assign the cloze passage after reading, it will help to reinforce concepts attained through reading.

Upon completing a short lecture on the causes of the Civil War, an American history teacher assigned the cloze passage below before students read the entire introduction for homework. See how well you fare with the exercise.

What caused the Civil War? Was it inevitable? To what extent and in what ways was slavery to blame? To what extent was each region of the nation at fault? Which were more decisive—the intellectual or the emotional issues?

Any consideration of the (1) of the war must include the problem of (2). In his Second Inaugural Address, Abraham Lincoln said that slavery was "somehow the cause of the war." The critical word is "(3)". Some (4) maintain that the moral issue had to be solved, the nation had to face the (5), and the slaves had to be (6). Another group of historians asserts that the war was not fought over (7). In their view slavery served as an (8) focal point for more fundamental (9) involving two different (10) of the Constitution. All of these views have merit, but no single view has won unanimous support.

Most historians agree that slavery was one among many issues that separated the two (11), and that an intertwining of (12), (13), (14), and (15) differences were just as significant. . . . Also, there is the question of the viability of (16) as a form of government. Compromise, so basic to democracy, failed. The (17)—the very concept of (18)—was openly challenged when the South refused to accept Lincoln's (19).*

Answers:

1. causes	7. slavery	14. political
2. slavery	8. emotional	15. psychological
3. somehow	9. issues	16. democracy
4. historians	10. interpretations	17. political system
5. crisis	11. regions	18. majority rule
6. freed	12. economic	19. election
	13. social	

OPIN

OPIN is a meaning-extending vocabulary strategy developed by Frank Greene of McGill University. OPIN provides another example of context-based reinforcement and extension. OPIN stands for *opinion* and also plays on the term *cloze*. Here's how OPIN works:

Have the class form groups of three. Distribute exercise sentences, one to each student. Each student must complete each exercise sentence individually. Then each member of a group must convince the other two members that his or her word choice is the best. If no agreement is reached on the "best" word for each

*SOURCE: Malcolm S. Langforde, Jr., *The American Civil War*. New York: Scholastic Book Services, 1968, pp. 8–9.

sentence, then each member of the group can speak to the class for his/her individual choice. When all groups have finished, have the class discuss each group's choices. The only rule of discussion is that each choice must be accompanied by a reasonable defense or justification. Answers like "because ours is best" are not acceptable.

OPIN exercise sentences can be constructed for any content area. Here are sample sentences from science, social studies, and home economics:

Science.

1. A plant's _____ go into the soil.
2. The earth gets heat and _____ from the sun.
3. Some animals, such as birds and _____ are nibblers.

Social Studies.

1. We cannot talk about _____ in America without discussing the welfare system.
2. The thought of _____ or revolution would be necessary because property owners would fight to hold on to their land.
3. Charts and graphs are used to _____ information.

Home Economics.

1. Vitamin C is _____ from the small intestines and circulates to every tissue.
2. Washing time for cottons and linens is eight to ten minutes unless the clothes are badly _____.

Answers:

Home Economics: 1. absorbed 2. soiled
Social Studies: 1. poverty 2. violence 3. organize
Science: 1. roots 2. radiation 3. rodents

OPIN encourages differing opinions about which word should be inserted in a blank space. In one sense the exercise is open for discussion, and as a result it reinforces the role of prior knowledge and experiences in the decisions that each group makes. The opportunity to "argue" one's responses in the group leads not only to continued motivation but also to discussion of word meanings and variations.

Context Puzzles and Related Activities

As we have suggested, context reinforcement encourages students to make decisions about key concept words. They must be able to recognize or apply technical terms in a meaningful context. Context reinforcement is valuable because it reinforces and extends an important skill (using context to get meaning) as well as an understanding of vocabulary terms.

Note the puzzle format used by a language arts teacher as she gave students structural clues which must be combined with context clues provided in the sentences:

Directions: Think of a word we have recently studied that fits in the blank space in each sentence below and has the same number of letters as the number of spaces provided in the corresponding line. Fill in the word on the line.

1. H __ __ D R __ __ __
2. A __ __ __ __ Y
3. __ __ __ __ U I
4. __ __ __ __ C O N __ __ __ __ __ __
5. __ O __ __ __ __
6. __ O M __ __ __

a. Charlie Brown tried to give up his _____ existence and lead a life of adventure.

b. Snoopy was in a state of _____ for weeks, showing no interest in anything.

c. Lucy showed her _____ by yawning throughout the baseball game.

d. The serious illness of Linus's grandmother left him _____; no one could comfort him.

e. The _____ in her expression was the very image of grief.

f. Such a _____ expression seems out of place on a young child.

In contrast to the puzzle format, examine several items from a high school English teacher's context reinforcement activity for his students. The sentences are illustrative of ones the teacher selected from several short stories that the class had read.

Directions: The sentences below are taken from short stories we are studying for this unit. Write a synonym and an antonym for each italic word below:

	Synonym	Antonym
1. After hitting the ground, Arvil rose with a slightly *vexed* expression.	_____	_____
2. Because I muffed the winning point, my teammates looked at me *truculently*.	_____	_____
3. Although he had eaten well the last few months, the years of eating just enough to survive made the dog *puny* in size.	_____	_____
4. The house too was *grotesque*, painted gray, its gables hung with daggerlike icicles.	_____	_____
5. In no hurry, I *sauntered* through Grant Park, observing the people as well as the flowers.	_____	_____
6. Usually we don't like people *meddling* with our personal business.	_____	_____
7. Having traveled all the world and lived all sorts of life styles, he was not bound to *provincial* ideas.	_____	_____

In another activity notice how the same English teacher reinforced contextual knowledge from the short stories read:

Directions: The sentences below are taken from the short stories we are studying for this unit. Using the context clues in these sentences, see if you can figure out the meanings of the italicized words below. Then record the clues that helped you determine the meaning of the word.

	Meaning	*Clues*
1. He got down and *pinioned* my arms with his knees.	————	————
2. I tried to kick him in the back of the head but could only *flail* my feet helplessly in the air.	————	————
3. Georgia made a *cutting* remark that hurt him.	————	————
4. . . . before we went to school she *plaited* my hair and I *plaited* hers before the mirror, in the same little twist of ribbons.	————	————
5. I liked his ease and the way that he accepted me immediately, *spontaneously* and freely, without waiting.	————	————
6. Feeling foolish, he lifted his face, baring it to an expected shower of *derision* from his brother.	————	————

Many other possibilities exist for context reinforcement and extension. Certainly, having students use words in sentences and paragraphs is a worthwhile application activity.

Word Puzzles

Word puzzles are helpful in reinforcing definitions. One of the best uses of these vocabulary exercises is to associate technical terms with more familiar words that convey meaning. For example, as part of a unit on geography, a social studies teacher developed a vocabulary matching activity to help students associate technical terms in the text material with known synonyms and more familiar language. The class first completed the exercise individually and then discussed it in small groups before reading text material.

Technical terms with multiple meanings pose problems to maturing readers. A math teacher anticipated the problem of meeting multiple-meaning words in a geometry unit she had organized. She prepared students for working with these terms through an exercise in *multiple meanings.*

As in the previous example, class discussion preceded reading. The math students quickly recognized that a given geometry term can refer to a different concept or different concepts outside mathematics. Two examples from the exercise are given below:

1. mean   (a) signify, (b) average, (c) bad tempered
2. point   (a) sharp end, (b) something that has position but is not extended, (c) place or spot

In addition to their value as definitional tasks, matching activities can reinforce technical vocabulary by helping students make visual associations. Notice in this example how a math teacher reinforced technical terms from a geometry unit by having students match them with visual counterparts:

Directions: Place the letter of the figure next to the definition that matches it correctly.

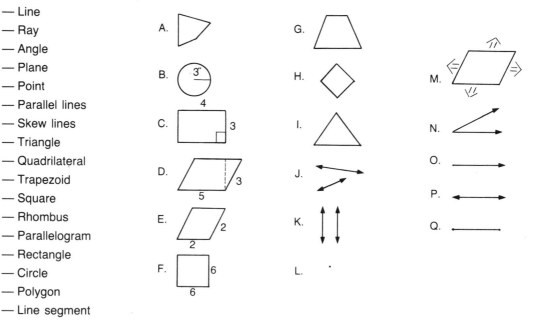

— Line

— Ray

— Angle

— Plane

— Point

— Parallel lines

— Skew lines

— Triangle

— Quadrilateral

— Trapezoid

— Square

— Rhombus

— Parallelogram

— Rectangle

— Circle

— Polygon

— Line segment

Magic Squares

A magic square exercise is by no means new or novel. Yet it has a way of reviving even the most mundane matching activity. We have seen the magic square used successfully in elementary and secondary grades as well as in graduate courses. Here's how a magic square activity works. An activity sheet has two columns, one for content area terms and one for definitions or other distinguishing statements such as characteristics or examples (see Box 9.3). Direct students to match terms with definitions. In doing so, they must take into account the alphabetic letters signaling the terms and the numbers signaling the definitions. The students then put the number of a definition in the proper space (denoted by the letter of the term) in the "magic square answer box." If their match-ups are correct, they will form a magic square. That is, the numerical total will be the same for each row across and each column down the answer box. This total forms the puzzle's "magic number." Students need to add up the rows and columns to check if they're coming up with the same number each time. If not, they should be directed back to terms and definitions to reevaluate their answers.

    Box 9.3 provides an example of a magic square exercise. Try it. The magic number for the exercise on literary terms is 34. Analyze the mental maneuvers that you underwent to determine the correct number combinations. In some cases you undoubtedly knew the answers outright. You may have made several educated guesses on others. Did you try to beat the number system? Imagine the possibilities for small-group interaction.

Box 9.3

MAGIC SQUARE: HOW WELL DO YOU KNOW LITERARY TERMS?

Directions: Select from the numbered statements the best answer for each of the literary terms. Put the number in the proper space in the magic square box. The total of the numbers will be the same across each row and down each column.

Literary Terms	*Statements*
A. Point of view	1. Mental pictures within a story
B. Symbolism	2. Events and happenings in a story
C. Theme	3. The "when" and "where" of the story
D. Mood	4. The overriding feeling in a work
E. Plot	5. When something stands for something else
F. Metaphor	6. An exaggeration of great proportions
G. Structure	7. That which unifies a story as a whole
H. Myth	8. Saying one thing but meaning another
I. Setting	9. The central insight
J. Simile	10. A comparison introduced by *as* or *like*
K. Hyperbole	11. An implied comparison
L. Allegory	12. Saying less, but meaning more
M. Foreshadowing	13. Clues to future happenings
N. Irony	14. A tale of human life told in supernatural proportions
O. Understatement	15. When objects and characters are equated with meanings that lie outside the story
P. Imagery	16. The vantage point from which everything is known or interpreted

Answer Box

A	B	C	D
E	F	G	H
I	J	K	L
M	N	O	P

Magic number = _____

Many teachers are intrigued with the possibilities offered by the magic square. But they remain wary of its construction: "I can't spend hours figuring out number combinations."

This is a legitimate concern. Happily, the eight combinations in Figure 9.4 make magic square activities easy to construct. You can generate many more combinations from the eight patterns simply by rearranging rows or columns. See Figure 9.5.

Figure 9.4
Model Magic Square Combinations

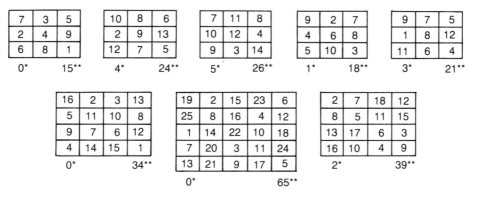

*foils needed in answer column
**magic number

Notice that the single asterisk in Figure 9.4 denotes the number of foils or distractors needed so that several of the combinations can be completed. For example, the magic number combination of 18 requires one foil in the number 1 slot that will not match with any of the corresponding items in the matching exercise. In order to complete the combination, the number ten is added. Therefore, when you develop a matching activity for combination 18, there will be ten items in one column and nine in the other, with item 1 being the foil.

Figure 9.5
More Magic Squares

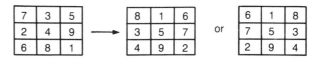

Puzzles such as those described are popular devices for reinforcing word meanings. A number of word puzzle formats work well to provide added recall and recognition of key terms. For additional examples, please refer to the Instructional Units in Appendix E.

Vocabulary Inquiry

Showing students how to inquire into the meanings of unknown words gives them the skills they need to build their own vocabularies. Demonstrating how to use several basic tools of inquiry—context analysis, structural analysis, and use of the dictionary—builds vocabulary principles which will guide students for a lifetime. With these tools readers can seek clues to word meanings on their own. These clues often reveal enough meaning to allow students to continue reading and not "short circuit" when they encounter an unknown word.

As we have emphasized throughout this book, teacher modeling often creates in students an awareness that is an extension of metacognitive functioning. It is, after all, the information within readers—their conceptual background and experience and knowledge of language—that enables them to inquire into the meaning of technical terms. Teachers who show students how to use information clues effectively do so by modeling meaning-getting strategies and then providing practice and feedback to students. Modeling provides insights into how to use context, a word's structure, or the dictionary to reveal sufficient meanings for the difficult terms students encounter while reading.

For example, you can guide students in the use of one or more of the vocabulary building skills before assigning material to be read. If a technical term (or more than one) in the material to be studied lends itself to a short demonstration, the teacher can walk students through the process necessary to derive meaning. As we will see in the following sections, these modeling demonstrations are brief and teacher directed. Often a walk-through takes no more than four or five minutes and makes use of visuals such as an overhead transparency or the chalkboard. As students are assigned to read, they are directed to practice and apply the meaning-getting strategy that was modeled. Often, teachers develop their own context sentences to help students deal with meanings of words.

Let's take a closer look at some of the specifics involved in vocabulary inquiry.

Context Analysis

Getting meaning from context is the major tool at the command of readers. It involves using information surrounding a troublesome word to help reveal its meaning. Every reader makes some use of context automatically. Instruction is needed, however, in cases where the author provides a deliberate context to help the reader with content area terminology that is especially difficult. Dulin (1970) suggested that

> as students progress in school and begin to encounter mature, technical, content-oriented reading materials, a different kind of contextual aid begins to appear. This occurs when an author or editor, consciously anticipating that a new word will be troublesome, purposely provides helpful context. Here the reader faces a true, deliberate context clue . . . and here he must know specifically how to approach it. *(p. 440–441)*

Even though textbook authors may consciously or unconsciously use deliberate contexts for unknown words, constraints in the material itself and/or the reader's own background limit the degree to which context reveals word meaning. The teacher and students must know how context operates to limit meaning as well as to reveal it.

Deighton (1970) identified several factors which limit the use of context: (1) what a context may reveal to a particular reader depends on the reader's experience; (2) the portion of context which reveals an unfamiliar word must be located reasonably close to the word if it is to act effectively; and (3) there must be some clear-cut connection between the unfamiliar term and the context which clarifies it.

Context analysis, as you have probably concluded, is mostly a matter of inference. Inference requires readers to see an explicit or implicit relationship between the unfamiliar word and its context or to connect what they know already with the unknown term. It can't be assumed that students will perceive these relationships or make the connections on their own. Most developing readers just don't know how to efficiently or effectively use a deliberate context provided by an author.

Classification schemes developed for contextual aids help teachers identify the prevalent contextual aids that authors use in textbooks (Quealy, 1969). These aids provide various kinds of information or clues to help illuminate the meaning of a troublesome word. Three kinds of information in particular are useful to readers: *typographic, syntactic,* and *semantic* aids.

Typographic Aids

Typographic or format aids make use of footnotes, italics, boldface print, parenthesized definitions, pictures, graphs, charts, and the like. A typographic aid provides a clear-cut connection and a direct reference to an unknown word. Many students tend to gloss over a typographic aid instead of using it to spotlight the meaning of a difficult term. The teacher can rivet attention to these aids with minimal expenditure of class time.

For example, consider the way a science teacher modeled a strategy for revealing the meaning of the word *enzymes,* which was presented in boldface type in the text. Before assigning a text section entitled "Osmosis in Living Cells," the teacher asked students to turn to page 241. Then he asked, "Which word in the section on osmosis stands out among the others?" The students quickly spotted the word *enzymes.* "Why do you think this word is highlighted in boldface type?" he asked. A student replied, "I guess it must be important." Another student said, "Maybe because it has something to do with osmosis—whatever that is." The teacher nodded approvingly and then asked the class to see if they could figure out what *enzymes* meant by reading this sentence: "Chemical substances called **enzymes** are produced by cells to break down large starch molecules into small sugar molecules."

The science teacher continued the modeling demonstration by asking two questions: "What are enzymes?" "What do they do?" The students responded easily. The teacher concluded the walk-through with these words: "Words that are put in large letters or boldface print are important. If you pay a little bit of attention to them as we just did, you will have little trouble figuring out what they mean. There are four other words in boldface type in your reading assignment. Look for them as you read and try to figure out what they mean."

Syntactic/Semantic Aids

Syntactic and semantic clues in content materials should not be treated separately, since one (syntactic information) usually triggers the other (semantic associations) for readers. That is to say, the grammatical relationships among words in a sentence or the structural arrangement among sentences in a passage often helps to clarify the meaning of a particular word.

Syntactic/semantic aids are much more subtle for readers than typographic aids. Dulin (1970) emphasized that "Even bright, generally skillful readers . . . are often unable to utilize this type of context clue to best advantage without help" (p. 444). Table 9.1 presents a summary of the most frequently encountered syntactic/semantic aids.

Table 9.1 Syntactic/Semantic Contextual Aids*

Type of Aid	Explanation	Examples
1. Definition	The author equates the unknown word to the known or more familiar usually by a form of the verb *be*.	*Entomology* **is** the study of insects, and biologists who specialize in this field **are called** *entomologists*. A *critical review* **is** an attempt to evaluate the worth of a piece of writing.
2. Linked synonyms	The author pairs the unknown word with familiar synonyms or closely related words in a series.	Kunte Kinte was the victim of **cruel, evil,** *malevolent,* and **brutal** slave traders. The Congressman from Connecticut possessed the traits of an honest and just leader: **wisdom, judgment,** *sagacity*.

3. Direct description:
   Examples
   Modifiers
   Restatements

The author reveals the meaning of an unknown word by providing additional information in the form of appositives, phrases, clauses or sentences.

Example clue: Undigested material **such as fruit skins, outer parts of grain, and the stringlike parts of some vegetables** form *roughage*.

Modifier clue: *Pictographic writing,* **which was the actual drawing of animals, people and events,** is the forerunner of written language.

Algae, **nonvascular plants which are as abundant in water as grasses are on land,** have often been called "grasses of many waters."

Restatement clue: A billion dollars a year is spent on *health quackery.* **In other words, each year in the United States millions of dollars are spent on worthless treatments and useless gadgets to "cure" various illnesses.**

4. Contrast

The author reveals the meaning of an unknown word by contrasting it with an antonym or phrase that is opposite in meaning.

You have probably seen animals perform tricks at the zoo, on television, or in a circus. Maybe you taught a dog to fetch a newspaper. **But learning tricks—usually for a reward—is very different from** *cognitive problem solving.*

It wasn't a *Conestoga,* like Pa's folks came

in. **Instead, it was just an old farm wagon drawn by one tired horse.**

5. Cause-effect	The author establishes a cause-effect relationship in which the meaning of an unknown word can be hypothesized.	The *domestication* of animals probably began when young animals were caught or strayed into camps. **As a result, people enjoyed staying with them and made pets of them.** A family is called *equalitarian,* **because a husband and wife will make decisions together and share responsibilities equally.**
6. Mood and tone	The author sets a mood, whether it be ironic, satirical, serious, funny, etc., in which the meaning of an unknown word can be hypothesized.	A sense of *resignation* engulfed my thoughts as **the feeling of cold grayness was everywhere around me.** The *tormented* animal **screeched with horror and writhed in pain** as it tried **desperately** to escape from the hunter's trap.

*NOTE: Italics denote the unknown word. Boldface type represents information clues that trigger context revelation.

Teachers need to be explicit in their modeling of strategies that will help students unlock meanings of unknown words through context analysis. Often the chalkboard or an overhead transparency is invaluable in helping students visualize the inquiry process necessary to reveal meaning. For example, if a *definition aid* is used, as in this example from Table 9.1: "Entomology is the study of insects, and biologists who specialize in this field are called entomologists"—it may be appropriate to first write the sentence on the board. During the modeling discussion, you can them show how *is* and *are called* provide information clues that will reveal meaning for *entomology* and *entomologists*. A simply strategy would be to cross out *is* and *are called* in the sentence and replace them with equal signs (=):

Entomology is the study of insects, and biologists who specialize in this field are called entomologists.

A brief discussion will reinforce the function of the verb forms *is* and *are called* in the sentence.

The definition clue is obviously the least subtle of the syntactic/semantic aids. However, all the aids in Table 9.1 require students to make inferential leaps of varying length. Consider one of the examples from the mood and tone aid: "The tormented animal screeched with horror and writhed in pain as it tried desperately to escape from the hunter's trap." Suppose this sentence came from a short story about to be assigned to a middle-grade English class. Assume also that many of the students would have trouble with the word *tormented* as it is used in the sentence. If students are to make the connection between *tormented* and the mood created by the information clues, the teacher will have to ask several effective clarifying questions.

The modeling walk-through begins with the teacher writing the word *tormented* on the board. She asks, "You may have heard or read this word before, but how many of you think that you know what it means?" Student definitions are put on the board. The teacher then writes the sentence on the board, "Which of the definitions on the board do you think best fits the word *tormented* when it's used in this sentence?" She encourages students to support their choices. If none fits, she will ask for more definitions now that students have seen the sentence. She continues questioning, "Are there any other words or phrases in the sentence which help us get a feel for the meaning of *tormented*? Which ones?"

The inquiry into the meaning of *tormented* continues in this fashion. The information clues (*screeched with horror, writhed in pain, desperately*) which establish the mood are underlined and discussed. The teacher concludes the modeling activity by writing five new words on the board and explaining, "These words are also in the story that you are about to read. As you come across them, stop and think. How do the words or phrases or sentences surrounding each word help to create a certain feeling or mood that will allow you to understand what each one means?"

When modeling the contextual aids in Table 9.1, it's important for students to discover the information clues. It's also important for the teacher to relate the demonstration to several additional words to be encountered in the assignment. Instruction of this type will have a significant cumulative effect. Imagine: if students are shown how to use contextual aids for two or three words per week, over the course of an academic year they will have about eighty to one hundred twenty applications in the process.

Morphemic Analysis

A word itself provides information clues about its meaning. The smallest unit of meaning in a word is called a morpheme. Analyzing a word's structure, *morphemic analysis* is a second inquiry tool that students can use to predict meaning. Page

(1975) noted that a reader encountering an unknown word can considerably reduce the number of feasible guesses about its meaning by approaching the whole word and identifying its parts. When readers use morphemic analysis in combination with context, they have a powerful meaning-getting strategy at their command.

A long word need not stop readers cold when they encounter it in print. Analyzing a word's structure will often produce enough meaning to allow the reader to continue. Well-timed instruction prior to reading assigned material can show students how to use word structure to advantage.

Word Structure

There are four categories of long or polysyllabic words identified by Olsen and Ames (1972):

1. Compound words made up of two known words joined together. Examples: *commonwealth, matchmaker.*
2. Words containing a recognizable stem to which an affix (a prefix, a combining form, or suffix) has been added. Examples: *surmountable, deoxygenize, unsystematic, microscope.*
3. Words that can be analyzed into familiar and regular pronounceable units. Examples: *undulate, calcify, subterfuge, strangulate.*
4. Words that contain irregular pronounceable units so that there is no sure pronunciation unless one consults a dictionary. Examples: *louver, indictment.*

Content vocabulary terms from categories 1 and 2 (compound words and recognizable stems and affixes) are the best candidates for instruction. Classroom teachers can readily demonstrate techniques for predicting the meanings of these words, because each of their isolated parts will always represent a meaning unit.

In some instances, a word from category 3 may also be selected for emphasis. However, there is no guarantee that students will bring prior knowledge and experience to words that comprise the third category. Long phonemically regular words lend themselves to syllabication. Syllabication involves breaking words into pronounceable sound units or syllables. The word *undulate*, for example, can readily be syllabicated (un-du-late). However, the syllable *un* is not a meaning-bearing prefix.

Many words from category 3 are derived from Latin or Greek. Many students will find these words especially difficult to analyze for meaning because of their lack of familiarity with Latin or Greek roots. Occasionally a word such as *strangulate* (derived from the Latin *strangulatus*) can be taught because students may recognize the familiar word *strangle*. They might then be shown how to link *strangle* to the verb suffix *-ate* (which means "to cause to become") to hypothesize a meaning for *strangulate*. Unfortunately, the verb suffix *-ate* has multiple meanings and the teacher should be quick to point this out to students. This procedure is shaky, but it has some payoff.

Words from category 2 warrant instruction, as English root words are more recognizable, obviously, than Latin or Greek ones. Whenever feasible, teach the principles of structural word analysis using terms that have English roots. Certain affixes are more helpful than others, and knowing which affixes to emphasize during instruction will minimize students' confusion.

Useful Affixes

The most helpful affixes are the combining forms, prefixes, or suffixes which have single, invariant meanings. Deighton's (1970) monumental study of word structure has helped to identify those affixes which have single meanings. (See Appendix A for a summary of Deighton's findings.)

In addition to the single, invariant meaning prefixes, there are many commonly used prefixes which have more than one meaning or have several shades of meaning. Because of their widespread use in content terminology you should also consider these variant meaning prefixes for functional teaching. (See Appendix B for a list of prefixes with varying meanings.)

The tables of affixes are resources for you. Don't be misled into thinking that studets should learn long lists of affixes in isolation because they ought to know them to analyze word structure. This approach is neither practical nor functional. We recommend instead that students be taught affixes as they are needed: to analyze the structure of terms that will appear in a reading assignment.

For example, an English teacher modeled how to analyze the meaning of *pandemonium* before students were to enounter the term in an assignment from *One Flew Over the Cuckoo's Nest*. She wrote the word on the board— pan*demon*ium—underlining the English base word *demon* and asking students for several synonyms for the word. Student responses included *witch, devil, monster, wicked people*.

Then she explained the *-ium* was a noun suffix meaning "a place of." "Now, let's take alook at *pan*. Sheila, have you ever heard of Pan American Airlines? If you were a Pan Am passenger, name several places that you might visit." Sheila and several other students answered the question as best they could. The teacher then explained than Pan American specialized in flights to all places in the Americas. Further discussion centered around the word *panoramic*. Through this process, relating the known to the unknown, students decided that *pan* meant *all*.

"Now, back to *pandemonium*. A place of all the demons. What would this place be like?" Students were quick to respond. The demonstration was completed with two additional points. The teacher asked the class to find the place in *One Flew Over the Cuckoo's Nest* where *pandemonium* was used and read the paragraph. Then she asked them to refine their predictions of the meaning of *pandemonium*. Next the teacher discussed the origin of the word—which the English poet John Milton coined in his epic poem *Paradise Lost*. Pandemonium was the capital of Hell, the place where all the demons and devils congregated— figuratively speaking, where all hell broke loose.

In addition to modeling, Readence, Baldwin, and Bean (1981) suggested a strategy in which known parts of familiar words are transferred to parts of unfamiliar words. They recommended these steps:

1. *Select unfamiliar words.* Identify words which may be troublesome to conceptual understanding and which lend themselves to morphemic analysis that students will encounter in their reading. Use the author's context or one you develop when presenting the words.

2. *Identify words with identical morphemes.* Similarly constructed words must be identified so the students may associate the new to the known. For example, with the word "matricide" you should identify words such as "maternal," "matriarch," "homicide," and "suicide."

3. *Present the unknown words.* Morphemes can best be taught if they are presented in an interesting format and use real words which, when analyzed, reinforce the meaning of the root or affix in question.

4. *Dictionary verification.* Volunteers can look up the word in the dictionary to verify the guesses offered by the class (p. 38).

Using the Dictionary

Context and structural analysis are skills which give insight into approximate meanings of unknown words. Rarely do these skills help to derive precise definitions for key words. Instead, readers use context or word structure to keep themselves in the ballpark—able to follow a writer's communication without bogging down on difficult terminology.

There are times, however, when context and word structure reveal very little, if anything, about a word's meaning. In these instances, or when a precise definition is needed, a dictionary is a logical alternative and a valuable resource for students.

Knowing when to use a dictionary is as important as knowing how to use it. A content teacher should incorporate dictionary usage into ongoing plans but should avoid a very common pitfall in the process of doing so. When asked, "What does this word mean?" the teacher shouldn't automatically reply, "Look it up in the dictionary."

To some students, "Look it up in the dictionary," is another way of saying "Don't bug me" or "I really don't have the time or the inclination to help you." Of course, this may not be the case at all. However, from an instructional point of view, that hard-to-come-by teachable moment is lost whenever we routinely suggest to students to look up a word in the dictionary.

One way to make the dictionary a functional tool is to use it to verify educated guesses about word meaning revealed through context or structural analysis as in Step 4 of the analytical strategy above. For example, if a student asks you for the meaning of a vocabulary term, an effective strategy is to bounce the question right back: "What do you think it means? Let's look at the way it's used. Are there any clues to its meaning?" Or should a difficult word have a recognizable stem and affix(es), take several minutes to guide students through an analysis of word structure to predict meaning.

Once a meaning is hypothesized through one or both of these strategies, students have a choice. If they are satisfied with an educated guess because it makes sense, the ritual of looking up a word in the dictionary ought not be performed. But if students are still unsure of a word's meaning, the dictionary is there.

Of course, the "teachable moment" shouldn't be overdone; it's effective when used sparingly. Sometimes it's perfectly valid just to tell a student a word's meaning when you're asked. Or even to say, "Look it up in the dictionary."

When students go into a dictionary to verify or to determine a precise definition, more often than not they need supervision to make good decisions. Keep these tips in mind as you work on dictionary usage.

1. Help students determine the "best fit" between a word and its definition. Students often must choose the most appropriate definition from several of many. This poses a real dilemma for maturing learners. As they act upon a word, your interactions will help them make the best choice of a definition and will provide a behavior model for making such a choice.

2. If you do assign a list of words to look up in a dictionary, choose them selectively: a few words are better than many. The chances are greater that students will learn several key terms thoroughly than that they will develop vague notions about a large number.

3. Help students with the pronunication key in a glossary or dictionary as the need arises. However, this does not mean that you will teach skills associated with the use of a pronunciation key in isolated lessons. Instead, it means guiding and reinforcing students' ability to use a pronunciation key as they study the content of your course.

Building Interest and Enthusiasm

We believe it's worthwhile to devote some class time to creating interest and enthusiasm in the language of a content area. Many of the preceding activities, because of their gamelike nature, build interest and enthusiasm for the study of words. Interested students are more likely to learn vocabulary. Deighton (1970) concurred when he argued that "A sense of excitement about words, a sense of wonder, and a feeling of pleasure—these are the essential ingredients in vocabulary development" (p. 59).

Focus on interesting words whose explanations are likely to arouse students' enthusiasm in other content area terminology. Consider the following "starter" activities.

Creating Word-Enriched Environments

Make bulletin boards and collages where key concept words can be illustrated through headlines, pictures, cartoons, jokes, advertisements, and the like.

Form student committees to preview reading assignments for new and unusual words and to explain them to the rest of the class. For example, an English class committee called the Word Searchers found this passage from *Flowers for Algernon*: "Sculpture with a living element. Charlie, it's the greatest thing since *junkmobiles* and *tincannia*." The Word Searchers introduced the terms *junkmobiles* and *tincannia* to the class. They explained that the two words would not be found in the dictionary. Then the committee challenged the class to come up with definitions that would make sense. To top off the presentation the committee prepared Exhibit A and Exhibit B to demonstrate the words—a mobile made of various assortments of junk and an *objet d' art* made from tin cans, jar lids, and the like.

Word Play

*The Reading Teacher's Lament**
George E. Coon

I tried teaching my students sequencing
skills, but I couldn't keep them in order.

I tried teaching word configuration, but my
lesson never took shape.

I tried teaching my students a lesson using
the kinesthetic approach, but they wouldn't touch it.

I tried a strong phonics approach, but I
found that wasn't too sound.

I wanted to teach my students vocabulary,
but I never found the words to do it.

I tried using a semantic approach to comprehension,
but my students never caught my meaning.

I did well in teaching palindromes because
I knew them backwards and forwards.

You wouldn't believe my unit on fantasy!

I tried teaching about vowels, but my students
never got the long nor the short of it.

I tried to teach about syllables, but they
broke up the lesson.

I tried working on predicting outcomes, but
they only guessed at the answers.

I tried teaching auditory discrimination, but they
wouldn't hear of it.

So I became a mathematics teacher and
my problems have really multiplied.

*SOURCE: *The Reading Teacher* 33 (1979): 154. Reprinted with permission of George E. Coon and The International Reading Association.

On occasion, word play will energize vocabulary study. Students' interest and enthusiasm for content terminology is sparked when they have the opportunity to play with words that are an integral part of their textbook materials.

Riddles

Several days before the start of a unit on shelled animals, a science teacher posted on the bulletin board a sign that read Coming Attractions. Each day students received a clue more specific than the one the day before as to what word represented the concept for the next unit of study.

> Day 1: What lives from 1 to 75 years . . .
> Day 2: on land or water . . . but likes to bury itself in sand . . .
> Day 3: prefers warm climates . . .
> Day 4: has no backbone . . . comes in many colors . . . a thing of great beauty . . .
> Day 5: and whose name begins with m, ends with k, and rhymes with *tusk*?
> Answer: m __ __ __ __ __ k

After each clue the teacher encouraged predictions, and discussion followed. She even made a number of resources on marine life available to interested students to extend their search. The students had converged upon the answer by the end of the fifth day. The teacher noted to the class that she was "shell shocked" by their enthusiasm.

Idiomatic and Slang Expressions

Discuss idiomatic and current slang expressions. Dale (1975) contended that "Slang is novel, vivid. It plays tricks with words. It attracts attention—both favorable and unfavorable. To describe the appeal of slang in slang terms is the desire to be with it, in the know, up-to-date" (p. 39). Slang comes from many sources: politics, the jargon of special groups, newspapers, magazines, sports, and so forth. To the extent that slang and idiomatic expressions relate to your subject matter, you might consider introducing them to the class. Students can play with slang words in a variety of ways: (1) making slang dictionaries; (2) interviewing adults about slang expressions that were "in" during their youth; (3) inventing new slang expressions to label events, behavior, phenomena that they were studying. (A business education student once described *high finance* as transactions involving "serious bucks." An English student called writing compositions an exercise in "dirtying paper.")

Figurative Language

Point out instances of figurative language in reading materials. The figurative use of words often transforms colorless textbook writing into vivid prose.

There are several common types of figurative language:

1. *Metaphor:* an implied comparison which often asserts that one thing is another or that it acts like or has some of the qualities of something else. Examples:

— *Meaning* is an arrow that reaches its *mark* when . . .

— The *Vietnam War* was a *creeping cancer* which *plagued* the American society.

— *The waves cast by a pebble of thought spread* . . .

2. *Simile:* an explicit comparison using *like* or *as*. Examples:

— The *logic of facts* penetrates *like a bullet*.

— A *perfect definition of comprehension* is *as elusive as the butterfly of love*.

3. *Oxymoron:* a seeming self-contradiction. Examples:

— hotbed of apathy

— gentle strength

— benign neglect

4. *Personification:* a figure of speech in which an object or quality or ideal is given some attributes of a human being (more commonly found in verse than in prose). Examples:

— The algae danced in the full light of the botanist's microscope.

— No computer could brag that it had programmed a human being.

5. *Hyperbole:* an exaggeration used to emphasize a statement or situation. Examples:

— There was something olympian in his snarls and rages, and there was a touch of hell-fire in his mirth.

— They felt like sleeping for a year, but the marathon dancers continued numbly across the killing floor.

Word Origins and Histories

A brief discussion of an unusual word derivation or history will usually give students a lasting impression of a word. Piercy (1976) recommended that a teacher accumulate word origins and use them as mnemonic devices. If you do so, there should be a clear connection between the word's "story" and the current meaning.

Students' enthusiasm for language (and therefore for the language of your content area) will increase when they know the derivations behind such words as:

1. *Assassin*. Originally, a drinker of hashish. The members of a secret order founded among a Mohammedan sect in ancient Persia used the drug hashish and, under its influence, secretly murdered people. A cult member was thus referred to as a hashshash. From that origin comes the English word *assassin*.

2. *Bombastic*. Metaphorically, speech stuffed with cotton. From the Latin *bombax* ("cotton") came the word *bombast,* which also meant "cotton." Later the meaning was expanded to include any material used as stuffing for garments. The word *bombast* was eventually used to mean a speaker's "inflated style"—figuratively speaking, speech that is stuffed with high-sounding words.

3. *Muscle*. Metaphorically, the scurrying of a mouse. The Latin word *musculus* means "mouse." The French adapted it because they associated the rippling of a muscle with the movement of a mouse.

4. *Calculate*. Originally, the counting stones of the Romans. The Latin word *calx* means "limestone." The ancient Romans used little stones called *calculus* to add and subtract. From this derived the English word *calculate* and its many variations.

5. *Broker*. Originally, a vendor of wine. From the French *brochier,* meaning "one who broaches or taps a cask" to draw off the wine. Although the word *broker* was first used to mean a vendor of wine, through the years the term came to mean any small retailer—for example, *pawnbroker*. In modern times, a broker has been associated with the more dignified financial transactions involving stocks and bonds.

6. *Easel*. Metaphorically, the artist's donkey, from the Dutch word *ezel,* "ass or donkey." Figuratively, a small stand or support for the artist's canvas.

[These capsule explanations were adapted from *Picturesque Word Origins* (Springfield, Mass.: G. and C. Merriam Company, 1933). More recent resources for teachers are given in Appendix C.]

You can also create awareness and interest with *eponyms:* words originating from persons or places (*pasteurize, bedlam, maverick, chauvinistic*) or from *acronyms*—pronounceable words formed from the beginning letters or groups of letters in words that make up phrases (*scuba* stands for *self-*contained *u*nderwater breathing *ap*paratus; *amphetamine* for *a*lpha *m*ethyl *ph*enyl *et*hyl *amine*; *Euromart* for *Euro*pean *Mar*ket; *snafu* for *s*ituation *n*ormal *all f*ouled *u*p). Interesting words abound. If they appear in a text assignment, don't miss the opportunity to teach them to students.

Looking Back, Looking Forward

Vocabulary instruction involves more than just looking up, defining, memorizing, and using words in sentences. Vocabulary study lays the groundwork for learning concepts. In this chapter we studied how teaching vocabulary in content areas combines the acquisition of word meanings with the development of concepts. Teachers who design and implement instructional techniques which capitalize on this relationship are enhancing their students' comprehension of content area reading materials.

Students need multiple experiences in which they use and manipulate words in differing instructional situations. Vocabulary reinforcement provides these opportunities for students to increase their grasp of the technical vocabulary of a subject. Teachers create an atmosphere for vocabulary reinforcement through the kinds of classroom activity that promote speaking, listening, writing, and reading. Moreover, vocabulary reinforcement exercises reinforce word meanings and relationships among technical terms. We saw numerous examples of how these reinforcement materials were developed by teachers and incorporated into their lessons.

In particular, conceptual tasks provide the framework needed to study words critically. Various types of categorizing activities such as word sorts, categories, concept circles, analogies, and post structured interviews reinforce and extend student's ability to perceive relationships among concepts they are studying.

Another aspect of vocabulary instruction is showing students how to inquire into the meaning of an unknown word in reading material. The teacher should model the inquiry process before students apply it during reading. The teacher can develop insights and principles on using context aids, word structure, and the dictionary to advantage through modeling. As a result of vocabulary building, students will develop a variety of skills which can be applied in reading.

Content area teachers should also create an interest in the languages of their disciplines. They can tell the history and derivation of interesting terms. They can develop word-enriched environments as well as engage students in word play. The study of words should be fun. Enthusiasm for words will lead to further word study in your content area. And this is what the awareness aspect of vocabulary instruction is all about.

In the next chapter the focus is on organizing for instruction. How do content area teachers "put it all together" as they integrate reading with subject matter instruction? As you approach the next chapter, reflect upon how you might organize the instructional strategies described in Part II of this book within a single text lesson or within the framework of a series of lessons.

Suggested Readings

Anderson, R. C., & Freebody, P. (1979). *Vocabulary Knowledge*. Urbana, Ill.: University of Illinois Center for the Study of Reading Technical Report No. 136.

Dale, E., & O'Rourke, J. (1971). *Technique of Teaching Vocabulary*. Palo Alto, Calif.: Field Educational Publications.

Deighton, L. (1970). *Vocabulary Development in the Classroom*. New York: Teachers College Press.

Humes, A. (1977). *The Use of Concept-Learning Techniques in Vocabulary Development*. Los Alamitos, Calif.: Southwest Regional Laboratory Technical Note 3-77-06.

Johnson, D., & Pearson, P. D. (1984). *Teaching Reading Vocabulary* (2nd ed.). New York: Holt, Rinehart and Winston.

Mezynski, K. (1983). Issues concerning the acquisition of knowledge: Effect of vocabulary training on reading comprehension. *Review of Educational Research, 53*, 253–279.

Pachtman, A., & Riley, J. (1978). Teaching the vocabulary of mathematics through interactions, exposure, and structure. *Journal of Reading, 22*, 240–244.

Readence, J., & Searfoss, L. (1980). Teaching strategies for vocabulary development. *English Journal, 69*, 43–46.

Smith-Burke, M. T. (1982). Entending concepts through language activities. In J. Langer and M. T. Smith-Burke (eds.), *Reader Meets Author/Bridging the Gap*. Newark, Del.: International Reading Association.

Part Three

Translating Knowledge into Practice

CHAPTER TEN

Planning Instruction

Ninety percent of your results come from activities that consume ten percent of your time.
—DEREK A. NEWTON

Organizing Principle

Something that isn't worth doing isn't worth doing well. This is especially true of passive and purposeless textbook reading. "Assigning and telling" are poor substitutes for content area reading instruction. Showing students how to read content material is worth doing—and worth doing well. The time it takes to plan for reading will get the results you want: active and purposeful learning of text materials. What planning does is give the teacher a blueprint for making decisions. The blueprint may be for a single text assignment or for multiple reading experiences involving a variety of reading material. However, lesson planning isn't teaching. The organizing principle makes this clear: *Teaching involves putting a plan to work in actual classroom situations.*

How teachers structure lessons and involve students actively in reading are cornerstones in content area reading. Study the Chapter Overview before reading. This chapter will help you answer the following pivotal questions:

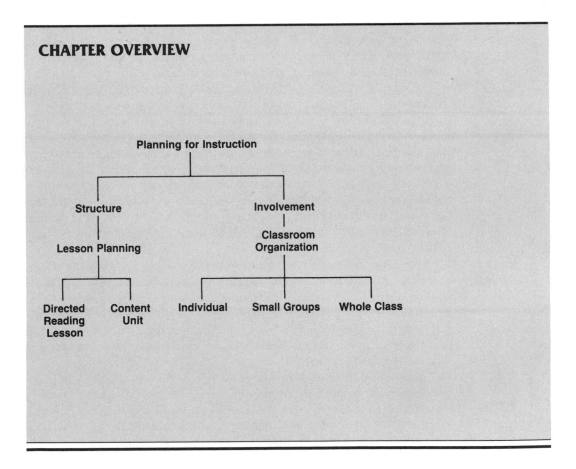

CHAPTER OVERVIEW

Planning for Instruction

Structure

Lesson Planning

Directed Reading Lesson

Content Unit

Involvement

Classroom Organization

Individual

Small Groups

Whole Class

1. How can content teachers plan instruction so that students will become actively involved in reading? Why do readers need structure?

2. What is involved in planning a directed reading lesson?

3. How does planning a content unit help the teacher to coordinate instructional activities and materials?

4. Why are small groups useful for reading-related discussions?

The faculty room is a special kind of gathering place. Observe, sometime, the pockets of human activity that form. When they are not talking about students or trading battle stories with one another, it's not surprising to see a group of teachers staking out territory along specialty lines. They delight in talking shop. During any given "free" period English teachers might be heard discussing the current best-seller, social studies teachers hotly debating the latest world crisis, or math teachers just talking algebra.

Good teachers know their subject matter. Professional competence is often judged according to how well informed and up to date a colleague is in a particular field. Good teachers also know that an intimate knowledge of a subject in itself isn't a sure ticket to success in the classroom. Another aspect of professional competence lies in "getting content across" to students.

Getting subject matter across to students is always a challenging task. The challenge is more pronounced than ever when reading becomes the vehicle for learning. To be able to show students how to read and learn actively from textbooks is never a small feat. But neither is it an impossible one.

Content teachers should organize instruction from texts for a singular purpose: to involve students actively in the reading of course materials. *Assign-read-answer-discuss* (ARAD) is a common but undistinguished practice that dominates textbook-learning. Students are assigned—to read a text selection—so that they can answer several questions—that become the basis for discussion in the next class session. More often than not, ARAD stifles involvement by fostering passive, purposeless reading.

A teacher shouting a reading assignment to students as they hustle out the door at the end of the period probably continues to happen more than we would like to admit. Under these conditions the reading assignment is purposeless. Why read it? The answer students give too frequently is "because it was assigned." The only real purpose for such reading is to get through the material. Getting through is the prime motivation when the assignment lacks any sense of where students are going and how they will get there.

Answering questions at the end of the selection is an important part of the getting-through syndrome. A favorite ploy of some students is to give the teacher a three-liner—an answer to a question that fills up three lines on a sheet of paper. Whether or not the response is thought out or fully developed, three lines suffice.

The class discussion that follows such an assignment usually slips quickly away from students to the teacher. If students can't or won't learn the material through reading, they'll get it through lecture or other means.

Mark Twain wrote in *Life on the Mississippi,* "I'll learn him or I'll kill him!" The same principle applies in spirit to assign-and-tell practices in classrooms. If students learn anything, they learn that they don't have to read course material because there are alternative routes to acquiring the information. The end result is passive reading or no reading at all.

Getting information across through reading demands more than assigning and telling. It requires that students act upon ideas in print. Stauffer (1975) commented that action on the part of students is a basic tenet in all learning. Students who act upon ideas as they read raise questions, make predictions, search for information, and reflect upon an author's message. The teacher's job is to activate and agitate thought. All activities, strategies, and materials which have been presented in this book are valuable only if they serve as springboards to thinking.

Not only must students act on ideas in print, but they must also interact with one another. Social interaction provides the framework within which readers can test, confirm, or reject ideas gained from reading. Students need a social context to articulate emerging concepts. This is why Stauffer (1975) noted: "Interaction means doing things in social collaboration, in a group effort . . . . This kind of interaction can lead to a critical frame of mind. Cooperation becomes co-operation when members of a group operate individually yet jointly upon a common provoked situation" (p. 32).

Readers' interactions with one another permit them to pool knowledge and to compare understandings. And in the process of interacting they will learn something about reading. Moffett and Wagner (1976) put it this way: "A light goes on in the head of a youngster who discovers that his peers understood a story differently from the way he did or that they don't agree about some idea he believed everyone took for granted. . . . The only way he can find out is to try to understand or express something and heed others' reactions" (p. 34).

Students who act upon ideas and interact with one another are involved in the subject matter. A reader who explains a point or justifies a response in effect shows others how to get information from the reading assignment. Students apply skills during reading; they demonstrate them during discussion.

No less important than the recognition that action and interaction are essential to learning from reading is the recognition that skilled and unskilled readers can work as intellectual equals when the teacher organizes the classroom to emphasize cooperation. A case in point illustrates how two teachers of American history teamed up to stimulate interaction among high, average, and low readers.

The two teachers, both at Lafayette High School in Williamsburg, Virginia, were dissatisfied with their students' performance during an inquiry-based unit on Colonial America (Devan et al., 1975). The students seemed to be unable to form workable hypotheses or to use library skills sufficiently to carry out the inquiry assignment. Their behavior in the media center was poor also. It was obvious to the teachers that the students were taking little interest in the assignment. To make matters worse, the feedback sessions in which students reported the results of their research efforts were little more than student lectures; many of the students just didn't participate.

After evaluating the situation, the two teachers decided that the problems in student performance and behavior were of an instructional nature. They decided they needed a way to stimulate interest and participation. So they devised a new game plan. They organized a new unit which called for differentiated research assignments on the causes of the American Revolution.

They developed four hypotheses, each related to a different cause of the Revolution and each containing a series of researchable items and events which may or may not have been associated with a particular cause. The distractor items were either completely out of historical context or did not relate to the causes under which they were grouped.

Then to each of several homogeneous groups of high, average, and low readers they assigned one of the hypotheses and a research task to complete. The high group performed at an evaluative or applied level of cognition on their inquiry task, the average group responded to an interpretive level task, and the low readers were to operate at a literal level on its research assignment.

The instructors further structured the inquiry unit by *not* telling the middle or high group about distractor items but telling the lower group of readers, who were assigned to identify and define each item. And throughout the inquiry the low readers were primed—that is, they received intense instruction on which items were related to a given hypothesis and which were not.

The teachers observed that the differentiated approach markedly improved performance during the information search in the media center. But the real payoff came during the feedback sessions when the middle and high groups were assigned to share the results of their inquiries with the low readers. It appeared that the organization of differentiated assignments, coupled with the priming of the low readers, created the "set" necessary for interaction. Here's what happened:

> With the presentation of the first distractor item by the high achieving group, the low achievement students began to question intensely the reporting group, demanding that they delineate and define the precise nature of the relationship existing between the distractor item and the hypothesis it was supposed to support. Discussion became rather heated, and at times, interest was so high that it was difficult to maintain the usual classroom atmosphere. In order to force the reporting group to defend its position, the low achievement group had to deal with the information at the same level of intellectual sophistication as did the reporting group. Instead of functioning at the literal level of comprehension, these low achieving students were now processing information at the applied level. *(Devan et al., 1975, pp. 145–146)*

Organizing the content classroom this way begins with the recognition that many problems related to content area reading *are instructional* in nature. The message behind the preceding illustration is twofold. First, the teacher should analyze conditions as they exist and then plan appropriate frameworks for instruction. Second, even supposedly poor readers will respond successfully to reading material at "higher levels" of comprehension under the proper instructional conditions. One of these conditions, as you might predict, involves the way teachers structure lessons.

The Directed Reading Lesson

What's the first thing that comes to mind when you think of lesson planning?

"That's as old as the ancient mariner."

"Restrictive!"

"Something I did way back when—during student teaching, not since."

"Picky. Picky. Picky."

We don't think any of these things, but neither do we suggest that a lesson plan must have a certain format, that objectives must be written a certain way, and so on and so forth. Instead, we contend that lesson organization is a blueprint for action, that having a plan in advance of actual classroom teaching is just good common sense.

The ability to organize a single lesson or a unit (a series of lessons) is a thread that runs throughout content area reading. A game plan is essential. Students respond well to structure. They need to sense where they are going and how they will get there when reading content materials. Classroom experiences without rhyme or reason won't provide the direction or stability that students need to enable them to grow as readers.

Lessons should be general enough to include all students, and flexible enough to allow the teacher to react intuitively and spontaneously when a particular plan is put to work in actual practice. In other words, organized lessons shouldn't restrict decisions about instruction that is in progress, but instead should encourage flexibility and change.

Some teachers, no doubt, will still argue that a lesson plan is an outdated educational artifact, that it's too restrictive for today's learners. Yet we're convinced that "to say that lesson planning is not appropriate is to say that thinking in advance of acting is inappropriate" (Mallan and Hersh, 1972, p. 41). Good lesson planning is a framework for making decisions—nothing more, nothing less.

Planning a Lesson

There's no one way to plan an effective content area reading lesson. Reading authorities have suggested several excellent lesson structures (Stauffer, 1975; Manzo, 1975; Herber, 1978). In this chapter we will examine what has been traditionally called the Directed Reading Lesson (DRL). The DRL offers the content teacher a fairly representative approach for lesson organization. In Chapter 5 two alternatives to the DRL, the Directed Reading-Thinking Activity (DR-TA) and the Guided Reading Procedure (GRP) were presented. Regardless of which type of plan is used, certain provisions must be made for any reading lesson to be effective. What the teacher does before reading, during reading, and after reading is crucial to active and purposeful reading. A discussion of the DRL clarifies this point.

The DRL can help teachers plan a single lesson involving reading. A single lesson doesn't necessarily take place in a single class session; several class meetings may be needed to achieve the instructional objectives of the lesson. Nor does each component of a DRL necessarily receive the same emphasis for any given reading assignment; the difficulty of the material, students' familiarity with the topic, and teacher judgment all play a part in deciding upon the sequence of activities you will organize. What the DRL tells you is that readers need varying degrees of guidance. As we have shown throughout this book, there are prereading, reading, and postreading activities which will improve comprehension as well as increase students' understanding of how that information can be gotten through reading. The components of a DRL can be examined in Figure 10.1.

Figure 10.1.
The Directed Reading Lesson in Content Areas

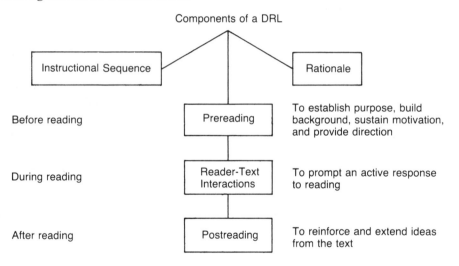

Prereading

A DRL which includes activity and discussion before reading reduces the uncertainty that students bring to an assignment. Prereading activities get students ready to read. Chapter 4 and sections from other chapters of this book were designed to help students to approach text material in a critical frame of mind; to seek answers to questions they have raised about the material.

During the prereading phase of instruction, a teacher often places emphasis on one or more of the following: (1) motivating readers, (2) building and activating background knowledge, (3) introducing key vocabulary and concepts, and (4) developing awareness of the task demands of the assignment and the strategies necessary for effective learning.

A key factor related to motivation involves getting students interested in the text reading. However, before taking into consideration "how to" motivate students, a fundamental question first needs to be raised: "Why should students be interested in this lesson?" Upon reflection, a teacher may even wish to consider whether he or she is interested in the material! If teachers are going to be models of enthusiasm for students, then the first step is to find something in the material to really get excited about. Enthusiasm—it is almost too obvious to suggest—is contagious. Many of the prereading activities and strategies presented in Chapter 4 have the potential to sustain interest in and establish purpose for reading. However, nothing is more motivating for students than to participate in these prereading activities *and* to experience first-hand the teacher's own enthusiasm and interest in the material.

Building and activating background knowledge for a lesson and presenting key vocabulary and concepts are also essential to prereading preparation. Many of the strategies in Chapters 4 and 9 spoke directly to this aspect of lesson planning and need not be belabored here. Suffice it to say, in making decisions related to building background knowledge, it's important to review previous lessons in light of present material. What does yesterday's lesson have to do with today's? Will students make the connection to previously studied material? Sometimes several minutes of review prior to forging ahead into uncharted realms of learning can make all the difference in linking "new" information to "old." Furthermore, when deciding which vocabulary terms to single out for prereading instruction, we emphasize three questions which should be considered: What key words will students need to understand? Are all the terms equally important? Which new words carry "heavy" concept loads?

Prereading might also include discussions which develop awareness of the reading task at hand and the strategies needed to handle the task effectively. These are *metacognitive discussions*. Providing direction is another way of saying that students will develop task-knowledge and self-knowledge about their own learning strategies. Helping students to analyze the reading task ahead of them or modeling a learning strategy that students will need during reading are two metacognitive activities that quickly come to mind. Questions to ask in planning for a metacognitive discussion are: What are the most important ideas in the lesson? What strategies will students need to learn these ideas? Are the students *aware* of these strategies?

Guiding Reader-Text Interactions

A directed reading lesson should also include provisions for guiding the search for and retrieval of information during reading. In other words, students need to be shown how to think through print.

Teachers easily recognize the important parts of a text assignment. Most students don't. Instead, they tend to read (if indeed they read at all) every passage in every chapter in the same monotonous manner. Each word, each sentence, each paragraph is treated with equal reverence. No wonder a distance exists between the reading material and the student.

Guidance during reading bridges the gap between students and textbook assignment so that students can learn how to read selectively, to distinguish important from less important ideas, perceive relationships, and to respond actively to meaning.

The various reading and study guides presented in this book were suggested within the spirit of guiding reader-text interactions. Note, however, that these adjunct aids should be used with difficult text material. At times, well-executed prereading instruction is enough to sustain most readers' active responses to text during reading.

Postreading

Ideas encountered before and during reading may need reinforcement and extension after reading. Postreading activities create the structure needed to refine emerging concepts. For example, a social studies teacher was nearing completion

---

Box 10.1

SOUTHEAST ASIA

I. *Directions:* A rice farmer, a Buddhist monk, a government official, and a geographer all feel competent to speak on any of the topics listed below. Who really is best qualified? Who is the specialist in each field? On the blank line preceding each topic place the letter of the correct specialist.

(a) rice farmer
(b) Buddhist monk
(c) government official
(d) geographer

___1. forested regions of Thailand

___2. the life of Siddhartha Gautama

___3. amount of rice exported each year

___4. monsoon rains in Southeast Asia

___5. harvesting rice

___6. causes of suffering

___7. the art of meditation

___8. the Menam river basin

___ 9. amount of rice produced per acre

___10. pagodas in Thailand

___11. number of Buddhists living in Bangkok

___12. virtues of a simple life

___13. the rice festival in Bangkok

___14. the Temple of the Emerald Buddha

___15. attainment of nirvana—perfect peace

II. *Directions:* Pretend you are either the rice farmer, the Buddhist monk, the government official, or geographer. Write a paragraph in which you reveal your professional attitude toward and opinion about the approaching monsoon season.

---

of a unit on Southeast Asia. She asked students to reflect upon their reading by using the activity in Box 10.1 as a springboard to discussion and writing. The writing and follow-up discussion refined and extended thinking about the ideas under study. The questions "Who is best qualified?" and "Who is the specialist in the field?" prompted students to sort out what they had learned. The teacher provided just enough structure by listing topics from various facets of Southeast Asian culture for students to focus thinking and make distinctions.

Activities such as the one in Box 10.1 reinforce and extend ideas. The writing and study strategies in Chapters 7 and 8 also help students "do something" with the ideas that they have read about. Writing activities, study guides, and other postreading activities such as semantic webbing and mapping are springboards to thinking and form the basis for discussing and articulating ideas developed through reading.

Some Examples of DRL Planning

At the Cleveland School of Science sixth graders were assigned a text selection on how bees communicate. The text told the story of Professor Karl von Frisch, an entomologist who had studied bees for years. The story focused on his experimental observations leading to the discovery of communication behavior among bees. The teacher's objectives were to (1) involve students in an active reading and discussion of the text assignment, and (2) have them experience some of the steps scientists go through when performing laboratory or field experiments. Her lesson plan follows:

I. Prereading
   A. Before introducing the text, determine what students presently know about bees:

      Who has observed bees in a close-up situation?

      What do you notice about bees that seems unique to them?

      When you see a bee, is it by itself, or usually in a group?

      Why do you think bees swarm in groups?

   B. Connect students' responses to the questions to the text assignment. Introduce the story and its premise.

   C. Form small groups of four students each and direct each group to participate in the following situation:

Professor Karl von Frisch worked with bees for many years. He was puzzled by something he had observed again and again. When he set up a table on which he placed little dishes of scented honey he attracted bees. Usually he had to wait for hours or days until a bee discovered the feeding place. But as soon as one bee discovered it, many more came to it in a short time. Evidently, the one bee was able to communicate the news of food to other bees in its hive.

Pretend you are a scientist helping Professor Karl von Frisch. How could you find out how the bees communicate? How do they tell each other where the food is located? List ten things you could do to find out the answers to these questions.

    D. Have the students share their group's top five ideas with the class. Write these on the chalkboard.

  II. Reader-Text Interactions

    A. Assign the selection to be read in class.

    B. During reading, direct students to note the similarities and differences between their ideas on the board and Professor von Frisch's experimental procedures.

 III. Postreading (Day Two)

    A. Discuss the previous day's reading activity. How many of the students' ideas were similar to von Frisch's procedures? Different?

    B. Extend students' understanding of the inquiry process that scientists, like von Frisch, follow. Divide the class into groups of four students to work on the following exercise:

All scientists follow a pattern of research in order to form answers for the questions they have about different subjects.

For example, von Frisch wanted to know about how bees communicated. He (1) formed a question, (2) formulated an experiment in order to answer the question, (3) observed his subjects in the experiment, and (4) answered the question based on the observations he made.

Now it's your turn! Tomorrow we are going on a field trip to the park to experiment with ants and food. Your first job as a scientist is to devise a question and experiment to fit your question. After we return, you will write your observations and the answer to your question. You will be keeping notes on your experiment while we are in the park.

Question:

Experiment:

Observations:

Answer:

    C. Conduct the experiment the next day at the park. Each group will be given a small amount of food to place near an existing anthill. They will record their notes and take them back to the classroom. Each group's discoveries will be discussed in class.

By way of contrast, study how a high school French teacher taught Guy de Maupassant's short story "L'Infirme" to an advanced class of language students. The story is about two men riding in a train car. Henry Bonclair is sitting alone in a train car when another passenger, Revalière enters the car. This fellow traveler is handicapped, having lost his leg due to a bullet during the war. Bonclair wonders about the type of life he must lead. As he looks upon the handicapped man, Bonclair senses that he has made his acquaintance a few years earlier. He asks the man if he is not the person he assumes him to be. Revalière is that man. Now Bonclair remembers that Revalière was to be married. He wonders if he had gotten married before the accident or after the accident or if at all. Bonclair inquires. No, Revalière had not married, refusing to ask the girl to "put up with" a deformed man. However, he is on his way to see her, her husband, and her children. They are all very good friends.

The French teacher formulated five objectives for the lesson;

1. to teach vocabulary dealing with the concept of infirmity;
2. to foster students' ability to make inferences about the reading material in the context of their own knowledge;
3. to foster students' ability to make predictions of what will happen in a story in light of their own background which they bring to the story;
4. to foster students' ability to evaluate their predictions in light of the story;
5. to use the story as a basis for writing a dialogue in French.

The steps in the plan are quite extensive and are outlined below:

I. Prereading
   A. Begin the lesson by placing the title of the story on the board: "L'Infirme." Ask students to look at the title and compare it to a similar English word (or words). Determine in a very general way what the story is probably about. (A handicapped person.)
   B. On the overhead, introduce key words used in the story by displaying a structured overview:

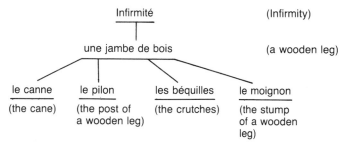

Infirmité	(Infirmity)
une jambe de bois	(a wooden leg)

le canne	le pilon	les béquilles	le moignon
(the cane)	(the post of a wooden leg)	(the crutches)	(the stump of a wooden leg)

   C. Use the structured overview to make predictions about the story.
   D. Use the Inferential Strategy. Ask and discuss with the class the following three sets of questions. Have the students write down their responses.
      (1a) Vous avez tous vu quelqu'un qui est très estropié à cause de la perte

d'une jambe ou d'un bras. Qu'est-ce qui traverse votre esprit? (De quoi est-ce que vous vous demandez?)

(You have all seen someone who is very crippled due to the loss of a leg or arm. When you see such a person, what crosses your mind? What do you wonder about?)

(1b) Dans l'histoire Bonclair voit cet jeune infirme qui n'a pas de jambe. Qu'est-ce que vous pensez traverse son esprit?

(In the story Bonclair sees a young cripple who has no leg. What do you think crosses his mind? What does he wonder about concerning this person?)

(2a) Quand vous voyez quelqu'un qui a l'air familier mais vague, qu'est-ce que vous voulez faire? Qu'est-ce que vous faites? Quels sont souvent les résultats?

(When you see someone who looks vaguely familiar, what do you want to do? What do you do? What are often the results?)

(2b) Dans cette histoire Bonclair se souvient vaguement qu'il a fait la connaissance de cet infirme. Prédites qu'il fait et prédites les résultats.

(In this story, Bonclair remembers vaguely having met this man Revalière. Predict what he does and the results.)

(3a) Imaginez que vous êtes fiancé(e) à un jeune homme ou à une jeune femme. Puis vous avez un accident et vous êtes estropié(e). Qu'est-ce que vous feriez? Voudriez-vous vous marier? Pourriez-vous compter sur l'autre de vous aimer encore?

Imagine that you are engaged to a young man or woman. Then you have a serious accident and are badly crippled. What would you do? Would you still want to marry? Could you still expect the other to love you?)

(3b) Dans notre histoire Revalière a eu un accident juste avant son marriage. Prédites ce qu'il a fait et ce qu'il a compté de la jeune fille. Prédites les résultats.

(In our story, Revalière had an accident just before his upcoming marriage. Predict what he did and what he expected of his intended. Predict the results.)

II. Reader-Text Interactions
   A. Assign the reading, instructing students to keep in mind their own background references and predictions, noting possible changes in their predictions.

III. Postreading
   A. Upon completion of the reading, conduct a follow-up discussion with the class. Relate their predictions to what actually happened, noting how our background knowledge and experience of the world leads us to think along certain lines.
   B. Through the discussion, note changes and refinement of student predictions and when they occurred.

C. Vocabulary exercise. Distribute a ditto on which is reproduced a vocabulary-context reinforcement exercise. All vocabulary items studied in the prereading section would be listed along with sentences taken from the story with blanks to be filled in with the appropriate word. There are fewer sentences than word choices listed. Seven or eight minutes are allowed for this exercise after which call for responses with students reading (in clear French) the complete sentence.

D. Have the class form groups of four with at least one male and female in each group. Establish the following situation:

Une jeune fille vient d'être estropiée dans un accident de natage. Son fiancé lui a téléphoné. Il veut lui parler. Qu'est-ce qu'il veut lui dire? On frappe à la porte. C'est lui.

(A young lady has been crippled for life in a swimming accident. Her fiancé has just called. He wants to come over and talk. What does he want to talk about? There is a knock at the door. It is he.)

Think together, drawing on your past knowledge and/or experiences of situations like this. Write a group dialogue in French between the girl and her fiancé of 15 to 20 lines. What might he have to tell her? How then might she react?

Select a boy and a girl to present the group's dialogue to the class.

A third lesson example involves a senior-level text assignment from *Invitation to Economics* (Scott, Foresman, 1982). The selection was six pages in length and dealt with the topic, "Trade Offs." A content analysis by the teacher yielded the following major ideas presented in the text:

1. When resources are used to produce one economic good or service, those same resources cannot be used simultaneously to produce another good or service: this opportunity has been "traded off."

2. In answering the basic economic questions, all countries must consider the question of (relative) value.

3. The trade offs that a consumer must make when buying different quantities of two items is shown graphically by a budget line.

4. The trade offs that a nation must make when producing different quantities of two items is shown graphically by the production-possibility frontier.

5. If the opportunity cost between two items is constant, this will be portrayed graphically by a straight line on a budget line or the production-possibility frontier.

6. If the opportunity cost between two products varies, this will be shown graphically by a curved line on the production-possibility frontier.

7. Any point (representing a combination of two items) that lies within or on a budget line is attainable with a given income; any point lying beyond the line is not attainable with that income.

8. Any point (representing a combination of two products) that lies within or on the production-possibility frontier for a particular nation is attainable, given that nation's existing amount of resources. Any point lying beyond the frontier is not attainable, given the existing amount of resources.

9. An increase in a nation's amount of resources or level of technology will push outward its production-possibility frontier.

Given the potential difficulty of the material, the teacher developed the following plan:

I. *Prereading*

Objectives:

A. Students will become aware of the key economic concepts of Chapter 1, Section 3: "Trade offs" (pp. 12–18).

B. Students will understand the graphic representation of economic concepts.

Procedure:

A. Have students preview this section by skimming; have them pay particular attention to the definitions of key concepts given in the page margins.

B. Have students examine and read the captions explaining a budget line (Figure 1.2, p. 14) and a production-possibility frontier (Figure 1.3, p. 15)

As an entire class, have them suggest the relationship of the concepts of trade offs and opportunity cost to these graphs.

II. *Reader-Text Interactions*

Objectives:

A. Students will comprehend the text at the literal, interpretive, and applied levels of comprehension.

Procedure:

A. Distribute to each student a mimeographed handout of a three-level reading guide (see Box 10.2); have them preview this guide to set their purpose for reading this section of the textbook.

B. Have students read pp. 12–18 and then individually complete the reading guide.

III. *Postreading*

Objectives:

A. Students will understand and extend the meaning of the economic concepts.

Procedure:

A. In pairs, have students take about 5 minutes to compare and discuss their marking of the items on the three-level reading guide. Then, in a class-sized group, answer any questions over the guide that students still have.

B. In groups of 4 or 5, give students about 5 minutes to list several specific examples from the news today of the following factors which could push the U.S. production-possibility frontier outward:

1. discoveries of additional resources;
2. advances which have raised our level of technology.

Then, have two students list these specific examples on the chalkboard during a whole-class discussion of them.

Finally, as a homework assignment, have students propose 2–3 of their own suggestions to:
1. increase the amount of productive resources in the U.S.; and
2. raise our level of technology.

(These will be discussed for 7–10 minutes in small groups to begin the next day's lesson; then, they will be shared with the entire class.)

Box 10.2

THREE-LEVEL READING GUIDE FOR "TRADE OFFS"

I. *Literal level*

Directions: Check the items you believe are *true,* given your reading of Section 3.

_____ 1. Since individuals cannot have everything they want, they must make trade offs.

_____ 2. In answering the basic economic questions, all countries must consider the question of value.

_____ 3. It is always simple for a nation to determine the relative value of different products.

_____ 4. The trade offs a consumer must make when buying different quantities of two items can be shown graphically by a budget line.

_____ 5. A production-possibility frontier shows graphically the relationship between a nation's existing resources and its level of technology.

_____ 6. A curved production-possibility frontier means varying opportunity costs.

II.   _Interpretive level_
Directions: Check the items that are logical inferences that can be drawn from Section 3.

_____ 1. Trade offs are necessary because productive resources are limited.

_____ 2. The opportunity cost of using steel to produce buses is the number of cars that could not be produced from the same steel.

_____ 3. The opportunity cost of working part time on school nights is the number of hours worked that cannot be used for other activities, such as studying or recreating.

_____ 4. The concept of a budget line implies that a person's income is never constant.

_____ 5. If the price of Item A is always twice the price of Item B, the budget line for these two items will be a straight line.

_____ 6. If a person's weekly income is $20, a combination of two rock albums (@ $7.00) and one cassette tape (@ $8.00) would lie either on or within their budget line.

III.   _Applied level_
Directions: Check the items which are logical applications of the economic concepts discussed in Section 3.

_____ 1. A nation's production-possibility frontier can be moved outward by discoveries of additional resources.

_____ 2. Increasing a nation's level of technology will move its production-possibility frontier inward.

_____ 3. In the long term, the increased use of robots in manufacturing would push a nation's production-possibility frontier outward.

The three lesson plans that we presented had the same underlying structure. Each plan provided a set of experiences designed to move students from preparation to read, to interaction with text, to extension and reinforcement of concepts integral to the material under study. The plans were developed by teachers for real instructional purposes. None of the lessons should be thought of as "perfect." However, they represent products which show how teachers translated knowledge about content area reading into plans for classroom practice. As such, the lessons were offered as working models.

How teachers translate knowledge of instructional strategies to single text assignments will vary by grade level and the sophistication of the students. The same is true of developing plans for a unit of study. In the next section, we go beyond considerations for planning single text lessons to decisions related to a series of lessons and multiple reading experiences.

Developing a Content Unit

While the DRL lends itself to a single lesson from a textbook, a *content unit* organizes instruction around a series of lessons which may include multiple reading materials. This doesn't mean that a predominant source of information such as the textbook will be excluded from a unit of study. Unit planning simply provides more options to coordinate a variety of information sources. Prereading, reading, and postreading activities become an integral part of unit teaching. When the teacher plans a series of lessons in advance, the mesh of activities will give students a sense of continuity, and they won't get a mishmash of unrelated experiences.

Listing instructional materials and resources is an important part of preparation in planning the unit. One reason why a unit is so attractive a means of lesson organization is that the teacher can go beyond the textbook—or for that matter, bypass it. Students often welcome the respite from continuous single-text instruction. Popular books, pamphlets, periodicals, reference books, newspapers, magazines, and audiovisual materials are all potential alternative routes to acquiring information. When a teacher organizes a unit topically or thematically with variable materials, students begin to assume the lion's share of responsibility for learning.

A content analysis is a major part of teacher preparation in the development of a unit of study. The content analysis results in the *what* of learning. It elicits the major concepts and understandings that students should learn from reading the unit materials. Through content analysis, the major concepts become the objectives for the unit. Earle (1976) pointed out that it doesn't matter whether these content objectives are stated in behavioral terms or not. What really matters is that the teacher knows which concepts must be taught. Therefore, it's important to decide upon a manageable number of the most important understandings to be gained from the unit. This means setting priorities; it's impossible to cover every aspect of the material that students will read or be exposed to.

A junior high science teacher's content analysis for a unit on the respiratory system yielded these major concepts to be taught:

1. Living things require oxygen.
2. Living things give off carbon dioxide.
3. Living things exchange oxygen and carbon dioxide during respiration.
4. When living things oxidize organic substances, carbon dioxide is given off.
5. When living things oxidize organic substances, energy is given off.
6. Sugars and starches are foods that store energy.

7. The respiratory system of living things is responsible for the exchange of gases.

8. Breathing is a mechanical process of living things and respiration is a chemical process that happens in the cells of living things.

9. The body uses only a certain part of the air that we take in during breathing.

Stating these content objectives forced the science teacher to select reading materials and plan the how of the unit: the instructional activities.

Organizing the Unit

The actual organizational framework of a unit will vary. For example, you might organize a unit entirely on a sequence of lessons from assignments from a single textbook. This type of organization is highly structured, and even restrictive in the sense that it often precludes the use of multiple text sources. However, an instructional unit can be planned so that the teacher will (1) use a single textbook to begin the unit and then branch out into multiple-text study and differentiated activities; (2) organize the unit entirely on individual or group inquiry and research; or (3) combine single-text instruction with multiple-text activities and inquiry.

Branching out provides the latitude to move from highly structured lessons to less structured ones. At the same time, the movement from single to multiple information sources exposes students to variable instructional materials that may be better suited to their needs and interests. Figure 10.2 shows the variability of a unit.

The science teacher organized the respiratory system unit following a branching-out pattern—around laboratory experiments, supplementary readings, and group research projects. The readings came from four information sources. Although students participated in the lab experiments as a whole class, the teacher devised *learning activity centers* for each of the supplementary reading materials:

Center 1: Gail G. Milgram, *The Teenager and Smoking*. New York: Richard Rosen Press, 1972.
Center 2: Arthur H. Cain, *The Use and Abuse of Cigarette Tobacco*. New York: John Day, 1964.
Center 3: Luther Terry and Daniel Horn, *To Smoke or Not To Smoke*. New York: Lothrop, Lee and Shepherd, 1969.
Center 4: Bernard Glemser, *All About the Human Body*. New York: Random House, 1958.

On days when the learning activity centers were in operation, students would open their classroom folders and read the schedules stapled to the inside covers of

Figure 10.2
Variability of a Content Unit

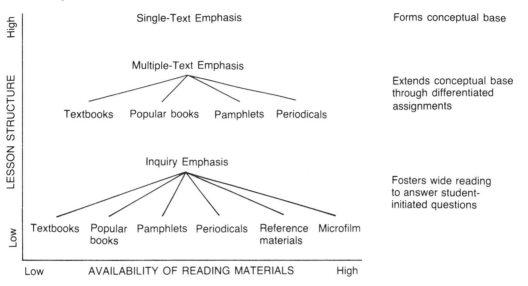

the folders. This helped determine which center each student was assigned to for a particular day. The centers were equipped with directions for individual and group work. The type of activities varied within each center. Reading guides, vocabulary reinforcement exercises, and outlining activities comprised the bulk of the reading assignments. The centers also included activities for writing and the interpretation of graphic materials. (Learning activity centers are discussed more fully later in this chapter.)

As part of the unit students also participated in group projects. Some projects required little or no reading; others required a great deal. For at least half the class, the classroom library and the school's learning resource center became built-in parts of the unit. Students were allotted class time to plan, research, and present their individual and group projects. Some of the inquiry projects included the following:

1. Your group represents the earth's top scientists. You have been invited to speak at the First Annual Interplanetary Conference on Life Support Systems. How would you explain the human breathing system to nonhuman scientists at the conference?

2. Conduct a cigarette survey of your classmates', neighbors', and teachers' attitudes toward smoking. To do this you must make up a survey questionnaire. Interpret and report the results of the survey to the class.

3. Write letters to the American Cancer Society or the American Lung Association requesting information on the effects of cigarette smoking. Make a classroom display of the literature they send you. Discuss the information in the display with the class.

4. What is SCUBA? How does it work? What is meant by "the bends"?

5. Research and construct comparison charts of the human breathing system and two other animal breathing systems. Explain to the class how the three animal systems differ and are alike.

6. Construct a model of the human respiratory system. You might use cardboard, papier mâché, or clay.

7. Write a column for the school newspaper on the history of tobacco.

8. If you were a talking fish, how would you explain the secret of breathing underwater to an interviewer from *People* magazine? Write the explanation in the form of an interview, with questions and responses.

The science unit followed a branching-out pattern, moving from whole-class reading and lab experimentation, to differentiated reading assignments in activity centers, to group inquiry and research projects requiring the use of multiple materials and resources.

Cross-Tabulating Concepts, Materials, and Activities

A unit of study is a planning tool for teachers; in all likelihood it will grow with use as you modify, refine, or add on instructional activities. In planning, a teacher often finds it difficult to coordinate content objectives with reading materials and resources and instructional activities. Estes and Vaughan (1985) suggested that teachers number the major concepts in the unit and then use a cross-tabulation system.

A unit on spatial relationships for a high school art class provides an example of how a teacher coordinated concept objectives, activities, and materials. First she listed the major concepts to be taught in the unit:

1. Humans are aware of space about them as functional, decorative, and communicative.

2. Space organized intuitively produces an aesthetic result, but a reasoned organization of space can also lead to a pleasing outcome if design is considered.

3. Occupied and unoccupied space have positive and negative effects on mood and depth perception.

4. The illusion of depth can be created on a two-dimensional surface.

5. The direction and balance of lines and/or forms creates feelings of tension, force, and equilibrium in the space that contains them.

6. Seldom in nature is the order of objects so perfect as to involve no focal point or force or tension.

Then she cross-tabulated these concepts with the activities and materials to be used in the unit. See Table 10.1.

Table 10.1
Sample of Cross-Tabulation

Activities	Materials	1	2	3	4	5	6
				Concepts			
1. Structured overview	Graham Collier, *Form, Space, and Vision*. Prentice-Hall, 1963	x	x	x	x	x	x
2. Vocabulary and concept bulletin board		x	x	x	x	x	x
3. Prereading exercise	Chapter 3				x	x	
4. Prereading exercise	Chapters 6 and 7	x	x	x			
5. Reading guide	Chapters 6 and 7	x	x	x			
6. Reading guide	Chapter 11						x
7. Vocabulary exercise	Chapter 3				x	x	
8. Vocabulary exercise	Chapters 6 and 7	x	x	x			
9. Vocabulary exercise	Chapter 11						x
10. Student's "choice" (list of projects for independent study)	H. Botten, *Do You See What I See*. Davis, 1965. H. Helfman, *Creating Things That Move*. Morrow, 1975. D. McAgy, *Going for a Walk with a Line*. Doubleday, 1959. L. Kampmann, *Creating with Space and Construction*. Reinhold, 1971. G. Le Frevre, *Junk Sculpture*. Sterling, 1973. J. Lynch, *Mobile Design*. Crowell, 1955.	x	x	x			
11. Hands-On:	Assortment of construction materials needed for activities						
Ink dabs		x	x	x			
Straw painting		x	x	x			
Dry seed arrangement		x	x	x			

Activities	Materials	Concepts					
		1	*2*	*3*	*4*	*5*	*6*
Cardboard sculpture					X	X	
Positive/negative cutouts		X	X	X			
Perspective drawing					X	X	
Large-scale class sculpture							X
Mobiles							X
Space frames							X
12. Filmstrip	*Calder's Universe.* Miller-Brody Productions #9-MB-808						X
13. Field trip to studio of a sculptress							X
14. Field trip to museum		X	X	X	X	X	X
15. Learning corner	Displays of artists' works with questionnaires to be filled out about them	X	X	X			

For additional sample units, with descriptions of activities and materials, see Appendix E. These units have been constructed by teachers for their own use.

The inquiry — as well as all other activities within the unit — can be initiated through different grouping patterns. Whole-class, small-group, and individual learning are all important means of classroom organization. Certain activities, however, are better suited to a particular grouping pattern than others. The next section explains why.

Classroom Organization

Effective classroom organization uses a combination of individual, small-group, and whole-class experiences. Small groups in particular facilitate active participation and should be a primary form of classroom organization when reading is the vehicle for learning. Students produce more ideas, participate more, and take greater intellectual risks in small-group or team learning situations. First, a small group, with its limited audience, provides more opportunity for students to contribute ideas to a discussion and take chances in the process. They can try out ideas without worrying about being wrong or sounding dumb — a fear that often accompanies risk taking in a whole-class situation. Second, team learning is generally more productive than individual learning.

Individualizing

Individual learning shouldn't be confused with individualized instruction. Moffett (1975) contended that individualized instruction often means "learning small things in small steps" (p. 23). Students actually complete the same program "except for some differences in pacing." Individual learning, however, in the context of this book, means providing enough differential guidance to help students read content materials successfully. Individual learning — individualizing — doesn't require a unique program for every member of the class. Nor does it suggest a different text for each student. The teacher can simply make adjustments in the lengths of reading assignments, the time given individual students to complete them, and the instructional activities related to the reading assignments.

The inquiry approach is one means of individualizing. The teacher's use of contracts and learning activity centers provide two additional approaches that will differentiate learning and offer students options.

Contracting

A contract is an agreement between two parties — here, the teacher and the student. Both teacher and students benefit from contracting. Through a contract, the teacher can differentiate instruction according to the competence, enthusiasm, and motivation of each student. For students, contracts foster a sense of commitment and responsibility and encourage them to pursue a variety of topics and interests through variable materials.

After introducing a unit and explaining the idea of the contract, the teacher and each student decide upon an acceptable contract between them. The teacher can set the terms of the contract, or teacher and student can set them together. The activities involved in the contract should be challenging but not frustrating. Teacher and student should then decide upon beginning and ending dates, resources needed, reasons for entering the contract, and a plan which includes when and where stages of work are to be accomplished. It is essential that the student understand all responsibilities in assuming the contract. The teacher's role is flexible enough to determine the degree of independence at which each student will function. If a student cannot work independently with certain tasks or materials, you can adjust the situation accordingly, providing the needed guidance and appropriate instruction.

As part of the general agreement, students are given a choice of evaluation options. They can contract to do so many activities for an A, a B, a C, and so on, as their contract grade. A method for evaluating the quality of student work should also be negotiated, as should criteria for final evaluation. Final evaluation may be based on daily conferences, classroom presentation or exhibit, written presentation, or a variety of other means. Evaluation is a vital aspect of the contract. If a student has lived up to his or her share of the bargain, then you must follow through accordingly. A trust can't be betrayed.

As students work to fulfill their contracts the teacher shouldn't remain detached. Your job is to guide, encourage, and give individual instruction depending on the nature of the task and a student's ability to handle it successfully. Such facilitation can best be handled through conferences.

A high school English teacher initiated a six-week literature unit on adolescent growth which she called "New Awareness Through Communication." Within the unit she devised a plan that combined contractual readings with obligatory readings. She introduced the unit to her students, explaining that it would operate partly on a contractual basis. They were required to make a commitment about the amount of reading they would do. Their contract grade would be based upon the number of short stories and novels they read: the more they read, the better their grades. To receive contractual credit for their reading, the students had to report on each of their selections on a five-by-seven inch index card, writing about some aspect of the unit theme. Each card contained the student's name, the title of the short story or novel, and a discussion of the theme with supporting evidence from the work. The teacher would not accept a plot summary.

Each Monday and Friday for four weeks students had silent reading days to do their contractual reading and complete their index cards. If they needed help in relating a story or novel to the unit theme, they could talk to the teacher.

The terms of the contract were: E = no contractual reading; D = one book, two short stories; C = one book, six short stories; B = one book, ten short stories; A = two books, ten short stories. The contract was to be fulfilled five weeks from the date of signing. See Box 10.3.

As you can see, the teacher provided plenty of structure but allowed students options in the quantity and choice of readings. It would have been possible for her to have provided even less structure by letting students decide on their own the terms of their contracts and means of reporting. This teacher chose, however, to operate a half-open classroom.

Learning Activity Centers

Learning activity centers (sometimes called stations) "decentralize" the content classroom. They offer an organizational arrangement for differentiating assignments and freeing the teacher to work with students individually or in small groups. For some teachers, decentralizing the classroom means changing their outlooks and attitudes. Yet in many respects a learning center approach will give you the best of two worlds for individualizing. On the one hand, you can devise centers where students explore interests in topics and materials related to a unit of study. Activities may revolve around self-selection of reading materials, listening and viewing, sustained silent reading and writing, inquiry, and exploratory study. On the other hand, you can develop activity centers which are more prescriptive in nature. Tasks that are designed with specific content objectives in mind will provide reinforcement and guidance for important concepts and skills to be developed in the unit.

The physical setting is the key to openness with stability in a classroom which organizes instruction around learning activity centers. Decentralization places a premium on classroom space, and how well it is to be utilized. Centers create a physical environment where student movement dramatically increases. Students assume responsibility for their own work; they are for the most part autonomous and self-directing.

Box 10.3

THE CONTRACT

I _____ contract to read _____ novel(s) and _____ short stories as listed below, for a contract grade of _____ .

Novel(s)	*Author*	*Teacher's Initials*
_____	_____	_____
_____	_____	_____
Short stories		
_____	_____	_____
_____	_____	_____
_____	_____	_____
_____	_____	_____
_____	_____	_____
_____	_____	_____
_____	_____	_____
_____	_____	_____
_____	_____	_____

Agreed:_____ (Student)
_____ (Teacher)

This means that the physical arrangement in the classroom should be adapted to reflect the tasks the students are assigned to participate in. Therefore, let the activities themselves determine the physical setup.

Operating the Centers

The secret to effective operation of learning activity centers lies in teacher organization and scheduling of students to designated activities. Four general organizational objectives must be achieved:

1. Students will operate independently in the classroom. Increased freedom means increased responsibility.

2. Students will be prepared to explain the operation of each activity center

2. in the classroom. The teacher, therefore, should spend some planning time walking students through a demonstration of each center, explaining its purpose and operation to the class.

3. Students will conduct themselves in a manner that reflects a consideration of each individual's right to think and read in a laboratorylike setting. Noise level will increase but students must respect one another's need for concentration.

4. Students will participate in the evaluation of their own progress. As students assume responsibility for their own learning, they should also assume responsibility for self-evaluation.

Activity centers may be philosophically appealing to many teachers, but how does philosophy mesh with the everyday mechanics of operating them in the classroom? How do you start, particularly if you're accustomed to having the whole class do the same thing at the same time?

Start small. Try introducing a limited number of centers at first and then gradually expand your offerings. Also try to visualize the process in which you expect yourself and students to become involved. Vacca and Vacca (1976) developed an organizational chart (Box 10.4) to help teachers visualize the use of learning centers in their classrooms. The chart takes into account several instructional concerns which are likely to become important as you plan centers: type of activity, available reading materials, number of students assigned to each center, and criteria for student placement. The chart may be shortened or lengthened or rearranged to accommodate specific classroom situations.

Box 10.4

---

*IMPLEMENTATION CHART**

	Type of Activity	Available Materials	Number of Students per Class Period	Criteria for Student Placement
1.	_____	_____	_____	_____
2.	_____	_____	_____	_____
3.	_____	_____	_____	_____
4.	_____	_____	_____	_____
5.	_____	_____	_____	_____
6.	_____	_____	_____	_____
7.	_____	_____	_____	_____

*SOURCE: Adapted from J. L. Vacca and R. T. Vacca, "Learning stations: how to in the middle grades." *Journal of Reading* 19 (1976): 563–567. Reprinted with the permission of J. L. and R. T. Vacca and the International Reading Association.

The first order of business is to decide upon the type of activities in the centers. Get them down on paper. You should make decisions based on curriculum guidelines, the subject under study, and your experience. What activities are feasible and manageable given your talents and resources and the needs and interests of your students? For each center you decide on, plan activities at varying levels of difficulty to ensure that all students can succeed with some of the tasks in each center. Earle and Morley (1974) recommended that you divide tasks into required and optional categories so that students will have some leeway to choose among activities and levels of difficulty. They should also have some freedom to determine the sequence in which they work on individual activities as well as the time it takes to complete work at a center. Some of the activities may be self-directing and self-correcting.

All activities and materials discussed in this book can be incorporated into learning activity centers in any content area. See Box 10.5 for sample learning center activities from Steurer (1978).

Box 10.5

SAMPLE LEARNING CENTER ACTIVITIES IN CONTENT AREAS*

Art:
Processes/following directions: rearrange mixed-up directions for making an art object.
Terminology: match pictures with words.

Business education:
Symbols: match them with words they represent.
Spelling test: listen to a tape-recorded list of words, write them.
Graphs and tables: interpret a tax schedule or balance sheet, answering questions.
Information search: under controlled and timed conditions, glean certain information from a tape.

Driver education:
Rules of the road: answer test questions for driver's permit.
Safe-driving attitude survey: take written survey, listen to answers and explanations on tape.
Road signs: match with words.

Foreign language:
Phonetics: listen to tape recording of minimal pairs, write on answer sheet "same" or "different."
Dictation: transcribe a passage from a recording.
Listening comprehension: listen to tape, answer written questions.
Gender/case: insert correct article before nouns in sentences, check by listening to tape recording of full sentences.

Health:
Vocabulary: match drug terms with pictures and definitions.
Following directions: from illustrated sheet, learn to do particular exercises (teacher evaluated).
Concepts: answer true/false questions on practices related to eating and drinking.

Home economics:
Nutrition: match foods and proportions to make a balanced menu for four people.
Following directions: make cookies from recipe, evaluate by taste and appearance.
Finances: use newspaper advertisements and checklist to select best buys for indicated items.

Industrial arts:
Concepts: review electrical principles by true/false questions.
Introduction to concepts: take pretest on diagnostic maintenance of autos.
Vocabulary: match items in a box with technical names.
Job overview: fill in job sheet with correct steps, tools, and parts needed to rebuild a carburetor.

Language arts:
  Sequence: arrange sentences of a paragraph in logical order.
  Main ideas: pick topic sentences from a series of paragraphs.
  Mechanics: correct mistakes in punctuation, spelling, or grammar in a paragraph (usually one skill at a time in each paragraph).
  Following directions: write a formal letter, evaluate it by a checklist of important letter elements.
Mathematics:
  Vocabulary: pair up roots and affixes used in math terms, test them by matching words and meanings.
  Word problems: do problems, check each step on answer sheet.
  Interpreting graphs: answer questions.
  Symbols: match math symbols with words.
Physical education:
  Reading comprehension: answer factual and inferential questions on sports articles.
  Interpreting diagrams: answer questions on field hockey or basketball play diagrams.
Science:
  Reading vocabulary: skim textbook chapter to find certain italicized words, copy those sentences, rewrite in own words (teacher evaluate).
  Search skills: find page number where particular questions are answered.
  Vocabulary: create technical terms by connecting roots and affixes.
  Comprehension: write formulas into sentence form, or rewrite sentences as formulas.
Social studies:
  Study: skim a chapter, answer questions about main items.
  Historical relationships: arrange related events of French Revolution in proper order.

*SOURCE: S. J. Steurer, "Learning centers in the secondary school." *Journal of Reading* 22 (1978): 134–139. Reprinted with permission of S. J. Steurer and the International Reading Association.

Scheduling Students to Centers. Once you decide on the number and type of activity centers, take stock of your materials to see what goes with what. The available materials column in the chart may include teacher-prepared guide exercises, vocabulary reinforcement and extension activities, visual aids, student-made items from previous classes, printed and nonprinted materials.

You will also need to decide the number of students that can participate effectively at one center and to assign students at each center. Three criteria will help you to assign students to centers:

1. *Random placement:* The types of activities are such that any student in the class can participate in them. For example, the teacher can randomly assign students to the reading area, the workshop area, to most centers that involve listening, viewing, and writing tasks. If the teacher varies the level of sophistication of reading tasks within a center, students can be placed at random.

2. *Affective placement:* The types of activities depend on students' interests, their ability to work together, personality traits, and so forth.

3. *Reading level placement:* If multilevel texts are available, the teacher can assign students appropriately.

Scheduling students at the learning activity centers is one of the most time-consuming but crucial tasks of the content teacher. Many teachers have found it efficient to staple a schedule to the inside front cover of each student's folder at the beginning of a new unit involving activity centers. The teacher gives each center a number and lists it on the blackboard or on a dittoed sheet. The first (and possibly the second) day of each student's schedule is blank: You can use this time to explain the directions for the operation of each center, to ask several students to select a center and describe how it functions to the rest of the class, and to have students work at centers of their own choosing. From the second or third day on, students will look at their own schedules at the beginning of a period and each will go to the center indicated for that particular day.

It's best to build a collection of centers over a long period of time, perhaps over a year or two. The commitment to a learning center approach requires a lot of time and energy. You may find centers most useful as an adjunct to more traditional classroom procedures. Steurer (1978) noted that centers "need not replace the teacher-directed format. . . . Learning centers add variation to the classroom and provide activities as well as independent study" (p. 134). Centers release teachers from the role of central performer in front of large groups of students so that they can give guidance when needed and provide emphatic instruction when a situation calls for it.

Small Groups

Organizing reading around small groups shifts the burden of learning from teacher to student. Small groups are particularly well suited to guided reading discussions. However, team learning is complex. Small groups don't run by themselves. Students must know how to work together and how to use techniques they have been taught. The teacher in turn must know about small-group processes. The practical question is "How will individual students 'turn into' groups?" Anyone who has ever attempted small-group instruction in the classroom knows the dilemma associated with the question. Many conditions can confound team learning if plans are not made in advance — in particular, teachers must decide on such matters as the size, composition, goals, and performance criteria of small groups.

The principle of "least group size" (Thelen, 1949) operates whenever you form learning teams. A group should be just large enough to include all the skills necessary to solve a problem or complete a task. A group that's larger than necessary provides less chance for individual participation and greater opportunity for conflict. If too many students are grouped together, there's bound to be a point of "diminishing returns." Group size for content area reading should range from two to six members (depending, of course, on the type of reading task). Since most small group activities will involve discussion and completion of guide materials, four-to-five-member groups are probably best.

Homogeneous grouping is often not necessary for discussion tasks. Both intellectual and nonintellectual factors will influence a small group's performance and the relationship between intelligence and small-group performance, as Davis (1969) attests, is often surprisingly low. (If this sounds like a pitch for heterogeneous discussion groups, it is.) Experiential and social background, interests, attitudes, and personality contribute greatly to the success of a small group. Grouping solely by reading or intellectual ability short-changes all students and robs discussion of its diversity.

Low-powered readers shouldn't be relegated to tasks that require minimal thinking or low-level responses to content material. What quicker way to incite riot and misbehavior than to group together students who are experiencing difficulty in reading? People learn from one another. A student whose background is less extensive than other students' can learn from them. The student who finds reading difficult needs good readers as models. Furthermore, the student who has trouble reading may in fact be a good listener and thinker who will contribute significantly to small-group discussion.

The most efficient formation of heterogeneous discussion groups is through random assignment. Students can count off in intervals to yield the appropriate size for each group. For example, a class of twenty-eight can count off in intervals of seven to form four-member groups. Or students can draw numbers from a box: number one through four form a group, five through nine another group, and so forth.

Small-group learning is goal- and task-oriented. The manner in which goals and paths to task completion are perceived affects the volume and quality of involvement by students in the group. If group goals are unclear, members' interest quickly wanes. Goals must also be directly related to the task. Roby (1968) noted that the conditions of the task must be "clearly defined with explicit objectives" and "understood and accepted by individual members" (p. 1).

Therefore, the teacher should explain criteria for task performance. For example, when students work with teacher-prepared guide materials such as those which are suggested in this book, they should attempt to adhere to criteria such as the following:

1. Read the selection silently and complete each item on the guide individually or with others in the group, depending on the teacher's specific directions.
2. Each item should be discussed by the group.
3. If there is disagreement on any item, a group member(s) must defend his or her position and show why there is a disagreement. This means going back into the selection to support one's position.
4. No one student dominates a discussion or bosses other members around.
5. Each member contributes something to each group discussion.

As students work on reading activities in their groups, the teacher can facilitate performance by reinforcing the criteria that have been established.

Cooperative Learning

Groups lack cohesiveness when learning isn't cooperative but competitive, when students aren't interdependent on each other for learning but work independently. However, social scientists and instructional researchers have made great strides since the 1970s at understanding the problems of the competitive classroom. Researchers at Johns Hopkins University in particular (Slavin, 1980, 1982) have studied the practical classroom applications of cooperative principles of learning. The bulk of their research suggests that cooperative small-group learning has positive effects on academic achievement and social relationships. The attempts below at creating cooperative classroom learning situations give insights into how to achieve interdependent learning.

Capuzzi (1973) reported the success of a procedure called *information intermix*. The intermix procedure directs students through a series of interactions with other group members. For example, students form four-member "growth groups" in which each member is given a "concept slip" containing a short excerpt from a text. They are told to learn their concepts and then "teach" them to the rest of the group. The intermix procedure continues in a similar manner with new group formations where members are mutually dependent on one another for their learning.

Psychology Today magazine popularized an attempt to ease the effects of busing and racial tension in schools in Austin, Texas, by making students dependent on one another for learning required materials (Aronson et al., 1975). Interdependent learning of text materials was achieved through the jigsaw-puzzle method, an activity that manipulated the way students responded to curriculum-based materials. Here's an example of jigsaw learning in action. A six-paragraph biography on the life of Joseph Pulitzer contained a major aspect of Pulitzer's life in each paragraph. The biography was then cut into six sections with one paragraph given to each member of a learning group. Because each student had no more than one-sixth of the biography, each was dependent on all the others to complete the picture. The jigsaw groups were cooperative because members had to work together to learn the materials for which they were responsible.

Vacca (1977) reported the influence of interdependent small groups in a social studies class. The teacher attempted to have students adhere to desired discussion behaviors during their interactions in small groups (these discussion behaviors were basically the same as those discussed in the previous subsection under performance criteria). Each small group earned a performance grade for discussing reading assignments in a six-week instructional unit. Here's how the group members earned their grades.

1. Each member in the group was observed by the teacher to see how well the desired discussion behaviors were exhibited.

2. On Friday of a week, each group earned a color reward worth so many points: green = 1 point; blue = 2 points; black = 3 points; red = 4 points. The color that a group earned was based on how well it had performed according to the criteria for discussion.

3. Each member of the group received the color (and the points that went with it) that the total group earned. This meant that if one or two members of the group did not carry out the appropriate discussion behaviors, the entire group was penalized.

4. The color for each student in the class was charted on a learning incentive chart.

5. Each week the small groups changed composition by random assignment.

6. The points attached to each color added up over the weeks. When the unit was completed, so many points resulted in a performance grade of A, B, C, or D.

A curious thing happened as a result of the reward system. On the Monday of each week that students were randomly assigned to new groups, they immediately went to the learning incentive chart to check the color received the previous week by each of the other members in their new group. Motivation was high. Group pressure was such that individual students who did not receive high points the previous week were intent on improving their performance in the new group.

We believe the main reason for the infrequent use of small groups is the frustration that teachers experience when teams lack cohesion. Uncooperative groups are a nightmare. No wonder a teacher abandons or is hesitant to use small groups in favor of whole-class instruction, which is easier to control. Small-group instruction requires risk taking on the part of the teacher as much as it encourages risk taking among students.

Whole-Class Instruction

As a means of classroom organization, whole-class instruction is significant because of its efficiency. A whole-class presentation is an economical means of giving information to large groups of students. A whole-class presentation can be used to set the stage for a new unit of study. The unit introduction, discussion of objectives, background building, and informal evaluation can all take place within the whole-class structure.

The chief limitation of whole-class instruction is that it limits active participation among students. While whole-class interaction provokes discussion to an extent, it cannot produce the volume of participation necessary to read and learn actively from content materials. The teacher often reverts to showmanship to enlist the active participation of the majority of students in a whole-class discussion. We often used to wonder why many teachers ended each working day totally exhausted. Although a little showmanship never hurt a lesson, no burden seems more difficult to carry or mentally fatiguing than to feel the need to perform in order to get students involved in learning.

Looking Back, Looking Forward

Content area teachers can organize for reading by planning instruction that will lead to active textbook learning. Students must act upon ideas in print but also interact with one another when studying, and so lesson organization is an important part of content area reading. The directed reading lesson and the unit plan provide the structure for teaching reading in content areas.

The directed reading lesson makes provisions for prereading, guided reading, and postreading instruction for a single lesson. The unit plan helps you to coordinate a series of reading lessons. It gives you much more latitude to coordinate instructional resource materials and activities. Unit activities can be organized around the whole class, small groups, or individuals. An effective content classroom combines all three grouping patterns to meet the individual and group needs and interests of students.

If content classrooms are to become effective learning environments, teachers will need support and reinforcement for the things they do. Staff development—planned opportunities to grow professionally—is the vehicle by which reading to learn strategies will become an integral part of the classroom context. The attention received by content area reading instruction has resulted in innovative teacher preparation programs, particularly at the preservice level. Colleges and universities are producing more prospective teachers equipped to teach reading within the context of subject matter instruction. But preservice education, at best, is only a beginning, albeit important, step toward learning a craft. Unless new teachers receive support and reinforcement from fellow teachers and administrators, they can soon find themselves eschewing what they have learned in "those method courses."

Staff development deals with the change process, with making decisions about which strategies to select and modify for individual classroom use. Attitudes about staff development and reading instruction have undergone much change during the 1980s. Teachers recognize problems facing text learners. Teachers want to know how to help students read textbooks effectively. They want to improve instruction with the help and advice of their colleagues. How teachers go about putting into practice the information contained in this book is the main focus of the next chapter. As a result, the final chapter of this book concentrates on working with teachers in the planning and implementation of successful staff development for content area reading.

Suggested Readings

Beyers, B. (1971). *Inquiry in the Social Studies Classroom*. Columbus, Ohio: Merrill.

Estes, T., & Vaughan, J., Jr. (1985). *Reading and Learning in the Content Classroom* (2nd ed.). Boston: Allyn and Bacon.

Mallan, J., & Hersh, R. (1972). *No g.o.d.s. in the Classroom—Inquiry into Inquiry.* Philadelphia: W. B. Saunders.

Moffett, J., & Wagner, B. J. (1976). *Student-Centered Language Arts and Reading, K-13* (2nd ed.). Boston: Houghton-Mifflin.

Peterson, P., Wilkinson, L., & Hallinan, M. (eds.). (1984). *The Social Contexts of Instruction.* New York: Academic Press.

Sharon, S. (1980). Cooperative learning in small groups: Recent methods and effects on achievement, attitudes and ethnic relations. *Review of Educational Research,* **50**, 241–271.

Slavin, R. (1980). Cooperative learning. *Review of Educational Research,* **50**, 315–342.

Slavin, R. (1982). *Cooperative learning: Student teams.* Washington, D.C.: National Education Association.

Webb, N., & Kenderski, C. (1984). Student interaction and learning in small-group and whole-class settings. In P. Peterson, L. Wilkinson, and M. Hallinan (eds.), *The Social Context of Instruction.* New York: Academic Press.

CHAPTER 11

Staff Development in Content Area Reading

You don't lead by hitting people over the head.
That's assault, not leadership.
—DWIGHT EISENHOWER

Organizing Principle

This chapter is for teachers who assume the responsibility for instructional leadership in content area reading. It should also be useful to reading specialists and consultants who, in collaboration with teachers, find themselves in the same role. Although the substance for staff development in content area reading has been provided in the preceding chapters of this book, instructional leaders who want a successful content area reading program recognize that they need more than knowledge and enthusiasm for this important aspect of reading instruction. There are certain things that they can do to ensure success.

Staff development provides the support and reinforcement that is essential for change in the school context. Professional development experiences are as important for teachers who have had a reading methods course as they are for the veteran in need of renewal. Both veteran and novice teachers, in collaboration, learn to become more effective and efficient at what they do. The organizing principle reflects this idea: *Participating in planned staff development in content*

CHAPTER OVERVIEW

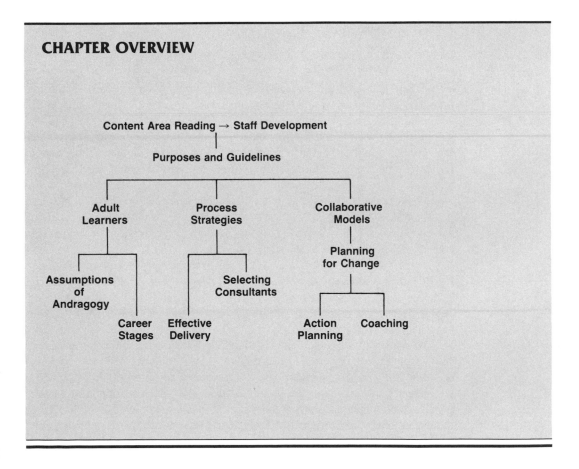

area reading leads to continued professional growth and improved instruction.
Use the questions below to guide your reading. When you finish the chapter,
return to the questions and see how well you can answer them.

1. What purposes should content area reading staff development serve?
2. What common characteristics do effective staff development programs share?
3. How do staff developers use the assumptions of andragogy in working with teachers?
4. How can staff developers increase participants' perceptions of effective delivery?
5. How can planners of staff development verify their selection of a consultant?
6. How does collaborative planning work and through what stages does the planning process move?
7. How do problem-solving teams operate in an action-planning model?
8. Why would coaching be effective in the adoption and use of content area strategies?

There's a paradox in the wake of recent publicity on the need to improve schools. At last, teachers and teaching are getting attention; unfortunately, much of this attention is negative. Despite this heavy dose of criticism, most teachers and administrators want to improve the quality of instruction. They want to convince the best and brightest persons to enter the teaching profession and they want to ensure veteran teachers continued opportunities for growth and reward. The time no longer exists when schools could count on ten percent staff turnovers to infuse new ideas and energy into the system. As a recent article in the *Ohio School Board Association Journal* put it, "What we've got staff-wise is what we've got" (King and Blough, 1982, p. 6). What have we got in relation to staff development in content area reading?

First, we have teachers who are dedicated to their profession, continuing to learn through graduate courses, seminars, workshops, or as cooperating teachers. There are others who update professionally by reading and talking with colleagues. And there are still others who are unreceptive to any change, even if it means growth. Next, we have a great deal of information—much of it research-based—in three related areas: content area reading, adult learning and development, and staff development. The content area reading strategies discussed in this book can be successfully implemented through a variety of means, not the least of which is well-planned staff development programs which use principles of adult learning.

So what have we got? We have what it takes: knowledge, willingness, process strategies, and, above all, a need. We have a need to attract and retain good teachers who will transfer content area reading into their schools and classrooms.

This chapter is intended to help teachers and other planners of staff development meet this need. It should guide their efforts to improve content area instruction through implementation of strategies *in collaboration with other teachers*. Teachers, administrators, specialists, consultants working together as a team can provide the real leadership needed—not the assault perpetrated by the leader "hitting people over the head" described by Eisenhower.

Purposes and Guidelines for Staff Development

Intentions are important. Before deciding to participate in the design of any staff development program in content area reading, it's essential to stop and take the time to ask "what is the intended result?" Many times, dissatisfaction with inservice programs can be traced back to a failure to come to grips with the real intention of the program. It stands to reason that if the purpose is unclear, the program's relevancy to participants will be less apparent.

Institutional vs. Personal Goals

What purposes will content area staff development serve? And, correspondingly, what outcomes do we expect to observe? It is the school building, according to Goodlad (1983), that is the largest and smallest unit for school improvement. This makes sense if staff development is truly participatory; teachers with common problems and interests can share as they develop content area reading strategies. District-wide programs, for example, can get unwieldy when they go beyond building-level concerns, while individual classroom intervention reinforces the isolation already inherent in the teaching profession.

Using the school as the frame of reference then, consider the range of purposes for staff development in content area reading on the continuum in Figure 11.1.

Figure 11.1
Purposes of Staff Development

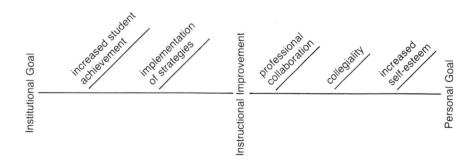

A focus on either end of this continuum could lead to a dichotomous and rather narrow view that staff development is intended either to result in improved student achievement or it is not. Or we might assume, as some program designers have in the past, that working toward an institutional goal is the sole and legitimate purpose for staff development, while working toward a personal goal is a frill. Our experiences and research on successful staff development tell us that this "either-or" assumption is rapidly changing. Staff development programs do not have to be one dimensional. Working toward staff collegiality in the school environment and developing new strategies to improve student learning are not mutually exclusive goals. Just as in the field of reading and language, we consider the affective and contextual factors in a student's reading development, we recognize the complexity of a teacher's professional growth in staff development.

Consequently, program designers are increasingly taking into account several different variables. They are beginning to design programs that incorporate more than the purposes on the left side of the continuum. School district planners and consultants are moving toward staff development in which persons improve themselves, their work, and their schools. The resulting programs are intended to address problems which may be of an institutional, instructional, and/or personal nature.

As such, purposes for content area reading staff development, which often deals with potential effects on instructional practices, can be drawn from several places on the continuum.

Institutional Goals

Traditionally, staff development programs are funded based on their expressed purpose to change teacher behavior and to improve student learning (Stallings, Needles, and Stayrook, 1979; Anderson, Evertson, and Brophy, 1979). Programs which have been successful in achieving this purpose are important in that they established the "soundest argument for the value of staff development"—a necessity with school policy-makers (Vaughan, 1983, p. 8). Studies which documented the programs' effectiveness in attaining institutional goals were controlled, expensive, dealt with basic skills, and are not likely to be repeated.

Nevertheless, they allow those interested in the research and practice of staff development to "explain a staff development activity in terms of its ultimate potential to influence student learning" (Vaughan, 1983, p. 8). Second, they in a sense legitimize the great bulk of research on staff development which does not directly aim to improve student learning, but deals more with potential effects on instructional practice. Most teachers have been involved in short-term inservice workshops or longer-term staff development programs based on attaining institutional goals through instructional improvement. Fewer teachers have been involved in programs based on attaining personal goals through collaboration.

Personal Goals

Recently we had an opportunity to converse with a group of content area teachers in Alaska. As professionals who were actively involved with staff development for several years in the Alaskan Content Reading Cadre, they seemed like the right group to validate some recent research findings about the personal side of staff development.

From the numerous studies available, we chose Spencer-Hall's 1982 report *Teachers as Persons: Case Studies of Home Lives and the Implications for Staff Development* to share with Cadre teachers. They responded in writing to the findings which they believed most relative to their own situations. Box 11.1 encapsulates their responses to each major finding.

Box 11.1

TEACHER'S RESPONSES TO THE PERSONAL SIDE OF STAFF DEVELOPMENT

1. *Teachers work long hard hours in job-related activities, yet feel isolated and unrewarded. Work often infringes on home life.*

"Our school district is addressing these problems with inservices on time management, stress, burnout and now effective school procedures."

"Since I began teaching, I forgot how to relax, but further, I discovered my teacher friends experienced the same duress."

"As teaching homemakers and/or mothers, we desperately need inservice in time-management so that we don't forget the importance of hobbies and recreation that are so important to bringing life and imagination to our teaching."

2. *Most teachers play traditional roles at home, facing a double workday; finances are often tight. They show an ability to cope simultaneously with a number of persons and situations.*

"As a working mother with two pre-school children it felt fantastic to hear verification of some of my frustrations."

"My wife has taught so I'm aware of the unfair division of labor . . . . We have tried to resolve that problem, but I think many men get too hung up on their male image to allow a successful resolution of the problem."

3. *Teachers are concerned about their weight, nutrition, exercise and illness.*

"There are good turnouts (when we're given a choice) on any sessions on health. It's like 'let *me* get squared away first before you lay something else on me.'"

"As soon as I go home I want to approach our principal to see if we could start putting together a 'keeping healthy' package."

4. *Teachers view staff development negatively, feel powerless about undesirable situations, yet are willing to work to develop professionally.*

"I really get irritated when poor planning by administrators upsets the careful balance I've tried to achieve by requiring workshops after the school workday."

"Principal-led teams at the building level would bring more open-mindedness."

"Your suggestion about interviewing the 'hard nuts' to keep them from being so negative in the session is creative and promises to be useful."

5. *Teachers are uncertain about how their efforts are viewed (by principals); their satisfaction is related to feelings of self-esteem. Some experience disillusionment and subtle sexism.*

"The non-involvement of many principals when it comes to a *real* understanding of the needs of staff . . . maybe principals are intimidated by teachers."

"We seem to have a lot of sexism—the 'Home Ec' teacher will take care of the pot luck social."

"I can relate to the problems—feeling of non-support and lack of self-esteem but at the same time feel very fortunate to teach in Alaska."

Exactly how findings such as these influence the design and implementation of future staff development sessions remains to be seen. It stands to reason, however, that personal areas such as health, nutrition, financial circumstances, living arrangements, and so on will have impact on teachers' personal goals and should not be ignored.

Guidelines for Planning

Over the years numerous reports and brochures have described in varying detail programs that were successful. Whether the goal of the program was "upgrading of teachers' skills in vocabulary reinforcement" or "instilling new energy as teachers help teachers," certain characteristics recur. These characteristics have been collected and analyzed by an assortment of groups, most notably the National Staff Development Council. This organization takes the position that certain program components best enhance staff skills. The council's suggestions which follow are sound guidelines for school districts in planning staff development in content area reading.

Effective staff development programs . . .

1. emphasize professional and personal growth and development rather than remediation;
2. initiate and support effective change based on an understanding of the change process;
3. support the stated goals of the district/school/classroom in terms of student outcomes;
4. support individual personal self-improvement efforts within the context of organizational goal setting and growth-oriented appraisal;
5. attend to the human needs of those for whom it is designed, modeling positive human interaction skills;
6. incorporate sound principles of adult learning and stages of concern with change reflected in research;
7. include a comprehensive planning process with extensive system building, and/or individual input;
8. provide continuously for all levels of staff, i.e., administrators, teachers, and classified staff;

9. provide for changes in subject matter, changes in methodology, and changes in the organization;

10. relate theory and application in a practical way, modeling (when appropriate) the kind of behavior which is desired as a result of participation in the activity;

11. suit the nature and length of the staff development activity to the purpose intended, i.e., orientation, short-term exposure, in-depth training leading to behavior change;

12. build on the preservice training of the teacher as the beginning of a continuum of development;

13. utilize a broad range of human resources from within schools, institutions of higher education, and the community where appropriate. *(Journal of Staff Development, 1984)*

In addition to learning from what works, we can also learn from what doesn't work. Staff development programs have had many problems, including lack of staff receptiveness and minimal financial resources. With these in mind, Griffin (1982) examined research studies of organization development, school change, adoption of innovations, and effective teaching to propose a list of "shoulds" for staff development. Here are his guidelines for improving teacher quality.

Staff development programs should . . .

1. be participatory, dealing with problems identified by teachers;

2. be situation-specific, considering differences between schools and grade levels;

3. be flexible and responsive to changes in participants and the setting;

4. mitigate to some degree status differences between teachers and administrators;

5. depend less on outsiders and more on insiders for content and procedural guidance;

6. be planned with an understanding of the influence of the context upon the program (perceptions, expectations, and beliefs already held by the staff). *(pp. 34–36)*

With these guidelines in mind, staff development in content area reading actually begins when the needs of teachers are identified. Staff development may at times appear to be a nebulous undertaking; there are no set prescriptions or prepackaged programs that will work for any one school in particular. An inservice program in content area reading is too individual a matter; it grows from within a school system based on the individual needs of teachers and their students.

Effective staff development is never automatically ensured; teachers' professional growth is brought about by mutual planning. Throughout this effort the integrity of teachers as adult learners must be maintained. Their feelings and perceptions matter. One of the major emphases of this chapter, therefore, is on adults as learners and as teachers at different stages of their careers.

Adult Learners

Teachers are adults and should be taught as such. And therefore, a staff development leader is an adult educator. Staff development is a learning situation—one in which teachers have been placed in a student relationship with the leader. While the dynamics of such a situation are not totally removed from the traditional student-adult teacher instructional paradigm, they merit a very different perspective.

Assumptions of Andragogy

The art and science of helping adults learn is called *andragogy*—"to teach adults"—from the Greek word for "man," *ander* and "leader," *agogos*. Use of the word *andragogy* can be traced back to Germany in the 1830s; in the same century the University of Amsterdam established a Department of Pedagogical and Andragogical Sciences. While andragogy is not a new term, Knowles (1973, 1978) has maintained that the assumptions and technology it is coming to identify are new.

Andragogy is based on several critical assumptions about the differences between children and adults as learners and differs from pedagogy essentially along four dimensions: (1) self-concept, (2) experience, (3) readiness, and (4) learning orientation.

Self-Concept and Experience

The heart of adultness is independence and self-direction. As people mature, their self-concepts change. They move from a psychological position of dependency to a position of increasing self-directedness. Children and even adolescents often remain dependent on their teachers in learning situations: "teacher knows best." This shouldn't be the case with adult learners.

The staff developer who prescribes what ought to be learned, how it will be learned, and the logical sequence in which it will be learned ultimately works against change, not for it. Newton (1977) was right on the mark when she asserted, "Any adult education situation involving the student in a role of dependency . . . will generate immediate and deep resistance and resentment" (p. 362). When working with fellow teachers, you may best view yourself as a gardener who creates good conditions for the growth of your plants. Once the growth process begins, step back and enjoy the results.

Another basic assumption in adult learning is that adults, with their rich store of experience, become invaluable resources for their own learning. The essence of one's identity is one's knowledge of the world. For many teachers, their teaching experiences are "who they are." The emphasis in staff development should be on techniques which tap those experiences and involve the participating teachers in analyzing them.

Once we observed a staff developer working with a teaching staff in a suburban high school. The teachers had voiced many concerns, the most ubiquitous being "Our students can't read." The teacher who led the session had anticipated the staff's general level of frustration and planned to clarify exactly what was meant by "They can't read." She asked the large group of teachers to form smaller groups by subject matter and gave each group two problems: (1) What do students actually do in class to indicate that they "can't read" assignments in your content area? (2) What would they need to do as far as you are concerned to successfully read assignments in your content area?

The leader hoped to use the staff's experiences to address some of the important issues related to content area reading. These teachers were facing, perhaps for the first time, the problem of reading their subject matter materials successfully.

The consultant then asked a member from each group to report the group's responses to the entire staff. The resulting banter and wisecracking was helpful: it broke the ice and led to discussion. Perhaps also for the first time, teachers from different content areas were sharing their opinions and perceptions about reading.

The leader skillfully incorporated the staff members' comments into her agenda. She used their insights to suggest that "teaching reading" is nothing more than good teaching. A third question—"How can we fine-tune our present skills to do what we are presently doing better?"—became the unifying principle for the remaining staff development sessions. The spirit of the staff development effort became "How can we continue to work on our craft?"

Readiness and Learning Orientation

In many cases education for children and adolescents assumes that students are ready to learn things they "ought" to learn based on their biological development and on social and academic pressures. Adult learning, on the other hand, assumes that adults are ready to learn what they "need" to learn in order to meet various situations they encounter throughout various phases in their lives. These situations are products primarily of the evolution of a person's social role as a worker, spouse, parent, or whatever. This is why Newton (1977) observed that "the requirements and demands of . . . the present situation and aspiring roles in real life must dominate and supersede all other considerations . . ." (p. 362).

Teachers respond differently to reading problems primarily because of their backgrounds and experiences, their attitudes toward teaching and learning, their attitudes toward students, and their values regarding education in general. This is why content area reading staff development can't be prepackaged for all the teachers on a staff. By prepackaged we mean each teacher "getting inserviced" by being introduced to the same thing at the same time. Some teachers will be readier than others for certain aspects of a content area reading program. Because of the nature of readiness among adults, the following "do's" for content area reading staff development are appropriate:

1. Individualize inservice through a variety of activities.

2. Respect the values and attitudes of teachers.

3. Offer open sessions for teachers of differing philosophies and values.

4. Make some sessions voluntary.

5. Provide released time.

6. Offer incentives for participation—additional released time, equivalency credit, stipends, recognition, certificates of completion, and so forth.

7. Reinforce the importance of internal incentives—teachers seeing students learn and feeling responsible for it.   *(Vaughan, 1983, p. 15)*

An adult's orientation to learning is problem-centered and in the here and now. Immediate application of learning is at a high premium since the learner "comes into an educational activity largely because he . . . wants to apply tomorrow what he learns today" (Knowles, 1973, p. 48). Whereas the curriculum for children and adolescents often involves a predetermined logical sequence, a curriculum for adults should be organized around problem areas. Newton (1977) affirmed this assumption by declaring that "postponed, logical, sequentially developed subject matter must be eschewed in favor of field-centered, work related learning" (p. 362). Learning about teaching innovations that cannot be transferred to the immediacy of their classrooms does not appeal to teachers.

"Show me what to do on Monday morning" is a legitimate demand. Often, however, this concern is misinterpreted to mean that classroom teachers are antitheoretical and antiresearch. Don't believe it for a moment. What teachers are actually saying is "Show me how to improve my craft. Let me experience the process you offer first, and if it makes sense, let's discuss why it works."

Staff development in content area reading must be based on teachers' motivations as adults to grow as fully as possible. Staff developers need to work at building an environment in which teachers have the opportunity to make discoveries significant to them. Such an environment contains teachers at different points in their careers and with different needs.

Career Stages

Teachers develop as adults and pass through different stages in their careers as they grow. We've all noticed the difference between teachers who see their jobs as rewarding and those who project the opposite. Some seem to readily restructure tasks to create challenge; they look for and find intrinsic rewards. Others simply are not at this point; they still have real needs in self-esteem and finding pleasure in learning activities. Can this group of teachers be helped to see their jobs as rewarding? A step in this direction is planning staff development according to needs of teachers at different levels or stages in their careers.

Most writers report three or four stages through which teachers' careers progress. Fuller (1969) described these as: survival (concern with personal adequacy); mastery (developing skills, methods, content); and impact (concern for students). Yarger and Mertens (1980) divided teachers into career levels according to years of experience (beginning, three to eight years, and highly experienced). Recently, Burke, Fessler, and Christensen (1984) proposed a career cycle that is affected by personal and organizational factors. They stress that teachers don't necessarily enter this cycle at the preservice level and move through the various stages in lockstep. In reality, teachers are "moving in and out of stages in response to both" personal environment (family, health, etc.) and organizational environment (school policies, recognition, etc.) (p. 14). This cycle is illustrated and defined in Figure 11.2.*

Figure 11.2
Teacher Career Cycle

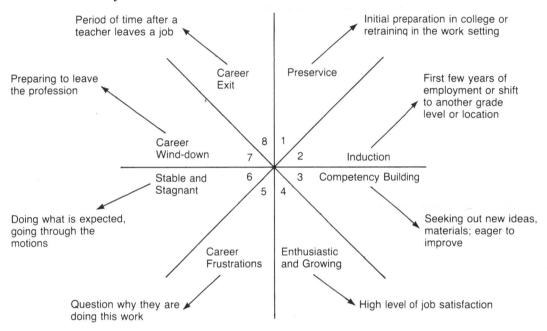

At the very least, content area reading staff developers who want to improve staff development based on these concepts of career stages would involve teachers at different career stages in program planning. The perceived usefulness of the planned activity is important and will most likely vary depending on the group's mix of experiences and career stages. A second-year teacher still sorting out the curriculum in fourth grade and the veteran down the hall going through the motions each needs and deserves to have relevant staff development activities.

Incorporating the basics of adult learning and development into our view of staff development broadens the scope of staff development activities and begins to get at answers to some rather provocative questions. To what extent are the problems identified in needs assessments problems that teachers can do something about? What can and cannot be changed? Should staff development be for the staff as a whole or individuals? Who determines the priorities?

*Source: Adapted from Peter Burke, Ralph Fessler, and Judith C. Christensen (1984). *Teacher Career Stages: Implications for Staff Development*. Bloomington, Ind: Phi Delta Kappa Educational Foundation.

Process Strategies

Whether you are a content area teacher or reading consultant, supervisor or administrator, it's likely you'll one day find yourself in the role of staff developer. As you assume responsibility for staff development and initiate collaboration, the preceding chapters in this book may provide a good deal of the program substance. But staff development leaders must also have a style: *how* we work with teachers is as important as the content we deliver.

Teachers respond favorably to competent delivery regardless of the topic of the staff development program.* Teachers want to be involved in staff development sessions in which their time is not wasted. They prefer ideas, strategies, and materials that relate directly to their own classrooms. These should be presented or demonstrated by someone who is knowledgeable and enthusiastic and who respects participants' experiences. Staff developers who are skilled in the use of process strategies are much more likely to be perceived by participants as effective. What distinguishes effective from ineffective delivery?

Effective Delivery

To determine how content area teachers perceive their staff development leaders, we conducted a study in six school districts around the United States. We collected examples of effective and ineffective staff developer behavior and classified these incidents into categories of effectiveness. Using a Critical Incident Record Form, we asked over 500 teachers to write their responses to two questions. Question 1 was designed to elicit specific examples of *effective* behavior on the part of staff development personnel:

> Think about your participation in staff development in the last two years. Describe a specific incident that caused you to feel that the session was very effective. Exactly what did the leader do that was so effective?

Question 2 was designed to elicit examples of ineffective behavior:

> Think of another inservice session; describe a specific incident that caused you to feel that the session leader was ineffective. Exactly what did the leader do that was so ineffective?

Here are several samples from the 904 usable incidents reported:

> "She had us actively involved playing the role of our students. The fact that we experienced the technique ourselves made it beneficial to the classroom."

> "It was very difficult to transfer the ideas into reality. There were no

---

*Portions of this section are adapted from: Jo Anne L. Vacca, "How to be an effective staff developer for content teachers." *Journal of Reading*, 26 (1983): 293–296.

guidelines for how to use strategies with kids; all grade levels were overlapping. I came away feeling extremely frustrated."

"He cited specific examples of how we could take back the suggestions and use them right away in the classroom."

"How could he expect us to work in small groups when we were seated in locking chairs? It was difficult to talk to others."

Figure 11.3 contains the categories we developed, percent of incidents in each category, along with the description of the category and excerpts of typical incidents reported in each category.

Figure 11.3
Categories of Staff Developer Behaviors

Category	Description	Excerpts	Percent of Total
Content delivery	Technique for involvement or participation; classroom relevance of strategy or materials.	"we participated," "lecture," "roleplaying," "didn't relate to my classroom," "meaningful."	37.5
Personal influence	Personality traits or characteristics; personal actions or responses to situations.	"dull," "exciting," "no enthusiasm," "alienated the participants," "motivated and inspired."	22.7
Professional competence	Background knowledge, preparation or organization; proficiency or clarity of directions; adherence to task.	"well-informed," "knew next to nothing about the topic," "no directions for small groups," "didn't stick to subject."	34.2
Arrangements	Assessment of needs; mechanics.	"subject applied to different audience," "session too long," "right after school."	5.6

Realistically, staff developers have a complex leadership role. It's unlikely they will be perceived as effective 100% of the time in any situation. Yet, when staff developers are aware of effective delivery strategies and show concern for the quality of their delivery, the implementation of any program is bound to improve. An effective staff development leader is sincerely trying to create an environment in which teachers are motivated to grow as fully as possible. Even in the best circumstances some teachers will be more ready than others to change.

There are times when teachers play a role in designing and planning staff development programs, yet have little commitment to participate. According to Lewin (1948) a three-step change process helps motivate individuals to change. Unfreezing, the first step, enlists their active participation.

Unfreezing*

Unfreezing is analogous to the readiness stage in a directed reading lesson; its purpose is to build an interest in and a state of readiness for the program steps that are to follow. (Unfreezing cuts across age levels and should be used with adults as well as with children and adolescents.) Staff developers use process skills to create relaxed settings, allay fears, and discuss problems, personal reservations, and participants' needs. They are interested in lessening feelings of discomfort and/or hostilities. They are after awareness. Above all, leaders seek the active involvement (mental as well as physical) of participants and their commitment—commitment fostered by a feeling of open-mindedness toward what is to follow in the program.

How does a leader unfreeze rather than "unglue" a group of fellow teachers? We posed this question to a group of more than 150 specialists, consultants, and supervisors involved in development of content area reading staff who met in April 1979 in Atlanta as part of an International Reading Association Preconvention Institute. During the institute the participants discussed their written responses to our questions, and three distinct categories of activity for unfreezing emerged. What follows is a representative sampling from each category.

1. *Ice Breakers*. These strategies vary in time from five to twenty minutes (time approximations refer to the application of the strategy and are not meant to imply that unfreezing would be completed within these time frames). They are intended to involve participants. These activities are generally fun. Not only do they get participants involved, but they also get teachers thinking about problems associated with the inservice topic. Examples:

   a. Use brainstorming. This strategy can be adapted easily to staff development objectives. Identify a broad concept that reflects the main topic to be discussed—for example, vocabulary—during the session. Then have participants work in small groups to generate lists of words related to the broad concept in x number of seconds. These two steps will help the staff developer instantly tap into what participants know about the topic.

*Portions of this section are adapted from: Jo Anne L. Vacca and Richard T. Vacca, "Unfreezing strategies for staff development in reading." *The Reading Teacher*, 35 (1980): 27–31.

b. Create conceptual conflict to arouse curiosity about the topic. Present teachers with a "situation that will cause puzzlement, doubt, surprise, perplexity, contradiction, or ambiguity ("case of a fifteen-year-old student who reads text material with perfect oral pronunciation . . . and near zero comprehension"), a situation, for example, that might challenge their present concept of reading. Once aroused, the teachers will be motivated to seek information to resolve the conflict.

c. Lead a magic circle to open up communication by making it possible for each member of the circle (a circle is a must so that everyone can see everyone else) to comment. Intersperse probing questions with questions of a lighter nature. For example, lead off with "What do you like best about your job?" Follow with "Complete this statement: If I had $1,000 to spend in one week in my classroom, I would. . . ." Your third question might be "What do you dislike most about teaching _____?" (fill in the blank with science, social studies, or whatever).

2. *Vicarious Experiences*. Strategies in this category are aimed at involving teachers with actual practices or materials that are used with their students. They usually serve as demonstration of a generalization and vary from fifteen minutes to almost an hour in length. Examples:

a. Set up several learning activity centers with examples of content area reading activities. Have teachers follow a minischedule in which they work through all centers in rotation. Allow about ten minutes at each, signaling the switch with a bell or timer.

b. Try out a teaching technique with volunteers in front of the whole group. Then ask pairs of teachers to analyze what has taken place. Share responses, being receptive to statements of "times when this won't work" as well as positive feedback.

c. Call on a volunteer to read a passage projected on an overhead screen. Choose a passage with unfamiliar vocabulary such as a difficult biology passage or a paragraph using an unfamiliar dialect. Ask first the reader and then the rest of the group to retell it in their own words.

d. Give a timed test to measure several reading skills of the teachers. Create a formal, quiet, serious atmosphere; use a timer. As the teachers score their tests, generalize about potential problem areas this test uncovers.

3. *Problem Solving*. In this category are strategies that lead participants to use their own experiences and knowledge in thinking through new concepts. Problem-solving activities can vary in time from fifteen minutes to just over an hour.
Examples:

a. Set up a hypothetical situation. Describe it to the whole group in a

a. concise manner ("It's 1997, and water sources have been discovered in abundance in all parts of this continent, including barren desert areas. How would this discovery change life as we know it?") Divide participants into groups of three or four. Allow about five minutes for group discussion, then pool answers, perhaps forming categories of statements on the board. As a follow-up to 2a above, form small groups and distribute to each a problem related to teaching reading in each content area. Be sure to allow enough time to review each group's answers.

b. Distribute a ten-statement prediction guide to reading instruction. Have teachers complete the guide independently, then form small groups or pairs and compare answers. Then read each statement aloud, eliciting discussion from the whole group. Part of the guide might look like this:

Directions: Consider the following statements and determine which are likely and which are unlikely. Check the column under Likely if you think the statement could be true. Check under Unlikely if you think the statement could not be true.

Likely   Unlikely

_____   _____   1. Students reading on the twelfth-grade level of a reading achievement test will have no difficulty with a physics text written on a twelfth-grade level.

_____   _____   2. Text pictures and diagrams are self-explanatory.

_____   _____   3. Silent reading is a habit that can be developed in content classrooms.

_____   _____   4. Purposes for reading need to be explained by the teacher before students read.

Once participants are willing to become actively involved, it's time to take the second step, moving forward.

Moving Forward

In this stage participants are introduced to a range of instructional options and alternatives—the techniques, strategies, and materials developed throughout this book. The program leader may arrange a series of workshop sessions to demonstrate them. Involvement is the key to this continuing process. Teachers sense the process of content area reading by playing the role of student. Once the participants have had the opportunity to experience certain strategies and materials, the leader follows with explanations involving the how and why of them.

As they demonstrate strategies, presenters need to sustain the rapport that has been established. Although no single technique will be effective in all situations, there are process strategies that teachers consistently associate with the effective delivery of staff development. These strategies are contained in Figure 11.4.

Figure 11.4
Process Strategy Implementation Chart

Type of Strategy	Materials	Facilities	Participants	Time
1. Brainstorming. Identify a broad concept with large group; small groups generate word lists; compare in large group.	Notepaper, pencils, chalkboard, or overhead projector	Student desks or tables and chairs	20–500; small groups of 5–8	10–20 minutes
2. Open-ended discussions. Set up hypothetical situation(s) or create conceptual conflict(s). Work through alternative solutions in groups; compare.	Paper, pencils worksheets	Movable furniture or auditorium and break out rooms	20–500; small groups of 5–8	15–30 minutes
3. Lecture-feedback. Present information first, then stimulate questions, discussion(s).	Lectern, or table; overheads; agenda or outline	Auditorium or classroom with chairs in semi circle	20–500	20 minutes each
4. Role-playing. Simulate a teaching situation; call on volunteer give test. Share feelings, responses of group, and relate to students.	Handouts, ditto; chalkboard; commercial tests, published books	Student desks; chairs and tables	20–100	30–40 minutes

(continued)

5. Demonstration teaching. Bring in student or visit classroom.	Outline; introduction reactions forms; anecdotes or checklist	Open space or stage; classroom or resource room	10–50; 5–10 depending on size of room	30–60 minutes
6. Videotapes. Preceded by introduction or by experiencing first the technique then watching, the comparing.	Tapes, color playback machine; outline or brochure	Comfortable seating; adjustable lighting	10–50	10–60 minutes
7. Materials-producing. Design strategy for a specific content and group of students. Produce in form it will be used.	Oak tag, ditto, typing paper, transparencies, markers, rulers, scissors, stapler	Tables, chairs, nearby office, thermofax, ditto or xerox machine, cutting board	10–50	60 minutes to 2 hours
8. Feedback or Gripe sessions. Allow time for "what's wrong with" or "why it won't work;" acknowledge problems so they won't dominate.	Feedback forms		Everyone or optional attendance	5–10 minutes
9. Learning Centers. Teachers follow a mini-schedule in which they work through centers, each with a different activity.	Sample teacher-made and commercial	Tables, plenty of space and light; large room or several classrooms	20–100	60 minutes to 2 hours; 15 minutes per station

Strategy	Materials/Form	Setting	Number	Time
10. Conferences. Individual teachers sign-up to meet with instructor . . . only if they feel a need.	Sign-up sheet with dates, times	Private area with desk, two chairs	1, possibly 2 (if paired) at a time	15–30 minutes each
11. Pairing. Have teachers work in pairs (or triads) according to grade level or interest area or count-off to get new combinations.	Match information from informal assessment on 5 by 8 cards or discussion; or match by number, etc.	Movable chairs or student desks	10–30	15–45 minutes
12. Observations. Teachers observe behaviors of one or a group of children in a clinic or regular classroom.	Checklist or anecdotal narrative form or time-sample form	One-way glass/mirror; classroom or resource room	2 or 3 in each	30–45 minutes
13. Interviewing. Interview one or two teachers in front of group or have teachers interview each other or students.	Schedule or open-ended, structured or unstructured questions	Two chairs in front; or regular seating	1 at a time or everyone in pairs	10–20 minutes

We designed the chart as a way to cross-check several important variables in staff development delivery. Each of the thirteen strategies can help accomplish certain objectives or meet typical staff development needs. Associated with each strategy are the necessary materials and facilities. Also indicated are the number of potential participants and the approximate time needed to complete the process. Elements such as time or numbers of teachers can be adjusted to accommodate specific situations.

Reflective questions should be encouraged during the Moving Forward step, on the part of teachers and staff developer. Teachers might ask, "Why should I do this?" "When should I use this approach rather than the other one?" "How can I construct these guide materials based on my content?" Staff developers might ask, "Is this delivery strategy producing the expected result?" "Is it increasing the willingness of content area teachers to continue participating?" "Is the process improving their ability to incorporate functional reading into content area instruction?"

Many projects in content area reading screech to a halt at this point. Time, funding, or staff constraints are some of the reasons typically given for the lack of follow-through and support that is essential to professional growth. Nevertheless, moving forward should also provide the time and shared expertise teachers need to actually produce classroom materials or design new strategies for their students. To complete the process of change successfully, a third step called refreezing is necessary.

Refreezing

Few things are more frightening than trying out a new idea for the first time, especially when teachers attempt to incorporate content area reading strategies into their lessons. Teachers need three kinds of assistance to attain closure to implementation: positive support, constructive criticism, and help with redesign or modification of strategies and materials.

Both feedback and follow-up are necessary to ensure that initial changes in behaviors, attitudes, or knowledge are being supported. If changes dealing with instructional strategies are to be meaningful, they must be refined and incorporated into the teachers' repertoire.

An illustration of refreezing as an integral part of the process was a recent institute we conducted. Thirty-five teachers, grades four through eight, participated in an intensive two-week summer workshop on vocabulary reinforcement through concept development. The institute followed this cycle: study instructional strategy, design strategy for a group of students, implement the strategy with students, evaluate the strategy and modify if necessary. Follow-up sessions were planned for the fall to coincide with implementation in the regular classroom.

In the fall verbal and written feedback occurred immediately following each classroom visit. This was a give-and-take process, with teachers reflecting on their use of vocabulary strategies and materials and the consultants reading and responding to their reflections. It corresponded to the coaching phase of the training model we discuss later.

Selecting Consultants

Who is going to deliver or present the content area reading staff development program? The choice of the person who will fill the role of staff developer is crucial. Local teachers and administrators tend to have a good record of success in staff development programs (Lawrence, 1974). Local talent should always be considered.

A staff development project in content area reading may make use of outside expertise such as that offered by a college- or university-based consultant. But staff development ultimately fails or succeeds because of the professional expertise of local talent—school-based personnel who work "inside" the system. The local staff developers for content area reading are often the reading consultants or reading teachers within a school or district. However, total responsibility need not and should not be exclusively theirs. The classroom teacher must play an integral role in content area reading staff development. An ideal situation, for example, may occur when a reading specialist teams up with a classroom teacher to lead an inservice program. The reading specialist may not feel comfortable with the content of a subject area but knows the reading process and how to apply it. The classroom teacher, on the other hand, knows the content but may not feel comfortable with the reading process. Each draws on the other's expertise and strengths to conduct the program.

Even greater time, attention, and deliberation are required when contracting with consultants outside the district because they are often unknown. Yet their behavior can "make or break staff development experiences" (Vacca, 1981, p. 53). Whether the consultant is to conduct a single session or work with a district over an extended period of time, his or her selection can have long-term effects.

Choosing skillful presenters is a difficult process. Ascertaining participants' needs and program objectives will help determine the criteria for the selection of consultants. But the criteria must often be supplemented and corroborated through telephone calls and colleagues' impressions.

For example, some characteristics may be verified in an indirect way via telephone conversations with prospective consultants. Are they interested in the topic being negotiated? Do they have clear and pleasant voices? Do they have a sense of humor? More direct conversation about the topic should reveal whether or not the consultant's knowledge is current. Do they inquire about audio-visual materials or seating arrangements? Do they want to know the results of the needs assessments? What cannot be learned on the telephone should be discussed with people who have previously heard or worked with the prospective consultant.

Using these techniques and formulating criteria cannot guarantee that a content area staff developer will be successful, but at least the probability of success is increased. A checklist for selecting and assessing consultants, derived from the categories of staff developer behaviors previously discussed, is an efficient guide which we include in Box 11.2.

Box 11.2

*A CHECKLIST FOR SELECTING AND ASSESSING CONSULTANTS**

The following checklist was compiled from a national survey of teachers' perceptions of successful presenters (Vacca, 1981). The characteristics represent an ideal type of consultant.

1. Content Delivery
_____ Uses active involvement techniques.
_____ Avoids straight lecture method.
_____ Maintains balance between group participation and presentation of information.
_____ Demonstrates ideas and strategies with classroom examples.
_____ Demonstrates materials that have immediate use in classroom.

2. Personal Influence
_____ Is enthusiastic and interested in the topic itself.
_____ Is dynamic and stimulates excitement.
_____ Relates to group in an open, honest, and friendly way.
_____ Answers questions patiently.
_____ Avoids alienating participants by talking down to them.
_____ Possesses a sense of humor.

3. Professional Competence
_____ Is knowledgeable about the topic.
_____ Has clear objectives in mind.
_____ Is well organized.
_____ Keeps on schedule.
_____ Explains procedures and gives directions for all activities.
_____ Adheres to the topic.
_____ Uses audio-visual materials skillfully.
_____ Allows time for questions.
_____ Provides opportunity for practice.

4. Arrangements
_____ Assesses needs of group in advance of presentation.
_____ Uses seating arrangements appropriate for group size and type of activity.
_____ Attends to comfort of group.
_____ Gives breaks as needed.
_____ Adjusts noise levels as needed.
_____ Schedules sessions other than directly after school if possible.

*Source: Jo Anne L. Vacca, "Program Implementation," in *Staff Development Leadership: A Resource Book*. Columbus, Ohio: Department of Education, 1983, pp. 51–58.

Materials and Facilities

In conjunction with the selection of consultants, attention should be paid to materials and facilities. Materials, whether they are the handouts of the district or the consultant, whether they are published or teacher-made, are important to effective program delivery. Materials, as much as any process strategy used by the consultant, can help make staff development successful. On the other hand, materials which appear unrelated to classroom or district concerns are associated with unsuccessful experiences. Handouts and other materials tend to be viewed more positively in all staff development activities if they describe local situations and examples (Patton and Anglin, 1982). Content area teachers want consultants who present relevant ideas, strategies, and materials that relate directly to their own classrooms.

When making arrangments for programs, staff development leaders should try to use facilities that will help make the staff development activities or process strategies as real as possible. The location of activities is important, according to Wood, 1981:

> The more the teachers see the students, school facilities, instructional materials, and equipment used in the training as similar to their own situation, the more likely they are to view the experiential activities and what is to be learned as real and applicable to them.   *(p. 77)*

Paying attention to arrangements such as facilities can be time-consuming. Facilities also may not take on the same importance as selecting the consultant and preparing materials. Yet, when teachers mention facilities in an evaluation of a staff development program, their comments are usually negative. They criticize the size of rooms, temperature, lack of breaks, and refreshments.

Facilities become even more important to participants when staff development activities are judged average or less successful. Then they are "quick to complain about noise, seating arrangements and temperatures" (Patton and Anglin, 1982, p. 167). Because facilities can have such a negative impact, staff development leaders should obtain early feedback from participants and step in to correct any immediate problems.

Although there are no panaceas in dealing with the complexities of staff development, there are some models we can rely on. They are particularly useful for content area reading staff development because they revolve around planning for change and depend on process strategies to implement.

Collaborative Models

"Going it alone" may have appeal in some aspects of school life, but it has no place in staff development planning. Collaboration is the watchword in staff development today. In fact, schools described as successful are places where teachers *and* administrators (1) plan, design, research, evaluate, and prepare teaching materials; (2) frequently observe teaching; and (3) teach each other the practice of teaching (Little, 1981). Further, they are places where "teachers engage in frequent, continuous, and increasingly concrete and precise talk about teaching practice" (Little, pp. 1–3).

Schools in which collaboration and mutual respect have been nurtured and maintained are often referred to as collegial. In these workplaces the norm is one of collegiality defined as a "state of mind" (Garman, 1982), and as "expectations and structures for shared work and shared responsibility" (Little, 1982). Indeed, the delivery of help and advice by colleagues is a feature frequently cited by teachers as effective in improving instruction (Pac-Urar and Vacca, 1984, p. 36).

The importance of the building principal and his or her role as instructional leader cannot be overemphasized in any successful staff development model. In a truly collegial situation, however, this doesn't mean one individual successfully fulfilling everyone's expectations.

> This is where the collegial approach comes in. . . . For example, a principal's strength might be in the active demonstration of desirable teaching behaviors; in other cases, a principal may be better at the managerial functions which bring about conditions which allow desirable teaching behaviors to occur. *(Vaughan, 1983, p. 12)*

Principals, then, need to welcome teachers and external building personnel into a collegial collective for instructional leadership. Above all, principals who support the norm of collegiality clearly describe their expectations, model desired behaviors, and defend the norm against internal and external pressures. To accomplish this, they must rely on meaningful communication in collaborative planning and data-based decision-making, "the foundation of good staff development programs" (Greenfield, 1983, p. 30).

Numerous informal opportunities for shared work and shared decision-making exist in the course of a school day between school-based staff developers and teachers. Perhaps the voluntary questions one colleague asks another in hope of securing some advice is the ideal situation for getting teachers involved in content area reading instruction through staff development. Most instances thought of as staff development, however, are of a more structured nature. They involve program development in which teachers and leaders plan change gradually.

Planning for Change

A model for staff development in content area reading should be general enough to invite adaptations which the circumstances of individual schools demand. The model should also be systematic enough to move classroom teachers through a planned sequence of activities that identify and facilitate those teachers' needs. And, finally, a model should be planned with change as its ultimate purpose and product.

Cunningham (1972) identified three phases of planning in a change-orientation to improve the instructional competencies of content area staff. As Figure 11.5 suggests, the planning process establishes a continuous involvement process for reading staff development in content areas.

Planning begins with a proposal to initiate a program for reading in the content areas. The proposal may come from the top via administrative mandate and

Figure 11.5
Planning Process

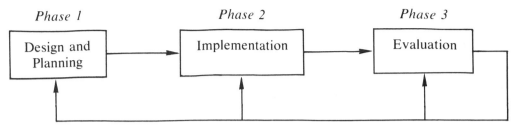

filter down, or it may come from teachers who feel the burden of working with students who they maintain won't or can't read content area materials. Or, it may come from teachers who wish to identify and pilot some new strategies.

Planning necessarily relies on information and ideas from a variety of sources, especially the group for whom the staff development is intended. An assessment can help a planning committee collect them.

Assessment helps identify needs, attitudes, interests, and potential resources for staff development. It takes many forms.

Attitude Scale

Teachers' attitudes toward reading in their classrooms is important. Vaughan (1977) contended that resolution of students' problems in reading content material "may well begin with the teacher's attitude toward the problem" (p. 606). To this end, Vaughan developed a scale to measure attitudes toward teaching reading in content classrooms and demonstrated through statistical procedures that it was reliable and valid in assessing teachers' attitudes toward reading in context areas.

Attitude scales can be used a number of ways to help plan a staff development project. First, you may agree with Vaughan's (1977) assumption that "teachers who are aware of and sympathetic to the difficulties their students may have reading their textbooks are likely to be the teachers who will learn" (p. 606). If this is the case, the attitude scale can help to determine the immediate target group for the staff development program. Second, the information derived from the attitude scale can indicate the scope and content of the workshop sessions within planning phase 2, implementation. Teachers with low or below-average scores, for example, may need more structured contact with each other to share mutual problems before additional content is presented. And third, the scale can be used as a post-test to measure changes in attitude at the end of a staff development program.

Surveys

Assessment may also include the use of surveys to get at the needs, concerns, and interests of a teaching staff. Obviously, multiple copies of a survey facilitate the collecting of information from large numbers of colleagues. Boxes 11.3 and 11.4 are two examples of assessment surveys for content area reading.

Box 11.3

SURVEY OF COMPETENCY NEEDS AND RESOURCES*

Directions: Listed below are competencies related to reading in content areas. Indicate whether you would like assistance in each area. If you are willing to help others, or if you know of resources that might be used for staff development activities in an area, please indicate this in the Resources column.

Competencies	Needs			Resources
	I feel confident in this area	I would like a little more help here	I would like lots of help here	
1. Differentiate reading assignments in a single text to provide for a range of reading abilities				
2. Plan instruction so that students know how to approach their reading assignments				
3. Help students identify various patterns of organization which a writer uses in text material				
4. Help students set purposes for their reading assignments				
5. Develop reading and study guides to help students comprehend text material				
6. Teach technical vocabulary before students meet terms in their reading				
7. Reinforce students' understanding of technical vocabulary by providing opportunities for their repeated use				

8. Use tradebooks to supplement the basic textbook

9. Determine the difficulty of my content area materials

10. Use informal content inventories to discover students' limitations in reading textbook assignments

11. Develop an instructional unit

12. List additional competency areas accordingly

*SOURCE: Adapted from *Right to Read Manual for Community Literacy Program Development.* Springfield, Ill.: Illinois Office of Education, 1975, p. G-11.

Box 11.4

SURVEY OF NEEDS AND CONCERNS

Directions: Please number in order of importance the areas in which you feel you need additional help in order to teach content through reading. Then, answer each question as completely as possible.

__ Determining the reading difficulty level of my content area materials.

__ Guiding students to comprehend their reading assignments.

__ Developing questions for a reading assignment.

__ Reinforcing technical vocabulary by providing opportunities for repeated use.

__ Developing vocabulary skills that will help students unlock the meaning of words independently.

__ Planning instruction so that students know how to approach their reading assignment.

__ Differentiating reading assignments in a single textbook to provide for a range of reading abilities.

__ Guiding students to read graphs, charts, maps and illustrations.

__ Teaching key vocabulary terms before students meet them in an assignment.

__ Showing students how to read content materials critically.

__ Teaching students how to outline text material.

__ Developing a unit which coordinates instructional resources and materials.

1. What is your area of greatest concern about your delivery of instruction in content area reading?

2. What is your area of least concern?

Interviewing colleagues is another way to collect additional or clarify existing information gleaned from attitude measures and other paper and pencil surveys. This technique provides less quantity for assessment, but often yields more quality information such as reasons behind areas of concern and requests for help. The final two questions in Box 11.4, for instance, could be used to probe teachers in an informal one-to-one interview.

At this point in the planning process basic goals and objectives are ready to be set. The implementation phase, what is actually done and how it will bring about change, is beginning.

Implementing a Model

We'd like to suggest two collaborative school-based models for the implementation phase of staff development in content area reading. We have found each effective in working with adult learners. Selection of one or the other depends mainly on the planning committee's assessment of the status quo, and on the content needs and delivery preferences of building personnel. Figure 11.6 illustrates first how some very basic questions can help a planning committee move toward the implementation of a model. Second, it shows two collaborative models actually identified for use in content area reading staff development.

Figure 11.6
Selecting a Collaborative Model

Status Quo	Needs	Delivery	Model
What is the current situation or climate in the building?	What is necessary to improve this?	How can this be done?	Which model can we follow or adapt?
There is little contact among faculty; problems are mentioned in the lounge but there is no opportunity to share possible solutions.	The faculty need a more structured way of sharing; they need to find ways to collaborate about specific instructional problems.	Setting up problem-solving teams would give structure and mutul support.	Action planning
The faculty will be participating in a funded program to introduce new strategies. In the past new ideas have not been put into practice.	The faculty need a step-by-step program on the adaption and use of an innovation with built-in support.	Training procedures that include a coaching phase to follow the new strategies into the classroom.	Training-coaching

Action Planning Model

Here's how one high school (School A) used an action planning model for staff development implementation. First, the planning committee collected needs assessment data and clarified the summarized data through interviews with teachers. Next the committee contacted members of the faculty from different subject areas and asked them to be on two problem-solving teams, each made up of four faculty and an assistant principal. These teams then met once a week during the fall semester following explicit procedures to develop an action plan. The results of one team's work are shown below:

1. *Define the problem.*
   a. We understand the problem to be . . .
      Large vocabulary and concept load in high school textbooks.
   b. The following people are involved in the problem . . .
      Teachers in selecting and teaching vocabulary terms and students' disinterest.
   c. Other factors relevant to the problem . . .
      Pressures to get through the content and produce acceptable test scores.
   d. One aspect of the problem we need to change . . .
      Finding more effective ways of teaching vocabulary to students.

2. *Plan for Change.*
   a. Exactly what are we trying to accomplish?
      Find better ways to use social studies and history subject matter as a natural context for the development of students' vocabularies.
   b. What behavior is implied?
      History and social studies teachers will identify key words, show students interrelationships, preteach, and guide students. Students will understand and use strategies they are shown.
   c. Who is going to do it?
      Each team member will meet with several other teachers to get their input, then come back to the team. Eventually most of the history and social studies staff and their students will be involved.
   d. Can it be done?
      Yes. There is every reason to expect support from the staff because the problem is a real one and we all expect improvement.
   e. What tangible evidence will indicate change?
      Teachers will be meeting to share what works and students will be observed improving their vocabularies in class and using this knowledge and skill in tests.

3. *Take Action Steps.*
   a. Actions that need to be taken:
      1. Discussions with and memo to faculty.
      2. Selecting consultant.
      3. Arranging workshops for faculty with and without consultant.

   4. Formative evaluations of progress.
   5. Concerted effort in classroom vocabulary instruction.
   6. Post assessment of teachers, consultant, and students; summative evaluation compiled.
 b. Persons responsible for each action:
   1. team and principal
   2. team and faculty
   3. principal
   4. team and principal
   5. team and faculty
   6. team, principal, and planning committee
 c. Timing of each action:
   1. January
   2. January
   3. February
   4. February, March
   5. April
   6. May
 d. Necessary human and financial resources:
   1. school office budget
   2. Team requesting money from district staff development committee
   3. principal
   4. released time for workshops budgeted; consultant
   5. materials reproduced
   6. principal; report disseminated

Training-Coaching Model

A middle school (School B) used a training-coaching model for staff development implementation. The reading consultant had secured a grant to introduce and implement teaching strategies to help students with content area materials. Working through the building staff development committee, she outlined a plan adapted from Bruce Joyce and his colleagues (1983) to systematically train the faculty in the adaption and use of identified instructional innovation in content area reading. Based on her recommendation they hired a university-based consultant to assist with the first phase of the project which began in October. Participation was voluntary, and substitute teachers were provided for day-long sessions. Twenty-four faculty agreed to participate for the duration out of a total teaching staff of thirty-two. The two phases of the training-coaching model are shown below:

Phase One: Training

Components	Place	Time
1. *Present the idea(s).* Talk about comprehension; technical vocabulary; prereading strategies.	Session #1, 2, 3	October, November, December

2. *Model or demonstrate.*
   Give examples; read short selections; share samples; do several strategies together.

   Session #1, 2, 3 — October, November, December

3. *Provide practice.*
   Teachers develop materials and strategies using their own materials, then try out in classroom.

   Session #2, 3 — November, December

4. *Provide feedback.*
   Teachers reflect on use of materials and strategies; refine and adapt strategies, get feedback from consultant and colleagues and try again; repeat cycle.

   Session #3, 4 — December, January, February

Phase Two: Coaching

5. *Coach for application.*
   Teachers expand and further adapt innovations to other areas of their teaching; meet in small groups in their own classrooms with consultant to discuss problems; visit one anothers' classrooms.

   Individual Classrooms — February, March

The two phases of the training-coaching model are similar to the sports analogy presented in chapter eight in connection with study strategies. The coach (colleague, consultant, master teacher) goes into classrooms to provide feedback, to guide, inspire, and share knowledge and experiences with those "in training." Training in this case, of course, refers to teachers learning, working on, and refining their techniques. The coach may, in the coaching phase, debrief the teachers with questions getting at how successful they feel they've been; journal entries might also be used. Just as with students and studying, this is a time for teachers to internalize the procedures and take control of the strategy!

Evaluating Change

At times it seems as if some school districts have jumped the gun in handling evaluation of staff development programs. In their haste to show the results of staff development programs, they have tended to confuse process with product. For example, are the goals of staff development aimed at showing automatic gain in student achievement even before the teachers' growth and the program designed to influence that growth have been carefully evaluated? One way of avoiding confusion between process and product of staff development is to plan for various levels of evaluation within the process itself. Figure 11.7 shows three levels for evaluation of a staff development program.

Figure 11.7
Levels of Evaluation in Staff Development

Level 1	Teacher		
Level 2	Teacher	Classroom	
Level 3	Teacher	Classroom	Student

Level 1 evaluates the process by which teacher skills are developed and fine-tuned, answering such questions as: What was the quality of individual workshops? Were the goals and objectives of the program achieved? Was the consultant or program leader effective?

Level 2 considers the effect of the staff development process on what teachers are actually doing in the classroom. Are teachers attempting to incorporate or implement content area reading activities into instruction? Have they modified their previous strategies and materials to fit their new purposes? Are their instructional units incorporating a wider range of instructional materials and resources?

Level 3 considers the effect of the staff development process on its ultimate product—improved student attitude toward and performance in content area reading.

Staff development programs sometimes move too quickly from teacher and classroom evaluation to student evaluation in a rush to prove their worth.

The push for visible returns is understandable; in the wake of the school improvement movement, it's probably inevitable. But programs which center predominantly on evaluation of levels 1 and 2 offer teachers the opportunity to grow professionally and improve the quality of their classroom instruction.

A number of evaluative tools can be used to determine the extent of teachers' professional growth. Pre- and post-testing of teachers' knowledge of reading on tests specifically constructed for the staff development program can yield evaluative insights if it is agreed that knowledge of reading is a good indicator of teacher growth. Changes in teachers' attitudes toward content area reading can be interpreted from pre- and post-tests with an attitude scale. Systems for analyzing and classifying interactions between teachers and students (some good ones can be found in *Second Handbook of Research on Teaching,* 1973) and observation check-lists can help evaluate the effect of the program on teachers' classroom activities.

We recommend using the same checklist developed for selecting consultants when you want to assess participants' perceptions of the staff developer's performance. For rating the quality and perceived effectiveness of individual workshop sessions, try a rating scale similar to the one in Box 11.5.

Box 11.5

RATING SCALE FOR WORKSHOPS

Directions: To determine whether this particular workshop met your needs and the established objectives of the program, please provide your honest opinion on its design, presentation, and value. Circle the number which best expresses your reaction to each of the items below.

1. The organization of the workshop was — Excellent   5 4 3 2 1   Poor

2. The objectives of the workshop were — Clear   5 4 3 2 1   Vague

3. The contribution of the workshop leader(s) was — Excellent   5 4 3 2 1   Poor

4. The ideas and activities presented were — Very Interesting   5 4 3 2 1   Dull

5. My participation in this workshop should prove — Very Beneficial   5 4 3 2 1   Of no benefit

6. Overall this workshop was — Excellent   5 4 3 2 1   Poor

7. The strongest feature of the workshop was:

8. The weakest feature of the workshop was:

9. Would you like further help on any of the topics presented at the workshop? If so, please list them.

Looking Back, Looking Forward

In this chapter we focused on the successful implementation of content area reading strategies through well-planned staff development programs. To attract and retain good teachers who will incorporate content area reading into their instructional repertoires, these programs are based on principles of adult learning. They are the result of collaboration—among teachers, administrators, specialists, and consultants.

Staff development programs with clear purposes are more likely to be perceived as relevant by participants. Hence, planners of staff development may deal with a range of purposes from improved student achievement, to instructional improvement, to personal growth of teachers. With clear purposes set, planners shouldn't import a prepackaged program; neither should they start from scratch.

We can learn from what works. Many successful programs are described in reports and brochures. Recurring characteristics of these programs are incorporated into guidelines for planning content area reading staff development. We can also learn from what doesn't work. Do not, for example, exclude teachers from initial decision-making. Use problem areas identified by teachers in a mutual planning process.

Staff development in content area reading (and other topics as well) needs to take into account teachers' orientation to learning as adults. A natural extension of this, albeit largely ignored, is the stage at which teachers are in their career cycle. Depending on the given mix of experiences and career stages in a group of teachers, the scope of staff development activities will vary.

The style of staff development leaders is important; how skilled they are in process strategies adds to the perceived effectiveness of program delivery. Process strategies can help accomplish certain objectives or meet typical staff development needs when used in conjunction with appropriate materials, facilities, and allocated time. The difficult process of selecting skillful presenters and consultants calls for the use of criteria such as the checklist we provide in the chapter for selecting and assessing consultants.

Working toward collegiality in schools is an ever-present goal, one enhanced by a collaborative planning process. We illustrated this with the selection and implementation of two collaborative models, action planning and training-coaching. And, just as purposes are rarely one dimensional, evaluation of staff development usually requires more than one measure. Where continued professional growth and improved instruction in content area reading are the payoffs, well-planned and implemented staff development is worth the effort.

Suggested Readings

Griffin, G. (ed.). (1983). *Staff Development*. 82nd Yearbook of the National Society for the Study of Education. Chicago: University of Chicago Press.

Joyce, B., Hersh, R., & McKibbon, M. (1983). *The Structure of School Improvement*. New York: Longman.

Knowles, M. (1978). *The Adult Learner: A Neglected Species* (2nd ed.). Houston: Gulf Publishing Company.

Staff Development Leadership: A Resource Book. (1983). Columbus, Ohio: Ohio Department of Education.

Bibliography

Alexander, J. E. (ed.) (1983). *Teaching Reading* (2nd ed.). Boston: Little, Brown and Company.

Allington, R. & Strange, M. (1980). *Learning through Reading in the Content Areas*. Lexington, Mass.: D. C. Heath.

Anderson, R., Evertson, C., & Brophy, J. (1979). An experimental study of effective teaching in first grade reading groups. *Elementary School Journal, 79* 193–222.

Anderson, R. C. & Biddle, W. (1975). On asking people questions about what they are reading. In G. Bower (ed.). *The Psychology of Learning and Motivation*. New York: Academic Press.

Anderson, R. C. & Freebody, P. (1981). Vocabulary knowledge. In J. T. Guthrie (ed.). *Comprehension and Teaching: Research Perspectives*. Newark, Del.: International Reading Association.

Anderson, R. C., Reynolds, R. E., Schallert, D. L., & Goetz, E. T. (1977). Frameworks for comprehending discourse. *American Educational Research Journal,* **14,** 367–382.

Applebee, A. N. (1984). *Contexts for learning to write: Studies of secondary school instruction*. Norwood, N.J.: ABLEX.

Applebee, A. N. (1981). *Writing in the Secondary School: English and the Content Areas*. Urbana, Ill.: National Council of Teachers of English.

Archer, A. (1979). Study skills. In D. Carnine and F. J. Silbert (eds.), *Direct Instruction: Reading*. Columbus, Ohio: Merrill.

Armbruster, B. B. & Anderson, T. H. (1981). *Content Area Textbooks*. Reading Education Report No. 23, Urbana, Ill.: University of Illinois Center for the Study of Reading.

Armbruster, B. B., Echols, C., & Brown, A. L. (1982). The role of metacognition in reading to learn: A developmental perspective. *Volta Review,* 1982, **84,** 45–56.

Aronson, E. (1975). Busing and racial tension: The jigsaw route to learning and liking. *Psychology Today*, **8,** 43–50.

Artley, A. (1948). General and specific factors in reading comprehension. *Journal of Experimental Education,* **16,** 181–186.

Artley, A. S. (1975). Words, words, words. *Language Arts,* **52,** 1067–1072.

Ausubel, D. P. (1968). *Educational Psychology: A Cognitive View*. New York: Holt, Rinehart and Winston.

Ausubel, D. P., Novak, J. D., & Hanesian, H. (1978). *Educational Psychology: A Cognitive View*. (2nd ed.). New York: Holt, Rinehart and Winston.

Baldwin, R. S., & Kaufman, R. (1979). A concurrent validity study of the Raygor readability estimate. *Journal of Reading, 23,* 148–153.

Barron, R. (1969). The use of vocabulary as an advance organizer. In H. L. Herber and P. L. Sanders (eds.), *Research in Reading in the Content Areas: First Report.* Syracuse, N.Y.: Syracuse University Reading and Language Arts Center.

Barron, R., & Earle, R. (1973). An approach for vocabulary development. In H. L. Herber and R. F. Barron (eds.), *Research in Reading in the Content Areas: Second Report.* Syracuse, N.Y.: Syracuse University Reading and Language Arts Center.

Barron, R., & Stone, F. (1973, December). *The effect of student constructed graphic post organizers upon learning of vocabulary relationships from a passage of social studies content.* Paper presented at the meeting of the National Reading Conference, Houston.

Bartlett, B. (1978). Top-level structure as an organizational strategy for recall of classroom text. Unpublished doctoral dissertation, Arizona State University.

Beck, I., McKeown, M., McCaslin, E., & Burket, A. (1979). Instructional dimensions that may affect reading comprehension: Examples of two commercial reading programs. Pittsburgh: University of Pittsburgh, Language Research and Development Center Technical Report.

Beck, I. L., & McKeown, M. G. (1983). Learning words well—A program to enhance vocabulary and comprehension. *The Reading Teacher, 36,* 622–625.

Beck, I. L., Perfetti, C. A., & McKeown, M. G. (1982). Effects of long-term vocabulary instruction on lexical access and reading comprehension. *Journal of Educational Psychology, 74,* 506–521.

Beebe, B. F. (1968). *African Elephants.* New York: McKay.

Bellows, B. (1980). Running shoes are to jogging as analogies are to critical thinking. *Journal of Reading, 23,* 507–511.

Berlyne, D. (1965). *Structure and Direction of Thinking.* New York: Wiley.

Bernhardt, B. (1977). *Just Writing.* New York: Teachers and Writers.

Betts, E. (1950). *Foundations of Reading* (rev. ed.). New York: American Book Company.

Bloom, B. (1956). *Taxonomy of Educational Objectives: Cognitive Domain.* New York: McKay.

Bloome, D. (1985). Reading as a social process. *Language Arts, 62,* 134–142.

Britton, J. N., Burgess, T., Martin, N., McLeod, A., & Rosen, H. (1975). *The Development of Writing Abilities (11–18).* London: MacMillan Education Ltd.

Brown, A. L. (1978). Knowing when, where, and how to remember: A problem of metacognition. In R. Glaser (ed.), *Advances in Instructional Psychology.* Hillsdale, N.J.: Erlbaum.

Brown, A. L. (1982). Learning to learn how to read. In J. Langer and M. T. Smith-Burke (eds.), *Reader Meets Author/Bridging the Gap.* Newark, Del.: International Reading Association.

Brown, A. L., Campione, J., & Day, J. D. (1981). Learning to learn: On training students to learn from texts. *Educational Researcher,* **10,** 14–24.

Brown, A. L., Day, J. D., & Jones, R. (1983). The development of plans for summarizing texts. *Child Development,* **54,** 968–979.

Brown, A. L., & Day, J. D. (1983). Macrorules for summarizing texts: The development of expertise. *Journal of Verbal Learning Behavior,* **22,** 1–14.

Brown, A. L., & Palincsar, A. A. (1982). Inducing strategic learning from texts by means of informed, self-control training. *Topics in Learning and Learning Disabilities,* **2,** 1–17.

Brown, A. L., & Smiley, S. S. (1977). Rating the importance of structural units of prose passages: A problem of metacognitive development. *Child Development,* **48,** 1–8.

Brown, J. E., & Abel, F. J. (1982). Revitalizing American history: Literature in the classroom. *The Social Studies,* **73,** 279–282.

Bruner, J. (1961). The act of discovery. *Harvard Educational Review,* **31,** 21–32.

Bruner, J. (1960). *The Process of Education.* Cambridge, Mass.: Harvard University Press.

Bruner, J., Goodnow, J. J., & Austin, G. A. (1977). *A Study of Thinking.* New York: Science Editions.

Burke, J., Fessler, R., & Christensen, J. C. (1984). *Teacher Career Stages: Implications for Staff Development.* Bloomington, Ind.: Phi Delta Kappa.

Burmeister, L. (1974). *Reading Strategies for Secondary School Teachers.* Reading, Mass.: Addison-Wesley.

Camp, G. (1982). *A Success Curriculum for Remedial Writers.* Berkeley, Calif.: The National Writing Project, University of California, Berkeley.

Campbell, A. (1979). How readability formulae fall short in matching student to text in content areas. *Journal of Reading,* **22,** 683–689.

Capuzzi, D. (1973). Information intermix. *Journal of Reading,* **16,** 453–459.

Castallo, R. (1976). Listening guide—a first step toward notetaking and listening skills. *Journal of Reading,* **19,** 289–290.

Chall, J. S. (1958). *Readability: An appraisal of research and application.* Columbus, Ohio: Ohio State University, Bureau of Educational Research.

Cianciolo, P. (1981). Yesterday comes alive for readers of historical fiction. *Language Arts,* **58,** 452–462.

Collette, A. (1973). *Science Teaching in the Secondary School.* Boston: Allyn and Bacon.

Cooper, C. R., & Odell, L. (eds.) (1977). *Evaluating Writing.* Urbana, Ill.: National Council of Teachers of English.

Crafton, L. (1983). Learning from reading: What happens when students generate their own background knowledge. *Journal of Reading,* **26,** 586–593.

Cunningham, R. (1972). Design, implementation and evaluation of an affective/cognitive model for teacher change through a staff development program. Unpublished doctoral dissertation, Syracuse University.

Cunningham, R., & Shablak, S. (1975). Selective reading guide-o-rama: The content teacher's best friend. *Journal of Reading*, **18**, 380–382.

Daigon, A. (1979). From reading to writing. In R. T. Vacca and J. A. Meagher (eds.), *Reading Through Content*. Storrs, Conn.: University Publications and the University of Connecticut Reading-Language Arts Center.

Dale, E. (1969). Things to come. *Newletter*, **34.**

Dale, E. (1975). *The Word Game: Improving Communications*. Bloomington, Ind.: Phi Delta Kappa.

Dale, E., and Chall, J. S. (1948). A formula for predicting readability. *Educational Research Bulletin*, **27**, 11–20.

Dale, E., O'Rourke, J., & Bamman, H. (1971). *Techniques of Teaching Vocabulary*. Palo Alto, Calif.: Field Educational Publications.

Davidson, J. L. (1982). The group mapping activity for instruction in reading and thinking. *Journal of Reading*, **26**, 52–56.

Davidson, J. L., & Bayliss, V. A. (1979). Mapping. *The Journal of Language Experience*, **1**, 6–9.

Davis, F. B. (1944). Fundamental factors of comprehension in reading. *Psychometrika*, **9**, 185–197.

Davis, F. B. (1941). Fundamental factors of comprehension in reading. Unpublished doctoral dissertation, Harvard University.

Davis, F. B. (1972). Psychometric research on comprehension in reading. *Reading Research Quarterly*, **7**, 628–678.

Davis, F. B. (1968). Research in comprehension in reading. *Reading Research Quarterly*, **3**, 429–445.

Davis, J. (1969). *Group Performance*. Reading, Mass.: Addison-Wesley.

Deighton, L. (1970). *Vocabulary Development in the Classroom*. New York: Teachers College Press.

Devan, S., Klein, R., & Murphy, T. V. (1975). Priming—a method to equalize difference between high and low achievement students. *Journal of Reading*, **19**, 143–146.

Devine, T. (1981). *Teaching Study Skills*. Boston: Allyn & Bacon.

Dillon, J. T. (1983). *Teaching and the Art of Questioning*. Bloomington, Ind.: Phi Delta Kappa.

Dole, J. A., & Johnson, V. R. (1981). Beyond the textbook: Science literature for young people. *Journal of Reading*, **24**, 579–582.

Draper, V. (1982). Formative writing: Writing to assist learning in all subject areas. In G. Camp (ed.), *Teaching Writing: Essays from the Bay Area Writing Project*. Montclair, N.J.: Boynton/Cook.

Drummond, H. (1978). *The Western Hemisphere*. Boston: Allyn and Bacon.

Duffy, G. G. (1983). From turn taking to sense making. Broadening the concept of reading teacher effectiveness. *Journal of Educational Research*, **76**, 134–139.

Dulin, K. (1970). Using context clues in word recognition and comprehension. *The Reading Teacher*, **23**, 440–445.

Dupuis, M. M., & Snyder, S. L. (1983). Develop concepts through vocabulary: A strategy for reading specialists to use with content teachers. *Journal of Reading,* **26,** 297–305.

Eanet, M., & Manzo, A. V. (1976). REAP—a strategy for improving reading/writing/study skills. *Journal of Reading,* **19,** 647–652.

Earle, R. (1969). Developing and using study guides. In H. L. Herber and P. L. Sanders (eds.), *Research in Reading in the Content Areas: First Report.* Syracuse, N.Y.: Syracuse University Reading and Language Arts Center.

Earle, R. (1976). *Teaching Reading and Mathematics.* Newark, Del.: International Reading Association.

Earle, R., & Morley, R. (1974). The half-open classroom: Controlled options in reading. *Journal of Reading,* **18,** 131–135.

Early, M. (1964). The meaning of reading instruction in secondary schools. *Journal of Reading,* **8,** 25–29.

Early, M. (1973). Taking stock: Secondary reading in the 1970's. *Journal of Reading,* **16,** 364–373.

Ebbinghaus, H. (1897). Ueber eine neue methode zur prufung geistiger fahigkeiten und ihre anwendung bei schulkindern. *Zeitschrift fuer Psychologie und Physiologie der Sinnesorgane,* **13,** 401–457.

Elbow, P. (1973). *Writing Without Teachers.* New York: Oxford University Press.

Estes, T. (1970). Use of guide material and small group discussion in reading ninth grade social studies assignments. Unpublished doctoral dissertation, Syracuse University.

Estes, T., & Vaughan, J., Jr. (1985). *Reading and Learning in the Content Classroom* (2nd ed.). Boston: Allyn and Bacon.

Frase, L. (1971). A heuristic model for research in prose learning. A paper presented at the annual meeting of the American Educational Research Association, New York.

Frayer, D., Frederick, W. A., & Klausmeier, H. J. (1969). *A scheme for testing the level of cognitive mastery.* Working Paper No. 16. Madison, Wisc.: Wisconsin Research and Development Center for Cognitive Learning, University of Wisconsin.

Freedman, G., & Reynolds, E. G. (1980). Enriching basal reader lessons with semantic webbing. *The Reading Teacher,* **33,** 677–684.

Fry, E. (1968). A readability formula that saves time. *Journal of Reading,* **11,** 513–516, 575–578.

Fry, E. (1977). Fry's readability graph: Clarifications, validity and extension to level 17. *Journal of Reading,* **21,** 242–252.

Fuller, F. (1969). Concerns of teachers: A developmental characterization. *American Educational Research Journal,* **6,** 207–226.

Gagne, R. (1970). *The Conditions of Learning* (2nd ed.). New York: Holt, Rinehart and Winston.

Gambrell, L. B. (1980). Think-time: Implications for reading instruction. *The Reading Teacher,* **33,** 143–146.

Garman, N. B. (1982). The clinical approach to supervision. In *Supervision of Teaching*. Alexandria, Va.: Association for Supervision and Curriculum Development.

Gibson, E., & Levin, H. (1975). *The psychology of reading*. Cambridge, Mass.: MIT Press.

Gillet, J., & Kita, M. J. (1979). Words, kids and categories. *The Reading Teacher*, **32**, 538–542.

Gillet, J., & Temple, C. (1982). *Understanding Reading Problems*. Boston: Little, Brown & Company.

Gold, P., & Yellin, D. (1982). Be the focus: A psycho-educational technique for use with unmotivated learners. *Journal of Reading, 25*, 550–552.

Goodlad, J. (1983). *A Place Called School*. New York: McGraw-Hill.

Goodman, K. (1976). The reading process: A psycholinguistic view. *Language and Thinking in School* (2nd ed.). New York: Holt, Rinehart and Winston.

Goodman, Y., & Burke, C. (1972). *Reading Miscue Inventory Manual: Procedure for Diagnosis and Evaluation*. New York: Macmillan.

Graves, D. (1978). *Balance to Basics: Let Them Write*. New York: The Ford Foundation.

Graves, M. F., Prenn, M. C., & Cooke, C. L. (1985). The coming attraction: Previewing short stories. *Journal of Reading, 28*, 594–597.

Graves, M. F., Cooke, C. L., & LaBerge, M. J. (1983). Effects of previewing difficult short stories on low ability junior high school students' comprehension, recall, and attitudes. *Reading Research Quarterly, 18*, 262–276.

Green, J., & Harker, J. (1982). Reading to children: A communicative process. In J. Langer and M. T. Smith-Burke (eds.), *Reader Meets Author/Bridging the Gap*, pp. 196–221. Newark, Del.: International Reading Association.

Greene, F. (1979). Radio reading. In C. Pennock (ed.), *Reading Comprehension at Four Linguistic Levels*. Newark, Del.: International Reading Association.

Greenfield, W. D. (1983). Collaborative planning and data-based decision making. In *Staff Development Leadership: A Resource Book*. Columbus, Ohio: Ohio Department of Education.

Greenslade, B. (1980). Awareness and anticipation: The DR-TA in the content classroom. *Journal of Language Experience, 2*, 21–28.

Griffin, G. (1982, November). Guidelines for improving teacher quality. *American Education*, 33–37.

Grove, N. (1981, March). Wild Cargo: The business of smuggling animals. *National Geographic, 159*, 287–315.

Guthrie, J. (1981). Forms and functions of textbooks. *Journal of Reading, 24*, 554–556.

Guthrie, J. (1973). Reading comprehension and syntactic responses in good and poor readers. *Journal of Educational Psychology, 65*, 294.

Guthrie, J. (1974). The maze technique to assess, monitor reading comprehension. *The Reading Teacher, 28*, 161–168.

Hahn, A. (1984). Assessing and extending comprehension: Monitoring strategies in the classroom. *Reading Horizons, 24*, 225–230.

Halliday, M., and Hasan, R. (1976). *Cohesion in English*. London: Longman.

Hansell, T. S. (1976). Increasing understanding in content reading. *Journal of Reading*, **19**, 307–311.

Hansell, T. S. (1978). Stepping up to outlining. *Journal of Reading*, **22**, 248–252.

Hansen, J. (1981a). The effects of inference training and practice on young children's comprehension. *Reading Research Quarterly*, **16**, 391–417.

Hansen, J. (1981b). An inferential comprehension strategy for use with primary children. *The Reading Teacher*, **34**, 665–669.

Hare, V. C., & Borchardt, K. M. (1984). Direct instruction of summarization skills. *Reading Research Quarterly*, **20**, 62–78.

Harste, J. (1978). Instructional implications of Rumelhart's model. In W. Diehl (ed.), *Secondary Reading: Theory and Application*. Bloomington, Ind.: School of Education, Indiana University.

Hayes, D. A., & Tierney, R. T. (1982). Developing readers' knowledge through analogy. *Reading Research Quarterly*, **17**, 256–280.

Healy, M. K. (1982). Using student response groups in the classroom. In G. Camp (ed.), *Teaching Writing: Essays from the Bay Area Writing Project*. Montclair, N.J.: Boynton/Cook.

Heathington, B. S. (1975). *The Development of Scales to Measure Attitudes Toward Reading*. Unpublished doctoral dissertation. The University of Tennessee, Knoxville.

Heathington, B., & Alexander, J. E. (1984). Do classroom teachers emphasize attitudes toward reading? *The Reading Teacher*, **37**, 484–488.

Heinly, B. F., & Hilton, K. (1982). Using historical fiction to enrich social studies courses. *The Social Studies*, **73**, 21–24.

Henry, G. (1974). *Teaching Reading as Concept Development*. Newark, Del.: International Reading Association.

Herber, H. L. (1970). *Teaching Reading in Content Areas*. Englewood Cliffs, N.J.: Prentice-Hall.

Herber, H. L. (1978). *Teaching Reading in Content Areas* (2nd ed.). Englewood Cliffs, N.J.: Prentice-Hall.

Herber, H. L., & Nelson, J. (1975). Questioning is not the answer. *Journal of Reading*, **18**, 512–517.

Hinchman, K. (1984, November). *Reading and the Plans of Secondary Teacher: A Qualitative Study*. Paper presented at the meeting of The National Reading Conference, St. Petersburg, Fla.

Hittleman, D. (1977). *Developmental Reading: A Psycholinguistic Perspective*. Chicago: Rand McNally.

Hittleman, D. (1973). Seeking a psycholinguistic definition of readability. *The Reading Teacher*, **26**, 783–789.

Hoffman, S. (1983). Using student journals to teach study skills. *Journal of Reading*, **26**, 344–347.

Holly, M. L. (1984). *Keeping a Personal-Professional Journal*. Deakin, Australia: Deakin University Press.

Homer, C. (1979). A directed reading-thinking activity for content areas. In R. T. Vacca and J. A. Meagher (eds.), *Reading Through Content*. Storrs, Conn.: University Publications and the University of Connecticut Reading-Language Arts Center.

Howey, K. R., & Vaughan, J. C. (1983). Current patterns of staff development. In G. Griffin (ed.), *Staff Development, Eighty-Second Yearbook of NSSE, Part II*, pp. 92–117.

Huey, E. (1908). *The Psychology and Pedagogy of Reading*. New York: Macmillan.

Ignoffo, M. (1980). The thread of thought: analogies as a vocabulary building method. *Journal of Reading,* **23,** 519–521.

Irwin, J. W., & Davis, C. A. (1980). Assessing readability: The checklist approach. *Journal of Reading,* **24,** 124–130.

Johns, J., & Galen, N. (1977). Reading instruction in the middle 50's: What tomorrow's teachers remember today. *Reading Horizons,* **17,** 251–254.

Johnson, D., & Pearson, P. D. (1978). *Teaching Reading Vocabulary*. New York: Holt, Rinhart and Winston.

Johnson, D., & Pearson, P. D. (1984). *Teaching Reading Vocabulary* (2nd ed.). New York: Holt, Rinehart and Winston.

Journal of Staff Development (1982, April), i.

Joyce, B. R., Hersh, R., & McKibbon, M. (1983). *The Structure of School Improvement*. New York: Longman.

Joyce, B. R., Weil, M., & Wald, R. (1972). *Three Teaching Strategies for the Social Studies*. Chicago: Science Research Associates.

Judy, S., & Judy, S. (1980). *Gifts of Writing: Creative Projects with Words and Art*. New York: Scribner's Sons.

Kelley, B., & Holmes, J. (1979). The guided lecture procedure. *Journal of Reading,* **22,** 602–605.

Kennedy, B. (1985). Writing letters to learn math. *Learning,* **13,** 58–61.

King, J., & Blough, J. (1982, November). School district workshops: Inservice or disservice? *Ohio School Board Association Journal,* 6–8.

Kinneavy, J. L. (1971). *A Theory of Discourse*. Englewood Cliffs, N.J.: Prentice-Hall.

Kintsch, W. (1977). On comprehending stories. In M. A. Just & P. A. Carpenter (eds.), *Cognitive Processes in Comprehension*. Hillsdale, N.J.: Erlbaum.

Kintsch, W., & van Dijk, T. (1978). Toward a model of text comprehension and production. *Psychological Review,* **85,** 363–394.

Kirby, D., & Liner, T. (1981). *Inside Out: Developmental Strategies for Teaching Writing*. Montclair, N.J.: Boynton/Cook.

Knowles, M. (1973). *The Adult Learner: A Neglected Species*. Houston: Gulf Publishing Company.

Knowles, M. (1978). *The Adult Learner: A Neglected Species* (2nd ed.). Houston: Gulf Publishing Company.

Labov, W. (1972). *Sociolinguistic Patterns*. Philadelphia: University of Pennsylvania Press.

Langer, J. A. (1981). From theory to practice: A prereading plan. *Journal of Reading,* **25,** November, 152–156.

Lawrence, G. (1974). *Patterns of effective inservice education.* Tallahassee, Fla.: Florida Department of Education.

Lehr, F. (1982). Identifying and assessing reading attitudes. *Journal of Reading,* **26,** 80–83.

Lester, J. D. (1984). *Writing Research Papers: A Complete Guide* (4th ed.). Glenview, Ill.: Scott, Foresman.

Levine, D. S. (1985). The biggest thing I learned but it really doesn't have to do with science. . . . *Language Arts,* **62,** 43–47.

Lewin, K. (1948). *Resolving Social Conflicts.* New York: Harper and Row.

Lewis, R., & Teale, W. (1980). Another look at secondary school students' attitudes toward reading. *Journal of Reading Behavior,* **12,** 187–201.

Lindemann, E. (1982). *A Rhetoric for Writing Teachers.* New York: Oxford University Press.

Lundsteen, S. (1976). *Children Learn to Communicate.* Englewood Cliffs, N.J.: Prentice-Hall.

Little, J. W. (1981). *Finding the Limits and Possibilities of Instructional Leadership: Some Possibilities for Practical and Collaborative Work with Principals.* Washington, D. C.: National Institute of Education.

Little, J. W. (1982). Making sure: Contributions and requirements of good evaluation. *The Journal of Staff Development,* **3,** 25–47.

Little, J. W. (1981). *School Success and Staff Development: The Role of Staff Development in Urban Desegregated Schools.* Washington, D.C.: National Institute of Education.

Macrorie, K. (1970). *Uptaught.* Rochelle Park, N.J.: Hayden.

Malinowski, B. (1954). *Magic, Science and Religion and Other Essays.* New York: Doubleday, Anchor Books.

Mallan, J., & Hersh, R. (1972). *No g.o.d.s in the Classroom: Inquiry into Inquiry.* Philadelphia: W. B. Saunders.

Mandler, J., & Johnson, N. (1977). Remembrance of things parsed: Story structure and recall. *Cognitive Psychology,* **9,** 111–151.

Manzo, A. V. (1975). Guided reading procedure. *Journal of Reading,* **18,** 287–291.

Manzo, A. V. (1969). The request procedure. *Journal of Reading,* **11,** 123–126.

Manzo, A. V., & Shirk, J. K. (1972). Some generalizations and strategies for guiding vocabulary learning. *Journal of Reading Behavior,* **4,** 78–89.

Marksheffel, N. (1966). *Better Reading in the Secondary School.* New York: Ronald Press.

McAndrew, D. A. (1983). Increasing the reality of audiences in the classroom. *Connecticut English Journal,* **14,** 49–56.

McLaughlin, H. (1969). SMOG grading—a new readability formula. *Journal of Reading,* **12,** 639–646.

McNeil, J. D. (1984). *Reading Comprehension: New Directions for Classroom Practice.* Glenview, Ill.: Scott, Foresman.

Meyer, B. J. F. (1975). *The Organization of Prose and Its Effect in Memory*. Amsterdam: North-Holland.

Meyer, B. J. F., Brandt, D., & Bluth, G. (1980). Use of top-level structure in text: Key for reading comprehension of ninth-grade students. *Reading Research Quarterly*, **16,** 72–103.

Meyer, B. J. F., & Rice, E. (1984). The structure of text. In P. D. Pearson (ed.), *Handbook of Reading Research*, pp. 319–352. New York: Longman.

Milton, J. W. (1982). What the student-educator should have done before the grade: A questioning look at note-taking. In A. S. Algier and K. W. Algier (eds.), *Improving Reading and Study Skills*. San Francisco: Jossey-Bass.

Moffett, J. (1975). An interview with James Moffett. *Media and Methods*, **15,** 20–24.

Moffett, J., & Wagner, B. J. (1976). *Student-Centered Language Arts and Reading K-13* (2nd ed.). Boston: Houghton-Mifflin.

Moffett, J., & Wagner, B. J. (1983). *Student-Centered Language Arts and Reading, K-13: A Handbook for Teachers* (3rd ed.). Boston: Houghton-Mifflin.

Moore, D. W. (1983). A case for naturalistic assessment of reading comprehension. *Language Arts*, **60,** 957–968.

Moore, D. W., Readence, J., & Rickelman, R. (1983). An historical exploration of content area reading instruction. *Reading Research Quarterly*, **18,** 419–438.

Moore, M. A. (1981). C2R: Concentrate, read, remember. *Journal of Reading*, **24,** 337–339.

Myers, J. (1984). Writing to learn across the curriculum. Bloomington, Ind., Phi Delta Kappa.

Nelson, J. (1978). Readability: Some cautions for the content area teacher. *Journal of Reading*, **21,** 620–625.

Newton, E. (1977). Andragogy: Understanding the adult as a learner. *Journal of Reading*, **20,** 361–364.

Niles, O. (1964). Developing basic comprehension skills. In J. Sherk (ed.), *Speaking of Reading*. Syracuse, N.Y.: Syracuse University Reading and Language Arts Center.

Niles, O. (1965). Organization perceived. In H. Herber (ed.), *Developing Study Skills in Secondary Schools*. Newark, Del.: International Reading Association.

Olsen, A., & Ames, W. (1972). *Teaching Reading Skills in Secondary Schools*. Scranton, Pa.: Intext Educational Publishers.

Ortiz, R. (1983). Generating interest in reading. *Journal of Reading*, **28,** 113–119.

Pac-Urar, I., & Vacca, J. (1984, May). Working toward collegiality: If at first you don't succeed. *Thresholds in Education*, 36–38.

Page, W. D. (1975). Inquiry into an unknown word. *School Review*, **83,** 461–477.

Palmatier, R. (1973). A notetaking system for learning. *Journal of Reading*, **17,** 36–39.

Palmatier, R., & Bennett, J. M. (1974). Notetaking habits of college students. *Journal of Reading*, **18,** 215–218.

Pany, D., & Jenkins, J. (1977). Learning word meanings: A comparison of instructional procedures and effects on measures of reading comprehension with learning disabled students. Urbana, Ill.: University of Illinois Center for the Study of Reading Technical Report No. 25.

Paris, S., & Meyers, M. (1981). Comprehension monitoring, memory, and study strategies of good and poor reader. *Journal of Reading Behavior,* **13,** 5–22.

Patton, W., & Anglin, L. (1982). Characteristics of success in high school inservice education. *The High School Journal,* **65,** 163–168.

Pauk, W. (1978). A notetaking format: Magical but not automatic. *Reading World,* **16,** 96–97.

Pearce, D. L. (1983). Guidelines for the use and evaluation of writing in content classrooms. *Journal of Reading,* **27,** 212–218.

Pearson, P. D. (1982a). *Asking Questions about Stories.* Ginn Occasional Papers, No. 15. Columbus, Ohio: Ginn and Company.

Pearson, P. D. (1982b). *A Context for Instructional Research on Reading Comprehension.* Urbana, Ill.: University of Illinois Center for the Study of Reading Technical Report No. 230.

Pearson, P. D. (1974–1975). The effects of grammatical complexity on children's comprehension, recall, and conception of certain semantic relations. *Reading Research Quarterly,* **10,** 155–192.

Pearson, P. D., & Johnson, D. (1978). *Teaching Reading Comprehension.* New York: Holt, Rinehart and Winston.

Pearson, P. D., & Spiro, R. (1982). The new buzz word in reading as schema. *Instructor,* **89,** 46–48.

Perry, W. G. (1959). Students' use and misuse of reading skills: A report to the faculty. *Harvard Educational Review,* **29,** 193–200.

Peters, C. (1975). A comparative analysis of reading comprehension in four content areas. In G. H. McNinch and W. D. Miller (eds.), *Reading: Convention and Inquiry.* Clemson, S.C.: National Reading Conference.

Pichert, J. W., & Anderson, R. C. (1977). Taking different perspectives on a story. *Journal of Educational Psychology,* **69,** 309–315.

Piercy, D. (1976). *Reading Activities in Content Areas.* Boston: Allyn and Bacon.

Pradl, G. M., & Mayher, J. S. (1985). Reinvigorating learning through writing. *Educational Leadership,* **42,** 4–6.

Preston, R. (1968). *Teaching Social Studies in the Elementary School* (3rd ed.). New York: Holt, Rinehart and Winston.

Protheroe, D. (1979). Gi-go: The content of content area reading. In R. T. Vacca and J. A. Meagher (eds.), *Reading Through Content.* Storrs, Conn.: University Publications and the University of Connecticut Reading-Language Arts Center.

Purves, A. C. (1983). Teachers are real, too. *Connecticut English Journal,* **14,** 43–44.

Quandt, I. (1977). *Teaching Reading: A Human Process.* Chicago: Rand McNally College Publishing Company.

Quealy, R. (1969). Senior high school students' use of contextual aids in reading. *Reading Research Quarterly,* **4,** 512–533.

Raphael, T. E. (1982). Question-answering strategies for children. *The Reading Teacher,* **36,** 186–191.

Raphael, T. E. (1984). Teaching learners about sources of information for answering comprehension questions. *Journal of Reading, 27,* 303–311.

Raygor, A. (1977). The Raygor readability estimate: A quick and easy way to determine difficulty. In P. D. Pearson (ed.), *Reading: Theory, Research and Practice.* Clemson, S.C.: National Reading Conference.

Readence, J., Baldwin, R. S., & Bean, T. (1981). *Content Area Reading: An Integrated Approach.* Dubuque, Ia.: Kendall/Hunt.

Rickards, J. (1976). Interaction of position and conceptual level of adjunct questions. *Journal of Educational Psychology, 68,* 210–217.

Rico, G. L. (1983). *Writing the Natural Way: Using Right-Brain Techniques to Release Your Expressive Powers.* Los Angeles: J. P. Tarcher.

Rieck, B. J. (1977). How content teachers telegraph messages against reading. *Journal of Reading, 20,* 646–648.

Riley, J., & Pachtman, A. (1978). Reading mathematical word problems: Telling them what to do is not telling them how to do it. *Journal of Reading, 21,* 531–533.

Robinson, F. (1961). *Effective Study.* New York: Harper and Row.

Robinson, H. A. (1975). *Teaching Reading and Study Strategies: The Content Areas.* Boston: Allyn and Bacon.

Robinson, H. A. (1983). *Teaching Reading, Writing, and Study Strategies: The Content Areas* (3rd ed.). Boston: Allyn and Bacon.

Roby, T. (1968). *Small Group Performance.* Chicago: Rand McNally.

Rodrigues, R. J. (1983). Tools for developing prewriting skills. *English Journal, 72,* 58–60.

Rothkopf, E. (1966). Learning from written materials: An exploration of the control of inspection behavior by test-like events. *American Educational Research Journal, 3,* 241–249.

Salisbury, R. (1934). A study of the transfer effects of training in logical organization. *Journal of Educational Research, 28,* 241–254.

Samples, R. (1977). *The Wholeschool Book.* Reading, Mass.: Addison-Wesley.

Sanacore, J. (1983). Improving reading through prior knowledge and writing. *Journal of Reading, 26,* 714–720.

Sargent, E., Huus, H., & Andresen, O. (1971). *How to Read a Book.* Newark, Del.: International Reading Association.

Sawyer, D. (1974). The diagnostic mystique—a point of view. *The Reading Teacher, 27,* 355–360.

Schacter, S. W. (1978). An investigation of the effects of vocabulary instruction and schemata orientation on reading comprehension. Unpublished doctoral dissertation, University of Minnesota.

School daze: From A to Z (1982). Kansas City: Hallmark Cards.

Shablak, S., & Castallo, R. (1977). Curiosity arousal and motivation in the teaching/learning process. In H. L. Herber and R. T. Vacca (eds.), *Research in Reading in the Content Areas: Third Report.* Syracuse, N.Y.: Syracuse University Reading and Language Arts Center.

Shepherd, D. (1973). *Comprehensive High School Reading Methods*. Columbus, Ohio: Merrill.

Shepherd, D. (1978). *Comprehensive High School Reading Methods* (2nd ed.). Columbus, Ohio: Merrill.

Sherer, P. (1975). Skimming and scanning: De-mything the process with a college student. *Journal of Reading, 19,* 24–27.

Slavin, R. (1980). Cooperative learning. *Review of Educational Research, 50,* 315–342.

Slavin, R. (1982). *Cooperative Learning: Student Teams*. Washington, D.C.: National Education Association.

Smith, F. (1975). *Comprehension and Learning: A Conceptual Framework for Teachers*. New York: Holt, Rinehart and Winston.

Smith, F. (1979). *Reading Without Nonsense*. New York: Teachers College Press.

Smith, F. (1978). *Understanding Reading* (2nd ed.). New York: Holt, Rinehart and Winston.

Smith, F., & Feathers, K. (1983). Teacher and student perceptions of content area reading. *Journal of Reading, 26,* 348–354.

Smith, N. B. (1964). Patterns of writing in different subject areas. *Journal of Reading, 7,* 31–37.

Smith, N. B. (1959). Teaching study skills in reading. *Elementary School Journal, 60,* 158–162.

Smith, S. L. (1982). Learning strategies of mature college learners. *Journal of Reading, 26,* 5–13.

Spencer-Hall (1982, March). Teachers as persons: Case studies of home lives and implications for staff development. Paper presented at annual meeting of American Educational Research Association, New York.

Spiegal, D. L. (1981). Six alternatives to the directed reading activity. *The Reading Teacher, 34,* 914–922.

Stahl, S. A. (1983, October). Vocabulary instruction and the nature of word meanings. Paper presented at the meeting of The College Reading Association, Atlanta, Ga.

Stake, R. E. (ed.). (1975). *Evaluating the Arts in Education: A Responsive Approach*. Columbus, Ohio: Merrill.

Stallings, J., Needles, M., & Stayrook, N. (1979). *How to Change the Process of Teaching Basic Reading Skills in Secondary Schools*. Menlo Park, Calif.: SRI International.

Stauffer, R. (1969). *Directing Reading Maturity as a Cognitive Process*. New York: Harper and Row.

Stauffer, R. (1975). *Directing the Reading-Thinking Process*. New York: Harper and Row.

Stein, N., & Glenn, C. (1979). An analysis of story comprehension in elementary school children. In R. Freedle (ed.), *New Directions in Discourse Processing*. Norwood, N.J.: ABLEX.

Steurer, S. (1978). Learning centers in the secondary school. *Journal of Reading,* **22,** 134–139.

Summers, E. (1965). Utilizing visual aids in reading material for effective learning. In H. L. Herber (ed.), *Developing Study Skills in Secondary Schools.* Newark, Del.: International Reading Association.

Taba, H. (1975). *Teacher's Handbook for Elementary Social Studies.* Reading, Mass.: Addison-Wesley.

Taylor, B. (1980). Children's memory of expository text after reading. *Reading Research Quarterly,* **15,** 399–411.

Taylor, B. (1982). A summarizing strategy to improve middle grade students' reading and writing skills. *The Reading Teacher,* **36,** 202–205.

Taylor, W. (1953). Cloze procedure: A new tool for measuring readability. *Journalism Quarterly,* **30,** 415–433.

Tchudi, S., & Yates, J. (1983). *Teaching Writing in Content Areas: High School.* Washington, D.C.: National Education Association.

Thelen, H. (1949). Group dynamics in instruction: Principle of least group size. *School Review,* **57,** 139–148.

Thelen, J. (1984). *Improving Reading in Science* (2nd ed.). Newark, Del.: International Reading Association.

Thelen, J. (1982). Preparing students for content reading assignments. *Journal of Reading,* **25,** 546–547.

Thorndike, E. (1917). Reading and reasoning: A study of mistakes in paragraph reading. *Journal of Educational Psychology,* **8,** 323–332.

Thorndyke, P. (1977). Cognitive structures in comprehension and memory of narrative discourse. *Cognitive Psychology,* **9,** 77–110.

Thurstone, L. L. (1946). A note on a reanalysis of Davis' reading tests. *Psychometrika,* **11,** 185–188.

Toch, T. (1984, March 7). Bell calls on educators to push publishers for better materials. *Education Week,* p. 11.

Tuinman, J. T., & Brady, M. C. (1974). How does vocabulary account for variance on reading comprehension tests: A preliminary instructional analysis. In P. Nacke (ed.), *Interaction: Research and Practice in College-Adult Reading, 23rd yearbook.* National Reading Conference.

Tullock-Rhody, R., & Alexander, J. E. (1980). A scale for assessing attitudes toward reading in secondary schools. *Journal of Reading,* **26,** 609–610.

Tutolo, D. (1977). The study guide: Types, purpose and value. *Journal of Reading,* **20,** 503–507.

Vacca, J. L. (1981). *Establishing Criteria for Staff Development Personnel.* Washington, D.C.: National Institute of Education.

Vacca, J. L. (1983). How to be an effective staff developer for content teachers. *Journal of Reading,* **26,** 293–296.

Vacca, J. L. (1983). Program implementation. In *Staff Development Leadership: A Resource Book.* Columbus, Ohio: Ohio Department of Education.

Vacca, J. L. (1976). Reading techniques to improve self-concept. *New England Reading Association Journal,* **11,** 28–32.

Vacca, J. L., & Sparks, C. (1981). The evaluation of adults seeking improvement in reading. *Reading World,* **20,** 197–200.

Vacca, J., & Vacca, R. T. (1976). Learning stations: How to in the middle grades. *Journal of Reading,* **19,** 563–567.

Vacca, J. L., & Vacca, R. T. (1983). Process strategies for effective staff development: In *Dissemination report: Systematic planning for school improvement.* Columbus, Ohio: Ohio Department of Education.

Vacca, J. L., & Vacca, R. T. (1980). Unfreezing strategies for staff development in reading. *The Reading Teacher,* **34,** 27–31.

Vacca, R. T. (1975). Development of a functional reading strategy: Implications for content area instruction. *Journal of Educational Research,* **69,** 108–112.

Vacca, R. T. (1977). An investigation of a functional reading strategy in seventh grade social studies. In H. L. Herber and R. T. Vacca (eds.), *Research in Reading in the Content Areas: Third Report.* Syracuse, N.Y.: Syracuse University Reading and Language Arts Center.

Vacca, R. T., & Johns, J. (1976). $R > S_1 + S_2 + \cdots S_n$, *Reading Horizons,* **17,** 9–13.

Vaughan, J., Jr. (1977). A scale to measure attitudes toward reading in content classrooms. *Journal of Reading,* **20,** 605–609.

Vaughan, J. C. (1983). Using research on teaching, schools and change to help staff development make a difference. *The Journal of Staff Development,* **4,** 6–24.

Walker, J. (1979). Squeezing study skills (into, out of) content areas. In R. T. Vacca and J. A. Meagher (eds.), *Reading Through Content,* pp. 77–92. Storrs, Conn.: University Publications and the University of Connecticut Reading-Language Arts Center.

Wechsler, D. (1958). *The Measurement and Appraisal of Adult Intelligence.* Baltimore: The Williams and Wilkins Co.

Winograd, P. N. (1984). Strategic difficulties in summarizing texts. *Reading Research Quarterly,* **19,** 404–425.

Wittrock, M. D., Marks, C., & Doctorow, M. (1975). Reading as a generative process. *Journal of Educational Psychology,* **67,** 481–489.

Wixson, K. (1983). Questions about a text: What you ask about is what children learn. *The Reading Teacher,* **37,** 287–294.

Wixson, K., Bosky, A., Yochum, M. N., & Alvermann, D. (1984). An interview for assessing students' perceptions of classroom reading tasks. *The Reading Teacher,* **37,** 346–353.

Wood, F. (1981). Designing effective staff development programs. In *Staff Development/Organization Development.* Alexandria, Va.: Association for Supervision and Curriculum Development.

Yarger, S., & Mertens, S. K. (1980). Testing the waters of school-based teacher education. In *Concepts to Guide the Education of Experienced Teachers.* Reston, Va.: Council for Exceptional Children.

Appendix A

Affixes with Invariant Meanings

AFFIX	MEANING	EXAMPLE
1. *Combining Forms*		
anthropo-	man	anthropoid
auto-	self	autonomous
biblio-	book	bibliography
bio-	life	biology
centro- centri-	center	centrifugal
cosmo	universe	cosmonaut
heter- hetero-	different	heterogeneous
homo-	same	homogeneous
hydro-	water	hydroplane
iso-	equal	isometric
lith- litho-	stone	lithography
micro-	small	microscope
mono-	one	monocyte
neuro-	nerve	neurologist
omni-	all	omnibus
pan-	all	panchromatic
penta-	five	pentamerous

AFFIX	MEANING	EXAMPLE
phil-	love	philanthropist
philo-		
phono-	sound	phonology
photo-	light	photosynthesis
pneumo-	air, respiration	pneumonia
poly-	many	polygon
proto-	before, first in time	prototype
pseudo-	false	pseudonym
tele-	far	television
uni-	one	unicellular

2. *Prefix*

apo-	separate or detached from	apocarpous
circum-	around	circumvent
com-	together or with	combine
co-		
col-		
con-		
cor-		
equi-	equal	equivalent
extra-	in addition	extraordinary
intra-	within	intratext
mal-	bad	malpractice
mis-	wrong	mistreatment
non-	not	nonsense
syn-	together or with	synthesis

3. *Noun Suffix*

Each Noun Suffix Functions to Indicate:

-ana	a collection of various materials that reflect the character of a notable place or person	Americana
-archy	rule or government	oligarchy
-ard	a person who does something to excess	drunkard
-art		braggart
-aster	inferiority or fraudulence	poetaster
-bility	quality or state of being	capability
-chrome	pigment, colored or color	autochrome
-cide	murder or killing of	insecticide
-fication	action or process of	classification
-ation		dramatization
-gram	something written or drawn	diagram
-graph	writing, recording, drawing	telegraph
		lithograph

AFFIX	*MEANING*	*EXAMPLE*
-graphy	a descriptive science of a specific subject or field	planography oceanography
-ics	the science or art of	graphics athletics
-itis	inflammation or inflammatory disease	bronchitis
-latry	the worship of	bibliolatry
-meter	a measuring device	barometer
-metry	the science or process of measuring	photometry
-ology	the science, theory	phraseology
-logy	or study of	paleontology
-phore	a bearer or producer	semaphore
-phobia	persistent, illogical, abnormal or intense fear	hypnophobia
-scope	an instrument for observing or detecting	telescope
-scopy	viewing, seeing or observing	microscopy
-ance	These noun suffixes are used	tolerance
-ation	to form abstract nouns	adoration
-ion	with the meaning of	
-ism	"quality, state, or	truism
-dom	condition," and action	
-ery	or result of an	
-mony	action.	matrimony
-ment		government
-tion		sanction
-er	These noun suffixes	helper
-eer	pertain to living	engineer
-ess	or nonliving agents.	countess
-grapher		geographer
-ier		
-ster		youngster
-ist		shootist
-stress		mistress
-trix		executrix

	Adjective Suffixes Function	
4. *Adjective Suffix*	*to Indicate:*	
-est	a superlative	greatest
-ferous	bearing, producing	crystalliferous
-fic	making, causing, or creating something	morbific

AFFIX	MEANING	EXAMPLE
-fold	division	fivefold tenfold
-form	having the form of	cuneiform
-genous	generating or producing	androgenous endogenous
-ic	a characteristic of	seismic microscopic
-wise	manner, direction, or position	clockwise
-less	lack of, free of or not having	toothless
-able -ible	worthy of or inclined to	debatable knowledgeable
-most	a superlative	innermost
-like	resemblance or similarity to something specified, characteristic of or appropriateness to something specified	lifelike
-ous	possessing, having or full of	joyous
-ose	possession of or having similiarity to	grandiose
-acious	a tendency toward or abundance of something	fallacious
-ful	fullness or abundance	masterful useful armful
-aceous -ative -ish	These adjective suffixes mean pertaining to	impish foolish
-ive -itious		additive fictitious

Appendix B

Commonly Used Prefixes with Varying Meanings

PREFIX	MEANING	EXAMPLE
ab-	from, away, off	abhor abnormal abdicate
ad-	to, toward	adhere adjoin
ante-	before, in front of, earlier than	antecedent antediluvian
anti-	opposite of, hostile to	antitoxin antisocial antisemite
be-	make, against, to a great degree	bemoan belittle befuddle
bi-	two, twice	biped bivalve
de-	away, opposite of, reduce	deactivate devalue devitalize
dia-	through, across	diameter diagonal
dis	opposite of, apart, away	dissatisfy disarm disjointed

PREFIX	MEANING	EXAMPLE
en-	cause to be, put in or on	enable engulf
epi-	upon, after	epitaph epilogue epidermis
ex-	out of, former, apart, away	excrete exposition
hyper-	above, beyond, excessive	hyperphysical hypersensitive
hypo-	under, less than normal	hypodermic hypotension
in- il- im- ir-	not, in, into, within	inept indoors
inter-	between, among	interscholastic interstellar
neo-	new, young	neophyte neo-Nazi
per-	through, very	permanent perjury
peri-	around, near, enclosing	perimeter perihelion
post-	after, behind	postlude postorbital
pre-	before, in place, time, rank, order	preview prevail
pro-	before, forward, for, in favor of	production prothorax pro-American
ortho-	straight, corrective	orthotropic orthopedic
re-	again, back	react recoil
sub- sur- sug- sup-	under, beneath, subordinate	subsoil substation
super-	above, over, in addition	superhuman superlative superordinate
syn-	with, together	synthesis synchronize

PREFIX	*MEANING*	*EXAMPLE*
trans-	across, beyond, through	trans-Atlantic transconfiguration transaction
ultra-	beyond in space, excessive	ultraviolet ultramodern
un-	not, the opposite of	unable unbind

Appendix C

List of Resources for Word Histories, Origins, and Derivations

Asimov, Isaac. *Words from History*. Boston: Houghton Mifflin Co., 1968.

_____. *Words from the Myths*. Boston: Houghton Mifflin Co., 1961.

_____. *Words of Science*. Boston: Houghton Mifflin Co., 1959.

_____. *Words on the Map*. Boston: Houghton Mifflin Co., 1962.

Blumberg, Dorothy R. *Whose What?* New York: Holt, Rinehart and Winston, 1973.

Ernst, Margaret S. *Words*. New York: Alfred A. Knopf, Inc., 1950.

_____. *More About Words*. New York: Alfred A. Knopf, Inc., 1951.

_____. *In a Word*. With drawings by James Thurber. Great Neck, New York: Channel Press, 1954.

Evans, Bergen. *Dictionary of Mythology*. Lincoln, Neb.: Centennial Press, 1970.

Ferguson, Charles W. *The Abecedarian Book*. Boston: Little, Brown and Co., 1964.

Funk, Charles E. *A Hog on Ice*. New York: Paperback Library, 1973.

_____. *Thereby Hangs a Tale*. New York: Harper, 1950.

Funk, Wilfred J. *Word Origins and Their Romantic Stories*. New York: Funk and Wagnalls, 1950.

Garrison, Webb B. *Why You Say It*. New York: Abingdon Press, 1955.

Lambert, Eloise. *Our Language, the Story of the Words We Use*. New York: Lothrop, Lee and Shepard Co., 1955.

Mathews, Mitford. *American Words*. New York: World Publishing Co., 1959.

Mathews, M. M. *Words: How to Know Them*. New York: Holt, Rinehart and Winston, Inc., 1956.

Morris, William and Mary Morris. *Dictionary of Word and Phrase Origins*. New York: Harper & Row, vol. 1, 1962; vol. 2, 1967; vol. 3, 1971.

Norman, Barbara. *Tales of the Table*. Englewood Cliffs, N.J.: Prentice-Hall, Inc., 1972.

O'Neill, Mary. *Words, Words, Words*. New York: Doubleday and Co., 1966.

Partridge, Eric. *Name into Word*. London: Secker and Warburg, 1949.

_____. *Origins, a Short Etymological Dictionary of Modern English*. London: Routledge and Kegan Paul, 1958.

Severn, Bill, *People Words*. New York: Ives Washburn, Inc., 1966.

_____. *Place Words*. New York: Ives Washburn, Inc., 1969.

Sorel, Nancy. *Word People*. New York: American Heritage, McGraw-Hill Co., 1970.

Appendix D

Magazines That Print Work by Student Writers

Adapted from Teachers and Writers Collaborative,
October 1984

This compilation is a listing and not an endorsement of magazines which print work by student writers (an asterisk indicates a purely literary magazine):

Action. Scholastic, Inc., 730 Broadway, New York, N.Y. 10003. Publishes student writing based on writing assignments in its previous issues. For students 12–14.

Alive! for Young Teens. Box 179, St. Louis, Mo. 63166. Christian education magazine. Ages 12–16.

*Chart Your Course. P. O. Box 6448, Mobile, La. 36660. Material by gifted, creative, and talented children. Ages 6–18.

Child Life. The Children's Better Health Institute, 1100 Waterway Blvd., Indianapolis, Ind. 46206. Ages 7–9.

Children's Digest. The Children's Better Health Institute, 1100 Waterway Blvd., Indianapolis, Ind. 46206. Ages 8–10.

City Kids. 1545 Wilcox, Los Angeles, Calif. 90028. Ages 11–14.

Cobblestone: The History Magazine for Young People. 20 Grove St., Peterborough, N.H. 03458. Each issue devoted to a particular theme. Ages 8–14.

Cricket. Box 100, LaSalle, Ill. 61301. Note: considers *only* material that complies with current contest rules and descriptions (see each issue for current contest rules). Ages 5–13.

District: Young Writers Journal. 2500 Wisconsin Ave., N.W., #549, Washington, D.C. 20007. For District of Columbia students and residents only. Ages 9–14. Currently in planning stages. Write for information.

Ebony Jr.! 820 S. Michigan Ave., Chicago, Ill. 60605. Specializes in material about Blacks. Ages 6–12.

English Journal. National Council of Teachers of English, 1111 Kenyon Rd., Urbana, Ill. 61801. Poetry, no fiction. Ages 12–17.

*Hanging Loose. 231 Wyckoff St., Brooklyn, N.Y. 11217. Since 1968 has included a special section of student poetry and fiction. Ages 14–18.

Just About Me. Ensio Industries, 247 Marlee Ave., Suite 206, Toronto, Ont., Canada M6B 4B8. For girls. Ages 12–19.

Paw Prints. National Zoo, Washington, D.C. 20008. Specializes in wild exotic animal conservation and other animal-related material. Ages 6–14.

Purple Cow. Suite 315, Lates Center, 110 E. Andrews Dr., N.W., Atlanta, Ga. 30305. Prefers nonfiction. Ages 12–18.

Scholastic Scope. 730 Broadway, New York, N.Y. 10003. Uses student manuscripts in the "Mini Mystery" and "Student Writing" pages. Ages 15–18.

Science World. Scholastic Inc., 730 Broadway, New York, N.Y. 10003. Uses material on life science, earth science, health, biology, etc. Ages 12–16.

Seventeen. 850 Third Avenue, New York, N.Y. 10022. Ages 13–21.

Sprint. Scholastic, Inc., 730 Broadway, New York, N.Y. 10003. Publishes student writing based on assignments in its previous issues. For students aged 9–11.

*Stone Soup. P.O. Box 83, Santa Cruz, Calif. 95063. Ages 6–12.

The Sunshine News. Canada Sunshine Publishing, Ltd., 465 King St., East, #14A, Toronto, Ont., Canada M5A 1L6. Ages 14–17.

Teenage Magazine. 217 Jackson St., P.O. Box 948, Lowell, Mass. 01853. Formerly *Highwire.* Ages 14–19.

Voice. Scholastic, Inc., 730 Broadway, New York, N.Y. 10003. Ages 12–18.

Wee Wisdom. Unity Village, Mo. 64065. Ages 6–13.

Appendix E

Sample Instructional Units

Our Solar System

Teacher: Elaine Sargent
Subject: Astronomy
Grade: Fifth

This instructional unit is designed for fifth graders with varying reading levels and scientific abilities. Its goal is to help students understand man's efforts to explain the universe through creative and scientific endeavors. Students therefore explore some very basic concepts about the solar system through materials and activities that focus on intellectual, creative, and physical experiences. Grouping arrangements vary from whole class to small groups based on interest and/or ability to "study buddies" to individual study. During this six- to eight-week unit, students will be expected to take some responsibility for planning, monitoring, and evaluating their learning. They will be expected to keep contracts for projects of their own choice or design and to confer with the teacher at regular intervals.

Major Concepts

1. The science of astronomy has a long history, including early man's various beliefs about the universe.
2. The sun, like all stars, is made up of hot gases that give off light and heat.
3. The sun is the center of our solar system, with the planets revolving in predictable orbits. The order of the planets from the sun outward is Mercury, Venus, Earth, Mars, Jupiter, Saturn, Uranus, Neptune, and Pluto.

4. The planets have both similarities and differences.

5. A satellite is a man-made or natural object that revolves around a planet.

6. The phases of the moon occur as the moon revolves around and reflects the sun's light.

7. There are two kinds of eclipses — solar and lunar.

8. Other members of our solar system include asteroids, meteoroids, and comets.

9. Scientists use different types of evidence to develop a theory.

10. Man has used his knowledge of space to create literature, art, and music.

Materials and Readings

Fiction

(All books in this section are listed under Concept 10.)

1. Beatty, Jerome, Jr. *Matthew Looney and the Space Pirates*. Glenview, Ill.: Young Scott, 1972.
2. Campbell, John W. *The Best of John W. Campbell*. Edited by Lester DelRay. Westminster, Md.: Ballentine, 1976.
3. Earnshaw, Brian. *Dragonfall 5 and the Empty Planet*. West Caldwell, N.J.: Lothrop, 1976.
4. _____ . *Dragonfall 5 and the Space Cowboys*. West Caldwell, N.J.: Lothrop, 1975.
5. Key, Alexander. *The Forgotten Door*. Philadelphia: Westminster, 1965.
* 6. L'Engle, Madeline. *A Wrinkle in Time*. New York: Farrar Straus, 1962.
7. MacGregor, Ellen. *Miss Pickerell and the Weather Satellite*. New York: McGraw-Hill, 1971.
8. _____ . *Miss Pickerell Goes to Mars*. New York: McGraw-Hill, 1951.
9. Morressy, John. *The Humans of Ziax II*. New York: Walker and Co., 1974.
10. Philipe, Anne. *Atom, the Little Moon Monkey*. New York: Quist, 1970.
11. Slobodkin, Louis. *The Space Ship in the Park*. New York: Macmillan, 1952.
12. _____ . *The Space Ship Returns to the Apple Tree*. New York: Macmillan, 1972.
13. _____ . *The Space Ship under the Apple Tree*. New York: Macmillan, 1972.

*To be read by teacher to class.

Nonfiction

*Concepts**

1. Adler, Irving. *The Sun and Its Family*. New York: 1 2 3 4   6 7
   John Day Co., 1969.
2. Asimov, Isaac. *The Moon*. Chicago: Follet, 1966.   5 6 7
3. Branley, Franklyn M. *A Book of the Milky Way* 1 2 3   9
   Galaxy for You. New York: Thomas Y. Crowell,
   1965.
4. _____ . *The Nine Planets*. New York: Thomas Y. 1 2 3 4   7
   Crowell, 1972.
5. _____ . *What Makes Day and Night?* New York:
   Thomas Y. Crowell, 1961.
6. Carlisle, Norman. *Satellites: Servants of Man.*   4 5 6
   Philadelphia: Lippincott, 1971.
7. Crosby, Phoebe. *Junior Science Book of Stars.* 1 2   4   6   9
   Champaign, Ill.: Garrard, 1960.
8. Fenton, Carroll Lane. *The Moon for Young Ex-*
   plorers. New York: John Day Co., 1963.
9. Fenton, Carroll Lane, and Mildred Adams Fen-   2 3 4 5 6 7 8
   ton. *Worlds in the Sky*. New York: John Day Co.,
   1963.
10. Feravolo, Rocco. *Wonders Beyond the Solar Sys-* 1 2 3 4   8 9
    tem. New York: Dodd, Mead and Co., 1968.
11. Freeman, Mae, and Ira Freeman. *Fun with As-*   2 3 4 5 6 7 8
    tronomy: Easy Projects for Young Scientists. New
    York: Random House, 1953
12. Gallant, Roy A. *Exploring the Moon*. New York: 1   5 6 7
    Doubleday, 1966.
13. Jobb, Jamie. *The Night Sky—An Everyday Guide* 1 2 3 4 5 6 7 8 9
    to Every Night. Boston: Little, Brown and Co.,
    1977.
14. Knight, David C. *Let's Find Out About Earth.* 1 2 3   5
    New York: Franklin Watts, 1968.
15. Lum, Peter. *The Stars in Our Heaven: Myths and* 1 2 3 4   9
    Fables. New York: Pantheon Books, 1961.
16. Lyon, Jene. *Astronomy: Our Sun and Its Neigh-* 1 2 3 4 5 6 7 8 9
    bors. Racine, Wis.: Western Publishing Co.,
    1974.
17. Munch, Theodore W., and B. Teidemann. *What*   2 3 4
    Is a Solar System? New York: Benefic Press,
    1961.

*These numbers refer to the concepts on pp. 441–442.

Concepts

18. Polgreen, John, and Cathleen Polgreen. *The Earth in Space*. New York: Random House, 1963.   2 3 4 5

19. Nussbaum, Hedda (ed.). *Charlie Brown's Second Super Book of Questions and Answers about the Earth and Space*. New York: Random House, 1977.   1 2 3 4 5 6 7 8 9

20. Rey, H. A. *Find the Constellations*. Boston: Houghton Mifflin, 1966.   2 4

21. *Stars and Planets—A Golden Stamp Book*, Racine, Wis.: Western Publishing Co., 1973.   1 2 3 4 5 6 7 8 9

22. Zim, Herbert S. *Comets*. New York: William Morrow and Co., 1957.   1 8 9

23. _____ . *The Sun*. New York: William Morrow and Co., 1975.   1 2 7 9

24. _____ . *The Universe*. New York: William Morrow and Co., 1961.   1 2 3 8 9

Textbooks

1. Gallant, Roy A., and Isaac Asimov. *Ginn Science Program: Intermediate Level A*. Lexington, Mass.: Ginn and Co., 1975, pp. 105–142.   1 2 3 6 9

2. Jacobson, Willard. *Thinking Ahead in Science Series: Learning in Science*. New York: American Book Co., 1965, pp. 98–128.   5 6

*3. MacCraken, Helen D., et al. *Science Through Discovery*. Singer Science Series, New York: Random House, 1968, pp. 125–159.   1 2 3 4 5 6 7 8 9

4. Navarra, John, and Joseph Zafforoni. *Today's Basic Science*. New York: Harper & Row, 1967, pp. 88–125.   1 2 3 4 5 6 8 9

5. Rockcastle, Verna N., et al. *Elementary School Science*. Menlo Park, Cal.: Addison-Wesley Publishing Co., 1972, pp. 186–209.   2

Audio-Visual Materials

Concepts

1. *Earth, Venus, and Mercury*. Jim Handy series, 1971. Filmstrip, intermediate, color.   2 3 4

*This is the major text. The others are to be used for advanced or slower study groups, and/or research on individualized projects.

*Concepts**

2. *Eclipse of the Moon*. Film Association of California. Film loop, color.		7
3. *Eclipse of the Sun*. Film Association of California. Film loop, color.		7
4. *Mars*. Jim Handy series, 1971. Filmstrip, intermediate, color.	3 4	
5. *Night and Day*. Encyclopaedia Britannica Films, 1955. Filmstrip, intermediate, color.	2	
6. *Outer Planets*. Jim Handy series, 1971. Filmstrip, intermediate, color.	3 4	
7. *The Earth and Its Moon*. Flannel Board Kit, intermediate.	5 6 7	
8. *The Planets: Family of the Sun*. Included in *The Universe*, National Geographic Society, 1972. Filmstrip, cassette, and teacher's guide; advanced; color.	2 3 4	8 9
9. *What a Scientist Sees Through the Telescope*. Educational Reading Service, 1968. Filmstrip, intermediate, color.	1	9

Instructional Activities

Activities	Materials Used†	Concepts
*1. Unit planning with students.	tm	1 2 3 4 5 6 7 8 9 10
*2. Contracts for individual projects.	tm	1 2 3 4 5 6 7 8 9 10
*3. Preassessment survey.	tm	1 2 3 4 5 6 7 8 9
*4. Cloze test and small group discussion.	tm	1 2 3
*5. Structured overview through class discussion.	tm	1 2 3 4 5 6 7 8 9 10
6. Find out about man's early beliefs about the universe. Write a report, make a diorama, give a play, plan a bulletin board.	nf15, nf7, t1, t4	1

*required.
†tm = teacher-made, nf = nonfiction, t = textbook, f = fiction.

Activities	Materials Used†	Concepts					
7. Look up information on instruments used by early astronomers. Illustrate and tell about the sextant, sundial, celestial sphere, dividers.	t1	1					
*8. Read pp. 125–126, directed lesson.	t3	1	2	3			
9. Discover about telescopes. Read pp. 93–100.	t4	1					9
10. Experiment with magnifying glass.	t4, nf10, nf11	1					9
*11. Use a telescope (community resource).	t4, 5, nf13, 20		2				
12. Make and label models of telescopes.	t4, nf3, 11	1					9
13. Construct a time line for early discoveries in astronomy.	t1, 4, av9, tm	1					
*14. Read and watch *What a Scientist Sees Through His Telescope* reading guide.	tm, av9	1					9
15. How did these men contribute to today's understanding of the universe? Individualized project.	t1	1					9
*16. Read pp. 127–128, directed reading.	t3		2				
17. Activity: making a sun calendar.	t1, nf11	1	2				
*18. Read and do three-level reading guide on *Junior Science Book of Stars*.	nf7, tm	1	2		4	6	
19. Project: make a sun camera	nf11		2				9
20. Experiment: air bends sunlight	nf11, t5		2				9
*21. Make a model of the sun. Label it. Be able to explain it.	nf23, 3, 9, 16, 21		2	3			
22. Vocabulary: sun word hunt.	tm		2				

Activities	Materials Used†	Concepts			
*23. Read pp. 128–129, directed reading.	t3		2		
24. Structured overview for #25.	tm		2		9
25. Read pp. 186–207 in small group.	t5		2		9
26. Simulate the twinkling of stars.	t5, nf3, 10		2		
27. Make dioramas of the constellations.	t5, nf20, t3, nf13	1	2		10
28. Use a constellation map.	map, nf13, 20		2		9
29. Experiment with light.	t5		2		9
*30. Draw and label one (minimum) constellation for the bulletin board.	t3, 4, 5, map, nf13, 19, 20		2		
*31. Join in listening while teacher reads aloud *A Wrinkle in Time*.	f6				10
*32. Read pp. 129–132, directed reading.	t3			3 4	
33. Experiment: direct light/ reflected light.	t5, 3		2		
*34. Demonstration: orbits of planets.	t3			3	
35. View filmstrip *Day and Night*.	av5		2		
*36. Read pp. 135–136, directed reading.	t3			3 4	
*37. Demonstration: Earth's rotation and revolution.					
38. Haiku: sun, stars, day, night.	tm, nf3, 9, 10, 15	1		3	10
*39. Read pp. 136–139.	t3			3 4	
*40. Learning center: a visit to the planets.	tm			3 4	9 10
41. View filmstrips on particular planet and/or *The Planets*.	av1, 4, 6, 8	1		3 4	
*42. Give an oral report on a planet of your choice.	av1, 4, 6, 8, t4, nf1, 4, 9, 11, 13, 15, 16, 17, 18, 19, 21, 24	1		3 4	9

Activities	Materials Used[†]	Concepts		
*43. Using diagrams and tables, three-level guide.	tm	3 4		
*44. Read pp. 98–126, cassette available.	t2		5	9
*45. Word puzzle: satellites.	t11		5	
*46. Satellites: True or False?	t10		5	
47. Experiment on gravity.	t2, nf11		5	9
48. Make models of satellites: Tiros, Telestar, Pioneer, etc.	nf6		5	9
49. Experiment: paths of falling object.	t2		5	9
50. Experiment: weightlessness.	t2, nf2, 19		5	9
51. Experiment: friction.	t2		5	9
*52. Read pp. 141–142, directed reading.	t3		5 6	
53. Picture study/three-level guide.	tm		5 6	
54. Read pp. 13–17 and write about your walk on the moon. Try to make it as authentic as possible. Tape your story.	nf11, 8, 12, 2, 19, 18, 16, 21		5 6	9 10
55. Learn some legends and folklore about the moon.	nf15, t4			10
56. Find out about moon exploration	nf2, 12, 16, 19, 21			9
57. Crossword puzzle: the moon.	tm		5 6 7	
58. Observe the moon. Look for seas and craters, different quarters, etc.	nf2, 12, 13, 16, field glasses		6	9
59. Record the times of moonrise.	newspaper nf2		6	
60. Draw a moon map. Locate places the U.S. has explored.	nf12, t4	1		9
*61. Listen to *Clair de Lune*. How did Debussy feel about the moon? Do you	recording of "Claire de Lune"	1		9 10

Activities	Materials Used[†]	Concepts
think moon explorations have changed the way people visualize the moon?		
*62. DRTA: phases of the moon.	tm, nf2	6
63. Read pp. 143–144.	t3	6
64. Read pp. 101–104.	t4	6
*65. Demonstration: phases of the moon.	t4	6 9
66. Use the flannel board to show the phases of the moon.	av7	6
*67. Read pp. 145–146, directed lesson.	t3	7
68. Watch film loop of lunar eclipse.	av2	7
*69. Make a model of a lunar eclipse and label. Write a brief explanation.	may use av7, nf2, 19, 11, 21, 15	7
*70. Read pp. 146–147, directed lesson.	t3	7
71. Watch film loop of solar eclipse.	av3	7
*72. Make a model of a solar eclipse and label. Write a brief explanation.	nf23, 19, 11, 21	7
*73. Read pp. 148–150, directed lesson.	t3	1 8 9
*74. Categories worksheet: comets, meteoroids, and asteroids.	tm	1 8 9
*75. Comets: cause and effect.	tm	1 8 9
*76. Read at least two science fiction works.	fl, 2, 3, 4, 5, 7, 8, 9, 10, 11, 12, 13	10
*77. Post-survey (can use as study device for test).	tm	1 2 3 4 5 6 7 8 9 10
*78. Final evaluation	tm	1 2 3 4 5 6 7 8 9 10

Activity 3*

SURVEY—BEFORE AND AFTER UNIT

This is not a test! Some of the information here may be totally new for you. However, you may know much more than you think! Place a *T* for true or an *F* for false in front of each statement. If you have no idea what the answer is put a *?* in front of the statement.

___ 1. Astronomy is the scientific study of the universe beyond Earth.

___ 2. The science is brand new. It was just developed during the last 50 years.

___ 3. Revolve means to orbit around a central point or spot.

___ 4. The sun is a planet.

___ 5. Stars are made up of hot gases and give off light and heat.

___ 6. The earth is at the center of the solar system.

___ 7. The solar system is a group of planets that revolve around the sun.

___ 8. There are seven planets in our solar system.

(continued at the top of the next page)

Activity 5

STRUCTURED OVERVIEW OF OUR SOLAR SYSTEM:

Part A

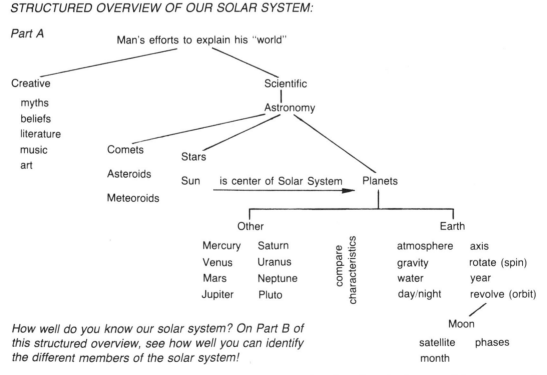

How well do you know our solar system? On Part B of this structured overview, see how well you can identify the different members of the solar system!

(continued on the bottom of the next page)

*The following are sample activities and therefore not necessarily numbered consecutively.

___ 9. All the planets are very much alike.

___ 10. A satellite is something that revolves around a planet.

___ 11. All satellites are made by man.

___ 12. The moon does not reflect the sun's light.

___ 13. Earth is the only planet that has a moon.

___ 14. The moon goes through eight phases each year.

___ 15. The spinning of the earth causes day and night.

___ 16. The earth takes one year to travel around the sun.

___ 17. When the earth casts a shadow on the moon, we call this a comet.

___ 18. A meteor is a piece of metal or stone traveling through space.

___ 19. Scientists use facts that they know are true to try to explain things, to make "educated guesses," about things we do not really know for sure.

___ 20. Everything you read about space and the universe is true.

When everyone has finished, we will discuss the statements and our answers.

Activity 5

Part B

Identify the members of the solar system and write their names correctly on the lines.

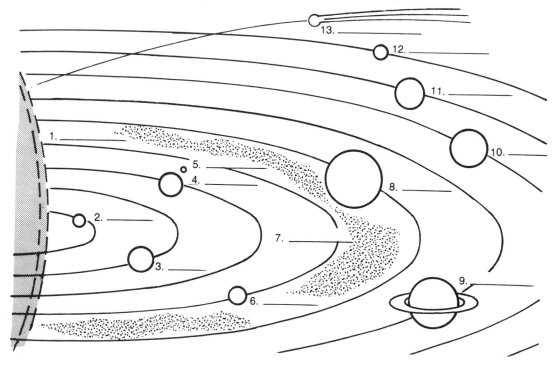

Activity 13

EARLY DISCOVERIES IN ASTRONOMY

Directions: To help you understand the development of astronomy as a science, list the order that the following events occurred. For extra credit, you may include the year the event happened. Check your answers in *Today's Basic Science* or the *Ginn Science Program* book.

_____ The Egyptians made a sun calendar.

_____ Nicholas Copernicus was a Polish astronomer. He introduced the theory that the sun was the center of the universe.

_____ When Galileo improved and perfected the telescope, a new era in astronomy began.

_____ Ancient people had only their eyes with which to study the stars. They had many beliefs about the heavens, but no real evidence for their beliefs.

_____ Tycho Brahe was an astronomer who lived in Denmark. He made the most accurate measurements of the changing positions of the moon and planets known to the world at that time.

_____ The Sumerians used mathematics in their study of the sky. They made accurate records of the changing positions of the stars, sun, and planets. This helped astronomy become a science.

_____ Johannes Kepler was a German mathematician and astronomer. He used Tycho Brahe's careful records to figure the first scale model of the solar system.

_____ As more powerful telescopes were developed, discovery after discovery was made, right up to the present day!

_____ Claudius Ptolemy was a Greek astronomer who lived in Alexandria, Egypt. He believed that the earth was the center of the whole universe. The sun, moon, and planets moved around the earth.

Activity 14

THREE-LEVEL STUDY GUIDE

What a Scientist Sees Through His Telescope
  I. Answer all three questions.
    1. Name three famous inventors of the telescope. _____
    _____
    2. List three things Galileo saw through his telescope. _____
    _____
    3. Who first used lenses to make a telescope? _____
  II. Check the statements that are true.
    _____ 1. Galileo's use of the telescope was for peaceful purposes.
    _____ 2. Most of what we know about space today would have been known even if the telescope had not been invented.
    _____ 3. Lippenshiem was trying to invent a telescope.
    _____ 4. Marco Polo's discovery of glass lenses used by the Chinese was important for the invention of the telescope.

III. Check the statements that tell what *What a Scientist Sees Through His Telescope* is about.

_____ 1. A new scientific discovery is often dependent on another earlier discovery.

_____ 2. Men can use their knowledge to learn more about their world.

_____ 3. Galileo started a new era in astronomy.

_____ 4. Astronomy has a long history.

Activity 38

HAIKU

Sun, Stars, Day, Night

Writing a poem is a fun way to express and share not only what you have learned, but also what you thought and felt about those things. An easy and interesting way to write a poem is to use the Japanese haiku (said "hi koo"). The purpose of haiku is to present a single thought or observation about nature. Try writing a haiku about the sun, stars, day, and/or night. Choose just one for starters. Then you may want to try others. Haiku must follow a special pattern:

Line One = 5 syllables
Line Two = 7 syllables
Line Three = 5 syllables

That's it!

Brainstorm with two or three friends to make a list of words and ideas for a topic you have chosen. Then use these words and phrases to write your own haiku. Share your haiku with the teacher or a friend. Ask for help if you get stuck. After sharing with the teacher, you may want to paint a watercolor to go with you poem. Also, you may want to display it on the bulletin board.

Activity 45

WORD PUZZLE

Directions: Answer the clues by filling in the appropriate spaces. When you have filled in all the blanks, the circled letters will spell the mystery word.

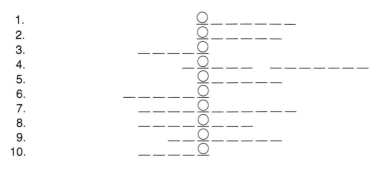

(*continued*)

1. Radio and television _____ are sent great distances around the earth by satellites.
2. The point in an orbit that is farthest from Earth.
3. Paths in which satellites travel around larger objects.
4. Name for things fired to push a satellite in the opposite direction and slow it down.
5. To push, especially a rocket.
6. To go from one place to another.
7. A force that tends to pull all things together.
8. When a moving object rubs against something and causes it to slow down and/or get hot.
9. Speed.
10. Natural satellites are sometimes called _____ .

Activity 46

SATELLITES

Directions: Determine whether the following statements are true or false. Mark *T* or *F* accordingly in the margins.

_____ 1. Gravity holds satellites in their orbits.

_____ 2. Moons are natural satellites.

_____ 3. You can see earth satellites in the daytime.

_____ 4. All orbits of satellites are shaped like perfect circles.

_____ 5. Satellites orbit at different speeds at different times.

_____ 6. A satellite moves at a slower speed as it moves toward the earth.

_____ 7. Three-stage rockets are used to put satellites into orbit.

_____ 8. Rockets give satellites a push straight up into space.

_____ 9. Satellites must travel at a speed of approximately 18,000 miles per hour to stay in orbit.

_____ 10. A satellite stays in orbit for only a few days, or a month at the longest.

Now, look over the statements you marked false. Use the space below to rewrite them to make them true. You may check your work by referring back to the book.

_____

_____

_____

_____

_____

_____

_____

_____

Activity 74

COMETS, OR METEOROIDS, OR ASTEROIDS?

Directions: Examine the following phrases and decide whether they describe comets, meteoroids, or asteroids. Write which object the phrase describes in the margin blank. Think carefully, especially in marking one item that seems to apply to all three!

_____ 1. It is a piece of metal or stone.

_____ 2. A famous one was named after an English astronomer, Edmund Halley.

_____ 3. Earth's atmosphere protects it from being hit constantly by them.

_____ 4. They are located between Mars and Jupiter.

_____ 5. They usually fall to Earth as fine dust.

_____ 6. Some are the size of tiny pebbles.

_____ 7. Their orbits are egg-shaped.

_____ 8. The first one was discovered in 1801.

_____ 9. The largest one is named Ceres.

_____ 10. They revolve around the sun.

_____ 11. They look like a star with streaming tails.

_____ 12. They are seen more in August and November.

_____ 13. Most have diameters of less than fifty miles.

_____ 14. They are sometimes called "shooting stars."

_____ 15. No one completely understands what they are made of.

_____ 16. Friction causes their surfaces to get hot, melt, and turn into glowing gases.

_____ 17. They are so far away that they can't be seen with a telescope.

_____ 18. They are considered minor planets.

_____ 19. People used to fear them.

_____ 20. They are pulled toward the earth when they come close.

Activity 75

COMETS

Cause and Effect
Match the effects in Part II with the causes listed in Part I.

Part I: Cause	Part II: Effect
___ a. In 1910, Halley's comet came very close to Earth so that	1. the comet's glowing tail is formed.
___ b. Most comets are so far away	2. ices in the head of the comet turn into gases.
___ c. When a comet moves toward the sun	3. now people are not afraid of comets.
___ d. By making observations and using early scientific records	4. astronomers were able to learn a great deal about comets.

(*continued*)

___ e. People thought if a comet came too close it would explode and destroy Earth;

5. People were afraid of comets.

___ f. The earth has passed through the tail of a comet and was not harmed;

6. they cannot be seen, even with the aid of a telescope.

___ g. The gases move away from the head of the comet

7. Edmund Halley correctly predicted the return of a comet.

Survival

Teacher: Sheila Peckham
Subject: Literature
Grade: Eleven

This literature unit combines an in-depth class study of a modern American novel, *One Flew Over the Cuckoo's Nest*, with team study of novels whose themes are similar to that of *One Flew Over the Cuckoo's Nest*, and individual inquiry of themes, topics, or issues evolving from class and team study. The lessons move from teacher-centered presentations in the class study to student-centered small group interactions, to individual research projects. Because of the nature of this unit, the teacher uses a content outline to organize learning experiences rather than a system of cross-tabulating concepts, activities, and materials.

Content Outline

   I. Major Topics of Study
   A. Conflict
      1. man vs. man
      2. man vs. society
      3. man vs. nature
      4. man vs. self
   B. Themes
      1. emasculation
      2. alienation
      3. control
      4. dehumanization
      5. civil disobedience
      6. the Christ figure
   C. Literary Devices
      1. imagery
      2. foreshadowing
      3. motifs
      4. metaphor

II. Reading Materials
   A. Class study: Ken Kesey's *One Flew Over the Cuckoo's Nest*
   B. Group study
      1. Glendon Swarthout's *Bless the Beasts and the Children*
      2. Conrad Richtner's *The Light in the Forest*
      3. James Dickey's *Deliverance*
      4. James Dickey's *First Blood*
III. Instructional Activities
   A. Teacher-prepared adjunct materials for *One Flew Over the Cuckoo's Nest*
      1. structured overview for unit
      2. assessment of students' existing knowledge and attitudes
      3. prereading guide: the uses of metaphor
      4. vocabulary awareness activity: acutes vs. chronics
      5. anticipation guide: mental institutions
      6. reading guide on imagery
      7. interpretive/applied guide
      8. vocabulary awareness: bedlam, berserk, pandemonium, eccentric
      9. vocabulary building: matriarchy, emasculation
      10. prereading guide: masculinity vs. femininity
      11. array depicting conflict between McMurphy and Big Nurse
      12. three-level reading guide
      13. vocabulary building: alienation, technocracy, foreshadow, micro-cosm
      14. pattern guide: cause and effect
      15. prereading guide: the Savior theme
      16. postreading guide: the Savior theme
      17. review of major themes
      18. assessment of students' understandings
   B. Team study of four novels: general reading guide
   C. Individual projects

SURVIVAL UNIT SCHEDULE

One Flew Over the Cuckoo's Nest

	M	T	W	Th	F
Week 1	Informal preassessment	Prereading activity on metaphor and imagery	Vocabulary Prediction activity for first assignment Assign 1–41 Read aloud	Postreading discussion of prediction activity Guide on imagery and literal statements Vocabulary	Level guide Discussion

Week 2	Prereading vocabulary Prereading guide on emasculation motif Assign 42–91	Postreading activity on emasculation motif: discussion of responses generated from students' lists	Continued discussion Assign 91–115	Postreading array activity: Conflict Make bulletin board (array)	Prereading vocabulary Assign 116–144
Week 3	Rearrange array on bulletin board Three-level guides	Discussion Prereading vocabulary Assign 145–173	Postreading activity: cause/effect guide	Discussion Prereading activity on Christ imagery Assign 174–218	Postreading activity: Christ motif guide
Week 4	Discussion continued using responses from Christ motif guide Assign rest of the novel	Discussion: pull together major themes previously presented	Review activity: poem	Postreading assessment	(composition)

Team Study of Four Novels

	M	T	W	Th	F
Week 5	Introduction of four novels and of team strategy and format Give class schedules Choose books Distribute guides	Reading period	Discussion I Group A Group B (teacher works with each group ½ period)	Discussion I Group C Group D	Reading period
Week 6	Discussion II Group A Group B	Discussion II Group C Group D	Reading period	Discussion III Group A Group B	Discussion III Group C Group D

Week 7

| Feedback session on each group's novel: Group A Group B | Feedback session Group C Group D | Tie together loose ends: synthesis of all five novels | Introduce individual inquiry projects | ⟶ |

STRUCTURED OVERVIEW OF UNIT

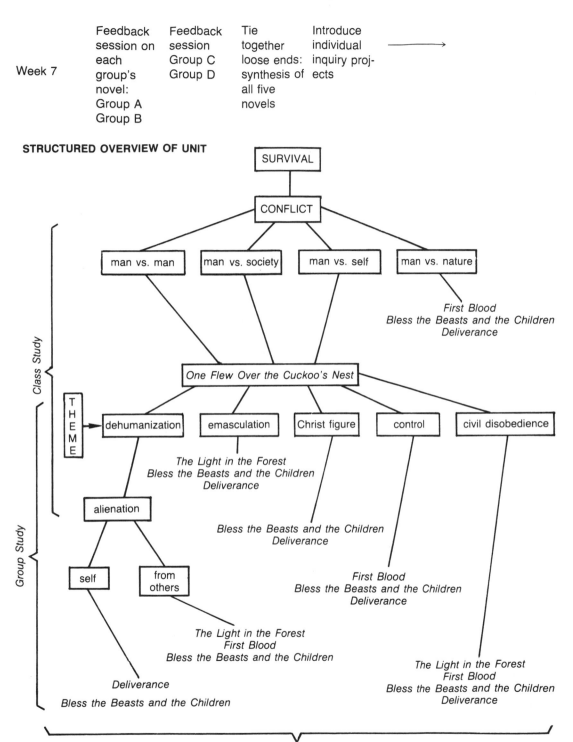

Activity 2

PREASSESSMENT

Purpose: This guide is designed to function as an informal inventory of students' present understandings of some of the major ideas, concepts, and themes they will encounter throughout the literature unit. Through small-group and whole-class discussions and reactions, the teacher can informally assess the degree to which these ideas have been thought out by the students.

A. Individual
Directions: Read each of the following statements. Place a check on the numbered line next to those statements you would be willing to defend. Try to think of specific examples you would use to defend those statements you agree with or to refute those statements you disagree with. This is not a quiz or a test. These statements are some of the ideas we will be discussing in the next few weeks.

_____ 1. There is no insanity; only behavior the majority won't tolerate.
_____ 2. A world with risks and choices and pain is worth more than a world of protection and safety.
_____ 3. A person can be alienated from himself.
_____ 4. It is never right to break a law.
_____ 5. It is society that decides who's sane and who isn't.
_____ 6. Power is the sum total of the strength of those dominated.
_____ 7. Modern technocracy softens men.
_____ 8. The majority is usually right.
_____ 9. Most men are sheep.
_____ 10. Every man is responsible for whatever happens to him.
_____ 11. Man creates his own gods and demons to suit his needs.
_____ 12. Violence is an acceptable strategy for change.
_____ 13. Most people dislike what is different.
_____ 14. The difference between right and wrong is largely a matter of point of view.
_____ 15. Few people are really capable of independence; most people seek a leader to follow.

B. Small group
Directions: In your small group, discuss those statements with which you disagree. Try to use concrete examples to convince others of your conclusions.

Activity 3

PREREADING GUIDE

Purpose: This activity is designed to lead students, through the use of metaphor, to understand that reality often exists on other levels than the plane of objective or literal occurrence. This prereading "organizer" is necessary to help students recognize the significance of the recurring mechanical images and motifs essential to their understanding of the first reading assignment in *One Flew Over the Cuckoo's Nest*, as well as of the entire novel.

Procedure: Put the following statements on the board.

Our school is a factory.
It is run by robots.
The student is the product being produced.
The student is being manufactured to fit into a bigger machine.

Divide the class into small groups. Instruct each group to list examples of the daily routine that support or refute the given statements.

Examples:
Everyone is regulated by bells.
Teachers sometimes have no sympathy.
Everyone is expected to do the same things well.

Resume a large group and list the examples the students give. During discussion of their metaphors, introduce Chief Brooms' statement:

"It's the truth even if it didn't happen." (p. 13)

Have students react to the statement. Students can use the previous discussion or give other examples to evaluate the credibility of Broom's statement.

Activity 5

ANTICIPATION GUIDE

Purpose: Motivation

Procedure: Introduce the novel *One Flew Over the Cuckoo's Nest* by telling the students it is about a mental institution. Then distribute the following anticipation guide:

Directions: Read the following statements and place a check next to those you believe you'll find to be true in the novel.

_____ 1. Mental hospitals have eliminated all old-fashioned cruelty.

_____ 2. The intention of the therapy is to allow the patients to remain as much a part of their own democratic, free neighborhood as possible.

_____ 3. The inmates are no crazier than anyone on the street.

_____ 4. It is society that decides who is sane and who is not.

_____ 5. The staff is just as interested in the patients' cures as the patients are.

_____ 6. A healthy, sane individual is one who can stand up for his or her own beliefs and rights.

   After a class comparison of prediction statements, assign pages 1–41.

Postreading activity: Reexamine the prediction statements in small groups. Students should be instructed to reevaluate the statements in light of the first reading assignment, and to extract specific examples from the reading to back up their opinions on the statements.

Activity 7

INTERPRETIVE/APPLIED-LEVEL GUIDE

Directions, Part A: McMurphy tells Harding, "Nurse Ratchet is trying to make you weak so she can get you to toe the line, and to follow her rules, to live like she wants you to. And the best way she does this, to get you to knuckle under is to weaken you be gettin' you where it hurts worst . . . to sap every bit of strength you got." (57)

Harding tells McMurphy, "Miss Ratchet is a sweet, smiling angel of mercy . . . unselfish as the wind, toiling thanklessly for the good of all . . . and desires our cures as much as we do." (56–58)

Below are some ward procedures and events. Put an *Mc* next to those descriptors which support McMurphy's theory. Put an *H* next to those which support Harding's theory. Use the page numbers given to refer to these procedures and events in context. Work through these together in your group.

_____ 1. the cooperative trophies awarded to the floor (22)

_____ 2. the use of the log book (19)

_____ 3. the therapeutic group session (43)

_____ 4. the orderly time schedule (32–34)

_____ 5. Miss Ratchet's screening procedure for hiring aides (44)

_____ 6. keeping the chronics and acutes separate (36)

_____ 7. Miss Ratchet's charitable deeds on the outside (38)

_____ 8. the staff's gentle coaxing behavior toward the patients (35)

_____ 9. Maxwell Taber's therapeutic treatment (40)

_____ 10. ward rules (28)

_____ 11. Chief Broom's therapeutic treatment (40)

Directions, Part B: Read each of the following statements aloud in your group. Decide whether each can be supported with information from the novel. Consider your discussion of the events in Part A. Put the numbers of those events from Part A which support the statements in Part B in the proper blanks.

_____ 1. The patients are proud of their record for cooperation.

_____ 2. The nurse maintains control by the dictum "divide and conquer."

_____ 3. By confiding their fears to fellow inmates, the patients will gain strength.

_____ 4. The Combine is a conspiracy to regiment the patients' lives, to control them through a hypnotic routine.

_____ 5. The log book is a means to destroy any individuality.

_____ 6. The men serve the "machine," not the reverse.

_____ 7. Nurse Ratchet's biggest fear is that a new admission will destroy her power.

_____ 8. Nurse Ratchet uses fear and hatred to maintain control.

_____ 9. Nurse Ratchet instills feelings of guilt.

_____ 10. Miss Ratchet's charitable deeds destroy the self-esteem of the receiver.

Directions, Part C: Read each of the following statements aloud. Check each statement that you find reasonable and can support by combining ideas contained in the reading selection with your own related ideas and experiences. Be ready to present evidence from both sources to support your decisions.

_____ 1. To the establishment, cooperation with authority is of highest value.

_____ 2. Self-control is a measure of sanity.

_____ 3. The world belongs to the strong. One must accept this as a law of the natural world.

_____ 4. The strong get stronger by making the weak weaker.

_____ 5. It is often painful to admit the truth. It is easier to believe what you want to believe.

Activity 11

ARRAY DEPICTING CONFLICT BETWEEN MCMURPHY AND BIG NURSE

Purpose: At this point the major conflict of the novel has surfaced. Through a visual display of the conflict between Big Nurse and McMurphy and the ideas each character represents, students should be able to see the general movements of the plot as well as the forces at conflict throughout the novel. When students finish constructing the array, it can be posted on a bulletin board and modified throughout the unit.

Directions: Examine the packet of cards in your small groups. Arrange and rearrange the cards into what you agree is a logical display of the story thus far.

conflict	emasculation
McMurphy	laissez-faire
individuality	order and regimentation
conformity	the pioneer
authority	confession
Big Nurse	Chief Broom
Combine	Cheswick
group over individual	Harding
masculinity	Billy Bibbit
femininity	

Students should work in small groups as they develop reasonable descriptions of the relationships between the above elements.

In the large group, compare and discuss arrays. The class should agree upon an array to display on the bulletin board. Throughout the rest of the unit, cards can be arranged according to the plot development, and new cards can be added.

An example of a possible starting array is shown on the next page.

This activity should help students see how ideas as well as people are at conflict.

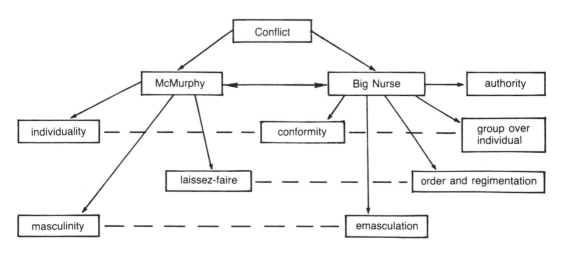

As students add the names of some of the other major characters to the array, interesting debates may develop in that some of the characters may clearly side with McMurphy but remain under the authority of Big Nurse. Their loyalties will fluctuate throughout the novel. Other students may want to arrange characters' names according to some concepts other than *loyalty* to the two major characters. For example, Harding could be included under *emasculation*, and Chief Broom with *order* and *regimentation*.

From this point on, a major portion of the novel is fueled by a series of small-scale battles between Nurse and McMurphy. Cards should be constructed representing each conflict. Students, through debate, are to decide who was the victor over each issue and place cards appropriately. This should lend itself to much debate because in many cases it may appear that one character is winning the battle, but losing the war.

Activity 13

VOCABULARY BUILDING

1. *alienation*
Use structural analysis. Students may recognize *alien*.

> *alien:*   foreign
> *-ation:*   abstract noun ending

Various forms and uses of *alienation* should be discussed (alienation from other, from self, etc.). Use examples from the book. (Chief Broom felt so alienated from society that he stopped talking. Characters who have lost their own will and identity in the novel are self-alienated.)

2. *technocracy:* management of society by technical experts
Students should recognize the suffix *-cracy* from words such as democracy and autocracy. After establishing that *-cracy* means rule, elicit such meanings for *techno-* as built, craft.

Use the context of the Combine from the novel to build an understanding of a technocracy and manifestations of it.

3. *foreshadow:* to represent; to typify beforehand
Upon examination of the word's parts, students may be led to see that this word practically defines itself. *Fore-* means ahead; a *shadow* is a representation or image.

Use examples from the novel of foreshadowing in literature:

The story of Uncle Holligan in the first assignment foreshadows McMurphy's treatment of Big Nurse. Ruckley's treatment for rebelling foreshadows McMurphy's treatment.

4. *microcosm*

> *micro:*   little
> *-cosm:*   world

Again, start with the meanings the students already attach to this word's parts. They will most likely recognize *micro-* from microscope, etc. They should recognize *-cosm* from cosmos. If they don't, give them the words microscope and cosmos to help them infer the meaning of the word.

Put the word in the context of the novel. One of Kesey's points is that the Ward is a microcosm for the outside society.

Elicit examples from the novel.

Activity 14

PATTERN GUIDE: CAUSE AND EFFECT (pp. 145–173)

Directions, Part A: McMurphy goes through two reversals in this episode. For each change, chart reasons why he changes and the effects of his changes. Choose from the list below. Many are used more than once. For example, an effect of one change can be a cause of another.

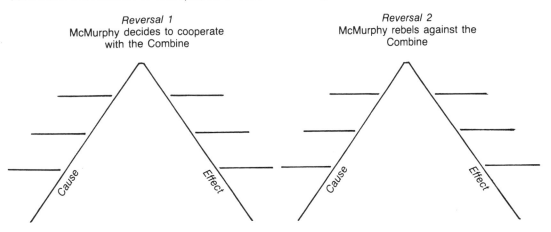

Reversal 1
McMurphy decides to cooperate
with the Combine

Reversal 2
McMurphy rebels against the
Combine

Cause — Effect — Cause — Effect

Choose from the following events:

1. McMurphy learns that the other inmates have committed themselves.
2. The lifeguard tells McMurphy that committed inmates can be kept in the institution as long as the institution sees fit.
3. McMurphy refuses to help Harding stand up the hydrocephalic patient.
4. Cheswick kills himself.
5. McMurphy scrubs the halls to please the nurse.
6. McMurphy witnesses the shock room.
7. The control panel is adjusted and running smoothly.
8. Big Nurse takes away the tub room privileges.
9. McMurphy breaks through Big Nurse's glass enclosure.
10. The fog thickens around Chief Broom once again.
11. The fog clears from around Chief Broom.
12. McMurphy dreams of faces.

Activity 18

POSTREADING ASSESSMENT

Directions: List I contains some statements that could be reasonable interpretations of the novel *One Flew Over the Cuckoo's Nest.* Read each statement carefully. If you think it is a valid point about the novel, put a *T* in the first numbered space. Then find actual events from the novel in List II which lend support to the statement. Put the number(s) of those events from List II in the second numbered space next to the statement in List I which support that statement. If you believe a statement in List I is not valid, leave the first blank empty, but provide numbers of events from List II in the second blank which support your rejection of the List I statement.

Example, List I: ____T____ __1,3__ 1. John is married.
List II: 1. John is wearing a wedding band.
       2. John likes to hunt.
       3. John has a joint checking account.

List I:

____ ____ 1. The major conflict of *Cuckoo's Nest* is between self-interest and self-sacrifice.

____ ____ 2. The inmates are victims of a matriarchy.

____ ____ 3. Influenced by McMurphy, Harding grows decisive and insightful.

____ ____ 4. Ellis, frozen in crucifixion against the Ward wall, is a live warning to McMurphy and foreshadows his fate.

____ ____ 5. McMurphy resurrects Billy Bibbit.

____ ____ 6. Big Nurse is victorious over McMurphy at the end of the novel.

____ ____ 7. Billy Bibbit plays the role of Judas in this novel.

____ ____ 8. The inmates will return to their submissive existences with McMurphy's death.

____ ____ 9. McMurphy's spirit is alive after his death.

____ ____ 10. McMurphy reveals Nurse's humanness and vulnerability before he dies.

____ ____ 11. Broom's murder of McMurphy is an act of love.

____ ____ 12. McMurphy's death is a victory over the Combine.

____ ____ 13. McMurphy's life is an allegory for the life of Christ.

____ ____ 14. Broom's battle for sanity and manhood is fought through is surrogate, McMurphy.

____ ____ 15. At the close of the novel, McMurphy and Broom are morally superior to the other inhabitants of the novel and to their earlier representations.

____ ____ 16. Broom chooses pain over safety.

____ ____ 17. McMurphy's tragic flaw is his pride in his own abilities.

____ ____ 18. McMurphy's tragic flaw is his compassion.

____ ____ 19. The asylum is a microcosm for the world.

____ ____ 20. McMurphy is responsible for Billy's suicide.

List II:

1. The men think McMurphy's body, after the lobotomy, is not his but a dummy of him.

2. Harding runs the gambling tables after McMurphy's lobotomy.

3. McMurphy waits for Billy rather than escaping while the time is opportune.

4. Chief Broom kills McMurphy.

5. McMurphy organizes a basketball team and coaches the inmates.

6. McMurphy organizes the game area in the tub room.

7. McMurphy smashes Nurse's glass enclosure after he talks to the lifeguard.

8. Nurse Ratchet threatens to tell Billy's mother about his affair with Candy.

9. The lifeguard warns McMurphy that he cannot release himself.

10. Big Nurse refuses to release McMurphy to another ward.

11. McMurphy refuses to help Cheswick defy Big Nurse.

12. Ellis is destroyed by shock treatment.

13. Broom's fog gradually subsides as the novel progresses.

14. McMurphy unsuccessfully tries to lift the control panel.

15. McMurphy convinces George to go on the fishing trip.

16. Chief Broom's father took his wife's name.

17. George tells McMurphy to be a fisher of men.

18. McMurphy attacks Washington in the shower to defend George.

19. Broom's family sold their land to the white man.

20. Chief throws the control panel through the window to escape from the institution.

21. Billy tells Nurse Ratchet that McMurphy forced him to sleep with Candy.

22. Harding leaves the insitution at the end.

23. McMurphy rips open Big Nurse's dress when he attacks her.

List III:

Directions: Listed below are statements which may relate in some way to the novel. Place a plus sign before each statement you believe expresses an idea that is implicitly or explicitly supported by the novel. Place a zero before any statement you believe is not supported by the novel. Below each statement, briefly cite specific examples from the novel to back your conclusion.

_____   1. Even when there is no hope of victory in terms of the score, if one undertakes an obligation to play against towering odds, he will earn a moral victory—at least over himself.

_____   2. A world of pain is better than a world of safety and protection.

_____   3. We must look beyond the surface when we measure a man.

_____   4. Violence is an acceptable strategy for change.

_____   5. Most men exercise little control over their fates.

_____   6. Men cannot be led to real self-sufficiency; they will always turn to leaders.

_____   7. When you lose your laugh, you lose your footing, your grasp on life.

_____   8. Bravado and courage are sources of power.

_____   9. Modern technocracy holds men in bondage, unawares.

_____   10. Modern society emasculates modern man.

_____   11. The American Indian culture was emasculated by the white culture.

Activity 20

PLAN FOR TEAM STUDY OF FOUR NOVELS

Introduction

Introduce *Bless the Beasts and the Children, The Light in the Forest, First Blood* and *Deliverance.* Each student should select one of the four novels to read. Explain to the class that they will be working in groups, each group being composed of students reading the same novel. Group work will include finding parallels with the themes studied in *One Frew Over the Cuckoo's Nest.*

   Give students a schedule of group discussions with the teacher. A general reading guide for all four novels should be distributed. Divide the reading of each novel into three sections for the purpose of group discussion. Assign the first section for the first discussion day scheduled.

Group discussions

The schedule allows the teacher three one-half hour sessions with each group, each session after students have read the one-third section assigned. During discussion days, other students can read in class. Those who finish early can begin individual reading on projects when their group isn't meeting.

Reading guide for group work

The following questions can be assigned for group discussion. Some groups will need more guidance and direction from the teacher than others. The teacher can monitor both the use of this guide and its requirements through interaction in the group discussions.

1. In what ways does the author expect us to generalize about the central character(s)?
    a. Who is (are) the central character(s)?
    b. What of importance happens to the central character(s)?
    c. Is it probable that the author wants the reader to extend these central events to all men or to every man in such a situation?
    d. Is the work mainly about the character's development or his deterioration?
    e. What is significant about physical appearance? social status?
    f. What are characteristics of his thought, speech, and action?
    g. What are the character's beliefs and convictions?
    h. Does the author seem favorable, critical, or noncommittal toward the character in question?
2. Who are the secondary characters? What are their chief traits? Are they developed characters or stereotyped ideas?
3. What conflicts constitute the main action of the story?
    Consider
    a. external conflicts:
       man vs. man
       man vs. nature
       man vs. society
    b. internal conflicts:
       man vs. himself
4. Are the conflicts resolved in the work?
5. Give a summary of the plot. Divide the material to indicate the growth and release of tension according to the following graph:

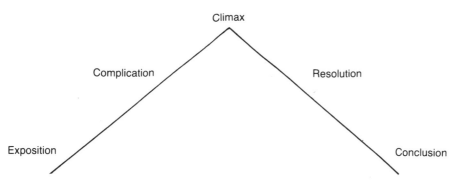

6. What are the various forces that account for the rising action, the turning point, and the climax?

7. Are there significant contrasts in the work between incidents in the plot? between characters? between moods?

8. What is the major theme of the work? Express this in a declarative statement. Theme is the author's judgment about or attitude toward his subject matter. Any expression of theme is correct that can justify itself from evidence in the work. Think of theme as the author's intention that guided him in writing the novel. Consider themes we found in *Cuckoo's Nest.*

9. Does the theme in any way contradict your basic beliefs and convictions about man and the world? Does the theme strengthen your beliefs?

10. How is the setting integrated with the theme? What are the details of the setting? Consider:
    historical period, season, etc.
    nation, city, or section of the nation
    social class and occupation of the characters
    mood and atmosphere (e.g., tense, gloomy)

11. What incidents could have happened only in this particular setting? What could have happened at any time or place?

12. Does the environment in the setting bring social, economic, political, or religious pressures to bear on the lives of the characters?

13. How does the author's use of figurative language and symbols affect the development of the theme?

14. How does the author use foreshadowing and suspense to grip the reader and urge him on to future moments in the story?

Activity 21

INDIVIDUAL PROJECTS

A list of suggested readings and projects can be a starting point for individual work. Students may design their own projects after their own ideas and interests. The teacher should, as in the small-group study, help steer students to reading selections and research sources appropriate to their abilities and interests.

Suggestions may include:

1. reading one of the four novels from small-group study.

2. pursuing the question of civil disobedience.
   Suggested readings:
   >Thoreau's *Walden* or "On Civil Disobedience"
   >Shaw's *Saint Joan*
   >Sophocles' *Antigone*
   >collected speeches of Martin Luther King, Jr.

3. pursuing the parable as a literary form.
   Suggested readings:
   >Steinbeck's *The Pearl*
   >selections from the Bible

4. pursuing the theme of control.
   Suggested readings:
   >Steinbeck's *The Pearl*
   >Steinbeck's *The Moon Is Down*
   >Orwell's *1984*

5. pursuing the theme of alienation.
   Suggested readings:
   >Salinger's *The Catcher in the Rye*

6. pursuing the question of the American Indians versus the white culture.
   Suggested readings:
   >*Bury My Heart at Wounded Knee*
   >*Little Big Man*
   >*When the Legends Die*
   >*Chief Joseph of the Nez Perce*

7. researching the treatment of patients in a mental institution—the questions of lobotomy, legal commitment, shock treatment.

8. reading literature dealing with the conflict man versus nature.
   Suggested readings:
   >Jack London's works
   >Crane's "The Open Boat"

9. selecting their own literature that is relevant to the survival unit themes.

Credits continued from page iv.

Amos Hahn for Questionnaire on Reading Strategies on p. 84. From "Assessing and Extending Comprehension: Monitoring Strategies in The Classroom." *Reading Horizons*, 1984, *24*, 225–230. By permission of *Reading Horizons*.

Maureen Wynter, special education teacher, Frederiksted, St. Croix, Virgin Islands, science comprehension inventory, pp. 89–90.

Chapter 4

Dora Bailey, Kent State University, Kent, Ohio, preview of Farenheit 451, pp. 110–111.

Henry Coe, social studies teacher, Durham, Connecticut, structured overview on propaganda, p. 115.

Ann Russo, business teacher, Durham, Connecticut, structured overview on data processing, p. 116.

Nancy Fishell, art teacher, Durham, Connecticut, structured overview on firing process, p. 117.

Judith Thelen for the structured overview on page 119. From "Preparing Students for Content Reading Assignments." *Journal of Reading*, March 1982, 25, 546–547. By permission of Judith Thelen and The International Reading Association.

Edward Murray, Sacred Heart College, Bridgeport, Connecticut, brainstorming activity on Civil War, p. 121.

Virginia Sazama, social studies teacher, Connecticut, prereading activity on Massachusetts settlers, p. 124.

Richard McManus, auto mechanics teacher, Durham, Connecticut, prereading activity on clutch situations, p. 124.

Karen Duhig, reading specialist, Deerfield, Illinois, prereading activity on "Atlas Babylon," p. 125.

Robert Ranieri, English teacher, Wheeling, Illinois, anticipation guide for Harris column, p. 129.

Mary Lou Getchman, social studies teacher, DeKalb, Illinois, anticipation guide to common soldier of Civil War, pp. 131–132.

Bruce Metzger, sixth grade teacher, New Philadelphia, Ohio, anticipation guide on weather clichés, p. 132.

Pat Wittaker, English teacher, Hudson, Ohio, anticipation guide for "It's Raining on Love," p. 133.

Chapter 5

Carol Barron, English teacher, Kent, Ohio, story map for "August Heat," p. 162.

Chapter 6

Ray Zeima, English teacher, Itaska, Illinois, three-level guide for *Flowers for Algernon*, p. 184.

Terry Gatlin, reading specialist, Palos Heights, Illinois, three-level guide for e.e. Cummings' poem, p. 185

Donald Burzler, Storrs, Connecticut, three-level guide for a mathematical word problem, p. 186.

Darrell Hohmquist, history teacher, New Lenox, Illinois, three-level guide for "Building First Cities, p. 188.

Pam Kenik, high school business teacher, Aurora, Ohio, three-level guide for "Down scaling of the American Dream," p. 189.

Teresa Gaziano, sixth grade teacher, Rockford, Illinois, three-level guide for "How do You Grow Up," p. 190.

Karen Duhig, reading specialist, Deerfield, Illinois, three-level guide for "Diffusion Through a Membrane."

Rafael Garcia, Jr., Spanish teacher, Durham, Connecticut, three-level guide for "Un Collegio," p. 192.

Richard McManus, auto mechanics teacher, Durham, Connecticut, pattern guide for "Power Mechanics," p. 195.

Karen Duhig, reading specialist, Deerfield, Illinois, pattern guide for "Split Cherry Tree," pp. 197–198.

William Healy, biology teacher, Durham, Connecticut, selective reading guide for "Mitosis," p. 201.

Laura Bania, Storrs, Connecticut, selective reading guide for "Advertising: The Permissible Lie," p. 203.

Chapter 7

Denise Stavis Levine for Jeremy's letter to the President and Josh's explanation of a lab experiment on p. 219. From "The Biggest Thing I Learned But It Really Doesn't Have to Do With Science." *Language Arts*, January 1985, *62*, 43–47. With permission.

Sarah Van Jura, special education teacher, Parma, Ohio, cluster for "Freed Slave," p. 235 and writing sample, p. 236.

David Liskey, English teacher, Canton, Ohio, jot-chart for "Stories About Heroes," p. 237.

Chapter 8

Kathy Rainier, Special Education Teacher, Kent, Ohio, semantic web for "The First Ohio Settlements," p. 269.

Mary Margaret Spear, Kent State University, Kent, Ohio, reading notes, pp. 275–277.

Chapter 9

Nancy Fishell, art teacher, Durham, Connecticut, open sort exercise on pottery, p. 312.

Joseph Campbell, business teacher, Durham, Connecticut, closed sort exercise on types of resources, p. 312.

Robert Ranieri, English teacher, Wheeling, Illinois, categorization exercise on tragedy, p. 314.

Debbie Kaprove, social studies teacher, Storrs, Connecticut, analogy exercise on geography, pp. 317–318.

Susan Lupo, math teacher, Roselle, Illinois, vocabulary matching exercise on geometric terms, p. 324.

Donna Kennedy Manolis, Crystal Lake, Illinois, magic square exercise on literary terms, p. 325.

Chapter 10

Kathleen Krispen, social studies teacher, Geneva, Illinois, postreading activity on Southeast Asia, p. 352.

Judy Serra, sixth grade teacher, Cleveland, Ohio, lesson plan, pp. 353–354.

Louis Porter, French instructor, Walsh College, Canton, Ohio, lesson plan, pp. 355–357.

Joseph Rottenborn, history teacher, Boardman, Ohio, lesson plan, pp. 357–360.

Marietta Raneri, art teacher, Castleton, New York, corss-tabulation chart for art unit, pp. 365–366.

Camille Fiduccia, English teacher, Westchester, Illinois, contract for fiction unit, p. 369.

Appendix E

Elaine Sargent, Storrs, Connecticut, unit on solar system, p. 441.

Sheila Peckham, Storrs, Connecticut, unit on *One Flew Over The Cuckoo's Nest*, p. 456.

Index

Carolyn Gordon, Cleveland, Ohio, pp. 473–480

Index